AN ANTHOLOGY OF

Beowulf Criticism

an anthology of BEOWULF CRITICISM

Edited by

LEWIS E. NICHOLSON

UNIVERSITY OF NOTRE DAME PRESS
NOTRE DAME LONDON

UNIVERSITY OF NOTRE DAME PRESS
Notre Dame, Indiana

Second Printing, 1964
Third Printing, 1966
Fourth Printing, 1971
Fifth Printing, 1976

Manufactured in the United States of America by
NAPCO Graphic Arts, Inc., Milwaukee, Wisconsin

To

Professor John T. Frederick,

in appreciation

CONTENTS

PREFACE

In this anthology there are eighteen scholarly and critical essays on *Beowulf,* ranging in time from Blackburn's famous essay on "The Christian Coloring in the *Beowulf,*" which appeared in 1897, to the recent studies of Morton W. Bloomfield and Margaret E. Goldsmith, both of whom stress the importance of the Latin fathers in the shaping of the Anglo-Saxon's mental world. The Blackburn and Chadwick essays are included as representative of earlier criticism which was interested more, perhaps, in the origins of the poem than what the poet did with it. Both Blackburn and Chadwick see the poem as one composed by a heathen which later underwent incidental changes at the hands of a minstrel or monkish scribe who was working with somewhat intractable material to bring it into conformity with new ideas. The redactor's piety may, on occasion, have exceeded his aesthetic interests, or so the essayists' interpretation holds, for in cloaking heathen ideas in Christian phraseology he produced inconsistencies in the text. Chadwick studies some seventy Christian passages in *Beowulf,* concludes that "the poet had little direct knowledge of the Christian religion," and that "the limitations of his theological equipment might be satisfactorily accounted for on the hypothesis that he knew only a few of Caedmon's works." A notably contrary point of view is offered by Schücking and Hamilton who both note the existence of the heathen-Germanic warrior ethic in the poem, but see the poet himself not as a random editor of pagan tales but one who exercised mental vigor to re-shape the old tradition in terms of Christian theology. Studying the poem against its rich Græco-Latin intellectual climate, Schücking observes that the ideal of kingship in the poem is primarily defined by Church literature, namely the "rex justus" of Augustine, and Hamilton finds that the poet revaluates his Germanic patrimony in terms of the Augustinian view of history.

Six recent articles reprinted here—those by Tolkien, Malone, Rogers, Wright, Kaske, and Goldsmith—focus on the meaning and value of the poem as a whole and make important contributions towards a better understanding of the poem's structure and unity. Tolkien's essay, widely recognized as a turning point in Beowulfian criticism, stresses the tragedy of the human condition and shows how this tragedy is set forth in artistic terms as "a balance of ends and beginnings," "the moving contrast of youth and age," with the monsters, embodying the forces of evil and chaos, appropriately placed in the center of the action. Rogers' view of the central theme of the poem is not essentially different from Tolkien's, though he understands the pattern of the poem to be not "an opposition of ends and beginnings" but a progression springing from Beowulf's three great fights. In spite of this emerging pattern, Rogers does not believe that the *Beowulf* can be regarded as an artistic unity in the modern sense primarily because the poet, constrained by his well-known pagan sources, was unable to re-shape all of his pagan motifs to harmonize with his Christian theme. For Goldsmith, the poem evidences no such pagan constraint, and she observes that "if a martial epic of *Beowulf* was known to our poet, he has taken pains to recast it in quite another mold." Goldsmith focuses on the moral and eschatological meanings of the poem, finds that the descriptions of wars, banquets, and feats of swimming are all subsumed by the poet under a higher purpose, which was (in the words of William Blake) to set forth imaginatively what "Eternally Exists, Really and unchangeably." Unlike Goldsmith, Malone sees the poet as a patriotic Englishman whose purpose in writing the poem was to glorify the heroic heritage which he inherited from ancient Germania. Concentrating upon the episodes in the poem rather than the main fable or plot, Malone maintains that certain of the episodes are drawn into the narrative while others remain external to it. Kaske, influenced by the earlier work of Ernst Curtius, argues that a formulary use of the "sapientia et fortitudo" theme not only governs the structure of the poem, but that the poet used this old ideal as an area of synthesis between Christianity and Germanic paganism. Wright's essay, unlike most of the essays discussed earlier which draw variously upon social history, literary history, or Biblical exegesis, restricts itself to a purely formal analysis of the poem. Wright studies the unity of the poem in terms of its imagery of light and darkness, and relates these concrete effects to contrasts of good and evil, joy and sorrow.

Five essays in this collection concentrate on a single character, scene, or in one instance, on a single passage. Bloomfield, citing instances of the allegorical method in Christian Latin poetry, suggests that the author of *Beowulf* is thinking of Unferth as *Discordia,* a personified abstraction after the allegorical manner of Prudentius, Martianus Capella, or Sedulius. (This interpretation, as Bloomfield points out, blends in with the suggestions made by Schücking in his article on the ideal of kingship, where the character of Beowulf is described as largely patterned after the Christian concept of the perfect ruler as set forth by Augustine, Gregory the Great, Pseudo-Cyprian, Hincmar of Reims, and others.) Cabaniss and McNamee call attention to the possible influence of the Holy Saturday Liturgy and the Harrowing of Hell tradition on the account of Beowulf's descent into Grendel's mere, and McNamee looks beyond this scene to find remarkable parallels between the outline of the *Beowulf* story and the Christian story of salvation. Robertson, drawing upon the meanings of gardens as found in mediaeval commentaries and encyclopedias, shows how a knowledge of these conventionally established meanings enables one to discern the Divine truth of the description of Grendel's mere. Bloomfield, in his recent article, "Patristics and Old English Literature," demonstrates, further, the relevance of the Latin fathers in Old English literary studies by viewing a single passage of the *Beowulf* against its varied background of patristic thinking.

Three of the anthologized essays—those by Wrenn, Magoun, and Baum—are on miscellaneous topics related to *Beowulf.* Wrenn identifies the designs on the Sutton Hoo standard, shield, and helmet as ritually significant elements, then suggests the possible significance that the designs and artefacts may have for the study of *Beowulf.* Magoun, drawing upon the earlier work of Parry and Lord to explain the recurrence of verses and verse-pairs in Anglo-Saxon poetry, analyzes the first twenty-five lines of *Beowulf* and lines 512-35 of *Christ and Satan* to demonstrate the pervasiveness of the oral formulaic patterns in narrative poetry. This important, but controversial study, has virtually given rise to a whole new school of Anglo-Saxon literary criticism. To conclude, Baum, emphasizing the poem's cryptic nature, remarks on the demands such a poem would make upon an audience: "He [the *Beowulf* poet] adopted a tense crowded style and a convoluted method of narration, the very antithesis of a minstrel's, most unsuited for oral recitation, and if he looked for an audience of listeners he was extraordinarily, not to say stubbornly, sanguine." Baum reviews interpretations of *Beowulf,* concludes that scholars have perhaps neglected criticism of the poem as a poem "because of uncertainty about the fundamental criteria of the poem."

AN ANTHOLOGY OF BEOWULF CRITICISM

The purpose of this anthology is to bring together in convenient form some of the best scholarly and critical essays on *Beowulf* to appear in recent years, some of which are not available in small libraries. The important critical studies of W. W. Lawrence, R. W. Chambers, Ritchie Girvan, Arthur G. Brodeur, Adrien Bonjour, and Dorothy Whitelock do not appear here, for their contributions have been published in book form and are easy to acquire. To aid the general reader, the editor has supplied translations of Latin, Old English, and Old Norse, placing these translations in brackets in the body of the text directly following the passage translated.

To R. E. Kaske, the editor owes a particular debt of gratitude for assistance and various helpful suggestions, and to Charles W. McCollester of the Notre Dame Press for his untiring support in preparing the manuscript for publication. W. H. Bennett, Joseph Milosh, Caroline Holmstrand, and Philip O'Mara gave additional assistance. For permission to reproduce the cover design, the editor wishes to acknowledge the courtesy of Urs Graf-Verlag, publishers of the facsimile edition of the *Codex Durmachensis,* and the Board of Trinity College, Dublin.

Notre Dame, Indiana
July, 1963

LEWIS E. NICHOLSON

AN ANTHOLOGY OF

Beowulf Criticism

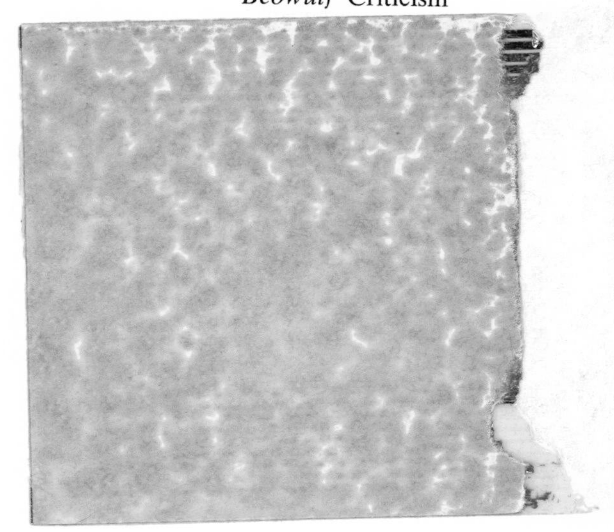

1

THE CHRISTIAN COLORING IN THE *BEOWULF* *

F. A. Blackburn

IT IS ADMITTED BY ALL CRITICS THAT THE *Beowulf* IS ESSENTIALly a heathen poem; that its materials are drawn from tales composed before the conversion of the Angles and Saxons to Christianity, and that there was a time when these tales were repeated without the Christian reflections and allusions that are found in the poem that has reached us. But in what form this heathen material existed before it was put into its present shape is a question on which opinions are widely different. In the nature of the case we can look for no entire consensus of opinion and no exact answer to the question; the most that one can expect to establish is at the best only a probability.

The following hypotheses are possible:

1. The poem was composed by a Christian, who had heard the stories and used them as the material for his work.

2. The poem was composed by a Christian, who used old lays as his material. (This differs from the first supposition in assuming that the tales had already been versified and were in poetical form before they were used by the author.)

3. The poem was composed by a heathen, either from old stories or from old lays. At a later date it was revised by a

* Reprinted, by permission of the Modern Language Association of America, from *Publications of the Modern Language Association of America* (*PMLA*), XII (1897), 205-225.

Christian poet, to whom we owe the Christian allusions found in it. (This hypothesis differs from the others in assuming the existence of a complete poem without the Christian coloring.)

The purpose of the present study is to contribute to the settlement of the question inferences drawn from a careful examination of the passages that show a Christian coloring. Whether the *Beowulf* is a unit or a compilation made from several poems originally distinct is not considered, except in so far as a conclusion may be drawn from the character of the Christian allusions, and all other questions in regard to the genesis of the Epic in general or of the *Beowulf* in particular are also left untouched.

It must be noted, however, at the beginning of the discussion, that it is not in all cases a simple matter to decide whether a passage under consideration is Christian in character. It is clear, I think, that we have no right to classify under this head those passages that are simply moral and ethical. The commandment not to bear false witness is regarded with good reason as a fundamental part of Christian doctrine, but when the dying Beowulf says, 'I sought not unrighteous strife nor swore oaths deceitfully,' we are justified in claiming the passage as Christian only by bringing proof that our forefathers, before they were enlightened by the instruction of Christian missionaries, thought false oaths right and proper. But when the hero continues, 'In all this I may rejoice, though sick with mortal wounds, for when my life hath left my body, the Ruler of men may not charge me with the murder of my kindred,' we may properly recognize the Christian coloring. This does not lie in the assertion of the speaker that he has kept the commandment not to kill, for Christianity can claim a monopoly of this no more than of the other just referred to, but in the apparent reference to a judgment after death and to the Ruler who is to try men for their deeds; a reference that seems to prove the writer's knowledge of the teaching of the Gospels.

Other passages are doubtful for a different reason. It is well known that the missionaries of the early Church took many words belonging to heathen beliefs and practices and applied them to corresponding conceptions and usages of the Christian system. In *Yule, Easter, God, hell,* etc., we still keep words thus adopted; others, now obsolete, are *hælend, nergend, drihten, metod, frea,* etc. To these may be added the various epithets applied to the Persons of the Trinity, which are used so freely by the Old English poets. Most of these are simply equivalents of Latin expressions, or imitations of them; e.g. *ælmihtig* (omnipotens); *ece drihten* (dominus æternus); *wuldorcyning* (rex gloriæ); and the like. This use of native words and epithets is nothing peculiar, of course; the same thing had already taken place in Latin and had given to *deus, dominus,* etc. their ecclesiastical meaning. But when such words are first used by the church, it is plain that something of the old meaning still clings to them and is suggested to the hearer. In some cases the older meaning vanishes after a time or becomes entirely subordinated to the later one; e.g. the word *Christ* has entirely lost, for most of those that use or hear it, its original meaning; *God* and *Saviour* have the older and more general meaning at times, but more often the later specialized one; *Father* and *Son,* as names of the Persons of the Trinity, are far less frequent than as ordinary names of relationship. We cannot always feel certain, therefore, in reading the *Beowulf,* whether the word is used by the writer with full consciousness of its later sense or with its older meaning. All cases of this kind are included in the following discussion; the question whether the earlier or the later meaning is to be assumed is considered in its place.

There are in the *Beowulf* sixty-eight passages in which the form of expression or the character of the thought seems to suggest something in Christian usage or doctrine, and we may properly assume that they had this effect on Christian readers at the time that the manuscript that has reached us was written. These passages may be classified according to content as follows:

1. Passages containing Bible history or allusions to some Scripture narrative.

2. Passages containing expressions in disapproval of heathen ideas or heathen worship.

3. Passages containing references to doctrines distinctively Christian.

4. Incidental allusions to the Christian God, to his attributes, and to his part in shaping the lives and fortunes of men. The fourth class is by far the most numerous; it comprises fifty-three cases, while under the first only three passages fall, under the second one, and under the third ten.

Of the three passages under the head of Scripture history, two refer to the Creation, the Fall, and the death of Abel; one contains an allusion to the Flood. They are found in vv. 90-113; 1261-1266; 1687-1693.

Under the second head, disapproval of heathenism, falls a single passage, vv. 175-178.

These four passages are of much greater length than those under the other two heads, and a closer study shows that they differ also in other respects. They will be taken up for consideration after we have examined the others.

The third class comprises ten allusions, more or less distinct, to Christian doctrines. Of these one refers to reward in heaven, six to hell or its inhabitants, and three to the day of judgment. They are the following:

756. deafla gedræg,
'the throng of devils.'

788. hellehæfton,
'hell's captive.'

808. feonda geweald,
'the power of fiends.'

852. hæþene sawle þær him hel onfeng,
'the heathen soul, there hell received him.'

977. ðær abidan sceal
maga mane fah miclan domes
hu him scir metod scrifan wille,
'there stained with crime must the man await the great doom, how the pure Lord will appoint for him.'

1274. gehnægde hellegast,
'crushed the hellish spirit.'

2741. for ðam me witan ne ðearf weldend fira
morðorbealo maga þonne min sceaceð
lif of lice,
'for when my life hath left my body, the Ruler of men may not charge me with the murder of my kinsmen'

2819. him of hwæðre gewat
sawol secean soðfæstra dom,
'his soul departed to seek the lot of the righteous.'

3069. oð domes dæg,
'until doomsday.'

3072. hellbendum fæst,
'fast in the bonds of hell.'

These passages, when studied in connection with the context, are found, with one or two exceptions, to lack the clearness that one would wish in deciding how far Christian influence has shaped them. For example, the reference in 977 ff. seems when standing by itself to be a clear allusion to the day of judgment, but in the poem it is put into the mouth of Beowulf, who assures Hrothgar that the escape of Grendel is a matter of no importance, since his wound is surely mortal. The doom that Grendel must abide seems therefore to be death. The allusions to hell in 788, 852 and 3072, become equally doubtful when we remember that Hel is the goddess of the world of the dead and corresponds to the classical Persephone. If we treat the word as a proper name we make the allusion entirely heathen. But "hellegast," in 1274, we may assume, would be used only by a Christian. Other passages receive their

Christian coloring from the use of the words *deofol* and *feond.* But it is not certain that *feond,* which strictly means 'foe,' has here the later sense that we now attach to the word 'fiend,' and *deofol,* though it was introduced from Latin with the coming of Christianity, does not refer in v. 756 to the devils of hell, but to the ocean monsters like Grendel, into whose company he wishes to escape. It is possible that the word, which is often used of nixies, kobolds, gnomes, etc., had already lost its meaning to such a degree that it could be used without suggesting anything in Christian teaching, in the way that a Protestant might use "Jesuit" in a sense that suggests nothing of the derivation or original sense of the term. Still we cannot suppose that any one but a Christian would use the word in this way, and it is, therefore, included among the Christian allusions.

Under the last head, incidental allusions to God and his power, goodness, etc., fall the great majority of the passages that show a Christian coloring. They are the following:

13. þone god sende,
'whom God sent.'

16. him þæs liffrea
wuldres wealdend woroldare forgeaf,
'the Lord of life, the Prince of glory, gave them prosperity thereafter.'

27. feran on frean wære,
'go into the Lord's keeping.'

73. swylc him god sealde,
'which God had given him.'

?169. for metode (reading not certain),
'because of the Lord.

227. gode þancedon,
'thanked God.'

316. fæder alwalda
mid arstafum eowic gehealde,
'the Almighty Father kindly keep you!'

381. hine halig god
for arstafum us onsende,
'the holy God hath sent him for our help.'

440. ðær gelyfan sceal
drihtnes dome se þe hine deað nimeð,
'he whom death shall take must yield him to the Lord's will.'

478. god eaþe mæg
þone dolsceaðan dæda getwæfan,
'God can easily keep the foe from his deeds.'

570. beorht beacen godes,
'God's bright sign' (the sun).

625. gode þancode,
'thanked God.'

670. metodes hyldo,
'the Lord's favor.'

685. witig god
on swa hwæþere hond halig drihten
mærðo deme swa him gemet þince,
'let the wise God, the holy Lord, adjudge honor on either side, as seemeth meet to him.'

696. ac him dryhten forgeaf
wigspeda gewiofu,
'but the Lord gave them victory.'

700. soð is gecyþed
þæt mihtig god manna cynnes
weold [w]ideferhð,
'the truth is shown, that the mighty God hath ever swayed the human race.'

706. þa metod nolde,
'since the Lord was unwilling.'

711. godes yrre bær,
'bore God's wrath.'

786. godes andsacan,
'God's adversary.'

811. fag wið god,
'hostile to God.'

928. alwealdan þanc,
'thanks to the Almighty.'

930. a mæg god wyrcan
wunder æfter wundre wuldres hyrde,
'ever can God, the glorious protector, work wonder on wonder.'

940. þurh drihtnes miht,
'through the might of the Lord.'

945. þæt hyre eald metod este wære,
'that the ancient Lord was kindly toward her.'

955. alwalda þec
gode forgylde,
'the Almighty repay thee with good!'

967. þa metod nolde,
'since the Lord was unwilling.'

1056. nefne him witig god wyrd forstode
ond ðæs mannes mod metod eallum weold
gumena cynnes swa he nu git deð,
'had not the wise God, fate and the man's courage withstood him. The Lord ruled all men, as he still doth.'

1271. ðe him god sealde,
'which God gave him.'

?1314. hwæþre him alfwalda æfre wille
æfter weaspelle wyrpe gefremman,
'whether the Almighty (alwalda by conj.) after a period of sorrow will work a change.'

1397. gode þancode
mihtigan drihtne,
'thanked God, the mighty Lord.'

1553. ond halig god
geweold wigsigor wihtig drihten
rodera rædend hit on riht gesced,
'and the holy God, the wise Lord, the Ruler of the skies, controlled the victory, adjudged it rightly.'

1609. þonne forstes bend fæder onlæteð
onwindeð wælrapas se geweald hafað
sæla ond mæla þæt is soð metod,
'when the Father, that hath control of times and seasons, that is the true Lord, looseth the fetters of the frost, etc.'

1626. gode þancodon,
'thanked God.'

1658. nymðe mec god scylde,
'had not God protected me.'

1661. ac me geuðe ylda waldend
þæt ic on wage geseah wlitig hangian,
'but the Ruler of men granted to me to see hanging on the wall, etc.'

1682. godes andsaca,
'God's adversary.'

1716. ðeah þe hine mihtig god mægenes wynnum
eafeþum stepte ofer ealle men
forð gefremede,
'though the mighty God had aided him with the joys of power and with might, etc.'

1724. wundor is to secganne
hu mihtig god manna cynne
þurh sidne sefan snyttru bryttað
eard ond eorlscipe he ah ealra geweald,
'wondrous is it to tell how the mighty God giveth to mankind wisdom, home, and rank. He hath power over all, etc.'

1751. þæs þe him ær god sealde
wuldres waldend weorðmynda dæl,

'after God, the glorious Ruler, hath given him much honor.'

1778. þæs sig metode þanc
ecean drihtne,
'for this thanks be to the Lord, the eternal Prince!'

1841. þe þa wordcwidas wigtig drihten
on sefan sende,
'the wise Lord hath put these words into thy heart.'

1997. gode ic þanc sege,
'I thank God.'

2182. ginfæstan gife þe him god sealde,
'the ample gifts that God had given him.'

2186.? drihten wereda,
'Lord of hosts'(?)

2292. se ðe waldendes
hyldo gehealdeð,
'who hath the favor of the Ruler.'

2329. þæt he wealdende
* * * * ecean drihtne
bitre gebulge,
'that he had angered the Ruler, the eternal Lord.'

2469. godes leoht geceas,
'chose God's light' (*i. e.* died).

2650. god wat,
'God knows.'

2794. ic ðara frætwa frean ealles ðanc
wuldurcyninge wordū secge
ecum drihtne,
'I thank the Lord of all, the King of glory, the eternal Lord, for these treasures.'

2857. ne ðæs wealdendes wiht oncyrran
wolde dom godes dædū rædan
gumena gehwylcū swa he gen deð,

'nor change the Ruler's will (willan by conj.); the power of God was to rule the fate of every man, as yet it doth.'

2874. hwæðre hi god uðe
sigora waldend þæt he hyne sylfne gewræc
'yet God, the ruler of victories, let him avenge himself.'

3054. nefne god sylfa
sigora soðcyning sealde þam ðe he wolde
he is manna gehyld hord openian
efne swa hwylcū manna swa hī gemet ðuhte,
'unless God himself, the true King of victories (he is the protection of men), should grant to whom he would to open the hoard, even to whomsoever he thought fitting.'

3109. on ðæs waldendes wære,
'into the Ruler's keeping.'

A careful reading of the passages under this head shows that nearly all of them receive their Christian tone simply from the use of the words *God* and *Lord* (god, frea, metod, drihten), or of some equivalent expression (wuldres wealdend, fæder alwalda, ylda waldend, or the like). In a few cases these terms are qualified by an epithet and in a few others there is a statement, always in very few words, in regard to God's power or goodness. A classification based on these variations in the form of expression gives the following results:

(a). Cases in which a simple name of Deity is used; 39, viz.: god, 23; metod, 7; waldend, 4; drihten, 2; frea, 2; fæder, 1.

(b). Cases in which this name of Deity is qualified by an epithet, either an adjective, a genitive, or a word compounded with the name-word, 28, viz.: god, 7; drihten, 8; waldend, 6; metod, 1; frea, 1; fæder, 1; cyning, 2; hyrde, 1; rædend, 1.

(c). Cases containing some Christian reflection, not simply a name or name accompanied by an epithet. Under this head fall seven cases, most of which have no more force than an epithet; in fact, in no one of them is more expressed than is stated by implication in the cases under the second head. Such a statement, for example, as 'he hath power over all' (he ah ealra geweald, 1727), has no more force than the epithet 'all-powerful' (alwalda, 316).

In all the Christian allusions of the poem, including those yet to be considered, there is one peculiarity that should not be overlooked. In no one of them do we find any reference to Christ, to the cross, to the virgin or the saints, to any doctrine of the church in regard to the trinity, the atonement, etc., or to the scriptures, to prophecy, or to the miracles. They might all have been written by Moses or David as easily as by an English monk. In fact, if it were not for the use of certain names and titles that have been appropriated by the church and thus given a technical meaning, it would not be difficult to find parallel expressions in Plato or Marcus Aurelius. This astonishing list of omissions seems to be without explanation if we assume that the poem first took its present shape at the hands of a Christian writer. We can well believe that many an inmate of the cloister had enough of the spirit of his fathers to find delight in tales of adventure by sea and land, and there is plenty of evidence that in many cases the monk was a kind of Friar Tuck, with only a thin veneer of Christianity, but we can hardly suppose that one could be found that would compose a poem and insert Christian reflections and yet fail to put in a single one on those phases of Christianity that were especially emphasized in the training of the time and that form the bulk of the poems professedly Christian.

The vague and colorless Christianity of these passages becomes very apparent if for the word *God* or equivalent epithet we substitute *fate* or the name of some heathen divinity. No further change is needed in many of the passages cited to remove the Christian tone and make them entirely heathen. For example, in describing the avarice and cruelty of Heremod (vv. 1716 ff.), the author says, 'Though the mighty God had exalted him with the joys of power and with strength, and had helped him more than all men, yet in his heart there grew up a cruel disposition, etc.' If for *God* we substitute *fate,* or some word of like meaning, the moral sentiment of the reflection remains, to be sure, but it is no longer a Christian sentiment. In fact, in many cases it is not necessary to change a word but only to assign to it its older meaning. When it is said that Grendel could not destroy the followers of Beowulf, *þa metod nolde* (v. 706), 'because the Lord willed it not,' it is quite natural to render the clause 'fate willed it not,' thus giving to *metod* its older meaning. The sentiment of this translation finds a parallel in many other passages of the poem. It would require but little skill to remove the Christian tone of the whole, with the exception of two or three passages, by making a few verbal changes and giving to certain words the older meaning instead of the later one.

Now if these passages can be heathenized by a few changes of this kind it is a very natural hypothesis that they were Christianized in the same way, and such a supposition explains their occurrence and their peculiarities. We may assume the existence of an older poem composed by a heathen Scop and containing moral sentiments and reflections of the same character as those of Homer or Virgil or the Edda. Later a Christian monk "edits" it for Christian readers. Where the author has spoken of the gods, he changes the word to the singular or makes some other change in the wording so that the God of the Christians may be referred to. He substitutes a verse of his own, or a portion of a verse, when necessary, possibly omits portions that do not readily yield to simple amendment, but does not materially change the general tone, which remains, therefore, essentially heathen. This method of incidental change explains the lack of all allusions to the leading doctrines of the Church and of any reference to Christ and his teaching, to say nothing of the many other things that we should expect to find, if we suppose that the work was composed in the first instance by a Christian.

This method of revision requires great skill, if it is to escape detection, and there are several of the passages quoted that seem to show that the task that the pious reviser took on himself was beyond his poetic skill. The Christian allusion often has the tone of a deliberate insertion rather than a reflection naturally suggested by the situation or the course of the thought. Moreover, the revision was not thorough, for there are many passages that still keep the heathen tone, especially those that name *Wyrd* as the controller of the destiny of men; in one case this word apparently stands as an appositive to a name of Deity. The lack of sequence, and in one or two cases even grammatical confusion, suggest that we shall not be far wrong if we assume that the changes are the work of some monkish copyist, whose piety exceeded his poetic powers. That this Christianizing of an older work is quite possible, hardly needs proof; if an illustration of the method is needed, it may be found in Alfred's *Boethius*.

This explanation, if accepted, will account for all the passages under the third and fourth heads, and for the allusion to the Flood under the first. It is not necessary to attempt to restore the older readings by conjecture; in some cases it is not hard to find traces that suggest a reconstruction, but in most of them only conjectures are possible. A trace of the older heathen version may be seen, I think, in the allusion to the Flood, just mentioned. The sinners that lost their lives by the waters are there called giants, and one or two peculiarities of expression lead me to hazard the suggestion that the passage, before it was Christianized, contained an allusion to the Northern tale of the war of the gods with the giants. The whole passage reads:

1688. on ðam wæs or writen
fyrngewinnes syðþan flod ofsloh
gifen geotende giganta cyn

frecne geferdon   þæt wæs fremde þeod
ecean dryhtne   him þæs endelean
þurh wæteres wylm   waldend sealde,

'thereon was written the beginning of the ancient strife, when the flood, the pouring sea, destroyed the race of the giants (shameless was their behavior); that was a people hostile to the eternal Lord; the Ruler gave them a reward therefor through the whelming of water.'

There are still left three passages for which the hypothesis of alterations by a scribe does not seem to suffice, and which must be regarded as interpolations in a broader sense, either by the supposed reviser or by some one else. The longest of these is found in vv. 90-113, and contains the story of the Creation and Fall, with a reference to Cain as the father of evil monsters like Grendel. The same reference to Cain occurs again in vv. 1261-1266. The third case is the reference to idol-worship and ignorance of the true God in vv. 175-188. I give this first.

175. hwilum hie geheton   æt hrærgtrafum
wigweorþunga   wordum bædon
þæt him gastbona   geoce gefremede
wið þeodþreaum   swylc wæs þeaw hyra
hæþenra hyht   helle gemundon
in modsefan   metod hie ne cuþon
dæda demend   ne wiston hie drihten god
ne hie huru heofona helm   herian ne cuþon
wuldres waldend   wa bið þæm ðe sceal
þurh sliðne nið   sawle bescufan
in fyres fæþm   frofre ne wenan
wihte gewendan   wel bið þæm þe mot
æfter deaðdæge   drihten secean
and to fæder fæþmum   freoðo wilnian,

'at times they vowed honors in their temples, prayed that the devil would give them help against their woes.

> Such was their custom, the hope of the heathen; they thought on hell in their hearts, they knew not the Lord, the judge of deeds; they knew not the Lord God, nor could they praise the Keeper of Heaven, the Ruler of glory. Sad is it for him that must thrust his soul into the embrace of fire in direful enmity, nor hope for comfort or change; well it is for him that shall be allowed after his death-day to visit the Lord and enjoy protection in the bosom of the Father.'

This passage does not call for extended comment. Its Christian tone lies in the reflection with which it closes, which brings it also under the third class, and in the implied condemnation of heathenism contained in the statement that the Danes worshipped the devil and knew not the true God. But Hrothgar, the king of these same Danes, says that the holy God has sent Beowulf to his aid, that God can easily keep Grendel from his evil deeds, and thanks God for the sight of Grendel's arm, which Beowulf has torn off in the fight. So, too, his queen, when she greets Beowulf, thanks God that her wish for a champion able to cope with the monster has been fulfilled, and the Danish coast-guard, after directing Beowulf and his comrades to the Hall, dismisses them with the pious wish, 'May the All-ruling Father keep you!' These and other instances are not in accord with the statement that the Danes knew not the true God, and seem to furnish good evidence that the passage containing the latter is an interpolation. I assume that the first reviser, in trying to put the poem in Christian garb, had left a little heathenism exposed here, as he has in other places, and that a later hand has added a moralizing passage on the wickedness of worshipping idols and the awful consequences to the worshipper.

There remains one case, the reference to Cain as the ancestor of Grendel and the other beings of earth, air and sea, who were put under ban by the coming of Christianity. This allusion, as was said, is found twice. The second passage is short and will be considered with the longer one. It contains a direct allusion to the murder of Abel, which is only implied in the first, and repeats the statement that Cain was the progenitor of the various monsters. The two passages may best be treated together, for it is safe to assume that they are from the same hand.

It is in these two passages that we find the most distinctly Christian coloring of the whole poem. The first one extends through about twenty-four verses, but seems to be intermingled with references to Grendel and to the Danes, and as it stands in the MS. offers serious difficulties of interpretation and confusion of thought to a much greater degree than we should expect, even in Old English poetry. This confusion is not sufficient, of itself, to warrant us in pronouncing the passage a later addition, though it raises suspicion of its genuineness, but when we find that a re-arrangement makes the whole clear, this suspicion is strengthened until it approaches the character of proof. It can at least lay claim to consideration as a very good hypothesis.

An interpolation may be an intentional insertion by the copyist, and the motive for such insertion may be what it may; or it may be unintentional, the scribe inserting the matter because he supposes that it belongs there. The latter is most often the case when additional matter has been written on the margin. The copyist supposes that this matter has been added because it was omitted by the former scribe, and therefore puts it in. He does in this way just what the compositor now does with the additions of the proof-reader, and misplacement is likely to occur, as it now does, if the position of the new matter is not carefully marked.

It is in this way, as I suspect, that the passage under consideration found its way into the text of the poem. The MS. of the Beowulf that has reached us is a copy of an older one, on the margin of which, I assume, some pious owner had written some twenty or more verses about the creation, the crime and punishment of Cain and the monsters like Grendel, whose origin was thus accounted for. This note occurs at the place where Grendel is first mentioned, and was supposed, no doubt, to make the work more fit for Christian readers and more edifying to Christian warriors. The copyist, supposing that this matter belonged to the story, copied it into the text, but in so doing he blundered badly and mixed the statements about Cain with those about Grendel into a story that is almost unintelligible.

The division and rearrangement that I propose is as follows:

Original; vv. 102-104a; 86-90a; 115 ff.

Interpolated; vv. 90b-101; 107-110; 104b-106; 111-114.

By putting the verses noted in this order and omitting those that I suppose to have been added later, we get what I suppose to have been the original form of the story. Hrothgar has built a hall and feasts there daily with his retainers. The writer goes on to say:

102. wæs se grimma gæst grendel haten
mære mearcstapa se þe moras heold
fen ond fæsten

86. ða se ellengæst earfoðlice
þrage geþolode se þe in þystrum bad
þæt he dogora gehwam dream gehyrde
hludne in healle þær wæs hearpan sweg
swutol sang scopes

115. Gewat ða neosian syþðan niht becom
hean huses hu hit hringdene
æfter beorþege gebun hæfdon
Fand þa ðær inne æþelinga gedriht
swefan æfter symble,

This arrangement leaves two verses incomplete, a result of the confused arrangement of the scribe who did not find it easy to fit the inserted matter to the old. But the story is clear and straight. It runs thus:

'There was a cruel spirit named Grendel, a famed mark-treader, who held the moors and the fen as his fastness. This mighty spirit, that dwelt in darkness, endured with difficulty for a time the daily hearing of loud revel in the hall; there was the melody of the harp, the bard's clear-sounding song. When then night came on he set out to visit the lofty house [and to see] how the Danes had occupied it after their banquet. He found there a troop of warriors sleeping after their feast,' etc.

The interpolation, arranged as indicated above, runs thus:

90. sægde se þe cuþe
frumsceaft fira feorran reccan
cwæð þæt se ælmihtiga eorðan worh[te]
wlitebeorhtne wang swa wæter bebugeð
gesette sigehreþig sunnan ond monan
leoman to leohte landbuendum
ond gefrætwade foldan sceatas
leomum ond leafum lif eac gesceop
cynna gehwylcum þara ðe cwice hwyrfaþ
Swa ða drihtguman dreamum lifdon
eadiglice oððæt an ongan
fyrene frem[m]an feond on helle

* * * * * *

107. in caines cynne þone cwealm gewræc
ece drihten þæs he abel slog
Ne gefeah he þære fæhðe ac he hine feor forwræc
metod for þy mane mancynne fram

104. fifelcynnes eard
wonsæli wer weardode hwile
siþðan him scyppend forscrifen hæfde

111. þanon untydras ealle onwocon
eotenas ond ylfas ond orcneas
swylce gigantas þa wið gode wunnon
lange þrage he him ðæs lean forgeald.

This passage, it will be seen, is entirely clear and consecutive, when thus arranged, except that two or three verses containing a reference to the Fall and the death of Abel are needed to make the proper connection between 101 and 107. It is noticeable that this gap is occupied in the MS. by the three verses in which Grendel and his dwelling-place are first mentioned. These verses, which in the rearrangement I have transposed to the beginning of the episode, where they naturally belong, have apparently crowded out a small portion of the interpolation. If the broken connection is restored by conjecture the story will run thus:

> 'He that knew how to tell the tale of the beginning of men from of old has said that the Almighty made the earth, the fair-shining plain which the water encircles, that the Victorious set the brightness of sun and moon for a light to men and decked with bough and leafage the regions of the earth; he also gave life to every living thing that dwells [therein]. Thus then mankind lived blessedly in joy, until one, the foe in hell, began to work mischief. [He beguiled them into disobedience, whereby they lost their home, and led Cain, their first-born, to slay his brother.] The Lord avenged on Cain's race the slaying of Abel, he was not pleased with the murderous deed, but he, the Lord, drove him into exile far from mankind. The wretched man, after the Creator had outlawed him, inhabited awhile the land of the monsters; from him sprang all the monsters, the Jotuns and elves and sea-beasts; also the giants that long fought against God; for that he gave them their meed.'

The other passage in which there is a reference to the descent of the various monsters from Cain contains about what we have supplied to make a consecutive story in the passage just given. It is as follows:

1261. siþðan camp wearð
to ecgbanan angan breþer
fæderenmæge he þa fag gewat
morþre gemearcod mandream fleon
westen warode þanon woc fela
geosceaftgasta wæs þæra grendel sum
heorowearh hetelic,

> 'after Cain (so by conj.) became the slayer of his own brother, his father's son; stained with murder and outlawed he fled the joys of men and dwelt in the desert. From him sprang many an accursed spirit; one of these was Grendel,' etc.

The conclusions reached in this study of the Christian allusions in the *Beowulf* are these:—

1. Of the passages in the *Beowulf* that show a Christian coloring, two are interpolated. The interpolation is proved in the case of one of these by the statements in it, which are contradicted by the evidence of the poem itself; in the case of the other by the dislocated arrangement, which shows an unskilful insertion of marginal matter. A small portion of this latter is repeated by interpolation farther on.

2. All the other passages in which any Christian tone can be detected have been made to suggest Christian ideas by slight changes such as a copyist could easily make. The evidence for this conclusion is found in the colorless character of the allusions, which appears in the entire lack of reference to anything distinctively Christian as contrasted with heathenism. Only on some such theory can we explain the entire lack of any reference to Christ, to New Testament narratives and teachings, and to Church doctrines and practices most in vogue at the time.

3. From these two conclusions there naturally springs a third; that the *Beowulf* once existed as a whole without the Christian allusions.

2

THE HEROIC AGE, AN EXCERPT*

H. Munro Chadwick

. . . I AM VERY MUCH INCLINED TO DOUBT WHETHER ANY SAFE conclusions as to the date of the poems can be obtained from metrical considerations, except of course as regards their final form.

Of far greater importance is the fact that with the exception of the Finn-fragment, which consists of only fifty verses, all our poems contain passages or references of a religious (Christian) character. In *Beowulf* alone there are about seventy such passages of which the significance is not open to question, and seven or eight others which may belong to the same category. Out of the total number thirty-three are limited to single verses or half-verses,[1] while another sixteen affect not more than two verses in each case.[2] The longest passage of all (v. 1724 ff.) contains at least 37 verses, the next longest (v. 175 ff.) fourteen.

* Reprinted, by permission of Cambridge University Press, from H. Munro Chadwick, *The Heroic Age* (New York: Cambridge University Press, 1912), pp. 47-56.

[1] vv. 27, 72, 101, 570, 670, 706, 711, 756 (?), 786, 788, 790, 801, 806, 811, 852, 940, 967, 975, 986 (?), 1201, 1255, 1379, 1626, 1658, 1680, 1682, 2088, 2182, 2216 (?), 2276 (?), 2469, 2650, 3083 (?).

[2] vv. 168 f. (?), 227 f., 440 f., 478 f., 588 f., 625 f., 945 f., 955 f., 1314 f., 1397 f., 1778 f., 1841 f., 1997 f., 2819 f., 2874 f., 3108 f.

The rest vary from three to nine verses.[3] The theology which appears in these passages is of a singularly vague type. There are four distinct references to incidents in the early part of Genesis, viz. one (v. 90 ff.) to the Creation, two (vv. 107 ff., 1261 ff.) to the story of Cain and Abel and one (v. 1688 ff.) to the Flood. Apart from these there appears to be no reference to any passage in the Bible except perhaps in v. 1745 ff., which are thought by some to be based on Ephes. vi. 16, and in v. 3069, which contains the phrase 'day of judgment.' We find also a few references to rewards and punishments in a future life.[4] The word *god* is of very frequent occurrence and always used in the Christian sense. The other epithets of the Deity are 'lord' (*frea, dryhten*), 'father' (*faeder*), 'creator' (*scyppend*), 'ruler' (*waldend*), 'almighty' (*alwalda, aelmihtiga*), 'ruler of men' (*ylda* or *fira waldend*), 'ruler of glory' (*wuldres waldend*), 'shepherd of glory' (*wuldres hyrde*), 'king of glory' (*wuldurcyning*), 'guider of the heavens' (*rodera raedend*), 'helm of the heavens' (*heofena helm*), 'ruler of victories' (*sigora waldend*), 'king of victories' (*sigora soðcyning*). On the other hand there is no example of the word *gast* in a religious sense (Holy Ghost), nor of the name *Crist,* nor of any epithet denoting 'Saviour' (*nergend, haelend* etc.). Hardly less curious is the total absence of the word *engel,* for expressions such as 'lord of angels' (*engla dryhten*)[5] are among the most frequent epithets of the Deity in Anglo-Saxon religious poems. Lastly, there are no references to the saints, to the cross or to the church, nor to any Christian rites or ceremonies.

[3] vv. 13—17, 90—8, 106—14, 316—8, 381—4, 665—7 (?), 685—7, 696—702, 928—31, 977—9, 1056—62, 1261—5, 1271—6, 1553—6, 1609—11, 1661—4, 1688—93, 1716—8, 2291—3, 2329—31, 2341—3 (?), 2741—3, 2794—7, 2855—9, 3054—7, 3069—73.

[4] vv. 588 f., 977—9, 2741—3, 2819 f.

[5] It is perhaps worth noting that in v. 2186 the expression *dryhten wereda* is used of Hygelac. Elsewhere in Anglo-Saxon poetry this phrase is applied only to the Deity.

It appears then that the religious utterances of the poem are of a singularly one-sided character. Indeed it has been observed[6] that, with the exception perhaps of vv. 977-9, "their theology is covered by the Old Testament, and a pious Jew would have no difficulty in assenting to them all." Certainly the facts are such as to call for some explanation, especially since the religious poems are pervaded by a wholly different tone.

One suggestion is that Beowulf was composed under the influence of the missionaries from Iona; but it is extremely doubtful whether the influence of Irish Christianity would tend in this direction at all.[7] Another is that the poet had little direct knowledge of the Christian religion, but that he was acquainted with some religious poems. This explanation certainly seems to fit the case much better than the other. Moreover there is one piece of positive evidence in its favour. In *Beow*. v. 89 ff. we hear of recitation to the accompaniment of the harp in Hrothgar's hall, and the subject of the recitation is the creation of the world. It appears to me highly probable that we have here an allusion to Caedmon's poem or poems on Genesis, which may very well have been among the earliest of that poet's productions. At all events it was by his hymn on the Creation that he first became known. The inference is strengthened by the rather close resemblance which the hymn bears to the phraseology of *Beowulf*. If the two poets were contemporary the author of *Beowulf* would have no other Christian poet on whom to draw, and the limitations of his theological equipment might be satisfactorily accounted for on the hypothesis that he knew only a few of Caedmon's works. As a matter of fact two or three out of the list given by Bede would have been quite sufficient to provide him with all the statements and terms that he uses.

There is another question however with regard to the composition of *Beowulf* which has aroused more controversy than this, namely whether the Christian passages formed an original

[6] Clark Hall, *Beowulf,* p. xxviii.

[7] If there is Celtic influence at all it is more probably Welsh.

part of the poem or not. In the former case of course the poem cannot have been composed before the second quarter of the seventh century. Indeed, if we grant the use of Caedmon's poetry the earliest possible date would be about 660. On the other hand if the Christian passages are due to interpolation the upper limit for the dating of the poem vanishes into air.

As to the possibility of such interpolation in principle we need scarcely entertain any doubt. It is true that the Christian passages or references cannot as a rule be removed without breaking into the rhythm. Consequently, if interpolation has taken place we must assume it to be the work of poets or minstrels, and not of scribes. But have we any reason for doubting that the minstrels of that period were capable of such 'interpolation.' Wherever poetry—at all events anonymous narrative poetry—is preserved exclusively by oral tradition, it is usually the case that the minstrel is allowed a certain amount of freedom in the presentation of his subject.[8] Now probably no one will suggest that it was only after their conversion to Christianity that the English began to compose poems about 'heathen kings.' But, if we grant that such poems were already in existence, does it really involve a greater amount of effort on the part of the minstrels to bring these poems up to date—by removing objectionable matter and introducing expressions in accordance with the new religion—than to compose an entirely new set of poems on the same subjects. I cannot think that such a view will be seriously maintained. Therefore we must consider the case of *Beowulf*—the only narrative poem which has come down to us entire—without prejudice on the general question; and we must endeavour to see whether it bears the stamp of a new composition or that of an old work which has been brought into conformity with new ideas. The probability or improbability

[8] The amount of freedom differs of course greatly from case to case; but it is only in communities which have elaborated the art of minstrelsy to a very high degree that the form of words can become absolutely stereotyped.

of the latter view will of course depend largely on the amount of inconsistency which the poem is found to contain.

Until within the last few years the majority of scholars believed that *Beowulf* was a composite work. This theory was most fully developed in the writings of Müllenhoff and ten Brink. According to the former[9] the poem was made up from four separate lays, though in its present form nearly half of it is the work of interpolators. The latter[10] likewise traced the origin of the poem to lays, but explained its inconsistencies as being due not to extensive interpolations but to the combination of two parallel versions. In regard to the relative antiquity of the various parts of the poem there was great divergence of opinion both between these scholars and generally. It is perhaps partly on this account that in recent years there has been a reaction in favour of believing that the poem as we have it is practically the work of one man, though it is allowed that he may have made use of earlier lays. But those who have adopted this view seem to agree that the author, whatever his precise date, belonged to the Christian period, and consequently that the religious passages are not due to interpolation.

Now in the first place it is clear that the story of Beowulf is derived from the Baltic, and the first question which we have to settle is as to the time at which the information on which it is based became known in England. The Angli themselves were originally a Baltic people, as I have tried elsewhere to show, and there is no doubt that down to the time of the invasion of Britain they were thoroughly familiar with all the surrounding regions. But we have no evidence whatever for believing that such was the case within the historical period. By the end of the sixth century, when the first missionaries arrived in this country, they had apparently ceased to be a seafaring people, and we have no record of any voyage made by an Englishman across the North Sea for several centuries. Again, the Danes

[9] *Beowulf* (1889), pp. 110—160.
[10] *Quellen und Forschungen,* LXII (1888); summarized p. 242 ff.

became familiar to the west of Europe during the sixth century; but from about 580 onwards we hear no more of their presence on the North Sea for fully two centuries. During the whole of this period their name is heard of only in connection with the missionary expeditions of St. Willibrord, early in the eighth century. I have suggested elsewhere[11] that their temporary disappearance was due to the maritime supremacy held by the Frisians. At all events we have archaeological evidence for a considerable amount of communication between southern Norway and the Frisian coasts during this period, while for the Baltic such evidence is almost wholly wanting.

Bearing these facts in mind we can hardly doubt that the information used by *Beowulf* was acquired before the end of the sixth century—in all probability we may say considerably before that date.[12] Next we have to notice that we have practically no trustworthy information regarding the history of the English kingdoms before the middle of the sixth century, and I think it will be the opinion of any attentive student of early English history that even the best informed persons of Bede's time were not much better off in this respect than we ourselves are. How then are we to account for the preservation of detailed information regarding the early kings of the Danes and Swedes? The only answer to this question, so far as I can see, is that the doings of such persons must have become embodied in stories which were preserved by recitation in a more or less fixed form of words. Such recitative pieces may have consisted of poetry alone or of poetry mixed with prose, like some of the pieces contained in the Older Edda. If we may trust the analogy of what appear to be the oldest pieces in this collection, such as Völundarkviða or Helgakviða Hundingsbana II, the speeches would be given in metre, while the connecting narrative might

[11] *The Origin of the English Nation,* p. 93, note.

[12] The references quoted previously preclude the possibility that these stories were first acquired from the Danes, when the latter again became known in this country about the close of the eighth century.

be partly or wholly in prose and quite brief. We have no evidence for believing that the early Teutonic peoples ever used entirely prose narratives, like the Icelandic and Irish sagas, for such purposes.

At all events it seems to me that if *Beowulf* is no older than the middle of the seventh century we are bound to assume the existence of earlier poems or narratives on the same subject. Such pieces may of course have been quite short, and it is likely enough that our epic has made use of more than one of them. One perhaps may have dealt with the hero's exploits at the Danish court and another with his last adventure, while in the scene between Beowulf and Hygelac it is possible that an older poem has been incorporated, more or less complete, in the text.[13]

But we have yet to take account of what is perhaps the most striking feature of the poem, namely the fact that, though it abounds in expressions of Christian sentiment, yet the customs and ceremonies to which it alludes are uniformly heathen. Among these we may mention the funeral ship in v. 27 ff., the offerings at the shrines in v. 175 f., the observation of the omens in v. 204 and the curious reference to hanging in v. 2444 ff. (cf. v. 2939 ff.), probably also the use of the boar on helmets (vv. 303 f., 1111 f., 1286, 1451 ff., 2152) and the burial of the treasure (v. 2233 ff.), together with the curse imprecated on the person who should disturb it (v. 3069 ff.). But most important of all are the descriptions of the disposal of the dead by cremation in vv. 1108 ff., 2124 ff., 3137 ff. In the long account of Beowulf's obsequies—beginning with the dying king's injunction (v. 2802 ff.) to construct for him a lofty barrow on the edge of the cliff, and ending with the scene of the twelve princes riding round the barrow, proclaiming the dead man's exploits—we have the most detailed description of an early Teutonic funeral which has come down to us, and one of which

[13] A different view is taken by Schücking, *Beowulfs Rückkehr,* xxi, *Studien zur engl. Philologie,* pp. 65 ff.

the accuracy is confirmed in every point by archaeological or contemporary literary evidence.[14] Such an account must have been composed within living memory of a time when ceremonies of this kind were still actually in use.

The significance of these passages seems to me to have been altogether misapprehended by recent writers. If the poem preserves its original form and is the work of a Christian, it is difficult to see why the poet should go out of his way in v. 175 ff. to represent the Danes as offering heathen sacrifices, for not long before he has introduced a song of the Creation at the Danish court, and in the sequel Hrothgar is constantly giving utterance to Christian sentiments. Again why should he lay Beowulf himself to rest with heathen obsequies, described in all possible detail, when in his dying speeches (vv. 2739 ff., 2794 ff.)[15] the hero has been made to express his faith and gratitude to the Almighty? On the other hand if the poem was originally a heathen work these inconsistencies are perfectly natural. If it was to retain its place after the change of faith and to be recited in the presence of bishops or clergy, all references to actual heathen worship or belief would of necessity have to be either accompanied by censure—as is the case in the homiletic verses following v. 175 ff.—or else suppressed altogether, and their place taken by expressions in accordance with Christian doctrine. Hence it seems to me probable that such expressions are frequently in the nature of substitutions for objectionable matter, rather than gratuitous additions; and in the same way I would account for the occasional survival of ideas which appear to be essentially heathen,[16] though they are cloaked in Christian phraseology. But references to practices

[14] We may refer especially to the account of Attila's funeral given by Jordanes, cap. 49 (from Priscus).

[15] Apart from certain expressions the general tone of these speeches, especially the last words of all (v. 2813 ff.), is scarcely Christian; but they contain nothing which is obviously opposed to Christian doctrine.

[16] E.g. in the imprecation, v. 3069 ff. The imprecatory formulae of charters can scarcely be regarded as analogous.

such as cremation which, though heathen, had long ago passed out of use, would not excite the same repugnance and consequently might be allowed to stand.

It may be urged[17] that cremation seems to have lingered on among the Old Saxons of the Continent until late in the eighth century. True: but it is quite incredible that a Christian poet should borrow from this quarter a method of funeral for his Christianised heroes. If the description of Beowulf's obsequies stood alone a bare possibility might be conceded to the suggestion that it had once formed a poem by itself, unconnected with *Beowulf,* and based upon a traveller's story. But cremation is clearly regarded as the normal rite throughout the poem, apart from the legendary story of Scyld. We have another description of it in the episode dealing with Finn (v. 1108 ff.), and above all there is the purely incidental reference in v. 2124 ff.: "Yet when morning came the knights of the Danes could not burn his (Aeschere's) lifeless form with fire, nor lay the man they loved on the pyre. She had carried the body away," etc. Here the poet realizes the significance[18] of the rite quite clearly and consequently notes that the inability of the Danes to carry it out added materially to their sorrow. In such a case the possibility of Christian authorship seems to me to be definitely excluded.

On the hypothesis that these descriptions had come down from the days of English heathenism all is easily explicable. At the time when the poem was Christianized it may very well not have been known that the rite of cremation was still practised among the heathen of the Continent, and in later days the verses of the old poet would be handed on in parrot fashion without their significance being generally understood. Well informed persons however, like Alcuin, who had travelled abroad, perceived clearly enough that, however much coated over with

[17] Cf. Brandl, in Paul's *Grundriss d. germ. Philol.,* II, 1003.

[18] The same idea is frequently expressed in the Homeric poems, e.g. Il. VII 79 f., XXII 342 f., XXIII 75 f., XXIV 37 f., Od. XI 71 ff., etc.

Christian phraseology, the heroic poems were in reality of an essentially heathen character.

Now cremation was widely prevalent in this country during the early days of the Saxon invasion—a fact attested by numerous cemeteries especially in the northern and midland counties, including the valley of the Thames. But it appears to have become a thing of the past when the Roman missionaries arrived here; otherwise it is difficult to account for the absence of any reference to the custom in the records which have come down to us. Indeed we may say with safety that it had passed out of general use, at least in the southern half of England, quite a generation before this time; for there are scarcely any traces of it to be found in those western districts which appear to have been conquered during the latter half of the sixth century. Consequently, if we are justified in believing that the descriptions of cremation ceremonies contained in *Beowulf* date from a time when the practice was still remembered, we must conclude that they were composed not later than the third or fourth decade of the seventh century.[19]

But it is not contended, so far as I am aware, by any scholar that the account of Beowulf's obsequies belongs to the earlier parts of the poem. It is the final scene of the story, it is not contained in any speech, and further it is of a thoroughly epic character and would be quite out of place in a short lay. Hence, if the line of argument which we have been following is legitimate, we shall be forced to admit that though the poem has undergone a fairly thorough revision in early Christian times, it must in the main have been in existence some time before the conversion. I do not mean to suggest that the 'revision' was entirely limited to the religious element. Other changes and addi-

[19] This date does not depend in any way on the question where the poem originated. Cremation may possibly have lingered in Northumbria longer than elsewhere; but that kingdom seems to have become entirely Christian between 626 and 642.

tions may have been made about the same time.[20] What I do mean is that the great bulk of the poem must have been in existence—not merely as a collection of lays or stories, but in full epic form—an appreciable time before the middle of the seventh century.

[20] E.g. possibly some of the elegiac passages (e.g. vv. 2236—2270, 2450—2464), which show a certain resemblance to such poems as the Ruin and the Wanderer.

3

THE IDEAL OF KINGSHIP IN *BEOWULF**

Levin L. Schücking

SO LONG AS WE HAVE CONSIDERED THE *Beowulf* EPIC A KIND OF intellectual coral-accumulation, which came about through the successive activity of many individuals, we could not well speak of an interpretation of the leading ideas underlying its composition. Even though Müllenhoff. for example, explained its fable as a nature-myth (that is, explained Beowulf's battles in terms of the opposition between summer and winter), his inquiry is still directed more to the origin of the materials out of which the poem is composed, than to the origin of the poem itself — a difference almost as great as that between the origin of the materials in a building, and the origin of the architectonic design expressed in it. But if one belongs to the increasing number of those who believe in a unitary individual origin of this poem, he will no longer avoid an investigation of this idea. In other words, for them the question arises what the unknown author intended by the poem and which special attitude to the world and life can be deduced from his work; in which connection, naturally, the sagacious word of Bernard Shaw remains of undiminished importance: "The existence of a discoverable and perfectly definite thesis in a poet's work by no means depends on the completeness of his own intellectual consciousness of it."

* Reprinted, by permission of the author and the Modern Humanities Research Association, from *MHRA Bulletin,* III (1929), 143-154. Originally entitled "Das Königsideal im *Beowulf,*" the essay appears here for the first time in translation.

In an earlier attempt ("Wann entstand der Beowulf?" ["When did the *Beowulf* originate?"] *Paul und Braunes Beiträge* 42, p. 399), I have already tried to prove that the author of *Beowulf* designed it as a kind of Fürstenspiegel ("mirror of a prince") — perhaps for the young son of a prince, a thought with which later Heusler (*Altgermanische Dichtung*, p. 184) also agreed. But if this is the case, it is still more appropriate and must then be the more possible to ascertain and interpret the image of a human ideal hovering before the author with respect to its most important features and their origin.

That such an idealistic picture reveals uncommonly much of the heathen-Germanic warrior ethic, is obvious at the start. In this respect, the end of King Beowulf is especially instructive. For no moment of human existence characterizes Christian and non-Christian attitudes so unequivocally as that of death. How does the dying Beowulf conduct himself? He throws a backward glance over his life, expresses satisfaction for having administered his kingdom so well that no enemy dared to attack it. Nor has he committed malicious deeds, broken an oath, or perpetrated wrong against his relatives. Great emphasis is placed, therefore, on the idea of performing that duty which also has first place in the code of morals of the Germanic people, namely *Treue* ["loyalty"]. (Cf. Heusler, *Altgermanische Sittenlehre*, p. 175; Neckel, *Altgermanische Kultur*, 76, 130). The Anglo-Saxon word "treow" itself has, by the way, just the three meanings with which we here are concerned:

1. Truthful behavior (Cf. "no malicious deeds")
2. Faithfulness, in the sense of loyalty (Cf. "relation to relatives")
3. Keeping of word or promise (Cf. "no oaths broken")

The concept that no enemy dared to attack him is, however, clearly also a traditional formula — not specifically Christian — for a glorious reign, as for example, the description of Edgar's reign contained in the *Peterborough Chronicle:* no enemy was so daring as to threaten his possessions, no army so strong as to devastate his country as long as he ruled over it. Thus, what one would expect of the dying Christian is lacking here. Even in the Byrhtnoth Poem — entirely filled with warlike spirit — at least there is put in the mouth of the leader at the moment of departing, the request to be admitted into Heaven (175). In contrast thereto, Beowulf's thought that the sight of the earthly goods which he acquired makes death easier for him is even decidedly un-Christian. There is little harmony between the Christian penitential axiom that we are all sinners, and the beautiful pride of duty-performed that emerges from his parting words with which he goes confidently before his Judge. The spirit which these words breathe is then much more what Heusler, relying primarily on Nordic materials, designates as the essence of the Germanic-heathen religiosity: "No terrified awareness of Deity, no humble submissiveness, but tones of comradely trust as between men and lords." Such a mental attitude occurs more than once in the poem. True pride, esteem for one's own achievement, dignity do not disappear in the religious relations. Byrthnoth, a shade more Christian, knows, for example, a prayer of entreaty for use before the battle (262), Beowulf by contrast only prayers of thanksgiving. Many other characteristic Germanic features are to be found in the poem; for example, the fatalistic belief in fate (Gæð a wyrd swa hio scel ["Fate goes ever as it must"]), which occurs throughout Germanic literature. This belief is also not infrequent in early Germanic Christianity, and there, as Ehrismann ("Religionsgeschichtliche Beiträge zum germanischen Frühchristentum," *Beiträge zur Geschichte der deutschen Sprache und Literatur,* XXXV [1909], p. 238) has shown, looks occasionally to the Augustinian doctrine of predestination only for fresh support for itself. An additional Germanic feature, not infrequent, is the emphasis on the duty of revenge which Heusler calls the greatest highlight of the old Germanic code, equal to loyalty of the vassal and heroic death. Many further examples of this kind, which make clear the connection with the rest of heroic literature and its unknown earlier stages, could be cited; thus, for example, the grim battle humor designed to show the fighter equal to the situation (Cf. line 451 and the corresponding passage in the *Waldere*. See L. L. Schücking, "Waldere und Waltharius," *Engl. Stud.*, 60, p. 21, and Hennig Brinkmann, "Ekkehards Waltharius als Kunstwerk," *Zeitschrift für deutsche Bildung*, 1928, p. 631), or also the cultivation of brotherhood by oath which one encounters in the relationship between Beowulf and Breca. All of this, as observed in large measure long ago, is distinctly Germanic.

However, if it had been the glorification of these features which mattered to the author, he could have written an Ermanarich epic. If he did not do so, he had obviously quite particular reasons for it. Here, too, Heusler has already indicated the right way by showing that Beowulf, the fighter of monsters, must have been a much better hero for a Christian mirror of princes, than a representative of the old heroic world of sagas. Looking at things in this manner it becomes especially clear that the specifically Germanic features enumerated disclose to a large extent a certain selection by which they are granted their place in a world view which in the last analysis is differently constituted. For there are in the poem very clearly un-Germanic features as, for example, the following. Neckel says (*loc. cit.*, p. 125 fn.): "It does not glorify champions and benefactors of the people as such." That, however, is precisely what it does. King Beowulf dies for his people, and his comfort in dying is to have acquired for his loyal people such precious possessions. Klaeber, who has the merit of having proved more exactly how Christian *Beowulf* is in fundamental conception, in spite of all its heathen Germanic elements, thinks he can even see in this motif an allegory of the Savior. He supports this parallel further by certain correspondences of the final action, namely the events at the sacrifice of the king's life, where the companions desert him in cowardice — and this is said to be a reminiscence of Gethsemane. The question is, however, whether the final action, like the whole concept, does not bring into being rather an ideal of kingship. Such an ideal has by degrees acquired an almost dominating character from the contemporary church literature, namely that of *imperator felix* ["successful emperor"] or *rex justus* ["just king"] of Augustine.[1]

The teaching of Augustine, which continues to live with only little change in Gregory the Great, Pseudo-Cyprian, Sedulius Scotus, Hincmar of Reims, etc., spiritualizes the authoritative office by asking from its bearer above all wisdom, piety, and kindness. The prince must be master of his desires and passions, and especially, not yield power over himself to the greatest and for him the most dangerous sin — pride (superbia), but remain modest and humble. His rule should be a service in love, benevolence, sympathetic care. "In domo cœlestis civitatis etiam qui imperant serviunt eis, quibus videntur imperare." ["In the house of the Heavenly State, those who rule also serve those whom they appear to command."] The "Pastor bonus" is the one of whom it may be said: "Non præesse sed prodesse vult." ["He does not want to command but serve."] He is indulgent and pardons easily. If he is forced to act harshly, he tries to compensate by mercy and ample charity. His purpose is to bring and keep for himself and his people the true peace of God on earth. For the highest purpose of life is harmony (ordinata concordia ["harmonious order"]) between states, within the state and within the family. In contrast to such a "rex justus" ["just king"] who always appears as a *good shepherd* and with the *qualities of a father,* is the "tyrannus" or "rex iniustus," who is ruled by the "radix vitiorum" ["root of vices"], "superbia" ["pride"] or "amor sui" ["love of self"] — *amor Dei* and *amor sui* are contrasted, for example, in XIV, Chapt. 13. Out of *amor sui* spring all other vices, such as "invidia, ira, tristitia, avaritia and ventris ingluvies" ["envy, wrath, sadness, avarice and gluttony"]. (Editor's note: Compare

[1] Compare to the following: St. Aurelii Augustini Episcopi, *De Civitate Dei,* Libri XXII, rec. E. Hoffmann, Vienna, 1900; Ernst Bernheim, *Mittelalterliche Zeitanschauungen,* Tübingen, 1918; Hugo Tiralla, *Das Augustinische Idealbild der christlichen Obrigkeit,* Greifswalder Diss., 1916.

Gregory, *Mor. in Job* [39:25], XXXI, xlv, 89 [*PL* 76, 621-2].) The teachers of the church already named express similar ideas, such as Sedulius Scotus who designates as the most perfect product of God's creation the "rex pacificus" ["peaceful king"] "in gloria regni sui" ["in the glory of his reign"] "quando in aula regia ostensis muneribus donisque traditis multa beneficia præstat" (Tiralla) ["when, in the royal court, he confers many benefits by bestowing offices and handing out gifts."] Charlemagne, an eager reader of Augustine, incidentally, adopted the attribute "pacificus" ["the peaceful"] as a title. Its most important continuer, however, is Gregory, who was also highly esteemed in the land of the Anglo-Saxons. Gregory praises ever more forcefully than Augustine the virtue of complete and humble devotion to God's will, the "obedientia" ["obedience"] of the Christian. Moreover, the Anglo-Saxon rule of the king also asks that the king, in the first place, be "folces frofor and rihtwis hyrde ofer cristene heorde" ("protector of the people and just shepherd over the Christian flock").[2]

But how far does the Augustinian interpretation of kingship shine forth in the *Beowulf* epic in spite of the indicated Germanic elements? First and foremost, it is evident in the conception of the theme, which shows a hero and king not only by great deeds but by the "prodesse" ["help"], which is according to Augustine the essence of the royal office. Beowulf, who kills the dragon, is the good shepherd, who perishes in protecting his flock. But the old King Hrothgar, too, in the first part of the poem embodies this ideal of "rex justus." He is a prince of peace, full of fatherly benevolence, caring for the welfare of his people. The "ordinata

[2] Compare "Institutes of Polity, Civil and Ecclesiastical" (*Ancient Laws and Inst. of England,* Vol. 2, 305); compare *ibidem,* the eight pillars of kingship (Be cynedome) with the same demands of "veritas, patientia, largitas, persuabilitas, correctio malorum, exultatio bonorum, levitas tributi and iudicii" ["truth, patience, generosity, gift of persuasion, correction of evil things, exultation of the good, lightness of tributes, and justice of judgments,"] as with Sedulius Scotus and Cathulf to Charlemagne, which Werminghoff cites (*Hist. Zeitschr.* 89, 198 ff.).

concordia" ["harmonious order"] is for him a high ideal. He rejoices in the treaty of peace between the Danes and the Gauts (1856) as well as the happy accord within the Danish community ("Her is æghwylc oþrum getrywe" ["Here is each loyal to the other"]. Further, like Beowulf, he accepts decisions from God's hands on most important matters without grumbling, and with Gregorian "obedientia." Especially remarkable, however, is his conduct towards his people. When his loyal Aeschere is torn away from him by death, he mourns for him in terms of highest praise just as he would for one of his peers. He even uses the designation "sincgifa" ("treasure-giver," line 1342) for the deceased as if speaking of a king, just as if he intended to bear out Gregory's demand: "Sit rector bene agentibus per humilitatem socius" ["Let the ruler be through humility a companion to those who conduct themselves well."] (Tiralla, 40). The final words of the epic celebrating the deceased as the kindest and friendliest of all men characterize most strongly this striving to show benevolence and warmth of heart in his relation with those around him.

Such strong emphasis on a prince's popularity and on good relations between a king and his people runs through the entire *Beowulf,* and perhaps contrary to what one might think, is in no way like the ideal of a king to be found in Vergil. King Latinus of the *Aeneid* is "pious, prudent, generous, just, tender of heart" (Heinze), but with the Latin poet, great popularity and the striving for popularity play no role. Evidently, Germanic conceptions are blended in the *Beowulf* to a high degree. That the king is, for example, always designated briefly as "wine" (Cf. "wine Scyldinga") means that the word for "friend" and "lord" is the same, evidently derived from the atmosphere of the life of the comitatus. Just this democracy within the governing class is typically Germanic. Still, the basis for the democracy is again Christian. The speech of Hrothgar against Pride ("superbia"), for example, breathes a typical Augustinian-Gregorian spirit (Cf. Gregory, *Cura Pastoralis,* XVII). Also the counter example of "tyrannus," who is more obedient to the devil than to God, — here, it is the gloomy Heremod — is in itself completely borrowed from the way of thinking of the Church Fathers, who, for example, liked to contrast Moses and Solomon or turn to account the picture of Saul (Hincmar, Pseudo-Cyprian); the details, it is true, are fitted out with the appropriate Germanic features. The basic vice of the evil ones is designated as "lufu" (1728), a word the use of which in this place has remained unexplained but which perhaps only renders Augustine's *amor sui*.

Finally, striking in the *Beowulf* is the strong emphasis on the king's intellectual powers. Likewise, in the picture of the ideal figure of the martyr king, Edmund, in Ælfric's Homily (*Lives of Saints,* Vol. II, E.E.T.S.O.S. 114, p. 316 ff.), prudence is cited in first place (*snotor* and wurðfull ["wise and worthy"]). This prudence, it is true, is of a very different kind (see further below). But the king is still in the first place the "wise one" — and to this, moreover, according to the proposition that wisdom presupposes age (*Wanderer,* 64, 65), is tied the notion of being well advanced in years, which is also customarily connected with other expressions for "prudent," namely "frod" and "snotor." Again and again, Beowulf is thus designated as "se wisa" (1318, 1400, 1698 etc.). His intellectual achievement in the epic is shown not the least by the fact that he is wise in a special way, namely, "wis wordcwida," that is, he is a good orator. But this, too, is neither foreign nor un-Germanic. "To be gifted as an orator," says Neckel (*loc. cit.* 76) "is always well-becoming to a Germanic king." In the Christian ideal of a king, however, this feature is particularly prominent. The "persuabilitas (in verbis)" belongs to the "eight pillars" of royalty. Such an ability for speaking is at the same time an ability for teaching, just as the deserted vassal in the *Wanderer* (38) yearns to return to the "*larcwidum*" ("teaching") of the king; indeed, sometimes, it passes over directly into the sermon. But to see so distinctly the teacher in the king is, I suppose — one should think of Gregory's *Cura Pastoralis*[3] — a clerical ideal.

With this a line of features is denoted, which, as we have seen, often make it difficult to answer in detail the question of native versus foreign origin, but it essentially discloses the ideal of a gentle prince of peace of Augustinian coinage. It is now instructive to see that this ideal is by no means limited to *Beowulf*.[4] Thus, we find, for example, a not unsimilar picture on German soil in *Ruodlieb*. *Ruodlieb* (first half of the 11th century) consists, as is well known, of three entirely unequal parts, of which one is usually only concerned with the main or middle piece, that is, the Novelle of the twelve teachings and the fully different end piece, which is closely allied with the heroic saga. But the introduction, moulded from a different type of narration from that which S. Singer once called the "heroic novel," describes how the hero goes into the realm of a neighboring king, whose favor he gains and, as leader of his army, wins victory for him. Then, as his ambassador in the country of the vanquished, he initiates

[3] Compare also *Bedas Widmung der Hist. Ecc. an König Ceowulf:* "Weil Dich Gott zum Könige erkor, geziemt es Dir, Dein Volk zu belehren." ["Since God chose you as king, it behooves you to teach your people."]

[4] The already quoted description of the ideal figure of the king-martyr Edmund, by Ælfric, shows rather completely the seven qualities which the English rule of kingship demands of the just king: fear of God and humility before God (eadmod and geþungen ["humble-minded" and "virtuous"]), love of justice (rihtwisnyss ["righteousness"]), sternness against evil (þam reþum styrde ["punished the wicked"]), care for the poor and oppressed (cystig wædlum and wydewum swa swa fæder ["charitable towards the poor and widows, just as a father"]), protection of the Church (?) (symble gemyndig þære soþan lare ["always mindful of the true teaching"]). In the place of a righteous judgment of friends and strangers, there is here a more thorough presentation of his goodness, of his deep compassion, of his abiding sense of responsibility for his people, as well as his democratic attitude (betwux mannum swa swa an man of him ["among men as one of them"]) and his willingness to sacrifice himself. Of his wisdom, finally, we have already spoken above (snotor and wurðfull ["wise and worthy"]).

negotiations for him, which find their conclusion in the personal meeting of the sovereigns.

If there was nothing else here to remind one of *Beowulf,* the remarkable correspondence of the narrative technique would do so. For the events here are told exactly as the Grendel battle — once how they came to pass, and then once more, in detail, as a report addressed to the king. This evidently follows a traditional scheme, which cannot be explained only by the tendency of early epic poetry to use the direct form of speech. But in the descriptions, too, the author may be seen moving in a literary tradition which touches with astonishing closeness on *Beowulf,* above all in the particulars of the description of the visit to the court. When, for example, the king delegates a steward, who then takes care of the guests' livelihood, brings and accompanies them to the frontier of the country, and receives for this a rich gift himself at their departure (IV, 70 ff.), one seems to be transplanted completely to *Beowulf.* After all this, one cannot be surprised if the features of the ideal of kingship also remind us most forcefully of those in *Beowulf,* except that they have become intrinsically softer in the course of rather 200 than 400 years. It is unnecessary to say that he is the personification of generosity and hospitality and keeps his promises reliably. It is more striking that he gives himself up completely to the care of his people. His first question when a messenger comes from war is, for example, "Are our men without wounds?" (III, 53). Indeed, even his subjects stand in the relationship of a friend to him (I, 131). He is completely *benevolent and warm of feeling,* undemanding for himself, he renounces all gifts, and full of modesty, he cannot utter a proud word about his triumphs (IV, 179). His magnanimity towards his enemies shows his highmindedness. He frees his captives and even decorates them (IV, 25, 106, 157, 242; V, 63), a feature of clemency which, as Naumann in his methodical but instructive essay about the state of research of the Nibelungs pointed out ("Stand der Nibelungenforschung," *Zeitschrift für Deutschkunde,* 1927), by no means "breathes the most modern spirit." He, too, is above all the pious prince of peace, who far removed from every "superbia," "achieves more victories by means of the spirit of the lamb and wisdom than others achieve by the sword." Like the king in *Beowulf,* he is able to find the proper rhetorical expressions to set forth his wisdom; he, also, gives advice — this is even the framework of the main tale — without, however, slipping into Hrothgar's sermon-like style.

The drawing of Attila's figure in certain parts of the Germanic epic exhibits another very conspicuous reflection of the literary predominance of this Augustinian ideal of kingship. Our research on the legends (Jiriczek, Heusler) usually attends to the fact that Attila appears very distinctly in one branch of the legends as a kind and mild prince, particularly in certain historical-political circumstances where he is shown serving many years as protector of the Ostrogoths. But the question is, how far the representation of the fatherly king, Attila, where the legend allows it, is in the spirit of a later time, a purely literary elaboration of an originally colorless mention of him as "huneo truhtin," ["lord of Huns"] as, for example, he is referred to in the *Hildebrandlied*. At least this literary elaboration is true of Ekkehard's *Waltharius*. The *Waltharius,* for example, describes Attila as decidedly a man of peace who prefers to enter into alliances rather than to fight battles with nations, prefers to reign in peace, and only regretfully fights rebels with arms (i. 68) (Walther, incidentally, likewise fights against rebels for Attila.). This conduct conforms entirely with the main tendency of the Augustinian "imperator felix," as described earlier in this paper. According to Augustine, a war may, of course, become inevitable, but he holds that it is much better "vicinum bonum habere concordem quam vicinum malum subjugare bellantem" ["to have a good neighbor in peace than to subdue a bad neighbor in war."]. Attila's benevolence toward his associates, the "anxious love" with which he as paterfamilias assists hostages and treats them like his own sons, so that Walther may address him as "best of fathers" — all of this agrees entirely with the basic character of the ideal king, which is now satisfactorily known to us and which one cannot designate otherwise than by the word "fatherly."

However, it is perhaps a mistake to consider this ideal so isolated, as has been done hitherto, without considering its broadest basis as is given in the general ideal of personality in the period. In a certain manner, the ideal is defined by the concept of virtue taught by the Church, which starts with the four cardinal virtues, prudence ("prudentia"), justice ("justitia"), courage ("fortitudo"), and temperance ("temperantia"). Of the demands of this doctrine of virtue, the one which exercised the strongest character-forming influence was evidently the ideal of *mensura* or *sobrietas* ("temperance"), which the Church took over with a certain change in coloration from the Latin Stoa and which appears set forth in detail in such works as the widespread "Formula Honestæ Vitæ" by Martin of Braga (6th century). The underlying idea of complete bridling of emotional drives, restraint and self-conquest, keeping to the middle way (in battle, for example, "nec timidum esse hominem nec audacem" ["for a man to be neither fearful nor rash"]) — these ideas assert themselves very early in literature as, for example, in the founding of epic tragedy on "desmesure." Quite wrongly, one is accustomed to interpret the *Chanson de Roland* as the first example of this "desmesure." For the fear of "desmesure" is to be found already in Hildegunde's speech of exhortation in the Anglo-Saxon *Waldere*,[5] which is still totally misinterpreted by research; "desmesure" is also the poet's explanation for the fall of alderman Byrhtnoth in the battle at Maldon in the year 991 (Cf. 1. 89). The Anglo-Saxon poem, "The Wanderer," (11. 65-69) already preaches right proportion, that is, virtue as the conscious mean between two extremes in the Aristotelian sense. But Beowulf is the first example of a design of a personality turned towards the "sobrietas" or "mensura"

[5] L. L. Schücking, "Waldere und Waltharius," *Engl. Stud.* 60, 22 ff. Remarkably, Hermann Schneider, *Germ. Heldensage*, 1928, 415, states: "Before [the year] 800, there was in England a Waltherlied and it soon became an epic." There is not a shade of proof for this!

ideal, and this is what gives him such an extraordinary interest. Here, a hero is described who unites in an ideal manner pride with modesty, devotion to God with self-confidence, daring with caution, joie de vivre with piety, who enjoys possessions but is not greedy, who is thankful, pious, and reverent towards age. Of the features which are especially striking, one should perhaps mention first prudence, the high estimation of which has already been remarked on in connection with the ideal of kingship. Indeed, the *Beowulf* poet once cites as God's main gifts prudence (snyttru), possession, and honor (dominion) (11. 1726-1727), where the traditional group is similar to that of Walther: "gotes hulde, êre und guot." Prudence (snyttru) is understood not only intellectually, but, as the knowledge of the just, is closely connected with the morally good and thereby acquires a special position. However, this prudence is also circumspection. Heusler says of the Germanic heroes: "Their first virtue is bravery, but this may also be blind courage, for heroic poetry loves bravado, overactivity, contempt of caution." In this sense only is Beowulf un-Germanic; he knows something similar as the Breca-episode indicates, but he looks at it as juvenile folly. His ideal does not allow "desmesure;" his ideal is discretion and circumspection. In the Grendel battle the hero shows just this when he seizes the demon only at a sure moment; he shows it again in the wise foresight of ordering an iron shield to be made for his encounter with the fire dragon; above all, however, when he realizes clearly from the beginning how difficult this struggle will be. And if it is a part of "prudentia": "præsentia ordinare, futura prævidere, præterita recordari," ["to order present matters, to foresee the future ones, to record the past ones,"], the hero performs these demands, too, in an exemplary fashion as his arrangements and speeches indicate.

The test of man is above all his relationship to the irascible impulses. He must be "continens in ira" ["continent in wrath"]. To show him as such was perhaps the main reason for the insertion of the Unferth-episode into the epic. It is true, he energetically averts the insults of the insolent one, but by no means does he allow himself to be carried away to acts of violence. Rather, he shows himself to be self-assured and soon makes Unferth his friend. Similarly, the good king in the German *Ruodlieb* is characterized quite consciously by the fact that no loss in the game of chess can annoy him (IV, 214). To suppress the passions of wrath is here too the first duty (III, 8).

Self-conquest leads then also to highmindedness. At one time, Naumann thinks (*loc. cit.* 11 ff.) he is able to distinguish clearly the ethics of the early Germanic time from the High Middle Ages by contrasting the generous attitude of Feirefiz in the fight against Parzival with Hildebrand and Asmund Kappabani. But Beowulf already shows such "chivalrous impulses" even towards a demon, where it is hardly in place, in his relationship with Grendel. (An example of highmindedness in *Ruodlieb* has already been mentioned.) Beowulf wants to renounce unequal conditions in the battle which would secure for himself an advantage. This is the same highmindedness with which he refuses the crown offered to him in favor of his relation; thus, he becomes a member of the virtuous society which supports the ideal of temperance.

Of the other virtues which stand out visibly, sound character which manifests itself in fixity of purpose should be emphasized. Again and again, we encounter in Anglo-Saxon literature praise of just this quality. Nothing is praised more than "fæstrædne geþoht" ["steadfast thought"]. But here again Germanic warrior-ideals flow together with Stoic-Christian ones. For example, the firmly stamped form of the typical "Gelübderede ["speech containing a vow"] ("beot," "beotword," also "gylp" [boastful speech," "boast," "boasting"]) which shows itself clearly in the Scandinavian as in Beowulf and Byrhtnoth (212), proves the special Germanic appreciation of resolution and firmness of will. One must explore and know oneself very thoroughly before one makes a resolution (*Wanderer,* 1. 70), but its pronouncement should then be tantamount to its execution.

Thus the personality ideal, just as the kingship ideal, shows itself to be a mixture of Germanic-heroic and Stoic-Christian ideas. If one compares the general relationships in the corresponding part of *Ruodlieb,* as Ehrismann has so brilliantly stated them (*Geschichte der deutschen Literatur,* I, 403), one sees with surprise that they really represent only a continuation of the development inaugurated here. I therefore doubt whether Ehrismann is right in designating *as hitherto unheard of,* the "self-discipline and more refined form of life" as well as "the touching tones of purely human feelings," which characterize "this world determined by the ideal of a power dominated by will, by moderation." One must rather point out how all this is in large part, already present in *Beowulf* beside the residues of heroic time, which at first are more conspicuous to the modern reader. How warmly and heartily, for example, does Hrothgar speak with the hero whom he embraces, weeping at his departure! How full of piety and at the same time kindred-friendly ("verwandschaftlich-freundlich") is the tone in which Beowulf addresses Hygelac, how decidedly tasteful and dictated by "mores iucundi" ["pleasing manners"], which Alcuin included in "temperantia," is his attitude on many occasions! Thus, the opinion must raise doubts whether *Ruodlieb* is, in these things, entirely outside any tradition and defies being placed in the inner development of the history of literature. There exists here a tradition — even a literary one! But the enticing task of drawing the most important conclusions from the indicated relationship for strictly literary-historical connections will not be undertaken here.

4

BEOWULF: THE MONSTERS AND THE CRITICS*

J. R. R. Tolkien

IN 1864 THE REVEREND OSWALD COCKAYNE WROTE OF THE Reverend Doctor Joseph Bosworth, Rawlinsonian Professor of Anglo-Saxon: 'I have tried to lend to others the conviction I have long entertained that Dr. Bosworth is not a man so diligent in his special walk as duly to read the books . . . which have been printed in our old English, or so-called Anglosaxon tongue. He may do very well for a professor.'[1] These words were inspired by dissatisfaction with Bosworth's dictionary, and were doubtless unfair. If Bosworth were still alive, a modern Cockayne would probably accuse him of not reading the 'literature' of his subject, the books written about the books in the so-called Anglo-Saxon tongue. The original books are nearly buried.

Of none is this so true as of *The Beowulf,* as it used to be called. I have, of course, read *The Beowulf,* as have most (but not all) of those who have criticized it. But I fear that, unworthy successor and beneficiary of Joseph Bosworth, I have not been a man so diligent in my special walk as duly to read all that has been printed on, or touching on, this poem. But I have read

* Reprinted, by permission of The British Academy, from *Proceedings of the British Academy,* XXII (1936), 245-295. The paper was first delivered by Professor Tolkien as the Sir Israel Gollancz Memorial Lecture of 1936.

[1] *The Shrine,* p. 4.

enough, I think, to venture the opinion that *Beowulfiana* is, while rich in many departments, specially poor in one. It is poor in criticism, criticism that is directed to the understanding of a poem as a poem. It has been said of *Beowulf* itself that its weakness lies in placing the unimportant things at the centre and the important on the outer edges. This is one of the opinions that I wish specially to consider. I think it profoundly untrue of the poem, but strikingly true of the literature about it. *Beowulf* has been used as a quarry of fact and fancy far more assiduously than it has been studied as a work of art.

It is of *Beowulf,* then, as as poem that I wish to speak; and though it may seem presumption that I should try with *swich a lewed mannes wit to pace the wisdom of an heep of lerned men,* in this department there is at least more chance for the *lewed man*. But there is so much that might still be said even under these limitations that I shall confine myself mainly to the *monsters* — Grendel and the Dragon, as they appear in what seems to me the best and most authoritative general criticism in English — and to certain considerations of the structure and conduct of the poem that arise from this theme.

There is an historical explanation of the state of *Beowulfiana* that I have referred to. And that explanation is important, if one would venture to criticize the critics. A sketch of the history of the subject is required. But I will here only attempt, for brevity's sake, to present my view of it allegorically. As it set out upon its adventures among the modern scholars, *Beowulf* was christened by Wanley Poesis — *Poeseos Anglo-Saxonicæ egregium exemplum*. But the fairy godmother later invited to superintend its fortunes was Historia. And she brought with her Philologia, Mythologia, Archaeologia, and Laographia.[2] Excellent ladies.

[2] Thus in Professor Chambers's great bibliography (in his *Beowulf: An Introduction*) we find a section, § 8. Questions of Literary History, Date, and Authorship; Beowulf in the Light of History, Archaeology, Heroic Legend, Mythology, and Folklore. It is impressive, but there is no section that names Poetry. As certain of the items included show, such consideration as Poetry is accorded at all is buried unnamed in § 8.

But where was the child's name-sake? Poesis was usually forgotten; occasionally admitted by a side-door; sometimes dismissed upon the door-step. '*The Beowulf*', they said, 'is hardly an affair of yours, and not in any case a protégé that you could be proud of. It is an historical document. Only as such does it interest the superior culture of to-day.' And it is as an historical document that it has mainly been examined and dissected. Though ideas as to the nature and quality of the history and information embedded in it have changed much since Thorkelin called it *De Danorum Rebus Gestis,* this has remained steadily true. In still recent pronouncements this view is explicit. In 1925 Professor Archibald Strong translated *Beowulf* into verse;[3] but in 1921 he had declared: '*Beowulf* is the picture of a whole civilization, of the Germania which Tacitus describes. The main interest which the poem has for us is thus not a purely literary interest. *Beowulf* is an important historical document.'[4]

I make this preliminary point, because it seems to me that the air has been clouded not only for Strong, but for other more authoritative critics, by the dust of the quarrying researchers. It may well be asked: why should we approach this, or indeed any other poem, mainly as an historical document? Such an attitude is defensible: firstly, if one is not concerned with poetry at all, but seeking information wherever it may be found; secondly, if the so-called poem contains in fact no poetry. I am not concerned with the first case. The historian's search is, of course, perfectly legitimate, even if it does not assist criticism in general at all

[3] *Beowulf translated into modern English rhyming verse,* Constable, 1925.

[4] *A Short History of English Literature,* Oxford Univ. Press, 1921, pp. 2-3. I choose this example, because it is precisely to general literary histories that we must usually turn for literary judgements on *Beowulf.* The experts in *Beowulfiana* are seldom concerned with such judgements. And it is in the highly compressed histories, such as this, that we discover what the process of digestion makes of the special 'literature' of the experts. Here is the distilled product of Research. This compendium, moreover, is competent, and written by a man who had (unlike some other authors of similar things) read the poem itself with attention.

(for that is not its object), so long as it is not mistaken for criticism. To Professor Birger Nerman as an historian of Swedish origins *Beowulf* is doubtless an important document, but he is not writing a history of English poetry. Of the second case it may be said that to rate a poem, a thing at the least in metrical form, as mainly of historical interest should *in a literary survey* be equivalent to saying that it has no literary merits, and little more need in such a survey then be said about it. But such a judgement on *Beowulf* is false. So far from being a poem so poor that only its accidental historical interest can still recommend it, *Beowulf* is in fact so interesting as poetry, in places poetry so powerful, that this quite overshadows the historical content, and is largely independent even of the most important facts (such as the date and identity of Hygelac) that research has discovered. It is indeed a curious fact that it is one of the peculiar poetic virtues of *Beowulf* that has contributed to its own critical misfortunes. The illusion of historical truth and perspective, that has made *Beowulf* seem such an attractive quarry, is largely a product of art. The author has used an instinctive historical sense — a part indeed of the ancient English temper (and not unconnected with its reputed melancholy), of which *Beowulf* is a supreme expression; but he has used it with a poetical and not an historical object. The lovers of poetry can safely study the art, but the seekers after history must beware lest the glamour of Poesis overcome them.

Nearly all the censure, and most of the praise, that has been bestowed on *The Beowulf* has been due either to the belief that it was something that it was *not* — for example, primitive, pagan, Teutonic, an allegory (political or mythical), or most often, an epic; or to disappointment at the discovery that it was itself and not something that the scholar would have liked better — for example, a heathen heroic lay, a history of Sweden, a manual of Germanic antiquities, or a Nordic *Summa Theologica*.

I would express the whole industry in yet another allegory. A man inherited a field in which was an accumulation of old stone, part of an older hall. Of the old stone some had already been used in building the house in which he actually lived, not far from the old house of his fathers. Of the rest he took some and built a tower. But his friends coming perceived at once (without troubling to climb the steps) that these stones had formerly belonged to a more ancient building. So they pushed the tower over, with no little labour, in order to look for hidden carvings and inscriptions, or to discover whence the man's distant forefathers had obtained their building material. Some suspecting a deposit of coal under the soil began to dig for it, and forgot even the stones. They all said: 'This tower is most interesting.' But they also said (after pushing it over): 'What a muddle it is in!' And even the man's own descendants, who might have been expected to consider what he had been about, were heard to murmur: 'He is such an odd fellow! Imagine his using these old stones just to build a nonsensical tower! Why did not he restore the old house? He had no sense of proportion.' But from the top of that tower the man had been able to look out upon the sea.

I hope I shall show that that allegory is just — even when we consider the more recent and more perceptive critics (whose concern is in intention with literature). To reach these we must pass in rapid flight over the heads of many decades of critics. As we do so a conflicting babel mounts up to us, which I can report as something after this fashion.[5] '*Beowulf* is a half-baked native epic the development of which was killed by Latin learning; it was inspired by emulation of Virgil, and is a product of the education that came in with Christianity; it is feeble and incompetent as a narrative; the rules of narrative are cleverly observed in the manner of the learned epic; it is the confused product of a committee of muddle-headed and probably beer-bemused Anglo-Saxons (this is a Gallic voice); it is a string of pagan lays edited by monks; it is the work of a learned but inaccurate Christian antiquarian; it is a work of genius, rare

[5] I include nothing that has not somewhere been said by some one, if not in my exact words; but I do not, of course, attempt to represent all the *dicta,* wise or otherwise, that have been uttered.

and surprising in the period, though the genius seems to have been shown principally in doing something much better left undone (this is a very recent voice); it is a wild folk-tale (general chorus); it is a poem of an aristocratic and courtly tradition (same voices); it is a hotchpotch; it is a sociological, anthropological, archaeological document; it is a mythical allegory (very old voices these and generally shouted down, but not so far out as some of the newer cries); it is rude and rough; it is a masterpiece of metrical art; it has no shape at all; it is singularly weak in construction; it is a clever allegory of contemporary politics (old John Earle with some slight support from Mr. Girvan, only they look to different periods); its architecture is solid; it is thin and cheap (a solemn voice); it is undeniably weighty (the same voice); it is a national epic; it is a translation from the Danish; it was imported by Frisian traders; it is a burden to English syllabuses; and (final universal chorus of all voices) it is worth studying.'

It is not surprising that it should now be felt that a view, a decision, a conviction are imperatively needed. But it is plainly only in the consideration of *Beowulf* as a poem, with an inherent poetic significance, that any view or conviction can be reached or steadily held. For it is of their nature that the jabberwocks of historical and antiquarian research burble in the tulgy wood of conjecture, flitting from one tum-tum tree to another. Noble animals, whose burbling is on occasion good to hear; but though their eyes of flame may sometimes prove searchlights, their range is short.

None the less, paths of a sort have been opened in the wood. Slowly with the rolling years the obvious (so often the last revelation of analytic study) has been discovered: that we have to deal with a poem by an Englishman using afresh ancient and largely traditional material. At last then, after inquiring so long whence this material came, and what its original or aboriginal nature was (questions that cannot ever be decisively answered), we might also now again inquire what the poet did with it. If we ask that question, then there is still, perhaps, something lacking even in the major critics, the learned and revered masters from whom we humbly derive.

The chief points with which I feel dissatisfied I will now approach by way of W. P. Ker, whose name and memory I honour. He would deserve reverence, of course, even if he still lived and had not *ellor gehworfen on Frean wære* upon a high mountain in the heart of that Europe which he loved: a great scholar, as illuminating himself as a critic, as he was often biting as a critic of the critics. None the less I cannot help feeling that in approaching *Beowulf* he was hampered by the almost inevitable weakness of his greatness: stories and plots must sometimes have seemed triter to him, the much-read, than they did to the old poets and their audiences. The dwarf on the spot sometimes sees things missed by the travelling giant ranging many countries. In considering a period when literature was narrower in range and men possessed a less diversified stock of ideas and themes, one must seek to recapture and esteem the deep pondering and profound feeling that they gave to such as they possessed.

In any case Ker has been potent. For his criticism is masterly, expressed always in words both pungent and weighty, and not least so when it is (as I occasionally venture to think) itself open to criticism. His words and judgements are often quoted, or reappear in various modifications, digested, their source probably sometimes forgotten. It is impossible to avoid quotation of the well-known passage in his *Dark Ages*:

> A reasonable view of the merit of *Beowulf* is not impossible, though rash enthusiasm may have made too much of it, while a correct and sober taste may have too contemptuously refused to attend to Grendel or the Fire-drake. The fault of *Beowulf* is that there is nothing much in the story. The hero is occupied in killing monsters, like Hercules or Theseus. But there are other things in the lives of Hercules and Theseus besides the killing of the Hydra or of Procrustes. Beowulf has nothing else to do, when he has killed Grendel and Grendel's mother in Denmark: he goes home to his own Gautland, until at last the rolling years bring the Fire-drake and his last adventure. It is too simple. Yet the three chief episodes are well wrought and well diversified; they are not repetitions,

exactly; there is a change of temper between the wrestling with Grendel in the night at Heorot and the descent under water to encounter Grendel's mother; while the sentiment of the Dragon is different again. But the great beauty, the real value, of *Beowulf* is in its dignity of style. In construction it is curiously weak, in a sense preposterous; for while the main story is simplicity itself, the merest commonplace of heroic legend, all about it, in the historic allusions, there are revelations of a whole world of tragedy, plots different in import from that of *Beowulf,* more like the tragic themes of Iceland. Yet with this radical defect, a disproportion that puts the irrelevances in the centre and the serious things on the outer edges, the poem of *Beowulf* is undeniably weighty. The thing itself is cheap; the moral and the spirit of it can only be matched among the noblest authors.[6]

This passage was written more than thirty years ago, but has hardly been surpassed. It remains, in this country at any rate, a potent influence. Yet its primary effect is to state a paradox which one feels has always strained the belief, even of those who accepted it, and has given to *Beowulf* the character of an 'enigmatic poem'. The chief virtue of the passage (not the one for which it is usually esteemed) is that it does accord some attention to the monsters, despite correct and sober taste. But the contrast made between the radical defect of theme and structure, and at the same time the dignity, loftiness in converse, and well-wrought finish, has become a commonplace even of the best criticism, a paradox the strangeness of which has almost been forgotten in the process of swallowing it upon authority.[7] We may compare Professor Chambers in his *Widsith,*

[6] *The Dark Ages,* pp. 252-3.

[7] None the less Ker modified it in an important particular in *English Literature, Mediæval,* pp. 29-34. In general, though in different words, vaguer and less incisive, he repeats himself. We are still told that 'the story is commonplace and the plan is feeble', or that 'the story is thin and poor'. But we learn also at the end of his notice that: 'Those distracting allusions to things apart from the chief story make up for their want of proportion. They give the impression of reality and weight; the story is not in the air . . . it is part of the solid world.' By the admission of so grave an artistic reason for the procedure of the poem Ker himself began the undermining of his own criticism of its structure. But this line of thought does not seem to have been further pursued. Possibly it was this very thought, working in his mind, that made Ker's notice of *Beowulf* in the small later book, his 'shilling shocker', more vague and hesitant in tone, and so of less influence.

p. 79, where he is studying the story of Ingeld, son of Froda, and his feud with the great Scylding house of Denmark, a story introduced in *Beowulf* merely as an allusion.

> Nothing [Chambers says] could better show the disproportion of *Beowulf* which 'puts the irrelevances in the centre and the serious things on the outer edges', than this passing allusion to the story of Ingeld. For in this conflict between plighted troth and the duty of revenge we have a situation which the old heroic poets loved, and would not have sold for a wilderness of dragons.

I pass over the fact that the allusion has a dramatic purpose in *Beowulf* that is a sufficient defence both of its presence and of its manner. The author of *Beowulf* cannot be held responsible for the fact that we now have only his poem and not others dealing primarily with Ingeld. He was not selling one thing for another, but giving something new. But let us return to the dragon. 'A wilderness of dragons.' There is a sting in this Shylockian plural, the sharper for coming from a critic, who deserves the title of the poet's best friend. It is in the tradition of the Book of St. Albans, from which the poet might retort upon his critics: 'Yea, a desserte of lapwyngs, a shrewednes of apes, a raffull of knaues, and a gagle of gees.'

As for the poem, one dragon, however hot, does not make a summer, or a host; and a man might well exchange for one good dragon what he would not sell for a wilderness. And dragons, real dragons, essential both to the machinery and the ideas of a poem or tale, are actually rare. In northern literature there are only *two* that are significant. If we omit from consideration the vast and vague Encircler of the World, Miðgarðsormr, the doom of the great gods and no matter for heroes, we have but the dragon of the Völsungs, Fáfnir, and Beowulf's bane. It is true that both of these are in *Beowulf*, one in the main story, and the other spoken of by a minstrel praising Beowulf himself. But this is not a wilderness of dragons. Indeed the allusion to the more renowned worm killed by the Wælsing is sufficient indication that the poet selected a dragon of well-founded purpose (or saw its significance in the plot as it had reached him), even as he was careful to compare his hero,

Beowulf son of Ecgtheow, to the prince of the heroes of the North, the dragon-slaying Wælsing. He esteemed dragons, as rare as they are dire, as some do still. He liked them — as a poet, not as a sober zoologist; and he had good reason.

But we meet this kind of criticism again. In Chambers's *Beowulf and the Heroic Age* — the most significant single essay on the poem that I know — it is still present. The riddle is still unsolved. The folk-tale motive stands still like the spectre of old research, dead but unquiet in its grave. We are told again that the main story of *Beowulf* is a *wild folktale*. Quite true, of course. It is true of the main story of *King Lear,* unless in that case you would prefer to substitute *silly* for *wild*. But more: we are told that the same sort of stuff is found in Homer, yet there it is kept in its proper place. 'The folk-tale is a good servant', Chambers says, and does not perhaps realize the importance of the admission, made to save the face of Homer and Virgil; for he continues: 'but a bad master: it has been allowed in *Beowulf* to usurp the place of honour, and to drive into episodes and digressions the things which should be the main stuff of a well-conducted epic.' [8] It is not clear to me why good *conduct* must depend on the main *stuff*. But I will for the moment remark only that, if it is so, *Beowulf* is evidently not a well-conducted epic. It may turn out to be no epic at all. But the puzzle still continues. In the most recent discourse upon this theme it still appears, toned down almost to a melancholy question-mark, as if this paradox had at last begun to afflict with weariness the thought that endeavours to support it. In the final peroration of his notable lecture on *Folk-tale and History in Beowulf* given last year, Mr. Girvan said:

> Confessedly there is matter for wonder and scope for doubt, but we might be able to answer with complete satisfaction some of the questionings which rise in men's minds over the poet's presentment of his hero, if we could also answer with certainty the question why he chose just this subject, when to our modern judgment there were at hand so many greater, charged with the splendour and tragedy of humanity, and in all respects worthier of a genius as astonishing as it was rare in Anglo-Saxon England.

[8] *Foreword* to Strong's translation, p. xxvi: see note 3.

There is something irritatingly odd about all this. One even dares to wonder if something has not gone wrong with 'our modern judgement', supposing that it is justly represented. Higher praise than is found in the learned critics, whose scholarship enables them to appreciate these things, could hardly be given to the detail, the tone, the style, and indeed to the total effect of *Beowulf*. Yet this poetic talent, we are to understand, has all been squandered on an unprofitable theme: as if Milton had recounted the story of Jack and the Beanstalk in noble verse. Even if Milton had done this (and he might have done worse), we should perhaps pause to consider whether his poetic handling had not had some effect upon the trivial theme; what alchemy had been performed upon the base metal; whether indeed it remained base or trivial when he had finished with it. The high tone, the sense of dignity, alone is evidence in *Beowulf* of the presence of a mind lofty and thoughtful. It is, one would have said, improbable that such a man would write more than three thousand lines (wrought to a high finish) on matter that is really not worth serious attention; that remains thin and cheap when he has finished with it. Or that he should in the selection of his material, in the choice of what to put forward, what to keep subordinate 'upon the outer edges', have shown a puerile simplicity much below the level of the characters he himself draws in his own poem. Any theory that will at least allow us to believe that what he did was of design, and that for that design there is a defence that may still have force, would seem more probable.

It has been too little observed that all the machinery of 'dignity' is to be found elsewhere. Cynewulf, or the author of *Andreas,* or of *Guthlac* (most notably), have a command of dignified verse. In them there is well-wrought language, weighty words, lofty sentiment, precisely that which we are told is the real beauty of *Beowulf*. Yet it cannot, I think, be disputed, that *Beowulf* is more beautiful, that each line there is more significant (even when, as sometimes happens, it is the same line) than in the other long Old English poems. Where then resides the special virtue of *Beowulf,* if the common element (which belongs largely to the language itself, and to a literary tradition) is deducted? It resides, one might guess, in the theme, and the spirit this has infused into the whole. For, in fact, if there were a real discrepancy between theme and style, that style would not be felt as beautiful but as incongruous or false. And that incongruity is present in some measure in all the long Old English poems, save one — *Beowulf.* The paradoxical contrast that has been drawn between matter and manner in Beowulf has thus an inherent *literary* improbability.

Why then have the great critics thought otherwise? I must pass rather hastily over the answers to this question. The reasons are various, I think, and would take long to examine. I believe that one reason is that the shadow of research has lain upon criticism. The habit, for instance, of pondering a summarized plot of *Beowulf,* denuded of all that gives it particular force or individual life, has encouraged the notion that its main story is wild, or trivial, or typical, *even after treatment.* Yet all stories, great and small, are one or more of these three things in such nakedness. The comparison of skeleton 'plots' is simply not a critical literary process at all. It has been favoured by research in comparative folk-lore, the objects of which are primarily historical or scientific.[9] Another reason is, I think, that the allu-

[9] It has also been favoured by the rise of 'English schools', in whose syllabuses *Beowulf* has inevitably some place, and the consequent production of compendious literary histories. For these cater (in fact, if not in intention) for those seeking knowledge about, and ready-made judgements upon, works which they have not the time, or (often enough) the desire, to know at first hand. The small literary value of such summaries is sometimes recognized in the act of giving them. Thus Strong (*op. cit.*) gives a fairly complete one, but remarks that 'the short summary does scant justice to the poem'. Ker in *E. Lit.* (*Med.*) says: 'So told, in abstract, it is not a particularly interesting story.' He evidently perceived what might be the retort, for he attempts to justify the procedure in this case, adding: 'Told in this way the story of Theseus or Hercules would still have much more in it.' I dissent. But it does not matter, for the comparison of two plots 'told in this way' is no guide whatever to the merits of literary versions told in quite different ways. It is not necessarily the best poem that loses least in précis.

sions have attracted curiosity (antiquarian rather than critical) to their elucidation; and this needs so much study and research that attention has been diverted from the poem as a whole, and from the function of the allusions, as shaped and placed, in the poetic economy of *Beowulf* as it is. Yet actually the appreciation of this function is largely independent of such investigations.

But there is also, I suppose, a real question of taste involved: a judgement that the heroic or tragic story on a strictly human plane is by nature superior. Doom is held less literary than ἁμαρτία. The proposition seems to have been passed as self-evident. I dissent, even at the risk of being held incorrect or not sober. But I will not here enter into debate, nor attempt at length a defence of the mythical mode of imagination, and the disentanglement of the confusion between myth and folk-tale into which these judgements appear to have fallen. The myth has other forms than the (now discredited) mythical allegory of nature: the sun, the seasons, the sea, and such things. The term 'folk-tale' is misleading; its very tone of depreciation begs the question. Folk-tales in being, as told — for the 'typical folk-tale', of course, is merely an abstract conception of research nowhere existing — do often contain elements that are thin and cheap, with little even potential virtue; but they also contain much that is far more powerful, and that cannot be sharply separated from myth, being derived from it, or capable in poetic hands of turning into it: that is of becoming largely significant — as a whole, accepted unanalyzed. The significance of a myth is not easily to be pinned on paper by analytical reasoning. It is at its best when it is presented by a poet who feels rather than makes explicit what his theme portends; who presents it incarnate in the world of history and geography, as our poet has done. Its defender is thus at a disadvantage: unless he is careful, and speaks in parables, he will kill what he is studying by vivisection, and he will be left with a formal or mechanical allegory, and, what is more, probably with one that will not work. For myth is alive at once and in all its parts, and dies before it can be dissected. It is possible, I think, to be moved by the power of myth and yet to misunderstand the sensation, to ascribe it wholly to something else that is also present: to metrical art, style, or verbal skill. Correct and sober taste may refuse to admit that there can be an interest for *us* — the proud *we* that includes all intelligent living people — in ogres and dragons; we then perceive its puzzlement in face of the odd fact that it has derived great pleasure from a poem that is actually about these unfashionable creatures. Even though it attributes 'genius', as does Mr. Girvan, to the author, it cannot admit that the monsters are anything but a sad mistake.

It does not seem plain that ancient taste supports the modern as much as it has been represented to do. I have the author of *Beowulf,* at any rate, on my side: a greater man than most of us. And I cannot myself perceive a period in the North when one kind alone was esteemed: there was room for myth and heroic legend, and for blends of these. As for the dragon: as far as we know anything about these old poets, we know this: the prince of the heroes of the North, supremely memorable — *hans nafn mun uppi meðan veröldin stendr* [his name shall live while the world lasts] — was a dragon-slayer. And his most renowned deed, from which in Norse he derived his title Fáfnisbani, was the slaying of the prince of legendary worms. Although there is plainly considerable difference between the later Norse and the ancient English form of the story alluded to in *Beowulf,* already there it had these two primary features: the dragon, and the slaying of him as the chief deed of the greatest of heroes — *he wæs wreccena wide mærost* [he was far and wide the most renowned of exiles]. A dragon is no idle fancy. Whatever may be his origins, in fact or invention, the dragon in legend is a potent creation of men's imagination, richer in significance than his barrow is in gold. Even to-day (despite the critics) you may find men not ignorant of tragic legend and history, who have heard of heroes and indeed seen them, who yet have been caught by the fascination of the worm. More than one poem in recent years (since *Beowulf* escaped somewhat from the dominion of the students of origins to the students of poetry) has been inspired by the dragon of *Beowulf*, but none that I know of by Ingeld son of Froda. Indeed, I do not think Chambers very happy in his particular choice. He gives battle on dubious ground. In so far as we can now grasp its detail and atmosphere the story of Ingeld the thrice faithless and easily persuaded is chiefly interesting as an episode in a larger theme, as part of a tradition that had acquired legendary, and so dramatically personalized, form concerning moving events in history: the arising of Denmark, and wars in the islands of the North. In itself it is not a supremely potent story. But, of course, as with all tales of any sort, its literary power must have depended mainly upon how it was handled. A poet may have made a great thing of it. Upon this chance must be founded the popularity of Ingeld's legend in England, for which there is some evidence.[10] There is no inherent magical virtue about heroic-tragic stories as such, and apart from the merits of individual treatments. The same heroic plot can yield good and bad poems, and good and bad sagas. The recipe for the central situations of such stories, studied in the abstract, is after all as 'simple' and as 'typical' as that of folk-tales. There are in any case many heroes but very few good dragons.

Beowulf's dragon, if one wishes really to criticize, is not to be blamed for being a dragon, but rather for not being dragon enough, plain pure fairy-story dragon. There are in the poem some vivid touches of the right kind — as *þa se wyrm onwoc, wroht wæs geniwad; stonc æfter stane* [when the dragon awoke, strife was renewed; he then moved quickly along by the rock], 2285 — in which this dragon is real worm, with a bestial life

[10] Namely the use of it in *Beowulf*, both dramatically in depicting the sagacity of Beowulf the hero, and as an essential part of the traditions concerning the Scylding court, which is the legendary background against which the rise of the hero is set — as a later age would have chosen the court of Arthur. Also the probable allusion in Alcuin's letter to Speratus: see Chambers's *Widsith*, p. 78.

and thought of his own, but the conception, none the less, approaches *draconitas* [dragon-ness)] rather than *draco* [dragon]: a personification of malice, greed, destruction (the evil side of heroic life), and of the undiscriminating cruelty of fortune that distinguishes not good or bad (the evil aspect of all life). But for *Beowulf*, the poem, that is as it should be. In this poem the balance is nice, but it is preserved. The large symbolism is near the surface, but it does not break through, nor become allegory. Something more significant than a standard hero, a man faced with a foe more evil than any human enemy of house or realm, is before us, and yet incarnate in time, walking in heroic history, and treading the named lands of the North. And this, we are told, is the radical defect of *Beowulf*, that its author, coming in a time rich in the legends of heroic men, has used them afresh in an original fashion, giving us not just one more, but something akin yet different: a measure and interpretation of them all.

We do not deny the worth of the hero by accepting Grendel and the dragon. Let us by all means esteem the old heroes: men caught in the chains of circumstance or of their own character, torn between duties equally sacred, dying with their backs to the wall. But *Beowulf*, I fancy, plays a larger part than is recognized in helping us to esteem them. Heroic lays may have dealt in their own way — we have little enough to judge by — a way more brief and vigorous, perhaps, though perhaps also more harsh and noisy (and less thoughtful), with the actions of heroes caught in circumstances that conformed more or less to the varied but fundamentally simple recipe for an heroic situation. In these (if we had them) we could see the exaltation of undefeated will, which receives doctrinal expression in the words of Byrhtwold at the battle of Maldon.[11] But though with sympathy and patience we might gather, from a line here or a tone

[11] This expression may well have been actually used by the *eald geneat* [old companion], but none the less (or perhaps rather precisely on that account) is probably to be regarded not as new-minted, but as an ancient and honoured *gnome* of long descent.

there, the background of imagination which gives to this indomitability, this paradox of defeat inevitable yet unacknowledged, its full significance, it is in *Beowulf* that a poet has devoted a whole poem to the theme, and has drawn the struggle in different proportions, so that we may see man at war with the hostile world, and his inevitable overthrow in Time.[12] The particular is on the outer edge, the essential in the centre.

Of course, I do not assert that the poet, if questioned, would have replied in the Anglo-Saxon equivalents of these terms. Had the matter been so explicit to him, his poem would certainly have been the worse. None the less we may still, against his great scene, hung with tapestries woven of ancient tales of ruin, see the *hæleð* walk. When we have read his poem, as a poem, rather than as a collection of episodes, we perceive that he who wrote *hæleð under heofenum* may have meant in dictionary terms 'heroes under heaven', or 'mighty men upon earth', but he and his hearers were thinking of the *eormengrund,* the great earth, ringed with *garsecg,* the shoreless sea, beneath the sky's inaccessible roof; whereon, as in a little circle of light about their halls, men with courage as their stay went forward to that battle with the hostile world and the offspring of the dark which ends for all, even the kings and champions, in defeat. That even this 'geography', once held as a material fact, could now be classed as a mere folk-tale affects its value very little. It transcends astronomy. Not that astronomy has done anything to make the island seem more secure or the outer seas less formidable.

[12] For the words *hige sceal þe heardra, heorte þe cenre, mod sceal þe mare þe ure mægen lytlað* [courage shall be the bolder, heart the keener, spirit shall be the greater, as our strength grows less] are not, of course, an exhortation to simple courage. They are not reminders that fortune favours the brave, or that victory may be snatched from defeat by the stubborn. (Such thoughts were familiar, but otherwise expressed: *wyrd oft nereð unfægne eorl, þonne his ellen deah* [fate often protects a man not yet fated to die, when his courage is good].) The words of Byrhtwold were made for a man's last and hopeless day.

Beowulf is not, then, the hero of an heroic lay, precisely. He has no enmeshed loyalties, nor hapless love. *He is a man, and that for him and many is sufficient tragedy*. It is not an irritating accident that the tone of the poem is so high and its theme so low. It is the theme in its deadly seriousness that begets the dignity of tone: *lif is læne: eal scæceð leoht and lif somod* [life is transitory: light and life together hasten away]. So deadly and ineluctable is the underlying thought, that those who in the circle of light, within the besieged hall, are absorbed in work or talk and do not look to the battlements, either do not regard it or recoil. Death comes to the feast, and they say He gibbers: He has no sense of proportion.

I would suggest, then, that the monsters are not an inexplicable blunder of taste; they are essential, fundamentally allied to the underlying ideas of the poem, which give it its lofty tone and high seriousness. The key to the fusion-point of imagination that produced this poem lies, therefore, in those very references to Cain which have often been used as a stick to beat an ass — taken as an evident sign (were any needed) of the muddled heads of early Anglo-Saxons. They could not, it was said, keep Scandinavian bogies and the Scriptures separate in their puzzled brains. The New Testament was beyond their comprehension. I am not, as I have confessed, a man so diligent as duly to read all the books about *Beowulf*, but as far as I am aware the most suggestive approach to this point appears in the essay *Beowulf and the Heroic Age* to which I have already referred.[13] I will quote a small part of it.

> In the epoch of *Beowulf* a Heroic Age more wild and primitive than that of Greece is brought into touch with Christendom, with the Sermon on the Mount, with Catholic theology and ideas of heaven and hell. We see the difference, if we compare the wilder things — the folk-tale element — in *Beowulf* with the wilder things of Homer. Take for example the tale of Odysseus and the Cyclops — the No-man trick. Odysseus is struggling with a monstrous and wicked foe, but he is not exactly thought of as struggling with the powers of darkness. Polyphemus, by devouring

[13] *Foreword* to Strong's translation, p. xxviii. See note 3.

his guests, acts in a way which is hateful to Zeus and the other gods: yet the Cyclops is himself god-begotten and under divine protection, and the fact that Odysseus has maimed him is a wrong which Poseidon is slow to forgive. But the gigantic foes whom Beowulf has to meet are identified with the foes of God. Grendel and the dragon are constantly referred to in language which is meant to recall the powers of darkness with which Christian men felt themselves to be encompassed. They[14] are the 'inmates of Hell', 'adversaries of God', 'offspring of Cain', 'enemies of mankind'. Consequently, the matter of the main story of *Beowulf,* monstrous as it is, is not so far removed from common mediaeval experience as it seems to us to be from our own. . . . Grendel hardly differs[15] from the fiends of the pit who were always in ambush to waylay a righteous man. And so Beowulf, for all that he moves in the world of the primitive Heroic Age of the Germans, nevertheless is almost a Christian knight.[16]

There are some hints here which are, I think, worth pursuing further. Most important is it to consider how and why the monsters become 'adversaries of God', and so begin to symbolize (and ultimately to become identified with) the powers of evil, even while they remain, as they do still remain in *Beowulf,* mortal denizens of the material world, in it and of it. I accept without argument throughout the attribution of *Beowulf* to the 'age of Bede' — one of the firmer conclusions of a department of research most clearly serviceable to criticism: inquiry into the probable date of the effective composition of the poem as we have it. So regarded *Beowulf* is, of course, an historical document of the first order for the study of the mood and thought of the period and one perhaps too little used for the purpose by professed historians.[17] But it is the mood of the author, the essential cast of his imaginative apprehension of

[14] This is not strictly true. The dragon is not referred to in such terms, which are applied to Grendel and to the primeval giants.

[15] He differs in important points, referred to later.

[16] I should prefer to say that he moves in a northern heroic age imagined by a Christian, and therefore has a noble and gentle quality, though conceived to be a pagan.

[17] It is, for instance, dismissed cursorily, and somewhat contemptuously in the recent (somewhat contemptuous) essay of Dr. Watson, *The Age of Bede* in *Bede, His Life, Times, and Writings,* ed. A. Hamilton Thompson, 1935.

the world, that is my concern, not history for its own sake; I am interested in that time of fusion only as it may help us to understand the poem. And in the poem I think we may observe not confusion, a half-hearted or a muddled business, but a fusion that has occurred *at a given point* of contact between old and new, a product of thought and deep emotion.

One of the most potent elements in that fusion is the Northern courage: the theory of courage, which is the great contribution of early Northern literature. This is not a military judgement. I am not asserting that, if the Trojans could have employed a Northern king and his companions, they would have driven Agamemnon and Achilles into the sea, more decisively than the Greek hexameter routs the alliterative line — though it is not improbable. I refer rather to the central position the creed of unyielding will holds in the North. With due reserve we may turn to the tradition of pagan imagination as it survived in Icelandic. Of English pre-Christian mythology we know practically nothing. But the fundamentally similar heroic temper of ancient England and Scandinavia cannot have been founded on (or perhaps rather, cannot have generated) mythologies divergent on this essential point. 'The Northern Gods', Ker said, 'have an exultant extravagance in their warfare which makes them more like Titans than Olympians; *only they are on the right side, though it is not the side that wins. The winning side is Chaos and Unreason'* — mythologically, the monsters — *'but the gods, who are defeated, think that defeat no refutation.'* [18] And in their war men are their chosen allies, able when heroic to share in this 'absolute resistance, perfect because without hope'. At least in this vision of the final defeat of the humane (and of the divine made in its image), and in the essential hostility of the gods and heroes on the one hand and the monsters on the other, we may suppose that pagan English and Norse imagination agreed.

[18] *The Dark Ages,* p. 57.

But in England this imagination was brought into touch with Christendom, and with the Scriptures. The process of 'conversion' was a long one, but some of its effects were doubtless immediate: an alchemy of change (producing ultimately the mediaeval) was at once at work. One does not have to wait until all the native traditions of the older world have been replaced or forgotten; for the minds which still retain them are changed, and the memories viewed in a different perspective: *at once they become more ancient and remote, and in a sense darker*. It is through such a blending that there was available to a poet who set out to *write* a poem — and in the case of *Beowulf* we may probably use this very word — on a scale and plan unlike a minstrel's lay, both new faith and new learning (or education), and also a body of native tradition (itself requiring to be learned) for the changed mind to contemplate together.[19] The native 'learning' cannot be denied in the case of *Beowulf*. Its display has grievously perturbed the critics, for the author draws upon tradition at will for his own purposes, as a poet of later times might draw upon history or the classics and expect his allusions to be understood (within a certain class of hearers). He was in fact, like Virgil, learned enough in the vernacular department to have an historical perspective, even an antiquarian curiosity. He cast his time into the long-ago, because already the long-ago had a special poetical attraction. He knew much about old days, and though his knowledge — of such things as sea-burial and the funeral pyre, for instance — was rich and poetical rather than accurate with the accuracy of modern archaeology (such as that is), one thing he knew clearly: those days were heathen — heathen, noble, and hopeless.

[19] If we consider the period as a whole. It is not, of course, necessarily true of individuals. These doubtless from the beginning showed many degrees from deep instruction and understanding to disjointed superstition, or blank ignorance.

But if the specifically Christian was suppressed,[20] so also were the old gods. Partly because they had not really existed, and had been always, in the Christian view, only delusions or lies fabricated by the evil one, the *gastbona,* to whom the hopeless turned especially in times of need. Partly because their old names (certainly not forgotten) had been potent, and were connected in memory still, not only with mythology or such fairy-tale matter as we find, say, in *Gylfaginning,* but with active heathendom, religion and *wigweorþung* [honor to idols]. Most of all because they were not actually essential to the theme.

The monsters had been the foes of the gods, the captains of men, and within Time the monsters would win. In the heroic siege and last defeat men and gods alike had been imagined in the same host. Now the heroic figures, the men of old, *hæleð under heofenum* [men under heaven], remained and still fought on until defeat. For the monsters do not depart, whether the gods go or come. A Christian was (and is) still like his forefathers a mortal hemmed in a hostile world. The monsters remained the enemies of mankind, the infantry of the old war, and became inevitably the enemies of the one God, *ece Dryhten,* the eternal Captain of the new. Even so the vision of the war

[20] Avoidance of obvious anachronisms (such as are found in *Judith,* for instance, where the heroine refers in her own speeches to Christ and the Trinity), and the absence of all definitely *Christian* names and terms, is natural and plainly intentional. It must be observed that there is a difference between the comments of the author and the things said in reported speech by his characters. The two chief of these, Hrothgar and Beowulf, are again differentiated. Thus the only definitely Scriptural references, to Abel (108) and to Cain (108, 1261), occur where the poet is speaking as commentator. The theory of Grendel's origin is not known to the actors: Hrothgar denies all knowledge of the ancestry of Grendel (1355). The giants (1688 ff.) are, it is true, represented pictorially, and in Scriptural terms. But this suggests rather that the author identified native and Scriptural accounts, and gave his picture Scriptural colour, since of the two accounts Scripture was the truer. And if so it would be closer to that told in remote antiquity when the sword was made, more especially since the *wundorsmiþas* [smiths who make wondrous things] who wrought it were actually giants (1558, 1562, 1679): they would know the true tale. See note 25.

changes. For it begins to dissolve, even as the contest on the fields of Time thus takes on its largest aspect. The tragedy of the great temporal defeat remains for a while poignant, but ceases to be finally important. It is no defeat, for the end of the world is part of the design of Metod, the Arbiter who is above the mortal world. Beyond there appears a possibility of eternal victory (or eternal defeat), and the real battle is between the soul and its adversaries. So the old monsters became images of the evil spirit or spirits, or rather the evil spirits entered into the monsters and took visible shape in the hideous bodies of the *þyrsas* [giants] and *sigelhearwan* [Ethiopians] of heathen imagination.

But that shift is not complete in *Beowulf* — whatever may have been true of its period in general. Its author is still concerned primarily with *man on earth,* rehandling in a new perspective an ancient theme: that man, each man and all men, and all their works shall die. A theme no Christian need despise. Yet this theme plainly would not be so treated, but for the nearness of a pagan time. The shadow of its despair, if only as a mood, as an intense emotion of regret, is still there. The worth of defeated valour in this world is deeply felt. As the poet looks back into the past, surveying the history of kings and warriors in the old traditions, he sees that all glory (or as we might say 'culture' or 'civilization') ends in night. The solution of that tragedy is not treated — it does not arise out of the material. We get in fact a poem from a pregnant moment of poise, looking back into the pit, by a man learned in old tales who was struggling, as it were, to get a general view of them all, perceiving their common tragedy of inevitable ruin, and yet feeling this more *poetically* because he was himself removed from the direct pressure of its despair. He could view from without, but still feel immediately and from within, the old dogma: despair of the event, combined with faith in the value of doomed resistance. He was still dealing with the great temporal tragedy, and not yet writing an allegorical homily in verse. Grendel inhabits the visible world and eats the flesh and blood of men; he enters their houses by the doors. The dragon wields a physical fire, and covets gold not souls; he is slain with iron in his belly. Beowulf's *byrne* [corslet] was made by Weland, and the iron shield he bore against the serpent by his own smiths: it was not yet the breastplate of righteousness, nor the shield of faith for the quenching of all the fiery darts of the wicked.

Almost we might say that this poem was (in one direction) inspired by the debate that had long been held and continued after, and that it was one of the chief contributions to the controversy: shall we or shall we not consign the heathen ancestors to perdition? What good will it do posterity to read the battles of Hector? *Quid Hinieldus cum Christo?* [What has Ingeld to do with Christ?] The author of *Beowulf* showed forth the permanent value of that *pietas* which treasures the memory of man's struggles in the dark past, man fallen and not yet saved, disgraced but not dethroned. It would seem to have been part of the English temper in its strong sense of tradition, dependent doubtless on dynasties, noble houses, and their code of honour, and strengthened, it may be, by the more inquisitive and less severe Celtic learning, that it should, at least in some quarters and despite grave and Gallic voices, preserve much from the northern past to blend with southern learning, and new faith.

It has been thought that the influence of Latin epic, especially of the *Aeneid,* is perceptible in *Beowulf,* and a necessary explanation, if only in the exciting of emulation, of the development of the long and studied poem in early England. There is, of course, a likeness in places between these greater and lesser things, the *Aeneid* and *Beowulf,* if they are read in conjunction. But the smaller points in which imitation or reminiscence might be perceived are inconclusive, while the real likeness is deeper and due to certain qualities in the authors independent of the question whether the Anglo-Saxon had read Virgil or not. It is this deeper likeness which makes things, that are either the inevitabilities of human poetry or the accidental congruences of all tales, ring alike. We have the great pagan on the threshold of the change of the world; and the great (if lesser) Christian just over the threshold of the great change in his time and place: the backward view: *multa putans sortemque animo miseratus iniquam* [thinking of many things and deploring the uneven lot].[21]

But we will now return once more to the monsters, and consider especially the difference of their status in the northern and southern mythologies. Of Grendel it is said: *Godes yrre bær* [he bore the anger of God]. But the Cyclops is god-begotten and his maiming is an offence against his begetter, the god Poseidon. This radical difference in mythological status is only brought out more sharply by the very closeness of the similarity in conception (in all save mere size) that is seen, if we compare *Beowulf,* 740 ff., with the description of the Cyclops devouring men in *Odyssey,* ix — or still more in *Aeneid,* iii. 622 ff. In Virgil, whatever may be true of the fairy-tale world of the Odyssey, the Cyclops walks veritably in the historic world. He is seen by Aeneas in Sicily, *monstrum horrendum, informe, ingens* [a dreadful monster, formless, huge], as much a perilous fact as Grendel was in Denmark, *earmsceapen on weres wæstmum . . . næfne he wæs mara þonne ænig man oðer* [the miserable creature in the form of a man except that he was larger than any other man]; as real as Acestes or Hrothgar.[22]

At this point in particular we may regret that we do not know more about pre-Christian English mythology. Yet it is,

[21] In fact the real resemblance of the *Aeneid* and *Beowulf* lies in the constant presence of a sense of many-storied antiquity, together with its natural accompaniment, stern and noble melancholy. In this they are really akin and together differ from Homer's flatter, if more glittering, surface.

[22] I use this illustration following Chambers, because of the close resemblance between Grendel and the Cyclops in kind. But other examples could be adduced: Cacus, for instance, the offspring of Vulcan. One might ponder the contrast between the legends of the torture of Prometheus and of Loki: the one for assisting men, the other for assisting the powers of darkness.

as I have said, legitimate to suppose that in the matter of the position of the monsters in regard to men and gods the view was fundamentally the same as in later Icelandic. Thus, though all such generalizations are naturally imperfect in detail (since they deal with matter of various origins, constantly reworked, and never even at most more than partially systematized), we may with some truth contrast the 'inhumanness' of the Greek gods, however anthropomorphic, with the 'humanness' of the Northern, however titanic. In the southern myths there is also rumour of wars with giants and great powers not Olympian, the *Titania pubes fulmine deiecti* [the youth cast down by a Titanic thunderbolt], rolling like Satan and his satellites in the nethermost Abyss. But this war is differently conceived. It lies in a chaotic past. The ruling gods are not besieged, not in ever-present peril or under future doom.[23] Their offspring on earth may be heroes or fair women; it may also be the other creatures hostile to men. The gods are not the allies of men in their war against these or other monsters. The interest of the gods is in this or that man as part of their individual schemes, not as part of a great strategy that includes all good men, as the infantry

[23] There is actually no final principle in the legendary hostilities contained in classical mythology. For the present purpose that is all that matters: we are not here concerned with remoter mythological origins, in the North or South. The gods, Cronian or Olympian, the Titans, and other great natural powers, and various monsters, even minor local horrors, are not clearly distinguished in origin or ancestry. There could be no permanent policy of war, led by Olympus, to which human courage might be dedicated, among mythological races so promiscuous. Of course, nowhere can absolute rigidity of distinction be expected, because in a sense the foe is always both within and without; the fortress must fall through treachery as well as by assault. Thus Grendel has a perverted human shape, and the giants or *jötnar*, even when (like the Titans) they are of super-divine stature, are parodies of the human-divine form. Even in Norse, where the distinction is most rigid, Loki dwells in Asgarðr, though he is an evil and lying spirit, and fatal monsters come of him. For it is true of man, maker of myths, that Grendel and the Dragon, in their lust, greed, and malice, have a part in him. But mythically conceived the gods do not recognize any bond with *Fenris úlfr* [Fenris wolf], any more than men with Grendel or the serpent.

of battle. In Norse, at any rate, the gods are within Time, doomed with their allies to death. Their battle is with the monsters and the outer darkness. They gather heroes for the last defence. Already before euhemerism saved them by embalming them, and they dwindled in antiquarian fancy to the mighty ancestors of northern kings (English and Scandinavian), they had become in their very being the enlarged shadows of great men and warriors upon the walls of the world. When Baldr is slain and goes to Hel he cannot escape thence any more than mortal man.

This may make the southern gods more godlike — more lofty, dread, and inscrutable. They are timeless and do not fear death. Such a mythology may hold the promise of a profounder thought. In any case it was a virtue of the southern mythology that it could not stop where it was. It must go forward to philosophy or relapse into anarchy. For in a sense it had shirked the problem precisely by not having the monsters in the centre — as they are in *Beowulf* to the astonishment of the critics. But such horrors cannot be left permanently unexplained, lurking on the outer edges and under suspicion of being connected with the Government. It is the strength of the northern mythological imagination that it faced this problem, put the monsters in the centre, gave them victory but no honour, and found a potent but terrible solution in naked will and courage. 'As a working theory absolutely impregnable.' So potent is it, that while the older southern imagination has faded for ever into literary ornament, the northern has power, as it were, to revive its spirit even in our own times. It can work, even as it did work with the *goðlauss* viking, without gods: martial heroism as its own end. But we may remember that the poet of *Beowulf* saw clearly: the wages of heroism is death.

For these reasons I think that the passages in *Beowulf* concerning the giants and their war with God, together with the two mentions of Cain (as the ancestor of the giants in general and Grendel in particular) are specially important.

They are directly connected with Scripture, yet they cannot be dissociated from the creatures of northern myth, the ever-watchful foes of the gods (and men). The undoubtedly scriptural Cain is connected with *eotenas* [giants] and *ylfe* [elves], which are the *jötnar* and *álfar* of Norse. But this is not due to mere confusion — it is rather an indication of the precise point at which an imagination, pondering old and new, was kindled. At this point new Scripture and old tradition touched and ignited. It is for this reason that these elements of Scripture alone appear in a poem dealing of design with the noble pagan of old days. For they are precisely the elements which bear upon this theme. Man alien in a hostile world, engaged in a struggle which he cannot win while the world lasts, is assured that his foes are the foes also of Dryhten, that his courage noble in itself is also the highest loyalty: so said thyle and clerk.

In *Beowulf* we have, then, an historical poem about the pagan past, or an attempt at one — literal historical fidelity founded on modern research was, of course, not attempted. It is a poem by a learned man writing of old times, who looking back on the heroism and sorrow feels in them something permanent and something symbolical. So far from being a confused semi-pagan — historically unlikely for a man of this sort in the period — he brought probably *first* to his task a knowledge of Christian poetry, especially that of the Cædmon school, and especially *Genesis*.[24] He makes his minstrel sing in Heorot of the Creation of the earth and the lights of Heaven. So excellent is this choice as the theme of the harp that maddened Grendel lurking joyless in the dark without that it matters little

[24] The *Genesis* which is preserved for us is a late copy of a damaged original, but is still certainly in its older parts a poem whose composition must be referred to the early period. That *Genesis A* is actually older than *Beowulf* is generally recognized as the most probable reading of such evidence as there is.

whether this is anachronistic or not.[25] *Secondly,* to his task the poet brought a considerable learning in native lays and traditions: only by learning and training could such things be acquired, they were no more born naturally into an Englishman of the seventh or eighth centuries, by simple virtue of being an 'Anglo-Saxon', than ready-made knowledge of poetry and history is inherited at birth by modern children.

It would seem that, in his attempt to depict ancient pre-Christian days, intending to emphasize their nobility, and the desire of the good for truth, he turned naturally when delineating the great King of Heorot to the Old Testament. In the *folces hyrde* [guardian of the people] of the Danes we have much of the shepherd patriarchs and kings of Israel, servants of the one God, who attribute to His mercy all the good things that come to them in this life. We have in fact a Christian English conception of the noble chief before Christianity, who could lapse (as could Israel) in times of temptation into idolatry.[26] On the

[25] Actually the poet may have known, what we can guess, that such creation-themes were also ancient in the North. *Völuspá* describes Chaos and the making of the sun and moon, and very similar language occurs in the Old High German fragment known as the *Wessobrunner Gebet.* The song of the minstrel Iopas, who had his knowledge from Atlas, at the end of the first book of the *Aeneid* is also in part a song of origins: *hic canit errantem lunam solisque labores, unde hominum genus et pecudes, unde imber et ignes* [he sang of the wandering moon and the sun's labors, whence came mankind and the cattle, whence came rain and flames]. In any case the Anglo-Saxon poet's view throughout was plainly that true, or truer, knowledge was possessed in ancient days (when men were not deceived by the Devil); at least they knew of the one God and Creator, though not of heaven, for that was lost. See note 20.

[26] It is of Old Testament lapses rather than of any events in England (of which he is not speaking) that the poet is thinking in lines 175 ff., and this colours his manner of allusion to knowledge which he may have derived from native traditions concerning the Danes and the special heathen religious significance of the site of Heorot (*Hleiðrar, æt hærgtrafum,* the tabernacles)—it was possibly a matter that embittered the feud of Danes and Heathobeards. If so, this is another point where old and new have blended. On the special importance and difficulty for criticism of the passage 175-88 see the Appendix.

other hand, the traditional matter in English, not to mention the living survival of the heroic code and temper among the noble households of ancient England, enabled him to draw differently, and in some respects much closer to the actual heathen *hæleð* [warrior], the character of Beowulf, especially as a young knight, who used his great gift of *mægen* [strength] to earn *dom* [glory] and *lof* [praise] among men and posterity.

Beowulf is not an actual picture of historic Denmark or Geatland or Sweden about A.D. 500. But it is (if with certain minor defects) on a general view a self-consistent picture, a construction bearing clearly the marks of design and thought. The whole must have succeeded admirably in creating in the minds of the poet's contemporaries the illusion of surveying a past, pagan but noble and fraught with a deep significance — a past that itself had depth and reached backward into a dark antiquity of sorrow. This impression of depth is an effect and a justification of the use of episodes and allusions to old tales, mostly darker, more pagan, and desperate than the foreground.

To a similar antiquarian temper, and a similar use of vernacular learning, is probably due the similar effect of antiquity (and melancholy) in the *Aeneid* — especially felt as soon as Aeneas reaches Italy and the *Saturni gentem . . . sponte sua veterisque dei se more tenentem* [the race of Saturn . . . maintaining itself in its own will and in the law of its old god]. *Ic þa leode wat ge wið feond ge wið freond fæste worhte, æghwæs untæle ealde wisan* [I know the people are firmly disposed toward both friend and foe, after the old fashion, in every respect blameless]. Alas for the lost lore, the annals and old poets that Virgil knew, and only used in the making of a new thing! The criticism that the important matters are put on the outer edges misses this point of artistry, and indeed fails to see why the old things have in *Beowulf* such an appeal: it is the poet himself who made antiquity so appealing. His poem has more value in consequence, and is a greater contribution to early mediaeval thought than the harsh and intolerant view that consigned all the heroes to the devil. We may be thankful that the product of so noble a temper has been preserved by chance (if such it be) from the dragon of destruction.

The general structure of the poem, so viewed, is not really difficult to perceive, if we look to the main points, the strategy, and neglect the many points of minor tactics. We must dismiss, of course, from mind the notion that *Beowulf* is a 'narrative poem', that it tells a tale or intends to tell a tale sequentially. The poem 'lacks steady advance': so Klaeber heads a critical section in his edition.[27] But the poem was not meant to advance, steadily or unsteadily. It is essentially a balance, an opposition of ends and beginnings. In its simplest terms it is a contrasted description of two moments in a great life, rising and setting; an elaboration of the ancient and intensely moving contrast between youth and age, first achievement and final death. It is divided in consequence into two opposed portions, different in matter, manner, and length: A from 1 to 2199 (including an exordium of 52 lines); B from 2200 to 3182 (the end). There is no reason to cavil at this proportion; in any case, for the purpose and the production of the required effect, it proves in practice to be right.

This simple and *static* structure, solid and strong, is in each part much diversified, and capable of enduring this treatment. In the conduct of the presentation of Beowulf's rise to fame on the one hand, and of his kingship and death on the other, criticism can find things to question, especially if it is captious, but also much to praise, if it is attentive. But the only serious weakness, or apparent weakness, is the long recapitulation: the report of Beowulf to Hygelac. This recapitulation is well done. Without

[27] Though only explicitly referred to here and in disagreement, this edition is, of course, of great authority, and all who have used it have learned much from it.

serious discrepancy [28] it retells rapidly the events in Heorot, and retouches the account; and it serves to illustrate, since he himself describes his own deeds, yet more vividly the character of a young man, singled out by destiny, as he steps suddenly forth in his full powers. Yet this is perhaps not quite sufficient to justify the repetition. The explanation, if not complete justification, is probably to be sought in different directions.

For one thing, the old tale was not first told or invented by this poet. So much is clear from investigation of the folk-tale analogues. Even the legendary association of the Scylding court with a marauding monster, and with the arrival from abroad of a champion and deliverer was probably already old. The plot was not the poet's; and though he has infused feeling and significance into its crude material, that plot was not a perfect vehicle of the theme or themes that came to hidden life in the poet's mind as he worked upon it. Not an unusual event in literature. For the contrast — youth and death — it would probably have been better, if we had no journeying. If the single nation of the *Geatas* had been the scene, we should have felt the stage not narrower, but symbolically wider. More plainly should we have perceived in one people and their hero all mankind and its heroes. This at any rate I have always myself felt in reading *Beowulf;* but I have also felt that this defect is rectified by the bringing of the tale of Grendel to Geatland. As Beowulf stands in Hygelac's hall and tells his story, he sets his feet firm again in the land of his own people, and is no longer

[28] I am not concerned with minor discrepancies at any point in the poem. They are no proof of composite authorship, nor even of incompetent authorship. It is very difficult, even in a newly invented tale of any length, to avoid such defects; more so still in rehandling old and oft-told tales. The points that are seized in the study, with a copy that can be indexed and turned to and fro (even if never read straight through as it was meant to be), are usually such as may easily escape an author and still more easily his natural audience. Virgil certainly does not escape such faults, even within the limits of a single book. Modern printed tales, that have presumably had the advantage of proof-correction, can even be observed to hesitate in the heroine's Christian name.

in danger of appearing a mere *wrecca* [exile], an errant adventurer and slayer of bogies that do not concern him.

There is in fact a double division in the poem: the fundamental one already referred to, and a secondary but important division at line 1887. After that the essentials of the previous part are taken up and compacted, so that all the tragedy of Beowulf is contained between 1888 and the end.[29] But, of course, without the first half we should miss much incidental illustration; we should miss also the dark background of the court of Heorot that loomed as large in glory and doom in ancient northern imagination as the court of Arthur: no vision of the past was complete without it. And (most important) we should lose the direct contrast of youth and age in the persons of Beowulf and Hrothgar which is one of the chief purposes of this section: it ends with the pregnant words *oþ þæt hine yldo benam mægenes wynnum, se þe oft manegum scod* [until old age which has often caused harm to many, deprived him of the joys of strength].

In any case we must not view this poem as in intention an exciting narrative or a romantic tale. The very nature of Old English metre is often misjudged. In it there is no single rhythmic pattern progressing from the beginning of a line to the end, and repeated with variation in other lines. The lines do not go according to a tune. They are founded on a balance; an opposition between two halves of roughly equivalent[30] phonetic weight, and significant content, which are more often rhythmically contrasted than similar. They are more like masonry than music. In this fundamental fact of poetic expression I think there is a parallel to the total structure of *Beowulf*. *Beowulf* is indeed the most successful Old English poem because in it the elements, language, metre, theme, structure, are all most nearly in har-

[29] The least satisfactory arrangement possible is thus to read only lines 1-1887 and not the remainder. This procedure has none the less been, from time to time, directed or encouraged by more than one 'English syllabus'.

[30] Equivalent, but not necessarily *equal,* certainly not as such things may be measured by machines.

mony. Judgement of the verse has often gone astray through listening for an accentual rhythm and pattern: and it seems to halt and stumble. Judgement of the theme goes astray through considering it as the narrative handling of a plot: and it seems to halt and stumble. Language and verse, of course, differ from stone or wood or paint, and can be only heard or read in a time-sequence; so that in any poem that deals at all with characters and events some narrative element must be present. We have none the less in *Beowulf* a method and structure that within the limits of the verse-kind approaches rather to sculpture or painting. It is a composition not a tune.

This is clear in the second half. In the struggle with Grendel one can as a reader dismiss the certainty of literary experience that the hero will not in fact perish, and allow oneself to share the hopes and fears of the Geats upon the shore. In the second part the author has no desire whatever that the issue should remain open, even according to literary convention. There is no need to hasten like the messenger, who rode to bear the lamentable news to the waiting people (2892 ff.). They may have hoped, but we are not supposed to. By now we are supposed to have grasped the plan. Disaster is foreboded. Defeat is the theme. Triumph over the foes of man's precarious fortress is over, and we approach slowly and reluctantly the inevitable victory of death.[31]

'In structure', it was said of *Beowulf,* 'it is curiously weak, in a sense preposterous,' though great merits of detail were allowed. In structure actually it is curiously strong, in a sense inevitable, though there are defects of detail. The general de-

[31] That the particular bearer of enmity, the Dragon, also dies is important chiefly to Beowulf himself. He was a great man. Not many even in dying can achieve the death of a single worm, or the temporary salvation of their kindred. Within the limits of human life Beowulf neither lived nor died in vain—brave men might say. But there is no hint, indeed there are many to the contrary, that it was a war to end war, or a dragon-fight to end dragons. It is the end of Beowulf, and of the hope of his people.

sign of the poet is not only defensible, it is, I think, admirable. There may have previously existed stirring verse dealing in straightforward manner and even in natural sequence with the Beowulf's deeds, or with the fall of Hygelac; or again with the fluctuations of the feud between the houses of Hrethel the Geat and Ongentheow the Swede; or with the tragedy of the Heathobards, and the treason that destroyed the Scylding dynasty. Indeed this must be admitted to be practically certain: it was the existence of such connected legends — connected in the mind, not necessarily dealt with in chronicle fashion or in long semihistorical poems — that permitted the peculiar use of them in *Beowulf*. This poem cannot be criticized or comprehended, if its original audience is imagined in like case to ourselves, possessing only *Beowulf* in splendid isolation. For *Beowulf* was not designed to tell the tale of Hygelac's fall, or for that matter to give the whole biography of Beowulf, still less to write the history of the Geatish kingdom and its downfall. But it used knowledge of these things for its own purpose — to give that sense of perspective, of antiquity with a greater and yet darker antiquity behind. These things are mainly on the outer edges or in the background because they belong there, if they are to function in this way. But in the centre we have an heroic figure of enlarged proportions.

Beowulf is not an 'epic', not even a magnified 'lay'. No terms borrowed from Greek or other literatures exactly fit: there is no reason why they should. Though if we must have a term, we should choose rather 'elegy'. It is an heroic-elegiac poem; and in a sense all its first 3,136 lines are the prelude to a dirge: *him þa gegiredan Geata leode ad ofer eorðan unwaclicne* [then the people of the Geats made ready for him a splendid pyre on the earth]: one of the most moving ever written. But for the universal significance which is given to the fortunes of its hero it is an enhancement and not a detraction, in fact it is necessary, that his final foe should be not some Swedish prince, or treacherous friend, but a dragon: a thing made by imagination for just such a purpose. Nowhere does a dragon come in so precisely where he should. But if the hero falls before a dragon, then certainly he should achieve his early glory by vanquishing a foe of similar order.

There is, I think, no criticism more beside the mark than that which some have made, complaining that it is monsters in both halves that is so disgusting; one they could have stomached more easily. That is nonsense. I can see the point of asking for *no* monsters. I can also see the point of the situation in *Beowulf*. But no point at all in mere reduction of numbers. It would really have been preposterous, if the poet had recounted Beowulf's rise to fame in a 'typical' or 'commonplace' war in Frisia, and then ended him with a dragon. Or if he had told of his cleansing of Heorot, and then brought him to defeat and death in a 'wild' or 'trivial' Swedish invasion! If the dragon is the right end for Beowulf, and I agree with the author that it is, then Grendel is an eminently suitable beginning. They are creatures, *feond mancynnes* [enemies of mankind], of a similar order and kindred significance. Triumph over the lesser and more nearly human is cancelled by defeat before the older and more elemental. And the conquest of the ogres comes at the right moment: not in earliest youth, though the nicors are referred to in Beowulf's *geogoðfeore* [youth] as a presage of the kind of hero we have to deal with; and not during the later period of recognized ability and prowess;[32] but in that first moment, which often comes in great lives, when men look up in surprise and see that a hero has unawares leaped forth. The placing of the dragon is inevitable: a man can but die upon his death-day.

[32] We do, however, learn incidentally much of this period: it is not strictly true, even of our poem as it is, to say that after the deeds in Heorot Beowulf 'has nothing else to do'. Great heroes, like great saints, should show themselves capable of dealing also with the ordinary things of life, even though they may do so with a strength more than ordinary. We may wish to be assured of this (and the poet has assured us), without demanding that he should put such things in the centre, when they are not the centre of his thought.

I will conclude by drawing an imaginary contrast. Let us suppose that our poet had chosen a theme more consonant with 'our modern judgement'; the life and death of St. Oswald. He might then have made a poem, and told first of Heavenfield, when Oswald as a young prince against all hope won a great victory with a remnant of brave men; and then have passed at once to the lamentable defeat of Oswestry, which seemed to destroy the hope of Christian Northumbria; while all the rest of Oswald's life, and the traditions of the royal house and its feud with that of Deira might be introduced allusively or omitted. To any one but an historian in search of facts and chronology this would have been a fine thing, an heroic-elegiac poem greater than history. It would be much better than a plain narrative, in verse or prose, however steadily advancing. This mere arrangement would at once give it more significance than a straightforward account of one king's life: the contrast of rising and setting, achievement and death. But even so it would fall far short of *Beowulf*. Poetically it would be greatly enhanced if the poet had taken violent liberties with history and much enlarged the reign of Oswald, making him old and full of years of care and glory when he went forth heavy with foreboding to face the heathen Penda: the contrast of youth and age would add enormously to the original theme, and give it a more universal meaning. But even so it would still fall short of *Beowulf*. To match his theme with the rise and fall of poor 'folk-tale' Beowulf the poet would have been obliged to turn Cadwallon and Penda into giants and demons. It is just because the main foes in *Beowulf* are inhuman that the story is larger and more significant than this imaginary poem of a great king's fall. It glimpses the cosmic and moves with the thought of all men concerning the fate of human life and efforts; it stands amid but above the petty wars of princes, and surpasses the dates and limits of historical periods, however important. At the beginning, and during its process, and most of all at the end, we look down as if from a visionary height upon the house of man in the valley of the world. A light starts — *lixte se leoma ofer landa fela* [its radiance gleamed over many lands] — and there is a sound of music; but the outer darkness and its hostile offspring lie ever in wait for the torches to fail and the voices to cease. Grendel is maddened by the sound of harps.

And one last point, which those will feel who to-day preserve the ancient *pietas* towards the past: *Beowulf* is not a 'primitive' poem; it is a late one, using the materials (then still plentiful) preserved from a day already changing and passing, a time that has now forever vanished, swallowed in oblivion; using them for a new purpose, with a wider sweep of imagination, if with a less bitter and concentrated force. When new *Beowulf* was already antiquarian, in a good sense, and it now produces a singular effect. For it is now to us itself ancient; and yet its maker was telling of things already old and weighted with regret, and he expended his art in making keen that touch upon the heart which sorrows have that are both poignant and remote. If the funeral of Beowulf moved once like the echo of an ancient dirge, far-off and hopeless, it is to us as a memory brought over the hills, an echo of an echo. There is not much poetry in the world like this; and though *Beowulf* may not be among the very greatest poems of our western world and its tradition, it has its own individual character, and peculiar solemnity; it would still have power had it been written in some time or place unknown and without posterity, if it contained no name that could now be recognized or identified by research. Yet it is in fact written in a language that after many centuries has still essential kinship with our own, it was made in this land, and moves in our northern world beneath our northern sky, and for those who are native to that tongue and land, it must ever call with a profound appeal — until the dragon comes.

APPENDIX

(*a*) *Grendel's Titles*

The changes which produced (before A.D. 1066) the medieval devil are not complete in *Beowulf*, but in Grendel change and blending are, of course, already apparent. Such things do not admit of clear classifications and distinctions. Doubtless ancient pre-Christian imagination vaguely recognized differences of 'materiality' between the solidly physical monsters, conceived as made of the earth and rock (to which the light of the sun might return them), and elves, and ghosts or bogies. Monsters of more or less human shape were naturally liable to development on contact with Christian ideas of sin and spirits of evil. Their parody of human form (*earmsceapen on weres wæstmum* [the miserable creature in the form of a man]) becomes symbolical, explicitly, of sin, or rather this mythical element, already present implicit and unresolved, is emphasized: this we see already in *Beowulf,* strengthened by the theory of descent from Cain (and so from Adam), and of the curse of God. So Grendel is not only under this inherited curse, but also himself sinful: *manscaða, synscaða, synnum beswenced* [evil-doer, malefactor, afflicted with sins]; he is *fyrena hyrde* [guardian of sins]. The same notion (combined with others) appears also when he is called (by the author, not by the characters in the poem) *hæþen* [heathen], 852, 986, and *helle hæfton, feond on helle* [captive of hell, enemy in hell]. As an image of man estranged from God he is called not only by all names applicable to ordinary men, as *wer, rinc, guma, maga,* but he is conceived as having a spirit, other than his body, that will be punished. Thus *alegde hæþene sawle*: *þær him hel onfeng* [he laid aside his heathen soul: there hell received him], 852; while Beowulf himself says *ðær abidan sceal miclan domes, hu him scir Metod scrifan wille* [there he shall await the great Judgment, how the glorious Lord will sentence him], 978.

But this view is blended or confused with another. Because of his ceaseless hostility to men, and hatred of their joy, his superhuman size and strength, and his love of the dark, he approaches to a *devil,* though he is not yet a true devil in purpose. Real devilish qualities (deception and destruction of the soul), other than those which are undeveloped symbols, such as his hideousness and habitation in dark forsaken places, are hardly present. But he and his mother are actually called *deofla,* 1680; and Grendel is said when fleeing to hiding to make for *deofla gedræg* [concourse of devils]. It should be noted that *feond* cannot be used in this question: it still means 'enemy' in *Beowulf,* and is for instance applicable to Beowulf and Wiglaf in relation to the dragon. Even *feond on helle,* 101, is not so clear as it seems (see below); though we may add *wergan gastes* [evil spirit], 133, an expression for 'devil' later extremely common, and actually applied in line 1747 to the Devil and tempter himself. Apart, however, from this expression little can be made of the use of *gast, gæst*. For one thing it is under grave suspicion in many places (both applied to Grendel and otherwise) of being a corruption of *gæst, gest* 'stranger'; compare Grendel's title *cwealmcuma* [murderous visitor], 792 = *wælgæst* [murderous sprite], 1331, 1995. In any case it cannot be translated either by the modern *ghost* or *spirit*. *Creature* is probably the nearest we can now get. Where it is genuine it applies to Grendel probably in virtue of his relationship or similarity to bogies (*scinnum ond scuccum* [demons and evil spirits]), physical enough in form and power, but vaguely felt as belonging to a different order of being, one allied to the malevolent 'ghosts' of the dead. Fire is conceived as a *gæst* (1123).

This approximation of Grendel to a devil does not mean that there is any confusion as to his habitation. Grendel was a fleshly denizen of this world (until physically slain). *On helle* and *helle* (as in *helle gast* 1274) mean 'hellish', and are actually equivalent to the first elements in the compounds *deaþscua, sceadugengea, helruna* [death-shadow, walker in darkness, one skilled in the mysteries of hell]. (Thus the original genitive *helle* developed into the Middle English adjective *helle, hellene* 'hellish', applicable to ordinary men, such as usurers; and even *feond on helle* could be so used. Wyclif applies *fend on helle* to the friar walking in England as Grendel in Denmark.) But the symbolism of darkness is so fundamental that it is vain to look for any distinction between the *þystru* [darkness] outside Hrothgar's hall in which Grendel lurked, and the shadow of Death, or of hell after (or in) Death.

Thus in spite of shifting, actually in process (intricate, and as difficult as it is interesting and important to follow), Grendel remains primarily an ogre, a physical monster, whose main function is hostility to humanity (and its frail efforts at order and art upon earth). He is of the *fifelcyn* [race of monsters], a *þyrs* or *eoten* [giant]; in fact the *eoten,* for this ancient word is actually preserved in Old English only as applied to him. He is most frequently called simply a foe: *feond, lað, sceaða, feorhgeniðla, laðgeteona* [enemy, enemy, injurer, mortal foe, hateful spoiler], all words applicable to enemies of any kind. And though he, as ogre, has kinship with devils, and is doomed when slain to be numbered among the evil spirits, he is not when wrestling with Beowulf a materialized apparition of soul-destroying evil. It is thus true to say that Grendel is not yet a real mediaeval devil — except in so far as mediaeval bogies themselves had failed (as was often the case) to become real devils. But the distinction between a devilish ogre, and a devil revealing himself in ogre-form — between a monster, devouring the body and bringing temporal death, that is inhabited by an accursed spirit, and a spirit of evil aiming ultimately at the soul and bringing eternal death (even though he takes a form of visible horror, that may bring and suffer physical pain) — is a real and important one, even if both kinds are to be found before and after 1066. In *Beowulf* the weight is on the physical side: Grendel does not vanish into the pit when grappled. He must be slain by plain prowess, and thus is a real counterpart to the dragon in Beowulf's history.

(Grendel's mother is naturally described, when separately treated, in precisely similar terms: she is *wif, ides, aglæc wif* [woman, lady, monster of a woman]; and rising to the inhuman: *merewif, brimwylf, grundwyrgen* [water-woman, she-wolf of the sea, accursed she-monster of the deep]. Grendel's title *Godes andsaca* [enemy of God] has been studied in the text. Some titles have been omitted: for instance those referring to his *outlawry,* which are applicable in themselves to him by nature, but are of course also fitting either to a descendant of Cain, or to a devil: thus *heorowearh, dædhata, mearcstapa, angengea* [accursed foe, persecutor, walker in the borderland, solitary journeyer]).

(*b*) *'Lof' and 'Dom'; 'Hell' and 'Heofon'*

Of pagan 'belief' we have little or nothing left in English. But the spirit survived. Thus the author of *Beowulf* grasped fully the idea of *lof* [praise] or *dom* [glory], the noble pagan's desire for the *merited praise* of the noble. For if this limited 'immortality' of renown naturally exists as a strong motive together with actual heathen practice and belief, it can also long outlive them. It is the natural residuum when the gods are destroyed, whether unbelief comes from within or from without. The prominence of the motive of *lof* in *Beowulf* — long ago pointed out by Earle — may be interpreted, then, as a sign that a pagan time was not far away from the poet, and perhaps also that the end of English paganism (at least among the noble classes for whom and by whom such traditions were preserved) was marked by a twilight period, similar to that observable later in Scandinavia. The gods faded or receded, and man was left to carry on his war unaided. His trust was in his own power and will, and his reward was the praise of his peers during his life and after his death.

At the beginning of the poem, at the end of the first section of the exordium, the note is struck: *lofdædum sceal in mægþa gehwære man geþeon* [by praiseworthy deeds a man shall thrive in every people]. The last word of the poem is *lofgeornost* [most eager for glory], the summit of the praise of the dead hero: that was indeed *lastworda betst* [the best memorial]. For Beowulf had lived according to his own philosophy, which he explicitly avowed: *ure æghwylc sceal ende gebidan worolde lifes; wyrce se ðe mote domes ær deaþe: þæt bið dryhtguman æfter selest* [each of us must await the end of life in the world; let him who may gain glory before death; that shall afterwards be best for the (unliving) warrior], 1386 ff. The poet as commentator recurs again to this: *swa sceal man don, þonne he æt guðe gegan þenceð longsumne lof: na ymb his lif cearað* [so must a man do, when he thinks to obtain in war long-lasting praise; he will have no care for his life], 1534 ff.

Lof is ultimately and etymologically *value, valuation,* and so *praise,* as we say (itself derived from *pretium*). *Dom* is *judgement, assessment,* and in one branch *just esteem, merited renown.* The difference between these two is not in most passages important. Thus at the end of *Widsith,* which refers to the minstrel's part in achieving for the noble and their deeds the prolonged life of fame, both are combined: it is said of the generous patron, *lof se gewyrceð, hafað under heofonum heahfæstne dom* [he gains praise and has under the heavens enduring glory]. But the difference has an importance. For the words were not actually synonymous, nor entirely commensurable. In the Christian period the one, *lof,* flowed rather into the ideas of heaven and the heavenly choirs; the other, *dom,* into the ideas of the judgement of God, the particular and general judgements of the dead.

The change that occurs can be plainly observed in *The Seafarer,* especially if lines 66-80 of that poem are compared with

Hrothgar's *giedd* or sermon in *Beowulf* from 1755 onwards. There is a close resemblance between *Seafarer* 66-71 and Hrothgar's words, 1761-8, a part of his discourse that may certainly be ascribed to the original author of *Beowulf,* whatever revision or expansion the speech may otherwise have suffered. The Seafarer says:

ic gelyfe no
þæt him eorðwelan ece stondað.
Simle þreora sum þinga gehwylce
ær his tid[d]ege to tweon weorþeð:
adl oþþe yldo oþþe ecghete
fægum fromweardum feorh oðþringeð.

[I do not believe that earthly riches will exist forever. In every case before his time may go away, one of three things is ever uncertain: disease or old age or sword hate takes away life from the doomed about to depart.]

Hrothgar says:

eft sona bið
þæt þec adl oððe ecg eafoþes getwæfeð,
oððe fyres feng, oððe flodes wylm,
oððe gripe meces, oððe gares fliht,
oððe atol yldo; oððe eagena bearhtm
forsiteð ond forsworceð. Semninga bið
þæt þec, dryhtguma, deað oferswyðeð.

[Soon in turn it will happen that sickness or the sword will deprive you of strength, or the embrace of fire, or the welling of the flood, or the attack of the knife, or the flight of the arrow, or terrible old age; or the brightness of eyes shall fail and grow dim. Very soon it is that death will overcome you, warrior.]

Hrothgar expands *þreora sum* [one of three things] on lines found elsewhere, either in great elaboration as in the *Fates of Men,* or in brief allusion to this well-known theme as in *The Wanderer* 80 ff. But the Seafarer, after thus proclaiming that all men shall die, goes on: 'Therefore it is for all noble men *lastworda betst* (the best memorial), and praise (*lof*) of the living who commemorate him after death, that ere he must go hence, he should merit and achieve on earth by heroic deeds against the malice of enemies (*feonda*), opposing the devil, that the children of men may praise him afterwards, and his *lof* may live with the angels for ever and ever, the glory of eternal life, rejoicing among the hosts.'

This is a passage which from its syntax alone may with unusual certainty be held to have suffered revision and expansion. It could easily be simplified. But in any case it shows a modification of heathen *lof* in two directions: first in making the deeds which win *lof* resistance to spiritual foes — the sense of the ambiguous *feonda* is, in the poem as preserved, so defined by *deofle togeanes* [against the devil]; secondly, in enlarging *lof* to include the angels and the bliss of heaven. *lofsong, loftsong* are in Middle English especially used of the heavenly choirs.

But we do not find anything like this definite alteration in *Beowulf*. There *lof* remains pagan *lof,* the praise of one's peers, at best vaguely prolonged among their descendants *awa to ealdre* [for ever and ever]. (On *soðfæstra dom* [judgment of the righteous], 2820, see below). In *Beowulf* there is *hell*: justly the poet said of the people he depicted *helle gemundon on modsefan* [they remembered hellish things in the thoughts of their hearts]. But there is practically no clear reference to *heaven* as its opposite, to heaven, that is, as a place or state of reward, of eternal bliss in the presence of God. Of course *heofon,* singular and plural, and its synonyms, such as *rodor,* are frequent; but they refer usually either to the particular landscape or to the sky under which all men dwell. Even when these words are used with the words for God, who is Lord of the heavens, such expressions are primarily parallels to others describing His general governance of nature (e.g. 1609 ff.), and His realm which includes land and sea and sky.

Of course it is not here maintained — very much the contrary — that the *poet* was ignorant of theological heaven, or of the Christian use of *heofon* as the equivalent of *caelum* in Scripture: only that this use was of intention (if not in practice quite rigidly) excluded from a poem dealing with the pagan past. There is one clear exception in lines 186 ff: *wel bið þæm þe mot æfter deaðdæge Drihten secean, ond to Fæder fæþmum freoðo wilnian* [well is it for him who is permitted after death to seek the Lord and ask for peace in the Father's embrace]. If this, and the passage in which it occurs, is genuine — descends, that is, without addition or alteration from the poet who wrote *Beowulf* as a whole — and is not, as, I believe, a later expansion, then the point is not destroyed. For the passage remains still definitely an aside, an exclamation of the Christian author, who knew about heaven, and expressly denied such knowledge to the Danes. The characters within the poem do not understand heaven, or have hope of it. They refer to *hell* — an originally pagan word.[33] Beowulf predicts it as the destiny of Unferth and Grendel. Even the noble monotheist Hrothgar — so he is drawn, quite apart from the question of the genuineness of the bulk of his sermon from 1724-60 — refers to no heavenly bliss. The reward of virtue which he foretells for Beowulf is that his *dom* shall live *awa to ealdre,* a fortune also bestowed upon Sigurd in Norse (that his name *æ mun uppi* [shall live forever]). This idea of lasting *dom* is, as we have seen, capable of being christianized; but in *Beowulf* it is not christianized, probably deliberately, when the characters are speaking in their proper persons, or their actual thoughts are reported.

The author, it is true, says of Beowulf that *him of hreðre gewat sawol secean soðfæstra dom* [his soul departed from his breast to seek the judgment of the righteous]. What precise theological view he held concerning the souls of the just heathen we need not here inquire. He does not tell us, saying simply that Beowulf's spirit departed to whatever judgement awaits such just men, though we may take it that this comment implies that it was not destined to the fiery hell of punishment, being reckoned among the good. There is in any case here no doubt of the transmutation of words originally pagan, *soðfæstra dom* could by itself have meant simply the 'esteem of the true-judging', that *dom* which Beowulf as a young man had declared to be the prime motive of noble conduct; but here combined with *gewat secean* it must mean either the glory that belongs (in eternity) to the just, or the judgement of God upon the just. Yet Beowulf himself, expressing his own opinion, though troubled by dark doubts, and later declaring his conscience clear, thinks at the end only of his barrow and memorial among men, of his childlessness, and of Wiglaf the sole survivor of his kin-

[33] Free as far as we know from definite physical location. Details of the original northern conception, equated and blended with the Scriptural, are possibly sometimes to be seen colouring the references to Christian hell. A celebrated example is the reference in *Judith* to the death of Holofernes, which recalls remarkably certain features in *Völuspá.* Cf. *Judith* 115: *wyrmum bewunden* [surrounded with serpents], and 119: *of ðam wyrmsele* [from the serpent-hall] with *Völ.* 36 *sá's undinn salr orma hryggjum*: which translated into O.E. would be *se is wunden sele wyrma hrycgum* [that hall is wound with backs of serpents].

dred, to whom he bequeathes his arms. His funeral is not Christian, and his reward is the recognized virtue of his kingship and the hopeless sorrow of his people.

The relation of the Christian and heathen thought and diction in *Beowulf* has often been misconceived. So far from being a man so simple or so confused that he muddled Christianity with Germanic paganism, the author probably drew or attempted to draw distinctions, and to represent moods and attitudes of characters conceived dramatically as living in a noble but heathen past. Though there are one or two special problems concerning the tradition of the poem and the possibility that it has here and there suffered later unauthentic retouching,[34] we cannot speak in general either of confusion (in one poet's mind or in the mind of a whole period), or of patch-work revision producing confusion. More sense can be made of the poem, if we start rather with the hypothesis, not in itself unlikely, that the poet tried to do something definite and difficult, which had some reason and thought behind it, though his execution may not have been entirely successful.

The strongest argument that the actual language of the poem is not in general the product either of stupidity or accident is to be found in the fact that we can observe *differentiation*. We can, that is, in this matter of philosophy and religious sentiment distinguish, for instance: (*a*) the poet as narrator and commentator; (*b*) Beowulf; and (*c*) Hrothgar. Such differentiation would not be achieved by a man himself confused in mind, and still less by later random editing. The kind of thing that accident contrives is illustrated by *drihten wereda,* 'lord of hosts', a familiar Christian expression, which appears in line 2186, plainly as an alteration of *drihten Wedera* 'lord of the Geats'. This alteration is obviously due to some man, the actual scribe of the line or some predecessor, more familiar with *Dominus Deus Sabaoth* than with Hrethel and the Weder-Geatish house. But no one, I think, has ventured to ascribe this confusion to the author.

That such differentiation does occur, I do not attempt here to prove by analysis of all the relevant lines of the poem. I leave

[34] Such as 168-9, probably a clumsily intruded couplet, of which the only certain thing that can be said is that it interrupts (even if its sense were plain) the natural connexion between 165-7 and 170; the question of the expansion (in this case at any rate skilful and not inapt) of Hrothgar's *giedd,* 1724-60; and most notably lines 175-88.

the matter to those who care to go through the text, only insisting that it is essential to pay closer attention than has usually been paid to the *circumstances* in which the references to religion, Fate, or mythological matters each appear, and to distinguish in particular those things which are said in *oratio recta* [direct discourse] by one of the characters, or are reported as being said or thought by them. It will then be seen that the narrating and commenting poet obviously stands apart. But the two characters who do most of the speaking, Beowulf and Hrothgar, are also quite distinct. Hrothgar is consistently portrayed as a wise and noble monotheist, modelled largely it has been suggested in the text on the Old Testament patriarchs and kings; he refers all things to the favour of God, and never omits explicit thanks for mercies. Beowulf refers sparingly to God, except as the arbiter of critical events, and then principally as *Metod,* in which the idea of God approaches nearest to the old Fate. We have in Beowulf's language little differentiation of God and Fate. For instance, he says *gæð a wyrd swa hio scel* [fate goes ever as it must] and immediately continues that *dryhten* holds the balance in his combat (441); or again he definitely equates *wyrd* and *metod* (2526 f.).[35] It is Beowulf who says *wyrd oft*

[35] Of course the use of words more or less equivalent to 'fate' continued throughout the ages. The most Christian poets refer to *wyrd,* usually of unfortunate events; but sometimes of good, as in *Elene* 1047, where the conversion of Judas is ascribed to *wyrd.* There remains always the main mass of the workings of Providence (*Metod*) which are inscrutable, and for practical purposes dealt with as 'fate' or 'luck'. *Metod* is in Old English the word that is most nearly allied to 'fate', although employed as a synonym of *god.* That it could be so employed is due probably to its having anciently in English an agental significance (as well as an abstract sense), as in Old Norse where *mjötuðr* has the senses 'dispenser, ruler' and 'doom, fate, death'. But in old English *metodsceaft* means 'doom' or 'death'. Cf. 2814 f. where *wyrd* is more active than *metodsceaft.* In Old Saxon *metod* is similarly used, leaning also to the side of the inscrutable (and even hostile) aspects of the world's working. Gabriel in the *Hêliand* says of John the Baptist that he will not touch wine: *so habed im* uurdgiscapu, metod *gimarcod endi maht godes* [so had destiny—the *metod*—and the might of God decreed for him.] (128); it is said of Anna when her husband died: *that sie thiu mikla maht* metodes *todelda, uured* uurdigiscapu [. . . that the great might of the *metod,* hostile destiny, dealt it (sorrow) out] (511). In Old Saxon *metod(o)giscapu* and *metodigisceft,* equal Fate, as O.E. *metodsceaft.*

nereð unfægne eorl, þonne his ellen deah [fate often protects a man not yet fated to die when his courage is good] (immediately after calling the sun *beacen Godes* [sign of God]), which contrasts with the poet's own comment on the man who escaped the dragon (2291): *swa mæg unfæge eaðe gedigean wean ond wræcsið, se ðe Wealdendes hyldo gehealdeþ* [thus may an undoomed man, one who retains the grace of the Ruler, survive easily woe and exile]. Beowulf only twice explicitly thanks God or acknowledges His help: in lines 1658-61, where he acknowledges God's protection and the favour of *ylda Waldend* [Ruler of men] in his combat under the water; in his last speech, where he thanks *Frean Wuldurcyninge . . . ecum Dryhtne* [the Ruler, the King of Glory, the everlasting Lord] for all the treasure, and for helping him to win it for his people. Usually he makes no such references. He ascribes his conquest of the nicors to luck — *hwæþre me gesælde* [anyhow it was granted to me], 570 ff. (compare the similar words used of Sigemund, 890). In his account to Hygelac his only explanation of his preservation in the water-den is *næs ic fæge þa gyt* [I was then not yet doomed] (2141). He does not allude to God at all in this report.

Beowulf knows, of course, of hell and judgement: he speaks of it to Unferth; he declares that Grendel shall abide *miclan domes* [the great judgment] and the judgement of *scir metod* [the glorious God]; and finally in his last examination of conscience he says that *Waldend fira* [Ruler of men] cannot accuse him of *morðorbealo maga* [the murder of kinsmen]. But the crimes which he claims to have avoided are closely paralleled in the heathen *Völuspá,* where the grim hall, *Náströndu á,* contains especially *menn meinsvara ok morðvarga* (perjurers and murderers).

Other references he makes are casual and formal, such as *beorht beacen Godes* [bright token of God], of the sun (571). An exceptional case is *Godes leoht geceas* [he chose God's light] 2469, describing the death of Hrethel, Beowulf's grandfather. This would appear to refer to heaven. Both these expressions have, as it were, inadvertently escaped from Christian poetry. The first, *beacen Godes,* is perhaps passable even for a heathen in this particular poem, in which the theory throughout is that good pagans, when not tempted or deluded by the devil, knew of the one God. But the second, especially since Beowulf himself is formally the speaker, is an item of unsuitable diction — which cannot be dismissed as a later alteration. A didactic reviser would hardly have added this detail to the description of the heathen king's death: he would rather have removed the heathen, or else sent him to hell. The whole story alluded to is pagan and hopeless, and turns on blood-feud and the motive that when a son kills his brother the father's sorrow is intensified because no vengeance can be exacted. The explanation of such occasional faults is not to be sought in Christian revision, but in the fact that before *Beowulf* was written Christian poetry was already established, and was known to the author. The language of *Beowulf* is in fact partly 're-paganized' by the author with a special purpose, rather than christianized (by him or later) without consistent purpose. Throughout the poem the language becomes more intelligible, if we assume that the diction of poetry was already christianized and familiar with Old and New Testament themes and motives. There is a gap, important and effective poetically whatever was its length in time, between Cædmon and the poet of *Beowulf*. We have thus in Old English not only the old heroic language often strained or misused in application to Christian legend (as in *Andreas* or *Elene*), but in *Beowulf* language of Christian tone occasionally (if actually seldom) put inadvertently in the mouth of a character conceived as heathen. All is not perfect to the last detail in *Beowulf*. But with regard to *Godes leoht geceas,* the chief defect of this kind, it may be observed that in the very long speech of Beowulf from 2425-2515 the poet has hardly attempted to keep up the pretence of *oratio recta* [direct discourse] throughout. Just before the end he reminds us and himself that Beowulf is supposed to be speaking by a renewed *Beowulf maðelode* [Beowulf spoke] (2510). From 2444 to 2489 we have not really a monologue in character at all, and the words *Godes leoht geceas* go rather with *gewat secean soðfæstra dom* [went to seek the judgment of the righteous] as evidence of the author's own view of the destiny of the just pagan.

When we have made allowance for imperfections of execution, and even for some intentional modification of character in old age (when Beowulf becomes not unnaturally much more like Hrothgar), it is plain that the characters and sentiments of the two chief actors in the poem are differently conceived and drawn. Where Beowulf's thoughts are revealed by the poet we can observe that his real trust was in *his own might*. That the possession of this might was a 'favour of God' is actually a comment of the poet's, similar to the comment of Scandinavian Christians upon their heathen heroes. Thus in line 665 we have *georne truwode modgan mægenes, metodes hyldo* [trusted firmly in his brave might, the favor of the Creator]. No *and* is possible metrically in the original; none should appear in translation: the favour of God *was* the possession of *mægen*. Compare 1272-3: *gemunde mægenes strenge, gimfæste gife ðe him God sealde* [he bore in mind the power of his might, the splendid gift which God had granted him].[36] Whether they knew it or not, *cuþon* (or *ne cuþon*) *heofena Helm herian* [they knew (or *knew not*) how to praise the Protector of heavens], the supreme quality of the old heroes, their valour, was their special endowment by God, and as such could be admired and praised.

Concerning Beowulf the poet tells us finally that when the dragon's ruinous assault was reported, he was filled with doubt and dismay, and *wende se wisa þæt he Wealdende ofer ealde riht ecean Dryhtne bitre gebulge* [the wise man thought that he, contrary to ancient law, had bitterly offended the Almighty, the everlasting Lord]. It has been said that *ofer ealde riht*, 'contrary to ancient law', is here given a Christian interpretation; but this hardly seems to be the case. This is a heathen and unchristian fear— of an inscrutable power, a *Metod* that can be offended inadvertently: indeed the sorrow of a man who, though he knew of God, and was eager for justice, was yet far estranged, and 'had hell in his heart'.

[36] Compare, for instance, the intrusive commentary in *Fóstbræðra saga* which observes in a description of a grim pagan character: *ekki var hjarta hans sem fóarn í fugli, ekki var þat blóð ult, svá at þat skylfi af hræðslu, heldr var þat hert af enum hæsta höfuðsmið í öllum hvatleik* (ch. 2); and again *Almáttigr er sá sem svá snart hjarta ok óhrætt lét í brjóst Þorgeiri; ok ekki var hans hugþryði af mönnum ger né honum í brjóst borin, heldr af enum hæsta höfuðsmið* [. . . his heart was not like the gizzard in a bird, nor was it full of blood so that it trembled from fear; rather, it was hardened by the supreme Master-Builder for all bold deeds (Ch. 2). Almighty is He who placed a bold and fearless heart in the breast of Þorgeirr; and his courage was not created by men or born with him in his breast, but rather (was created) by the supreme Master-Builder] (ib.). Here the notion is explicitly (if unseasonably and absurdly) expressed.

(*c*) *Lines 175-88*

These lines are important and present certain difficulties. We can with confidence accept as original and genuine these words as far as *helle gemundon on modsefan* [they remembered hell in their hearts] — which is strikingly true, in a sense, of all the characters depicted or alluded to in the poem, even if it is here actually applied only to those deliberately turning from God to the Devil. The rest requires, and has often received, attention. If it is original, the poet must have intended a distinction between the wise Hrothgar, who certainly knew of and often thanked God, and a certain party of the pagan Danes — heathen priests, for instance, and those that had recourse to them under the temptation of calamity — specially deluded by the *gastbona,* the destroyer of souls.[37] Of these, particularly those permanently in the service of idols (*swylce wæs þeaw hyra* [such was their custom]), which in Christian theory and in fact did not include all the community, it is perhaps possible to say that they did not know (*ne cuþon*), nor even know of (*ne wiston*), the one God, nor know how to worship him. At any rate the hell (of fire) is only predicted for those showing malice (*sliðne nið*), and it is not plain that the *freoðo* [protection] of the Father is ultimately obtainable by none of these men of old. It is probable that the contrast between 92-8 and 175-88 is intentional: the song of the minstrel in the days of untroubled joy, before the assault of Grendel, telling of the Almighty and His fair creation, and the loss of knowledge and praise, and the fire awaiting such malice, in the time of temptation and despair.

But it is open to doubt whether lines 181-88 are original, or at any rate unaltered. Not of course because of the apparent discrepancy — though it is a matter vital to the whole poem: we cannot dismiss lines simply because they offer difficulty of such a kind. But because, unless my ear and judgement are wholly at

[37] It is not strictly true to say, as is said, for instance, by Hoops that he is 'identified' with their heathen god. The Christian theory was that such gods did not exist, and were inventions of the Devil, and that the power of idols was due to the fact that he, or one of his emissaries, often actually inhabited them, and could be seen in their real hideousness if the veil of illusion was removed. Compare Aelfric's homilies on St. Bartholomew, and St. Matthew, where by the power of an angel or saint the devil residing in idols was revealed as a black *silhearwa* [ethiopian].

fault, they have a ring and measure unlike their context, and indeed unlike that of the poem as a whole. The place is one that offers at once special temptation to enlargement or alteration and special facilities for doing either without grave dislocation.[38] I suspect that the second half of line 180 has been altered, while what follows has remodelled or replaced a probably shorter passage, making the comment (one would say, guided by the poem as a whole) that they *forsook* God under tribulation, and incurred the danger of hell-fire. This in itself would be a comment of the *Beowulf* poet, who was probably provided by his original material with a reference to *wigweorþung* [honor to idols] in the sacred site of Heorot at this juncture in the story.

In any case the *unleugbare Inkonsequenz* (Hoops) of this passage is felt chiefly by those who assume that by references to the Almighty the legendary Danes and the Scylding court are depicted as 'Christian'. If that is so, the mention of heathen *þeaw* [custom] is, of course, odd; but it offers only one (if a marked) example of a confusion of thought fundamental to the poem, and does not then merit long consideration. Of all the attempts to deal with this *Inkonsequenz* perhaps the least satisfactory is the most recent: that of Hoops,[39] who supposes that the poet had to represent the Danish prayers as addressed to the Devil for the protection of the honour of the *Christengott,* since the prayers were not answered. But this attributes to the poet a confusion (and insincerity) of thought that an 'Anglo-Saxon' was hardly modern or advanced enough to achieve. It is difficult to believe that he could have been so singularly ill instructed in the nature of Christian prayer. And the pretense that *all* prayers to the *Christengott* are answered, and swiftly, would scarcely have deceived the stupidest member of his audience. Had he embarked on such bad theology, he would have had many other difficulties

[38] Similarly it is the very marked character already by the poet given to Hrothgar which has induced and made possible without serious damage the probable revision and expansion of his sermon. Well done as the passage in itself is, the poem would be better with the excision of approximately lines 1740-60; and these lines are on quite independent grounds under the strongest suspicion of being due to later revision and addition. The actual joints have, nevertheless, if that is so, been made with a technical competence as good as that which I here assume for the earlier passage.

[39] *Kommentar zum Beowulf,* p. 39.

to face: the long time of woe before God relieved the distress of these Christian Danes by sending Scyld (13); and indeed His permission of the assaults of Grendel at all upon such a Christian people, who do not seem depicted as having perpetrated any crime punishable by calamity. But in fact God did provide a cure for Grendel — Beowulf, and this is recognized by the poet in the mouth of Hrothgar himself (381 ff.). We may acquit the maker of *Beowulf* of the suggested motive, whatever we may think of the *Inkonsequenz*. He could hardly have been less aware than we that in history (in England and in other lands), and in Scripture, people could depart from the one God to other service in time of trial — precisely because that God has never guaranteed to His servants immunity from temporal calamity, before or after prayer. It is to idols that men turned (and turn) for quick and literal answers.

5

THE RELIGIOUS PRINCIPLE IN *BEOWULF**

Marie Padgett Hamilton

REFLECTIVE ENGLISHMEN OF THE SEVENTH AND EIGHTH CENturies, living under the transforming influence of classical and Christian ideas, must have satisfied a special need by revaluating their Germanic patrimony in terms of the new culture. In that process the Teutonic heritage naturally took on an added lustre wherever it lent itself to Christian interpretation. *Beowulf* more fully than any other English poem reflects that effort to assimilate and reappraise whereby the Germanic tradition from the Continent was ennobled by the new theology, as by a light flashed backward into the heroic past.[1] Thus the career of the Danish king Heremod becomes an exemplum for a Christian homily on pride; Grendel, creature of northern fantasy, is placed in a Biblical lineage of evil reaching back to the first murder. The poet probably recognized, however, that his illumination of the past stopped short of perfect fusion of new and old, to say nothing of historical fidelity. Doubtless he was less disturbed than we are by vestiges of his pagan sources that lie awkwardly in the matrix of his Christian prepossessions. He had the ad-

* Reprinted, by permission of the Modern Language Association of America, from *Publications of the Modern Language Association of America* (*PMLA*), LXI (June 1946), 309-331.

[1] "*Beowulf* . . . stands like Hervör at the tomb of Angantýr, 'between the worlds' " (R. W. Chambers, *Beowulf, An Introduction*, rev. ed., p. 489).

vantage of knowing what he meant when, for example, he used terms of various and elastic connotation like *wyrd* [fate, chance, fortune]. Also, if I am not mistaken, he saw his divergent materials in relation to a great central truth, an underlying principle which enabled him to recognize a larger unity in his fabulous tales than appears on the surface, and which made them in his eyes more worthy to survive in a reflective poem of epic magnitude.

This conception of *Beowulf* is, of course, not new. Professor Klaeber speaks of "the problem of finding a formula which satisfactorily explains the peculiar spiritual atmosphere of the poem."[2] Its didactic nature has given rise to the theory that it was designed to be a mirror for princes, to allegorical explanations, and to Klaeber's conception of the hero as a deliverer and redeemer, battling against the powers of darkness, and "suggesting the most exalted hero-life known to Christians."[3] Professor Gerald G. Walsh, pushing this thesis beyond the bounds discreetly set by Klaeber, regards *Beowulf* as "a single allegorical song intimating the Divine Mystery of Redemption." More specifically he writes:

> Grendel is the Devil; Beowulf offering himself for others is Christ redeeming man by self-sacrifice. . . . The suggestion throughout the epic is that man falls and needs a Saviour who will redeem him by the conquest of evil.[4]

Yet the reserve of the Christian poet in recasting his heathen tales is an arresting feature of the transformed narrative, and no small factor in the problem of interpretation. Whereas the Englishman and his circle could not have tolerated a hero loyal to Woden and Thunor, they would not have understood a man with no religious allegiance. At the same time, lovers of heroic verse who were equipped to follow *Beowulf* in its bridled allu-

[2] F. Klaeber, *Beowulf*, 3rd. ed., p. cxxi., n. 28.

[3] *Beowulf*, 3rd ed., pp. l-li; cf. *"Die Christlichen Elemente im Beowulf," Anglia*, XXXV, 111-136; 249-270, 453-482; *ibid.*, XXXVI, 169-199.

[4] Gerald G. Walsh, *Medieval Humanism*, pp. 45-46.

sions, its irony, and its rich vocabulary[5] could hardly have relished a story presenting Scandinavians of pre-conversion days as orthodox Catholics; such outright transformation of pagan Teutonic lore was reserved for later times and the more popular audience of the *Nibelungenlied.* The Beowulf-poet may be resolving the dilemma when he avoids reference to Christian worship or the saints and merely represents his nobler agents as intelligent monotheists. Except for temporary apostasy under great stress, they are loyal to the one true God (*sóð metod*), like the chosen people of the Old Testament.[6]

Even leaving that anachronism out of account, *Beowulf* "remains to us a singular and, in a sense, problematic poem."[7] As Klaeber comments, the heroic legends in the hands of the Christian poet "assumed a markedly edifying character which requires to be analyzed and explained."[8] The solution is to be sought not, I think, in any dominant message that the writer sought to convey, but rather in assumptions governing his vision of the past, imaginative moulds into which history or legend must be poured before either might become significant or viable for him.

Among the beliefs that underlie the poet's treatment of his heathen narratives, the most inclusive is the Christian doctrine of Providence, the conception of God as having governed all races of mankind since the creation, and as bestowing all favors, natural or supernatural, that men enjoy. Few would challenge this truism concerning the poet's philosophy, notwithstanding

[5] The "sophisticated style" and "respectable scholarly attainments of the author" are no longer matters for debate, and these, of course, presuppose a 'fit audience.' (Cf. J. S. P. Tatlock, "Layamon's Poetic Style in Its Relations," *Manly Anniversary Studies,* pp. 3-4; F. Klaeber, *Beowulf,* pp. lxviii, cxxi; W. W. Lawrence, *Beowulf and Epic Tradition,* pp. 3-4; C. W. Kennedy, *The Earliest English Poetry,* p. 14, etc.)

[6] Cf. Klaeber, *Beowulf,* p. cx, on "the Old Testament atmosphere" of the poem.

[7] *Ibid.,* p. cxx.

[8] *Ibid.*

his disturbing references to *wyrd*.[9] But the orthodox view of Providence known to the English converts also included the dogma of election and grace, which analysts of *Beowulf* have neglected. I wish to suggest here that the theory of grace, alongside the doctrine of Providence, conditioned the poet's view of the past and influenced his interpretation of events and agents in his stories. Actual proof being out of the question, the only tests at hand are harmony with the prevailing tenor of the poem and congeniality to the intellectual climate in which it flowered. Without forgetting either, I turn first to the intellectual climate, disregarding for the moment any pagan survivals that may have colored the early English attitude to Christian teaching.

I

Beowulf probably belongs to that golden age of early English libraries[10] to which King Alfred looks longingly back in his Preface to *The Pastoral Care*. In those libraries, Professor Ogilvy tells us, poets and scholars might have found, alongside other treasures, "a very respectable collection of pagan Latin poets and an extraordinarily complete one of their Christian successors," many saints' lives, and "an enormous number of Patristic works, including those of the greatest Fathers of the Church,

[9] Among witnesses to the essentially Christian character of *Beowulf*, such as Chambers, Rankin, Pizzo, Klaeber, Batchelor, a recent spokesman is Professor C. W. Kennedy, who describes the transmutation of pagan materials as "a deeply pervasive infusion of Christian spirit coloring thought and judgment, governing motive and action, a continuous and active agent in the process of transformation" (*Beowulf, the Oldest English Epic* [1940], p. xlix; *The Earliest English Poetry* [1943], p. 87).

[10] See J. D. A. Ogilvy, *Books Known to Anglo-Latin Writers from Aldhelm to Alcuin (670-804)*, p. 95, who concludes that English education was in better case than has been assumed before the coming of Hadrian and Theodore in 668 (pp. 103-104), and places the golden age of Anglo-Saxon libraries between the arrival of those scholars and the death of Benedict Biscop (p. 95). Ogilvy is convinced that not a great many books were added to English libraries between the years 735 and 790 (p. 94), probably because the English already "had possessed themselves of a large proportion of the works then current in Western Europe" (p. 96).

both Latin and Greek."[11] Among these writers by far the most influential on the religious thought of the early English were Gregory, Jerome, and Augustine;[12] more particularly Augustine. In this respect England was, to be sure, not exceptional at a time when religious dogma throughout Roman Christendom was dominated by Augustine,[13] and "the all-important topic in men's minds was that of God's grace."[14]

In England a prime favorite among Augustine's writings was his analysis of the past, viewed *sub specie aeternitatis* [in the light of eternity], wherein the principles of predestination and grace are most amply described in their effects upon history.[15] *The City of God,* Ogilvy concludes, "must have been known in England from the very beginning of the eighth century at the latest, and probably reached the island as early as the times of Hadrian and Theodore. It is continually cited, and quoted without cita-

[11] *Ibid.,* p. 97.

[12] King Alfred practically equates these Fathers with Biblical writers when he refers to heaven as "the everlasting home which He hath promised us through Saint Augustine, Saint Gregory, and Saint Jerome and through many other holy Fathers" (*King Alfred's Old English Version of Saint Augustine's Soliloquies,* tr. by H. L. Hargrove, Yale Studies in English, 22.1). For a statement regarding the influence of Augustine, Gregory, and Jerome on Anglo-Latin writers of the eighth century, see Ogilvy, pp. 13-14, 40-43, 49-55, and his summary, p. 97: "In the last analysis, . . . the importance of the eighth-century English for their immediate successors (and perhaps for us) was very largely due to their study of the greatest of the Fathers of the Church."

[13] For a convenient statement of this commonplace see, e.g., Harnack, *A History of Dogma* 5.3, or Cushman, *A Beginner's History of Philosophy* 1.335-337.

[14] The statement appears in a summary by Cushman (*op. cit.,* 1.335) of philosophical trends in Western Europe for the entire period between the years 476 and 1000. "The intellectual world," he writes, "was dominated by Neo-Platonic idealism, and the all important topic in men's minds was that of God's grace. Augustine stood at the beginning of the period and organized its conception of grace for it."

[15] Ogilvy, p. 14.

tion," by Anglo-Latin writers from Aldhelm[16] to Alcuin.[17] By all odds the most popular section of the *Civitas Dei* in England was Book 15,[18] Augustine's account of the two societies, or divisions of God's creatures, which have existed side by side since the Fall of the Angels, and are destined to go on in continual warfare to the last trump of doom. In short, the Righteous and the Reprobate: "the one predestined to reign eternally with God, the other condemned to perpetual torment with the Devil";[19] the heavenly citizen, as typified by Abel, "by grace predestined and by grace elected," and the carnal citizen, as typified by Cain.[20]

Grace in the theological sense is often referred to by Old English writers,[21] and frequently in an off-hand fashion which

[16] For the suggestion that the Beowulf-poet was influenced by Aldhelm, see A. S. Cook, "The Possible Begetter of the Old English *Beowulf* and *Widsith*," *Transactions of the Connecticut Academy of Arts and Sciences,* xxv, 281-346; and his briefer articles: *"Beowulf 1422," MLN,* xxxix, 77-82, and "Aldhelm and the Source of *Beowulf* 2523," *MLN,* xl, 137-142.

[17] Ogilvy, p. 14 and n. 26.

[18] *Ibid.*, n. 26.

[19] *De Civitate Dei* 15.1, ed. by Welldon. Here, and in most other quotations, my English renderings follow Healey's translation.

[20] *Ibid.*

[21] Since this fact is seldom noted, I append a list of allusions to grace in the theological sense, compiled from a partial survey of pertinent O.E. poems and of the O.E. Bede (i.e., *Eccl. Hist.* and *Life and Miracles of St. Cuthbert*). The terms for 'grace' in these passages are *ár, ést, giefu* and its compounds, *gifnes, hyldo, liss, milts* (cf. Bosworth-Toller):

ÁR: *Andreas* 979; *Christ* 335; *Guthlac* 620, 766; *Prayer* III 110; *Wanderer* 1 (?), 114.

ÉST: *Elene* 985; *Gifts* 87; *Guthlac* 826; *Phoenix* 46.

GIEFU: *Andreas* 530, 548, 575; *Christ* 42, 80, 480, 649, 710, 860, 1243; *Christ and Satan* 571, 644; *Daniel* 199, 420; *Eccl. Hist.* I 7, 13, 16, II, 5, 9, III. 1, 3, IV. 3, 18, 21, 22, 25, 29, V. 20; *Elene* 182, 199, 966, 1032, 1057, 1143, 1156, 1246; *Genesis* 2331, 2811; *Gifts* 21; *Guthlac* 100, 124, 530, 772, 1115, 1303; *Juliana* 316, 447, 517; *Phoenix* 557; *Solomon* 65; *St. Cuthbert*, Chapters 1, 4, 5, 11, 23, 46.

ÉADGIFU: *Juliana* 316.

HǼLOGIFU: *Christ* 3748.

SUNDUR-GIFU: *Christ* 80.

indicates what would be expected, that the doctrine of grace, like the related dogma of election, was taken for granted. Such doubtless would have been the case even though *The City of God* and other treatises by Augustine had not been read in England,[22] and yet they must have increased the interest of the English in those doctrines. The Augustinian emphasis on predestination and grace may, indeed, have served a special need of the Germanic converts by easing for them the ascent from pagan fatalism to the Christian belief in Divine Providence.[23] And the popularity of Book 15 of the *Civitas Dei,* added to and reinforcing the influence of its Biblical sources, may be reflected

---

WULDORGIFU: *Elene* 107; *Gloria* 44.
GIFNESS: *Prayer* III. 110, 114.
HYLDO: *Azarias* 13, 22; *Daniel* 292, 439.
LISS: *Christ* 1646.
MILTS: *Azarias* 50; *Andreas* 140, 544; *Exodus* 292; *Guthlac* 21; *Juliana* 657; *Wanderer* 2.

For a survey of Aelfric's view of grace see N. O. Halvorson, *Doctrinal Terms in Aelfric's Homilies,* University of Iowa Humanistic Studies, 5.1, pp. 53-63. See also A. Keiser, *The Influence of Christianity on the Vocabulary of Old English Poetry,* University of Illinois Studies in Language and Literature, 5.1, pp. 75-76, under "Gifts."

[22] The works of Gregory, who accepted Augustine's views of predestination, election, and grace (F. H. Duddon, *Gregory the Great,* 374, 400-403), would alone have insured the currency of the doctrines in England. They are assumed in *The Pastoral Care,* which was used by the English clergy from the time of Augustine's mission (H. Sweet, *Gregory's Pastoral,* E.E.T.S., 45, 50, p. 8). For references to election and grace see *ibid.,* pp. 50, 218, 219, 237, 381, and more especially, pp. 465, 467-469. I have made no survey of allusions to election in O.E., but see Bede, *Eccl. Hist.,* O.E. version 2.110, and mentions of the elect in *Christ* 1635; *Daniel* 150, 735; *Gloria* 42; *Guthlac* 59, 769; *Juliana* 16-17, 605; *Phoenix* 593-594.

[23] Cf. the evolution of the term *wyrd.* A. Keiser, discussing its use in O.E. poetry, says: "In the case of *wyrd* we observe that the mythological force has been lost almost completely. The word takes a two-fold development under Christian influence, being used in the sense of God and predestination, and in that of the fallen angel or devil" (*The Influence of Christianity on the Vocabulary of Old English Poetry,* p. 11; cf. pp. 52-53, 80, 87).

in the sharp dualism of Old English religious verse and its preoccupation with the destiny of the elect (*ðā gecorenan*) and the doomed (*ðā wyrgedan*). The Augustinian categories, or the Scriptural categories illumined and brought into greater prominence by Augustine, doubtless became a part of cultured men's equipment for analyzing experience and judging conduct in life or legend. And the unifying principle in Augustine's view of history — the conception of Divine Providence as ruling all peoples from the beginning and as bestowing all gifts and graces — supplied a key to understanding the past of the Germanic tribes, as well as that of the Hebrews or the pagan nations that are discussed in *The City of God*.[24]

In any case, the theme of the Beowulf-poet must have risen to higher levels of meaning when he recognized the hand of God in his tales of pre-Christian Scandinavia. He delighted to observe that the Christian deity always had ruled mankind:

Soð is gecyðed,
ðæt mihtig God manna cynnes
wéold wídeferhð (700-702).

[The truth is well known, that God Almighty has always ruled over the race of men.]

Metod eallum wéold
gumena cynnes, swá hé nú gít deð (1057-1058).

[The Measurer ruled all of the race of men, as he still does now.]

Wolde dóm Godes dǽdum rǽdan
gumena gehwylcum swá hé nú gén deð (2858-59).[25]

[The judgment of God would govern the deeds for each of men as he still does now.]

Thus the poet states his premise for seeing God's provident care of Geats and Danes as the deciding factor in various turns of events in the narrative.

[24] The transfer to Teutonic history and legend may have been aided by the current belief that the Germanic peoples were descended from Japheth. Aelfric says of Noah's sons: "Of Japhet ðám gingstan, ðe wæs gebletsod ðurh Noe, cóm ðæt norðene mennisc be ðǽre norðsǽ [From Japhet the youngest, who was blessed by Noah, came the northern people along the north sea] (*De Veteri Testamento*, ed. by Grein, p. 4).

[25] See also *Beowulf*, 1610-11, 1724-27, and cf. *Civitas Dei* 2.22, 4.33, 5.11-12, etc.

The orthodox Christian belief that the Divine mercies never have been reserved exclusively for the faithful would have left a poet free to represent the Creator as conferring grace on Scandinavian men of good will and as withholding it from the criminal kind of Grendel. It is most unlikely that the author of *Beowulf* deliberately set out to illustrate that dogma; yet obviously he has reconceived his legendary tales in terms of the Christian dualism, probably because he had come to sort all experience by that principle. He likewise appears to have had in mind the doctrine of grace, which was hardly separable from that dualism, as a postulate for understanding the past. Reexamined in the light of grace, certain troublesome passages in *Beowulf* become less obscure and the figure of Grendel, in particular, emerges in sharper relief.

II

For the Christian author reinterpreting Teutonic folklore, Grendel may have suggested the first link with the Bible. The classical giants that warred against the gods had been readily identified by Patristic writers, and thence by English commentators, with the subversive giants of *Genesis* 6.4,[26] whose final habitation was held to be the watery inferno described in *Job* 26.5-6:

> *Ecce gigantes gemunt sub aquis, et qui habitant cum eis;*
> *nudus est infernus coram illo, et nullum operimentum perditioni.*[27]

[See how the giants and those who live with them groan beneath the waters; hell is naked before him (God), and there is no cover for perdition.]

These monsters "under the waters, and those who dwell with them," are identified by Jerome with "the Devil and proud men under the earth; that is, all the unfaithful in Hell."[28] Gregory,

[26] O. F. Emerson, "Legends of Cain, Especially in Old and Middle English," *PMLA,* XIV (1906), 909.

[27] See S. J. Crawford, "Grendel's Descent from Cain," *MLR,* XXIII, 207; XXIV, 63, for the earliest suggestion that the poet had this Scriptural passage in mind in describing Grendel's abode.

[28] Migne, *Patrologia Latina* 23.1509.

whose *Moralia* on the Book of Job "was enormously popular in England"[29] in the seventh and eighth centuries, further relates the giants of *Job* 26 to *Isaiah* 26.14: *Mortui non vivant; gigantes non resurgant.* [The dead will not live; the giants will not rise again.] Gregory explains that "the giants will not rise again" from the dead because excessive pride bars them from the remedy of penitence; and he further cites *Proverbs* 21.16, to the effect that the erring man is destined to dwell in the company of the giants.[30] Whether or not the Beowulf-poet knew these commentaries on the Bible at first hand,[31] he not unnaturally associated his Scandinavian giants (*entas, eotenas, ðyrsas*) in their haunts beneath the waters with the *gigantes* of *Genesis,*[32] for ever doomed to the sub-aquatic Sheol of *Job* 26. The highly figurative conception of Grendel and his abode probably owes much to semi-symbolic Biblical giants.

In Patristic exegesis, as in *Beowulf* 111-114, the evil giants of *Genesis* were identified with the descendants of Cain,[33] and Grendel likewise had been condemned by the Creator among Cain's kind (*him Scyppend forscrifen hæfde/in Cáines cynne*) [the Creator had condemned them among the race of Cain].[34] Professor Tolkien regards this similarity as the initial point of contact in the poet's mind between heathen lore and Christian theology; here "new Scripture and old tradition touched and

[29] Ogilvy, p. 42. The *Moralia,* he says, probably came to England not much later than the mission of Augustine (*ibid.*).

[30] *Vir qui erraverit a via doctrinae in coetu gigantum commorabitur* [The man who has strayed from the path of doctrine will dwell in the company of giants] (Vulgate). The comment by Gregory is in *Moralia* 17.21.

[31] For a convincing argument that *Beowulf* 1724-68 was inspired by Gregory, see Cook, "Cynewulf's Part in Our *Beowulf,*" *Transactions for the Connecticut Academy of Arts and Sciences,* XXVII, 385-406.

[32] *Beowulf,* 111-114; see 1687-93 for another reference to the giants of *Genesis, gígantas.*

[33] Emerson, pp. 888-929; also *De Civitate Dei* 15.23 and Bede, *Commentaria in Scripturas Sacras,* ed. by Giles, I, 92.

[34] *Beowulf,* 106-107.

ignited."[35] The analogy between Cain and Grendel is well sustained. Guilty alike of envy, anger, murder, and impenitence, both were outlaws from the genial fellowship of men and estranged from the favor of God. The connection of Grendel and his mother with magic, as in their power to put a spell on swords, the magic sword in their possession, or Grendel's bag made by *déofles cræftum* [by the skills of the devil], further suggests the progeny of Cain, who were credited with the invention of magic and weapons.[36]

But the author of *Beowulf* belonged to a society that was accustomed to allegorical interpretation of the Scriptures. He, moreover, is given to cryptic allusion and ironic understatement, and is often intent upon the inner significance of his narrative. He is not the person to range Grendel and his dam literally among the kinsmen of Cain, as has been assumed. The complete destruction of Cain's actual descendants is referred to in that very passage wherein Grendel is said to have been condemned among their kind,[37] and their annihilation in the Deluge is again alluded to in the inscription on the magic sword by means of which Beowulf dispatches Grendel's mother.[38] The poet never quite affirms that Grendel was descended from Cain, unless his vague 'thence' (*ðanon*) may mean 'from him' in lines 111 and 1265. In the former passage, after numbering his villain with *Cáines cynne* (105-107) and then describing the exile of Cain, the poet adds: "Thence sprang all evil progeny, giants, etc., including

[35] J. R. R. Tolkien, *Beowulf: The Monsters and Critics,* British Academy Lecture, (London, 1936), p. 27.

[36] See Emerson, pp. 915-916. The legend that Cain's descendants originated weapons is, of course, to be traced to the mention in *Genesis* 4.22 of Tubal Cain as "an instructor of every artificer in brass and iron."

[37] *Beowulf,* 104-114.

[38] *Ibid.,* 1688-93.

the giants that strove against God."[39] In the second instance, having alluded again to Cain's proscription, the poem reads: "Thence sprang many accursed souls, including Grendel, hateful, savage reprobate."[40]

In identifying the Grendel family with "the race of Cain," the poet, I take it, is merely employing a metaphor for the society of reprobates, which is tersely contained in St. Guthlac's condemnation of his fiendish tempters: *Vae vobis, filii tenebrarum, semen Cain!*[41] [Woe to you, sons of darkness, seed of Cain!] The conception underlies Bede's *Commentary on Genesis,* Chapters IV and V. Therein Abel is presented as a type of Christ incarnate, Christ on the cross, all Christian martyrs, and the elect, who are but pilgrims on the earth.[42] Cain is interpreted as a type of those who persecute the just and, setting their hearts on earthly treasure, are shut out from the grace of Divine cognition and from the faith and hope of the elect.[43] Thus Bede sees in the murder of Abel the origin of that dualism that is to persist to the end of time: the suffering of the saints and the crimes of the reprobate, who are figuratively designated by the city that Cain built.[44] In

[39] Ðanon untýdras ealle onwócon
eotenas ond ylfe ond orcneas,
swylce gígantas, ðá wið Gode wunnon
lange ðráge (111-114).

[Thence all the evil brood arose, giants and elves and monsters, also the giants who fought against God for a long time.]

[40] Ðanon wóc fela
geó-sceaftgásta; wæs ðǽra Grendel sum,
heorowearh hetelíc (1265-67).

See note 73 below for my rendering of *geó-sceaftgásta.*

[41] *Vita Guthlaci,* c. 19, quoted by Klaeber, *Anglia,* XXXV, 262.

[42] *Venerabilis Bedae Commentaria in Scripturas Sacras,* ed. by J. A. Giles, I, 67, 70-71, 74-75, 78-79.

[43] *Ibid.,* I, 74-75, 77, 78-79.

[44] *Ibid.,* I, 78-79. "With the blood of Abel," says Gregory, "began the passion of the Church, and the Church of the elect before and after Christ is one" (F. H. Duddon, *Gregory the Great,* II, 293-294). Aelfric also speaks of the slaying of Abel as betokening the Crucifixion (*De Veteri Testamento,* p. 3).

the destruction by the Flood, also, Bede recognizes that city of the impious, the universal society of reprobates (*diluvio deleta, in quo spiritualiter insinuatur quod impiorum civitas, id est, societas tota reproborum* [The flood passed, in which was spiritually taught that the state of the impious, i.e. the whole society of the reprobate, will become corrupt . . . and will perish]).[45]

The figure of speech making Cain the patriarch of reprobates and heretics persisted throughout the Middle Ages. Note the expressions for 'Cain's kindred' in the following passages, and compare the 'semen Cain' of the *Vita Guthlaci* and the 'Caines cynne' of *Beowulf:*

> And of Sab, the duk Mauryn,
> He was of *Kaymes kunrede.*
> (*Kyng Alisaunder* 1932-33).
>
> And yif he livede ðo foule theves,
> Ðat weren of *Kaym kin* and of Eves,
> He scholde hange by ðe necke.
> (*Havelok the Dane* 2044-46)
>
> The forest fast ðan wold he seke,
> And als the karl of *Kaymes kyn.*
> (*Ywaine and Gawin* 588-589)
>
> As to live in lust, in lechery to leyke:
> Such caitives count to be come of *Cains kind.*
> (*Little John Nobody* 22-23)[46]
>
> Of the *kynrede of Caym* he [Satan] caste the freres.
> (*Peres the Ploughmans Crede* 486)[47]

The same notion must underlie the mediaeval jibe at friars contained in the acrostic CAIM, spelled from the names of the principal Orders,[48] as it doubtless accounts for the practice in the *Chansons de geste* of making Cain the progenitor of Saracen in-

[45] Bede, *Commentaria,* 1.80.

[46] Emerson, pp. 885-887, quotes line 23 of this excerpt and also the three quotations that precede it here. He frequently speaks of Grendel as one of "Cain's devil descendants," or "the devil kin of Cain." Emerson, however, never relates the metaphor *Cáines cynne* to the most elaborate development thereof, Book 15 of *The City of God.*

[47] Piers also calls the elaborate minsters of the friars "here hyghe hellehous of Kaymes kynde" (I, 559). Cf. Wyclif's name for friars' dwellings: "Caymes castle" (*English Works Hitherto Unprinted,* pp. 129, 211, 420).

[48] E.g., in *Political Poems,* ed. by Wright, I, 266.

fidels.[49] This convention of the *chansons* also ascribes to the Moslem opponents of Christian warriors traits shared by Grendel, but not by the Biblical Cain: gigantic stature, flaming eyes,[50] cannibalism,[51] and a knowledge of sorcery. These analogies, which obviously cannot result from the influence of *Beowulf* on the French poems, point to a common tradition, compounded of European giant-lore and Christian doctrine, which was already clear in its major outlines in the person of Grendel, and persisted into the Renaissance in the portrayal of pagan giants.

Cain as a limb of Satan and founder of evils is a commonplace of Scriptural exegesis, both Rabbinical and Patristic, as Emerson has abundantly shown.[52] The idea doubtless reverts mainly to I *John* 3.12: "Not as Cain, who was of that wicked one, and slew his brother." Obviously, to be of "Cain's kindred" is equivalent to being "of that wicked one." However, it is in *The City of God* that the metaphor of Cain as patriarch of the reprobate is most elaborately and memorably set forth;[53] the later use of the convention in European letters is, perhaps, but one more testimony to the commanding influence of Augustine's masterpiece. In Book 15, more especially, Augustine sees the origin of the dual parties of mankind in the murder of Abel. "Cain," he writes, "belongs to the City of Man; Abel belongs to the City of God.[54] . . . Cain conceived of God's command like a wicked reprobate, and, yielding to his height of envy, lay in wait for his

[49] William Wistar Comfort, "The Literary Rôle of the Saracens in the French Epic," *PMLA*, LV (1940), 629, 652.

[50] Grendel's eye flames with an ugly light (*Beowulf*, 726-727), whereas the eyes of the Saracen giants are "red as coals of fire" (Comfort, pp. 650-651).

[51] Comfort, pp. 650-652. See also C. M. Jones, "The Conventional Saracen of the Songs of Geste," *Speculum*, XVII (1942), 205 and n. 2, 218-219.

[52] Emerson, pp. 835-837, 916-926.

[53] Oddly, Emerson, in his "Legends of Cain," mentions the *Civitas Dei* only in relation to unimportant details, and never alludes to the rôle of Cain as founder of the Satanic City.

[54] *Civitas Dei*, 15.1.

brother and slew him. This was the founder of the fleshly society."[55] "Thus out of Adam's condemned race, as out of a putrefied lump, God elected some vessels to mercy and some to wrath, giving due pains unto the one, and undue grace to the other."[56] After the death of Abel, Cain and Seth became the heads of the rival factions;[57] and, the actual descendants of Cain having perished in the Flood, the Earthly City was repaired by Cham (Ham),[58] and perpetuated by his grandson, Nimrod, *gigans venator contra Dominum* [a giant hunter against the Lord].[59]

Book 15 of the *Civitas Dei* was, as we have seen, a favorite of Anglo-Latin authors. It is cited by Bede in some half-dozen of his works[60] and was a major inspiration for pertinent sections of his *Commentary on Genesis.*[61] There, as we likewise have noted, Bede refers now and again to the dual factions stemming from the first murder: the faithful, prefigured by the innocent Abel, whose sacrifice was pleasing to God; the wicked, typified by the exiled Cain, whose "envy and persecution . . . foreshadow the crimes of the reprobate."[62]

Bede has much to say also of Ham (Cham), "that wicked one, alien to the society of the just,"[63] from whose seed came

[55] *Ibid.,* 15.7.

[56] *Ibid.,* 15.2.

[57] *Ibid.,* 15.17.

[58] *Ibid.,* 15.20, 16.1-3.

[59] *Ibid.,* 16.3; cf. 16.4-5, 10. Ishmael, who is likewise mentioned in the *Chansons de geste* as an ancestor of the Saracens, is described by Augustine as a spiritual descendant of Cain, "a son of the bondwoman, born of the flesh," as opposed to "the sons of promise" (*ibid.,* 15.2). The influence of the *Civitas* alone was great enough to account for the tradition that both Cain and Ishmael were progenitors of Saracens and other infidels.

[60] According to a list of citations which Professor Ogilvy graciously sent me, as a supplement to those mentioned in *Books Known to Anglo-Latin Writers,* p. 14, n. 26.

[61] Ogilvy, p. 14, n. 26, citing Migne's notes, but the similarities are obvious.

[62] Bede, pp. 78-79, more particularly, but see also notes 42-45 above.

[63] *Ibid.,* p. 136.

Nimrod, "that accursed one, who perverted anew that state of human intercourse"[64] by building Babylon, "the city of the Devil; that is, the universal multitude of the reprobate."[65] That "lost city," which is peopled by "exiles and transgressors and tyrants," and "wanders a vagabond through the corruptions of this life,"[66] suggests both Cain and the proscribed Grendel, notorious *mearc-stapa,*[67] "fated wretch, treading the paths of exile in the likeness of a man."[68] Further, the circumstance that Augustine and Bede alike represent Cain and Cham as successively founders of the line of reprobates may explain why early English authors and scribes sometimes confused Cham with Cain, as in Alcuin's *Interrogationes et Responsiones in Genesin*[69] and in the *Beowulf* manuscript, where Grendel is said to have been condemned among *Cames cynne,* instead of the *Cáines cynne*[70] of emended texts.[71]

The quality of the Beowulf-poet, as well as the currency of the tradition that Cain was spiritual father of the reprobate, makes it unlikely that Grendel was identified with the race of Cain with any save figurative intent. Grendel is a typical denizen

[64] *Ibid.,* p. 133.

[65] *Ibid.,* pp. 143-145, 146.

[66] *Ibid.,* p. 146.

[67] *Mǽre mearcstapa, Beowulf* 103. *Mearcstapa,* usually glossed 'wanderer in the waste borderland,' but literally 'boundary-stepper,' looks like an equivalent of the Latin 'transgressor.' Cf. 'trespasser.'

[68] *Beowulf,* 1351-52.

[69] *Emerson,* p. 925.

[70] However, as Professor Henning Larsen reminds me, orthography may have assisted in the confusion, the *in* of mss. being similar to the letter *m.*

[71] Tertullian also mentions the tradition connecting Cham with Cain (*Liber De Praescriptionibus,* Cap. 1; quoted by Emerson, p. 925), but Augustine's treatise was better known. The fact that Augustine and Bede both hold Cham and Cain responsible for the reprobate disposes of the suggestion that English writers were led to confuse the two only through an Irish legend that Cham had inherited the curse and reputation of Cain. On the subject see Klaeber, *Anglia,* xxxv, 259; *Beowulf,* note to 1.107; Emerson, p. 925; Cook, "The Possible Begetter of the Old English *Beowulf* and *Widsith,*" *loc. cit.*

of the Earthly City: foe to God (*fág wið God,* 811; *Godes andsaca,* 786), fated wretch (*earmsceapen,* 1351), accursed spirit (*werig gást,* 133), hateful savage reprobate (*hearowearh*[72] *hetelíc,* 1267), one of those *geósceaftgástas*[73] whose line reverts to the crime and proscription of Cain. The point of the epithet *dréamum bedǽled,* twice applied to Grendel (721, 1275), is not merely that he is deprived of the joys of human fellowship, but rather that he is shut out from eternal blessedness.[74] The phrase and its synonyms are commonplaces for alienation from God and the bliss of the elect.[75] (Compare line 1227, where Beowulf is described as 'blessed,' *dréamhealdende.*)

Bearing the Divine wrath (*Godes yrre bær,*[76] 711), treading the paths of exile (1352), Grendel and his dam, *grim and grǽdig* [fierce and greedy] (121, 1499), *gífre and galgmód* [greedy and sad at heart] (1277), are compelled, as akin to Cain, to inhabit cold streams (1261) and windy headlands (*windige næssas,* 1358). Thus are they conceived in much the same terms as the apostate angels, *grédige and gífre,* in the poem *Christ and Satan*

[72] *Heorowearh,* 'savage reprobate' (Klaeber, *Anglia,* xxxv, 253).

[73] *Geósceaftgásta,* l. 1266, often translated 'demons sent by fate.' However, since *geósceaft* means something 'determined of old,' the most direct meaning of *geósceaftgást* would seem to be 'spirit predetermined,' 'predestinate soul.'

[74] Gummere, I note belatedly, makes this observation in *The Old English Epic,* p. 25.

[75] Thus in *Christ and Satan,* which has many phrases in common with *Beowulf,* the Saviour denounced the apostate angels and denied them the bliss of Heaven, *i.e.,* "deprived them of joy" (*dréamum bedélde,* 68). Satan, described like Grendel as *atol ǽglǽca* [terrible monster] (161), and like Grendel condemned "to tread the paths of exile" (*wadan wræclástas,* 121, 259), is "bereft of glory" (*wuldre benemed, duguðum bedéled,* 119-121) and "deprived of everlasting joy" (168). After the Judgment the souls of the Blest will shine "freed from sorrow" (*sorgum bedélde,* 294-296); but "the adversaries of God" (*Godes andsacan*) "will be sheared of glory, shut out from bliss" (*wuldres bescyrde, dréamum bedélde,* 242-243). So also in *Guthlac* the devil tempters of the saint are "deprived of bliss" (*dréame bidrorene,* 626, 901); "joy has been far removed from them" (667-669). Cf. Keiser, pp. 127-128, on *dréam* as 'heavenly joy.'

[76] Cf. *John,* 3.36; *Romans,* 9.21-22 (Vulgate).

(32, 192); for the angels also had been proscribed (*forscrifen,* 32-33), doomed to wander in the paths of exile (120), and to dwell *niðer under nessas* [down under the headlands] (31, 90, 134), *in ðissum neowlan genipe* [in this deep gloom] (101, 179; cf. *Beowulf* 1360: *under næssa genipu* [under the mists of the cliffs]).

The reprobation of Grendel, who was too fast in the toils of crime to repent,[77] may be mentioned also in that crux of long standing, *Beowulf* 166-169:

Heorot eardode
sincfáge sel sweartum nihtum.
(Nó hé ðone gifstól grétan móste,
maððum for Metode; né his myne wisse).
[He dwelt in Heorot, the richly adorned hall on dark nights. . . .]

Deep in an account of the monster's reign of terror, his nightly usurpation of the gift-hall Heorot, the poet, let us suppose, was reminded of the central ceremony of treasure-giving of which the lord Hrothgar and his thanes were deprived. This thought, perhaps, suggested the spiritual *gifstól* [gift throne] (cf. *gǽsta gifstól, Christ* 572), the throne of grace, to which Grendel had no access; and so the poet paused in characteristic fashion to remind us that the triumph of that evil one was circumscribed and temporary: "He might not approach the throne of grace, precious treasure, in the presence of God; he knew not His favor" (168-169).[78] If, however, *maððum* and *gifstól* merely signify Hrothgar's treasure-hoard and throne, the passage would seem to refer,

[77] Naes hit lengra fyrst,
ac ymb áne niht eft gefremede
morðbeala máre, *ond nó mearn fore,*
fæhðe ond fyrene; *wæs tó fæst on ðám* (134-137).
[It was no longer time but a single night that he again committed greater deeds of murder, and he did not shrink from hostility and crime; he was too confirmed in them.]

[78] Emerson, p. 863, also regards the passage as a reference to the reprobation of Grendel, and translates *gifstól* 'throne of grace,' as in *Christ,* 572. For *gif, gifu (giefu),* meaning 'Divine grace,' see Bosworth-Toller and note 21 above. Might *Beowulf* 168-169 be reminiscent of God's rejection of Cain's offering at the altar?

nevertheless, to the exclusion of Grendel from Divine favor. Compare Kennedy's rendering in *Beowulf, the Oldest English Epic:*

> But throne or treasure he might not touch,
> Finding no favor or grace with God.

Walsh's contention that Grendel is the devil often seems to be justified. *Helle-gást, helle-hæfta* [spirit of hell, captive of hell], Grendel is branded with familiar kennings for Satan and his peers: *féond on helle* [fiend in hell], *scucca* [demon], *scinna* [evil spirit], *atol ǽglǽca* [terrible monster], *féond mancynnes* [enemy of mankind], *hel-rúne* [one skilled in the mysteries of hell, demon], *deorc déaðscua* [dark death-shadow], *sceadu-genga* [walker in darkness], waiting to entrap and drag men "under darkness" (707), or eager to flee the grip of Beowulf and seek the concourse of fiends (*sécan déofla gedræg,* 756). The association of the Grendel pair with demons is the clearer by reason of the nature of their dwelling place, which plainly resembles the Hell described by Old English writers,[79] and which may be reminiscent of the subaquatic Sheol of *Job.* 26.

Yet the Satanic epithets for the Scandinavian water-monsters need not be taken too literally; for Lucifer and his followers, whether apostate angels or reprobate mortals, are described in much the same language by Old English and later mediaeval writers. The convention, ultimately Biblical, which makes little or no distinction between earthly and otherworld servants of the Fiend, is thus explained by Gregory:

Now as this same Saviour of us is one Person with the assembly of the

[79] See p. 121 above, for parallels between the abode of the apostate angels and that of Grendel; also Klaeber's notes on *Beowulf,* 1357-66, and Carleton Brown, "*Beowulf* and the *Blickling Homilies* and Some Textual Notes," *PMLA,* LIII (1938), 905-909. As regards Lawrence's suggestion that the desolate moors were added to the Beowulfian scenery as features in keeping with Grendel's descent from the exiled Cain, cf. the Vulgate version of *Job.* 30.6, wherein godless outlaws are said to dwell "in the desert places of the torrents and the caverns of the earth," a fairly accurate description of the site of Grendel's abode, and as figuratively conceived.

good, for He himself is the Head of the Body and we are all the Body of the Head; so our old enemy is one person with the whole company of the damned. . . . And so it is meet that all that is said . . . of our old enemy should be applied to his body, *i.e.*, to all wicked persons.[80]

The theory is elaborated in *The City of God*. Though the impious City had Cain as its earthly founder, the apostasy of Lucifer, symbolized by the separation of light from darkness, marked the beginning of the dual cities.[81] Thus are there but two societies of souls in all the universe. The citizens of the Heavenly state are God and his angels and all righteous men, whether living or dead; those of the Earthly state are Satan and the rebel angels, all wicked men still living and all the wicked dead.[82]

In the life temporal Grendel is but a cannibalistic monster in the likeness of a man, a stranger to grace, a murderous outlaw who meets death at the hands of a better wrestler. Hell then receives his heathen soul (850-852). Yet in the mind of the poet, his folklore giants, like those in *Genesis*, seem to have become associated with "the whole company of the damned," the Body of Satan. One is tempted to surmise that the author of *Beowulf*, in the manner of Bede and Augustine, envisioned the race of Cain in its timeless as well as its transitory state, and thus, as by a bold metaphor, conceived of Grendel and his dam as already denizens of Hell. Compare Dante's Tolomea, and the Man of Law's judgment on the fiendish Donegild:

Fy, feendlych spirit, for I dar wel telle,
Thogh thou heere walke, thy spirit is in helle.

III

Equating the figures of evil in new creed and old legend was less hazardous than the task of making a Teutonic Hercules like Beowulf square with Christian tradition. And yet in a realm of

[80] *Moralia*, Book 4; *Library of Fathers of the Holy Catholic Church* (Oxford, 1845), I, 196.

[81] *Civitas Dei*, 11.19, 33.

[82] *Ibid.*, 12.1. Aelfric (*Homilies*, 1.4.14-16) explains that the Fiend as Antichrist will come, as Christ came, in human likeness, *mennisc mann and soð déofol* ['mannish' man and true devil].

fantasy and epic grandeur, where a hero might have in his hand-grip the strength of thirty warriors, the poet was bound only by the larger outline of his inherited stories and the canons of heroic verse. So long as his poem contained nothing offensive to the tastes of the courtly, and perhaps ecclesiastical, circles to which he belonged, he had no cause to strain out gnats of theological or historical improbability. By presenting Scandinavian men of good will as looking in the main to the governance of God he might bring them within the sympathetic ken of their English cousins.[83] At the same time, the highly fanciful and romantic cast of his poem gave him leave to add color and a semblance of realism to his picture of the Heroic Age by describing the splendor of pagan funerals. ("The City taketh no heed of what is diverse in manners or in laws and institutions.")

As we turn from Grendel the reprobate to those who enjoyed Divine favor, and so to the brighter aspect of our poet's vision of an overruling Providence, the spectre of *Wyrd* appears and demands attention. What is the relation of *Wyrd* to the *mihtig God* who had governed mankind from the beginning and who, by withholding or conferring favors, controls much of the action of the narrative? Although the nature of the evidence admits of no definitive answer, a partial one must be sought for in any consideration of the view of destiny expressed or implied in the poem.

Students of *Beowulf* often approach references to *wyrd* with preconceptions of the "blind and inexorable power" of the Teutonic goddess of destiny; but uses of the term in Old English, including those in *Beowulf,* justify that notion only here and there.[84]

'Fate' sounds inexorable enough in the maxim of *Beowulf* 455: *Gǽð á wyrd swá hío scel!* [Fate goes ever as it must!] How-

[83] Shakespeare displays a similar tact in foregoing historical accuracy as regards the religion of his agents in *King Lear.* As inhabitants of pre-Christian Britain, in a social order where justice seems to be inactive, they acknowledge only pagan gods; but invoke Roman gods known to Elizabethan audiences, rather than unfamiliar deities of early Britain.

[84] See note 23 above.

ever, a *wyrd* that goes as she or it *must* does so in obedience to a superior power, as Alfred observes in paraphrasing Boethius:

Ðíos wandriende wyrd ðe wé wyrd háteð fǽrð ǽfter his [*God's*] *forðonce and ǽfter his geðeahte, swá swá hé tíohhað ðǽt hit síe.*[85]
[This changing Fate which we call *wyrd* proceeds according to His forethought and according to His design, just as He determines that it should be.]

Beowulf, who uses the maxim about *wyrd* in line 455 to comment on his approaching encounter with Grendel, has already affirmed in the same speech that he whom Death takes in the contest must be resigned to *Dryhtnes dóme* [judgment of God] (440-441). In a later speech Beowulf asserts that *wítig God* [wise God] will decide the outcome of the struggle (685-686).

'Fate' also appears to have had a hand in the death of Beowulf. *Wyrd* did not grant him victory in the battle with the Dragon (2573-75). In attacking the monster against the advice of friends, the aged king *héold on héahgesceap* [held to his high destiny] (3079-84); and the fate (*gifeðe*) that drew him to the Dragon's hoard was 'too strong' or, perhaps, 'too harsh' (*tó swíð,* 3085-86). Yet here again we do not know what conception of destiny lay back of the poet's words, nor to what extent the sense of doom that attends the passing of *Beowulf*[86] was dictated by literary art. Needless to say, a pattern of destiny setting heroes apart from ordinary men is a feature of epic tradition which is not peculiar to the pagan Germans or the early English.[87] The Beowulf poet, in conceiving his materials imagina-

[85] *King Alfred's Old English Version of Boethius,* 39.6, p. 128 in Sedgefield's edition. Cf. n. 91 below.

[86] Professor R. J. Menner (*The Poetical Dialogues of Solomon and Saturn,* p. 63), who sees in *Solomon and Saturn,* 364-366, an allusion to the belief that a man must endure his "hour of fate," refers the notion to Teutonic paganism, and probably rightly. Yet the idea is also Biblical (*Job,* 14.5). Cf. *Guthlac,* 1030-32.

[87] Nor to the Greeks and Romans, as mediaeval Christians knew when they conceived and nurtured the legends of the Christian King Arthur; and as the Nun's Priest of Chaucer knew when, with an apostrophe to "destinee that mayst not been eschewed," he pictured the mock-heroic Chauntecleer as a victim of disaster "by heigh imaginacioun forncast."

tively, also must have felt privileged to use *wyrd* in a figurative sense (as it is used, for example, in *Guthlac* 1351 and in *Phoenix* 210) wherever the rich connotations of the symbol might deepen his perspective.

Few now would contend that he drank "from the chalice of the Lord and the chalice of demons," or that he mixed his drinks in a confused compromise. That view does not accord with his evident sincerity or his mental vigor, nor with the main tenor of the poem. Now and again, as Professor Kennedy notes, "*God* and *Wyrd* are brought into juxtaposition in such manner as to imply control of Fate by the superior power of Christian divinity."[88] Indeed, at times the poet seems to have been at pains to make the point clear,[89] doubtless from the vantage-point of some principle of synthesis that was taken for granted also by the circle for which he wrote.

In the execution of Pope Gregory's policy of tolerance towards Germanic tradition, wherever it might be turned to account in converting the English, *Wyrd* may have been pressed into the service of the new faith. In her malign aspect she might easily share the common 'fate' of heathen gods and become a Christian demon; as such she appears in *Andreas* 613-614. Or she might be identified with the element of mutability, sorrow, and death which came into the world as a result of the Fall, a rôle which approaches that ascribed to her in *Solomon and*

[88] *Beowulf, the Oldest English Epic,* p. 1; *The Earliest English Poetry,* p. 88.

[89] In lines 477-479, 569-573 (?), 1055-58; also in 2525-27 if *metod* here means 'God,' as it does elsewhere in *Beowulf* and almost everywhere else in O.E. writings (cf. Keiser, p. 67). In lines 569-573, the 'Fate' that delivers the gallant, undoomed earl actually is the subsiding of the waters and the rising of the sun, *beorht beacen Godes.* Thus here, too, *wyrd* may have been associated with Providence, if the utterance is more than a faded proverb. Cf. *Beowulf* 2291-93, where the *unfæge* [undoomed] is easily saved from woe and exile through the grace of the Ruler, *Waldendes hyldo.*

Saturn 416-668.[90] Again, in her larger pagan function as goddess of destiny *wyrd* might be associated with the doctrine of Providence, as in *Elene* 1046-49 and 1122-23, and more elaborately in the Alfredian *Boethius* 39.4-8.[91] Boethius and Alfred

[90] The revolt and fall of the angels is here given as the explanation for the presence in the world of "wyrd the mighty"—beginner of evils, scather of the soul, waker of woe, bringer of years, mother of feud, daughter of death, father and mother of every capital sin (*frumscylda gehwæs:* of every original sin?). Professor Menner doubtless is right in concluding that here *wyrd* is not identical with Satan; "the implication is rather that the evils men endure are the result of Lucifer's rebellion" (*op. cit.,* p. 139). This conception of *wyrd* foreshadows the mediaeval notion of Fortune, as set forth in Boccaccio's *De Casibus Virorum.* Cf. Professor Farnham's resumé: "The power of Fortune came into being because of Adam's and Eve's disobedience to God. . . . Through that first Fall all miseries entered this world of ours, all misfortunes, all of those things by which men post along the road towards an inescapable death: in a word, all the mockery of Fortune" (*The Medieval Heritage of Elizabethan Tragedy,* p. 85). In keeping with his Christian interpretation of Fate, Solomon in the dialogue with Saturn holds that whereas *Wyrd* is hard to change, a wise man may meet each blow of circumstance (*wyrda gehwylce*) by means of prudence, the help of friends, and the power of the Divine Spirit (*Solomon and Saturn,* 427-433), a solution which Menner (p. 63, n. 4) compares with "the compromises of the Beowulf-poet," as reflected in *Beowulf,* 2291, 2574, and 979; 2625-27; 1056. Professor B. C. Williams relates the passage in *Solomon and Saturn* to *Beowulf,* 572 (*Gnomic Poetry in Anglo-Saxon,* p. 65).

[91] The system of Boethius does not preclude the narrower view of *wyrd* as a demon, nor the related conception in *Solomon and Saturn.* The Boethian Fate, which is but the working out in time of the divine Prescience, may be executed through the various devices of demons, as well as by divine spirits, the human soul, and the instrumentality of nature (*De Consolatione Philosophiae,* 4. Pr. 6.36-65). Here Alfred's rendering follows the Latin rather closely, using *wyrd* to signify both Fortune and Fate, *foreðanc* for *providentia,* and *foretíohhung* probably in a reminiscence of the *predestinatio* used earlier by Boethius (4. Pr. 6.12-13). After explaining that the fickle Fortune we call *wyrd* merely follows the Providence of God, as he has ordained, Alfred continues: Siððan wé hit hatað wyrd siððan hit geworht bið; ǽr hit wæs Godes foredanc and his foretíohhung. Ðá wyrd hé ðonne wyrcð oððe ðurh ðá gódan englas, oððe ðurh monna sawla, oððe ðurh óðerra gesceafta líf, oððe ðurh héofenes tungl, oððe ðurh ðára scuccena mislíce lotwrencas; hwílum ðurh án ðára, hwílum ðurh éall ðá. [Afterwards we call it Fate (wyrd) since it has been done; before, it was God's forethought and His pre-

assert that not everything in the world is subject to Fate, but that Fate and all that is subject to it are controlled by Divine Providence;[92] and *wyrd* in the passage cited from *Elene* seems to be identical with Providence.[93]

It would be rash to conclude that the Beowulf poet was familiar with the synthesis of Boethius, at first or second hand, although *The Consolation of Philosophy* apparently was known to Bede, as to Alcuin.[94] Yet, notwithstanding our ignorance of the chronology of most Old English verse, we may infer that *Beowulf* is not much older than *Andreas* and *Elene,* and that any principles of harmony between *Wyrd* and Christian philosophy which were accepted by the author, or authors, or those poems may well have been familiar also to the author of *Beowulf.*

IV

The conclusion that he regarded 'fate' as subordinate to the Divine will is, of course, the only theory that would be consistent with the poet's frequent reference to God's protecting care of the Geats and Danes and his control of their fortunes. The King of Glory, in special concern for the safety of the Danes, provides the mighty Geat as hall-guard against the giant (665-669), shields Beowulf (1658) after endowing him with

destination. Fate, he works either through good angels, or through the souls of men, or through the life of other creatures, or through the stars of heaven or through the deceptions of various demons; sometimes through one of them, sometimes through all] (39.6, pp. 128-129 in Sedgefield's edition).

[92] *Consolatio* 4. Pr. 6.60-65; Alfred's *Boethius,* 39.6, p. 129 in Sedgefield's edition.

[93] Keiser, p. 62, commenting on *Elene,* 1046-49, says; "One is tempted to identify the word *wyrd* with foreordination or predestination. Such an interpretation is placed upon *wyrd* by Old English homilists. In glosses *forewyrd* has the sense of predestination."

[94] Ogilvy, p. 22. Cf. Earle's contention that Providence and fate in *Beowulf* are harmonized under the influence of Boethius (*The Deeds of Beowulf,* p. 144).

fabulous strength, and grants him the victory over Grendel's mother (1553-56). The safe emergence of the refugee who took the fatal cup from the Dragon's hoard inspires the comment that a man undoomed and enjoying Divine grace may easily escape woe and exile.[95] Hrothgar attributes Beowulf's timely arrival to the favor of God (381-384), and moralizes on the liberality of *mihtig God* to erring mankind (1724-34). Beowulf, relying on supernatural aid, including his own Heaven-sent physical strength, gives *hálig Dryhten* credit for his triumphs in combat.[96]

One or two passages suggest that Beowulf and his companions are recipients of supernatural grace, Divine solicitude for their souls. Close upon a reminder that *mihtig God* has for ever ruled mankind (701-702), the poet describes the Geats asleep in Heorot, but assures us of their security from the malignant Grendel: "It was well known amongst men that the demon might not draw them under the shades, as God would not have it so" (705-707). The protection here referred to can hardly be mere bodily safety, for one of the sleeping Geats, Hondscio, is promptly devoured by Grendel. That we have, instead, a theological commonplace on the Creator's protection of the

[95] *Beowulf,* 2291-93:

Swá mæg unfǽge éaðe gedígan
wéan ond wrǽcsið, sé ðe Waldendes
hyldo gehealdeð!

[Thus may an undoomed man, one who retains grace, survive easily woe and exile.]

[96] *Beowulf,* 669-670, 685-687, 440-441 and possibly 958-960, where Beowulf speaks of his defeat of Grendel:

Wé ðæt ellenweorc éstum miclum
feohtan fremedon, frécne genéðdon,
eafoð uncúðes.

[Through abundant grace, we performed that deed of daring, that fight; daringly, we ventured on the might of the unknown.]
Here *éstum miclum* may signify 'throuºh abundant grace' and thus the glory would be God's. Note that Beowulf is replying to Hrothgar's speech of gratitude and congratulation, which repeatedly credits the deliverance of the Danes to divine intervention.

just from the power of demons seems to be indicated by the context of the similar expression, "thrust under the shades," in St. Guthlac's speech to devils come to tempt him: "Sinful creatures, cut off from glory, ye need not hope by cunning devices to thrust me under the shades, nor to draw me backward into the fiery blaze, the house of Hell." Note the similarities between the two:

Ðæt wæs yldum cúð,
ðæt híe ne *móste,* ðá Metod nolde,
se scynscaða, *under sceadu bregdan.*
(*Beowulf* 705-707)

[It was known to men that the demon-foe *could* not *drag them to the shades below* when the Creator did not will it.]

Ne ðurfan gé wénan, wuldre biscyrede,
ðæt gé mec synfulle mid searocræftum
under scæd sconde scúfan *mótan*
ne in bǽl blǽsan *bregdon*[97] on hinder,
in helle hús.
(*Guthlac* 673-677)

[You may not hope, bereft of glory, that you, sinful, with cunning craft, *may* shamefully thrust me *under shade,* nor in fiery blaze, *snatch* me backwards into hell's house.]

In both passages the phrase *under sceadu* (*scæd*) may be reminiscent of the kindred *in obscurum* of the Offertory in the Daily Mass for the Dead:

Domine, Jesu Christe, Rex gloriae, libera animas omnium fidelium defunctorum de poenis inferni, et de profundo lacu: libera eas de ore leonis, ne absorbeat eas tartarus, ne cadant in obscurum. [Lord Jesus Christ, King of glory, deliver the souls of all the deceased faithful from the pains of hell, and from the infernal lake. Deliver them from the lion's mouth, let not Tartarus engulf them, let them not fall into darkness.]

Light on the English expression, as used in *Guthlac* and in *Beowulf,*[98] is found also in an explanation of the equivalent *sub umbra* of *Job* 40.22 by Gregory, who relates the convention to *Apocalypse* 6.8:

[97] On infinitives ending in *on,* a characteristic of *Guthlac,* see *The Exeter Book,* ed. by G. P. Krapp and E. V. K. Dobbie, p. 265.

[98] Cf. *ðéostrum forþylmed* [enveloped by darkness], *Elene* 766: and *under dimscuan* [under dark shadows], *Andreas* 140-141.

It is written of the ancient enemy, "His name was death." All reprobates are therefore the shadow of death . . . when they take on themselves a resemblance to his malice. And they cover the Elect of God when they gain strength against them . . . in the cruelty of persecution.[99]

Grace also seems to have delivered Beowulf from the consequences of the incantation dooming any one who should disturb the Dragon's hoard to the torments of Hell, unless he were granted leave by "the true King of Victory." The listed provisions of the curse that is to be visited upon the plunderer are followed by lines usually emended to read:

næfne goldhwǽte georwor hæfde
Ágendes ést ǽr gescéawod (3074-75).

So emended, the passage is freely rendered as follows by Kennedy:

Except the invader should first be favored
With the loving grace of the Lord of all.

But this interpretation converts the lines into a virtual repetition of *Beowulf* 3054-57.[100] The Ms. reading of the so-called *locus desperatus* (3074-75), as punctuated by Wyatt, is

Næs hé gold-hwǽte; gearwor hæfde
Ágendes ést ær gescéawod.

Divine favor annuls the curse in either version. But is not the manuscript (with *gold-hwǽt* instead of *gold-hwǽte*) to be preferred, as explaining why the malediction had no power over

[99] Gregory, *Moralia*, Bk. 33; *Library of the Fathers*, III, 559. The elect may be tempted by "the cunning enemy," but not fully deceived by him. (*Gregory's Pastoral*, ed. by Sweet, p. 464.)

[100] nefne God sylfa
sigora Sóð-cyning, sealde ðám ðe hé wolde
(hé is manna gehyld) hord openian,
efne swá hwylcum manna swá him gemet ðúhte.

[unless God Himself, the True King of Victories — He is the protection of men — granted to whom He would to open the hoard, even thus to such of men as seemed to Him fitting.]

the soul of Beowulf, although he disturbed the treasure?[101] Thus, in the words of Professor Tinker: "But Beowulf was not greedy for gold; rather had he looked for the grace of the Almighty."[102]

Beowulf — *secg betsta, wígend weorðfullost, wyruld-cyninga manna mildust ond monðwǽrust* [best of men, most worthy warrior, of earthly kings the mildest and gentlest of men] — in virtue approaches the Virgilian Ripheus, whom Dante assigns to Paradise, to illustrate the grace of God to a pagan who "placed all his love below on righteousness."[103] But our English poet, whose genius lay rather in indirection, understatement, and the power of suggestion, merely asserts that the soul of Beowulf departed from his breast to seek *sóðfæstra dóm*.[104] 'The glory of the saints,' are we to suppose? Or, perhaps, 'the judgment meted out to the righteous'? Or merely 'whatever reward awaits just men in Beowulf's situation'?[105]

Beowulf's membership in the society of the just, needless to say, is implied in the persistent metaphor of his opposition to the kindred of Cain. He who wrestles with the powers of darkness naturally suggests "the most exalted hero-life known to Christians." The warfare against destruction with which the

[101] Klaeber's contention that Beowulf's death is brought about by "a mysterious, hidden spell" (*Beowulf*, p. xlix) hardly seems justified. The curse may have been represented as the cause of the hero's death in the source used by the poet, but he everywhere speaks of the malediction as limited or made powerless by Divine Mercy, which even seems to have saved the thief of the goblet from "woe and exile" (2289-93). Certainly the specific terms of the curse were not visited on Beowulf.

[102] Cf. Lawrence: "he . . . had very zealously given heed in the past to the grace of the Lord," as quoted in Klaeber's copious note on the passage.

[103] *Paradiso*, 20.118-119. Cf. *St. Erkenwald.*

[104] *Beowulf*, 2819-20.

[105] Cf. Tolkien, pp. 41-42. At all events, *ðá sóðfæstan* was a familiar kenning for the Blest; hence early English admirers of the Geatish warrior doubtless envisioned him safe among the *sóðfæstan* at the right hand of the Saviour, as they appear in *Christ and Satan* (611-613); or soaring up to Heaven, as in *Guthlac* (790-796); or at least among the Blessed described in *Elene* (1289-91) as uppermost in the flame that purges righteous souls for Paradise.

poem is concerned neither began nor ended with the magnanimous purging of Hrothgar's realm. Already Beowulf had rid his own people of the subversive monster kind;[106] and he was to meet death at grips with the Dragon, before ruin should overtake his kingdom through the invading armies of Franks, Frisians, and Swedes.

"Our counsel to the beloved lord, that he approach not the goldwarden, was of no avail," Wiglaf laments. "He held to his high destiny."[107] By reason of the singleness and consistency of that struggle, the "high destiny" of Beowulf, the several episodes are welded into a harmony transcending mere "unity of hero."[108] Thereby the fabulous tales achieve an epic dignity as the core of a reflective poem which might be said to resemble the Scriptural drama only in the sense that each is concerned with the emergence of evil and its rectification, through Divine intervention, by the self-sacrifice of a single hero. This potentiality of the theme, superadded to its other attractions, may have moved the English poet to salvage the story for his countrymen, and scribes to copy his poem as late as the end of the tenth century.

Here combined were the literary ingredients most to the taste of the early English. For here, told with gnomic comment, was hazardous adventure exhibiting physical and moral heroism, cherished loyalties, and a satisfying dualism, wherein the enlightened Christian might recognize the hand of Providence

[106] *Beowulf,* 415-424.

[107] *Beowulf,* 3079-84:

Ne meahton wé gelǽran léofne ðéoden
ríces hyrde ræ̃d ænigne,
ðæt hé ne grette gold-weard ðone. . . .
Héold on héahgesceap.

[We might not teach the dear prince, the guardian of the kingdom, any counsel, that he should not attack the keeper of the gold. . . . He held to his high destiny.]

[108] See Lane Cooper, *Aristotle on the Art of Poetry,* p. 30; also *The Poetics of Aristotle, Its Meaning and Influence,* p. 42.

and illustrations of the doctrine of grace. Not that the blend is allegory. The iron shield of Beowulf is "not yet the breastplate of Righteousness";[109] Grendel and the Dragon are fleshly inhabitants of the impious City, not symbols of it. Nevertheless, that adherence suggests a timeless element in the rôle of antagonists and hero, as they move against a circumstantial background of Scandinavian dynasties and semi-historical events.

[109] Tolkien, p. 24.

6

BEOWULF*

Kemp Malone

THE LITERARY HISTORY OF ENGLAND FALLS INTO TWO GREAT divisions, commonly called medieval and modern but better named in terms of the Protestant Reformation, an upheaval which had revolutionary effects not only on English religious life but also on English literature, as indeed on every aspect of English civilization. The works of literary art which have come down to us from the England of pre-Reformation times vary markedly, of course, in many ways, but they go together at bottom: they are rooted and grounded in the Latin Christianity which dominated the culture of western Europe from the post-classical period to the sixteenth century. The Church, however, had grown up and taken form in the midst of a powerful pagan culture, the civilization of classical antiquity, and the Roman and Irish missions of the sixth and seventh centuries planted the Church of England in the midst of another pagan culture, that of the ancient Germanic peoples. The new religion did not scorn the literary tradition either of classical or of Germanic paganism. Aldhelm, the first Englishman to compose religious verse in Latin, and Cædmon, the first Englishman to compose religious verse in English, were contemporaries, and both followed essentially the same procedure. Each sang the praises of the Christian

* Reprinted, by permission of the author, and the editor of *English Studies*, from that journal, XXIX (1948), 161-172.

God in an artistic medium inherited from paganism. Each poured new wine into old bottles.

In one respect, nevertheless, the two pioneers differed greatly. Christian literature in the Latin tongue was no novelty when Aldhelm and Cædmon began to sing. On the contrary, by the seventh century a large body of Latin Christian prose and verse had come into being, and Aldhelm had many Christian as well as pagan literary models at his disposal; that is to say, his task was one of imitation rather than of innovation. Cædmon, on the other hand, showed great originality, an originality which deserves the name of genius, when he seized upon the inherited native English way of composing poetry and used it in making poems Christian in theme and spirit. Nothing of the kind had ever been thought of before, so far as we know. Cædmon himself, indeed, had no thought of such a thing in his waking hours; his inspiration came to him in sleep, and took the form of a dream, in which a messenger of God made a poet of him and told him what to sing. It took a miracle to show Cædmon and his fellows that the native English poetical technique was worthy of use in serving God. One is reminded of St. Peter's vision at Joppa when he

> saw heaven opened, and a certain vessel descending unto him, as it had been a great sheet knit at the four corners, and let down to the earth: wherein all manner of four-footed beasts of the earth, and wild beasts, and creeping things, and fowls of the air. And there came a voice to him, Rise, Peter, kill, and eat. But Peter said, Not so, Lord; for I have never eaten anything that is common or unclean. And the voice spake unto him again the second time, What God hath cleansed, that call not thou common. [Acts 10:11-15].

In the seventh century and for many centuries thereafter, Latin was the language of the Church of England. The Latin tongue was the tongue of God, the natural and proper medium for high and holy thoughts. English was associated with worldly matters, and the English way of making poetry in particular could hardly have been turned to religious purposes without specific revelation from on high.

This revelation came to Cædmon, and its authenticity was duly accepted by the Church. In consequence, English poetry, from the earliest times of which we have record down to the Protestant Reformation, was predominantly religious poetry, and throughout Old English times this predominance was overwhelming. Or perhaps it would be safer to say that only a small part of the Old English verse which survives to us can be reckoned purely secular. The custom of using the vernacular, alongside Latin, for religious poetical purposes, spread to the Continent in the eighth century, thanks to the English missionaries who in that century converted the Germans to Christianity and reformed the Gallican Church. Cædmon, then, may be looked upon as the father, not only of English religious poetry, but also of the religious poetry in the other vernaculars of western Europe.

Here we are primarily concerned not with Old English religious poetry in general but with a particular poem: *Beowulf*. This poem holds a unique place in the literature of Europe. Its fundamentally Christian orientation is now widely recognized, and needs no discussion in this paper. Nevertheless, one cannot properly classify it as a religious poem in any strict or narrow sense. The action of the poem takes place in a part of ancient Germania and at a time thought of by the poet as ancient and therefore pagan. The characters are not Christians and know nothing of Christianity. The hero is a virtuous pagan. He is made as Christ-like as the setting permits, but all his virtues can be explained quite naturally as growing out of the heroic ideals of conduct traditional among the English as among the other Germanic peoples.

The monkish author, devout Christian though he is, finds much to admire in the pagan cultural tradition which, as an Englishman, he inherited from ancient Germania. It is his purpose to glorify this heroic heritage, this spiritual heirloom, this precious birthright of his nation. He accomplishes his purpose by laying stress upon those things in Germanic tradition which agree with Christianity or at any rate do not clash seriously with the Christian faith. In particular, his hero in all he says and does shows himself high-minded, gentle, and virtuous, a man dedicated to the heroic life, and the poet presents this life in terms of service: Beowulf serves his lord, his people, and all mankind, and in so doing he does not shrink from hardship, danger, and death itself. In many passages the poet's own Christianity comes to the surface; most notably, perhaps, in the so-called sermon of the aged King Hrothgar, who out of the fulness of his wisdom warns the youthful hero against the sin of pride. But even here the king's words, though obviously based on Christian teaching, are not put in specifically Christian terms, and most of the time the author keeps his Christianity below the surface. Nor does he falsify Germanic paganism by leaving out those features of it inconsistent with the Christian faith. Thus he puts in the mouth of Beowulf himself the following piece of pagan wisdom:

> it is better for every man
> to avenge his friend than to mourn much [1384b-1385].

The poet's picture of the Germanic past is idealized but not distorted. The devil-worship of the Danes (as the medieval Christians conceived it to be) is mentioned with perfect frankness in a famous passage (lines 175 ff.). Anachronisms are fewer and less serious than one would expect in a poem of the eighth century. Indeed, perhaps the most remarkable though not the most important feature of the poem is the relative high standard of historical accuracy which it maintains. The author was clearly a man learned in the traditional lore of his people, and concerned to tell the truth as he saw it.

We have seen that the earliest Christian poets of England, whether they composed in Latin or in English, took over the poetical manner traditional for the language of composition (and pagan in origin) but supplied their own matter: namely, Christian story or Christian teaching. For the matter handed down in the old pagan poetry they had no use; indeed, they objected strongly to what the old poets had to say, much though they admired and imitated their way of saying it. For illustration, I shall have to limit myself to two utterances of Alcuin, an Englishman of the eighth century best known for the help he gave Charlemagne in the so-called Carolingian revival of learning. In one of his poems, Alcuin compares the Song of Songs most favorably with the poetry of Vergil, saying,

I urge you, young man, to learn these canticles by heart. They are better by far than the songs of the mendacious Vergil. They sing to you the precepts of life eternal; he in his wickedness will fill your ears with worthless lies [*Carm.* 78, 5].

Alcuin condemns with equal severity the stock of traditional story drawn upon by the English scops of his day. In a letter of his he has this to say about one of these stories:

What has Ingeld to do with Christ? Narrow is the room, and it cannot hold both. The heavenly king will have nothing to do with so-called kings, heathen and damned, because that king reigns in heaven, world without end, but the heathen one, damned, laments in hell. [*MGH, Epist.* IV, 183 (No. 124)].

This attitude toward pagan literature prevailed, on the whole, down to the rise of humanism in fourteenth-century Italy. The humanists, however, found admirable in, say, Cicero, not only his artistic skill as a writer of Latin prose, but also his philosophy of life. This widening of interest served to accentuate, in the humanists, that reverence for classical antiquity so characteristic of the Middle Ages in general. The new movement brought the cult of classicism to the verge of idolatry, and humanistic thinking may be looked upon as the last and most extreme phase of medieval chronological primitivism.

Let us now go back to the *Beowulf* poet. It would hardly do to think of him as an eighth-century humanist, born 600 years before his time, since his interest lay, not in the philosophy of life of classical antiquity but in that of Germanic antiquity. Nevertheless his case is not unlike Petrarch's, in that both authors, Christians though they were, sought and found spiritual as well as stylistic values in a pagan literary culture: each in the particular culture which was his own by inheritance. In this matter the *Beowulf* poet did not stand alone. The author of *Deor* taught the virtue of patience under affliction by exempla[1] drawn from pagan Germanic story, and the author of *Maldon* sang a Christian lord and dright who fought and died for the faith, inspired and sustained by the same heroic ideals that their heathen forefathers had cherished. These ideals held their own to the very end of Old English times, and made many a man a hero in life and death not merely by force of ordinary tradition but also, and in large measure, by the force of poetic tradition. The scops kept the old ideals strong by singing the heroes of the past. The very attack which Alcuin made on heroic story tells us that in his day the old songs were still sung even in the citadels of English Christian piety: the monasteries. Such performances became impossible, of course, after the monastic reform in the latter part of the tenth century, a reform which swept western Europe and established a more rigorous pattern of monkish life wherever it went. But the English monk of that same century who composed the poem on the Battle of Maldon still knew and loved the traditional poetry of his people and we may be sure that he was one of many.[2]

The complex and sophisticated art of the *Beowulf* poet calls for a correspondingly elaborate analysis, an analysis which we cannot make at this time. We shall have to content ourselves here with a mere glance at the main fable or plot, before going on to a somewhat narrower study of the episodes.

The action of the poem falls into two main parts. In part one, the hero Beowulf, then young, goes from his homeland to Heorot, the hall of the Danish king Hrothgar, in order to cleanse it of Grendel, a troll who for years had haunted it at night; he overcomes Grendel single-handed and afterwards slays Grendel's mother, who sought to avenge her son. In part two, the hero, now grown old, goes out to defend his own kingdom against the ravages of a dragon; with the help of a faithful young kinsman he kills the dragon but himself falls in the fight. About two thirds of the poem are devoted to part one; about one third is devoted to part

[1] See *E.S.*, XIX, 198 (top and bottom).

[2] For further discussion, see "The Old English Period," Chapter V, in Baugh, Brooke, Chew, Malone, and Sherburn, *A Literary History of England* (New York, 1948).

two. The course of events in part one takes six days; in part two, one day (excluding preliminaries in both cases). Between the two parts there is an interval of many years.

It will be seen that the poet deals in detail with two chapters only of the hero's life, and that these two chapters stand in sharp contrast. In the first, the hero is young; he is represented as an ideal retainer; he undertakes a task which he is not in duty bound to perform; full of the generous spirit of youth, he goes out of his way to do good; he fights single-handed against two foes (taken one at a time); he wins, and goes home in triumph. In the contrasting chapter, the hero is old; he is represented as an ideal king; the task which he undertakes is one which he cannot avoid without failing in his duty to his own people; sad at heart, he meets the issue without flinching; he fights, with a helper beside him, against a single foe; he wins, but at the cost of his own life.

The two chapters, however, have one feature in common: in both, Beowulf fights as the champion of mankind, against monstrous embodiments of the forces of evil, adversaries so formidable that only the greatest of heroes could possibly cope with them. Our Christian poet makes much of the hero as a monster-queller, not only because a fight with a monster in the nature of the case is more dangerous and therefore more heroic than a fight with another man, but also, and chiefly, because the struggle between hero and monster symbolizes the struggle between good and evil in our earthly life. Mere man-to-man fighting lends itself far less readily to treatment in terms of right and wrong, and the poet accordingly makes little of his hero's military career. Here our author goes his own way, the way of a Christian moralist, departing deliberately and radically from the practice usual in heroic story, where the hero's exploits in battle get plenty of attention.

The poet's neglect of Beowulf's deeds of valor in ordinary warfare must have been deliberate. Certainly he was well informed about them. He tells us himself, though with the utmost brevity, about one of the many battles which his hero had survived with honor. In this particular battle, fought in the Low Countries, Beowulf had covered himself with glory: he had killed no less than thirty of the enemy in hand-to-hand conflict;[3] one of them, the Frankish champion Dæghrefn, he slew with his bare hands. The poet informs us further that Beowulf was the only man on his side to survive the battle. His own triumph over the enemy was so complete that, though his fellows all lay dead, he held the field alone and stripped from the bodies of the thirty men he had slain the armor to which his victory over them gave him honorable title, the surviving Franks not daring to interfere and allowing him to fall back to the sea unmolested. The story of King Hygelac's ill-fated expedition to the Netherlands, and in particular the story of the last stand of the doomed army, the fall of Hygelac, and the death of man after man of the king's devoted dright, until at the end Beowulf stood alone — this was surely a fight worthy of celebration in song. The *Beowulf* poet, in four scattered passages, has something to say about the expedition and its outcome. But he fails to make even an episode of it, much less a major part of the poem. Some poets would have thought it enough for a whole epic.

But I do not wish to blame the poet for what he left undone. He knew what he was about. Hygelac's expedition had no high moral purpose. The king and his men were out for booty, and our pious poet, though he loved a good fight as well as anybody, chose for extended treatment tasks undertaken and carried through by the hero for the benefit of mankind.

One exploit of Beowulf's remains to be considered: his swimming match with Breca. This match makes a clean-cut episode, to which more than 100 lines are devoted. The story of the match is not told as such, however. It is set in a frame: the fliting between Unferth and Beowulf. The integration of frame and story is beautifully complete: the swimming match is the subject of the fliting, each contender in the war of words giving us his own version of the story of the match. In consequence, this story

[3] See *E.S.*, XV, 151.

is told twice. The repetition is characteristic of the *Beowulf* poet, who loves to tell a story more than once. We have already seen that Hygelac's expedition up the Rhine is spoken of no less than four times. The most elaborate piece of repetition in the poem, of course, is Beowulf's report to Hygelac when he comes back from Denmark; this report amounts to a retelling of the story of the fight with Grendel and Grendel's mother. Many other cases of repetition occur in the course of the narrative. The poet repeats himself in a masterly fashion; the device as he employs it not only emphasizes and clarifies but also gives esthetic pleasure. When we come to a given repetition we know what to expect in a general way, but we always find novelty enough in word and thought. The two versions of the swimming match differ markedly, of course, in point of view, and therefore are highly differentiated, much more so than is the case with the other repetitions in the poem.

But why does the poet make so much of the swimming match? It comes under the head of the hero's *enfances,* or exploits of boyhood, a familiar feature of heroic story, but one fundamentally trivial in character. Beowulf mentions some other boyish feats of his when he first addresses King Hrothgar. His speech begins,

> Be thou hale, Hrothgar! I am Hygelac's kinsman and retainer. I did many glorious deeds when I was a boy [407-409a].

This is pretty vague, of course, but later on in the speech he tells Hrothgar, more specifically, that he had been a giant-killer, that he had taken five giants captive, that he had slain sea-monsters by night, and that he had fought with success against certain unnamed foes of his own people. Obviously if Beowulf fought monsters as well as that in his boyhood he ought to be able to cope with Grendel now that he has become a full-grown man. In other words, Beowulf's catalogue of his early exploits is meant to convince the king that here at last is the man he needs. The catalogue serves also to instruct the reader or hearers of the poem; they learn out of Beowulf's own mouth — that is, from the most authoritative source possible — that he is a redoubtable champion; in particular, that he is a monster-queller. This device of self-characterization is familiar in literary art. One finds it in Shakespeare, for example. The *Beowulf* poet's use of it is, in all likelihood, highly traditional and conventional.

Beowulf's mention of sea-monsters which he had slain by night takes us back to the swimming match with Breca, one detail of which is precisely this monster-quelling on the part of the hero. The quelling, as Beowulf himself points out, is of benefit to mankind, and may be taken for a kind of prelude to the more important quelling which is to follow at the Danish court. But after all, the two boys, when they agreed and vowed to swim to sea, had no thought of rendering a service to their fellow men. They risked their lives in this swimming match on the high seas in a spirit of recklessness. They were showing off. In Beowulf's story of the swim we catch the apologetic note: "we were both still in our boyhood" [536b-537a], he says. The implication is clear that the Beowulf who had reached young manhood would not have undertaken such a match. One should not risk one's life in vain.

It now becomes clearer why the poet makes a good deal of the swimming match. The story of the match gives us a short but vivid view of the adolescent hero in action. We get other glimpses of him as a boy, but nowhere else is any event of his boyhood told in detail. The poet reserves the main fable for his hero as a young man and as an old man, but in one episode he presents him in his immaturity. Here the future champion of mankind against the world of monsters is already a monster-queller, though not yet informed with a high moral purpose.[4] He plays with the heroic life to which, later on, he will dedicate himself in earnest.

Most of the episodic matter in the poem, however, is concerned, not with the hero himself but with his setting. The author, as we have seen, was not only a Christian moralist. He

[4] See my paper, "Young Beowulf," in *JEGP*, XXXVI, 21 ff.

was also an Englishman; that is, a man of Germanic stock and traditions. He chose a hero of his own race, and gave him for setting the golden age of ancient Germania, that glorious period of migration when the Germanic tribes overran the Roman Empire and made its provinces into Germanic kingdoms. A well-known American scholar, after remarking upon the intense patriotism characteristic of the English, adds,

> It is very surprising, then, in turning to the oldest English epic, to find that there is nothing patriotic about it at all. We call it an English poem, and rightly. It was written on English soil, for Englishmen, and in the English tongue. . . . Yet the epic deals neither with English people nor with English heroes. . . . The peoples whom it celebrates are foreigners, Scandinavians. . . . In short, *Beowulf* is a story dealing with foreign subject matter, borrowed from an alien and even hostile people, with no trace of English patriotism about it. How is this strange situation to be explained? [W. W. Lawrence, *Medieval Story*, p. 30]

Our answer must be that the question is ill conceived, arising as it does out of a mistaken view of eighth-century England. In those days the English, so far as their culture was concerned, still belonged, in part, to a commonwealth of nations, the Germania of their Continental forefathers. Within that commonwealth they were at home, and felt the Goth, the Swede, the Langobard alike to be cultural fellow-countrymen. The *Beowulf* poet was intensely patriotic; his poem shows at every turn the warmth of his love for his native culture and his native race. But his patriotism embraced Germania as a whole; it was no narrowly English affair. It is particularly significant, I think, that his hero lived and died in southern Scandinavia, the heart of the old Germanic homeland, the cradle of the race, the region least affected by foreign influences. Moreover, it was from the Jutland peninsula, a part of this very region, that the English themselves had come, in their great migration to Britain. We must not forget that England in its earliest centuries was still colonial territory. The stream of settlers from the Germanic motherland had probably stopped flowing by the time of the *Beowulf* poet, but the English had not forgotten their origin nor yet the source of their cultural traditions. Above all, *Beowulf* is a poem of the past, of a past thought of by the poet as remote. The action of such a poem obviously must take place in the homeland, not in a colony of recent foundation.

It may be worth our while, however, to speculate about the poet's reasons for not making King Offa the hero of his poem. Offa is the only English king of the Continental period about whom we have much information. We learn of him both in *Beowulf* and in *Widsith*. The *Beowulf* poet calls him the best of all mankind, and adds that he was held in high esteem far and wide because of his generosity and his success in warfare. The poet also tells us that Offa ruled his country with wisdom. In *Widsith* we get more specific information about Offa's achievements: while still a boy he overthrew "with single sword" (that is, by his own efforts, without help from others) the kingdom of the Myrgings, and dictated a boundary between his own kingdom and theirs, a boundary which his successors were able to keep. Moreover, we have reason to think that Offa was the first English king whose realm included western as well as eastern Sleswick. As I have said elsewhere (*MLR*, XXXIX, 56),

> The extension of the English king's authority to the North Sea coast of Sleswick made possible the later migration of the Angles to Britain, a migration which obviously would never have taken place had the English holdings remained strictly Baltic. Offa's war with the Myrgings, then, must be reckoned one of the great turning-points of English history, . . .

It seems clear that Offa was a man eminently suitable for celebration in song. An English poet in particular might be expected to make Offa the hero of a poem set in the Germania of the migration period, the heroic age of the Germanic peoples. Why did our poet choose Beowulf instead? The answer, I think, is simple. Beowulf was famous chiefly as a queller of monsters, whereas Offa won his fame as a queller of men. The poet, pious Christian that he was, found spiritual values in Beowulf's monster-quelling which he could not find in Offa's man-quelling. Nevertheless he did not like to leave Offa out of his poem altogether. The great hero of his own tribe must be brought in somehow. The episode in which Offa figures I describe elsewhere as having been introduced by a *tour de force,* and this may well be a correct statement of the case. But the poet's technic of linkage here has a parallel in at least one other episode. I will take up Offa first.

King Offa is introduced, not directly but by way of his wife, Queen Thrytho, and most of the episode is devoted to the lady, whose unorthodox behavior makes her more interesting than her pattern of a husband. The introduction of a husband through his wife, however, is certainly no *tour de force.* It is the introduction of Thrytho herself which makes trouble for modern readers. The poet gets her in by contrasting her with Hygd, wife of King Hygelac. Beowulf has come back home after his Grendel adventure and is approaching Hygelac's hall to make his report of the journey. The author stops at this point to comment on the hall, the king, and the king's wife. But he disposes of hall and king in a line and a half; Queen Hygd is the one he gives most of his attention to. She is characterized in accordance with the etymology of her name. *Hygd* means 'thought' and the queen is represented as thoughtful indeed: wise, well behaved, and mindful of other people's wishes and feelings. The poet explains Hygd's exemplary conduct as the fruit of deliberation, study, and mental activity. He says,

> The good queen of the people [i.e., Hygd] bore in mind (wæg) the haughtiness, the terrible violence of Thrytho [lines 1931b—1932].

In other words, Hygd took warning by the example of Thrytho. She took care to behave differently. This brings the poet to Thrytho's own behavior, which was certainly not very encouraging to would-be suitors, for she objected so strongly to the attentions of men that if one of them so much as looked at her she had him put to death. The poet goes on to say, "that is no way for a lady to do." We learn, however, that Thrytho turned over a new leaf after her marriage to Offa, whom she loved dearly. King Offa, it would seem, proved master of the situation at home as well as on the field of battle.

Linkage by contrast also serves to bring in the second Heremod passage (lines 1709-1722), a part of the so-called sermon of Hrothgar. The aged king after praising Beowulf speaks of Heremod as Beowulf's antithesis. He brings the passage to an end by exhorting Beowulf to profit by the evil example that Heremod has set. The sad fate of Heremod should be a lesson to the young hero. The same device of contrast is used in the first Heremod passage (lines 901-915), but here this type of linkage comes at the end of the passage; the poet, by contrasting Heremod with Beowulf, brings the narrative back to his hero. This passage about Heremod is introduced by the use of a different device: sequence in time. The poet has been speaking of the famous hero Sigemund, the dragon-slayer. He shifts to Heremod very simply, saying that Sigemund flourished after Heremod had had his day. We get no hint that the two men are connected in any other way, and the device which serves to link them in the poem strikes us as artificial enough. In this case, however, the Scandinavian evidence makes it clear that Sigemund and Heremod were traditionally associated, though just what the association was we are unable to make out. This information, gained from a study of Icelandic poetry, forces us to revise our opinion of the artistic technic of the *Beowulf* poet. We now see that the true linkage between Sigemund and Heremod was left unexpressed and needed no expression, since it was already firmly fixed by tradition in the minds of the poet's audience, to be evoked at will by a mere mention of the names. It is our misfortune, but not the poet's fault, that we in our ignorance miss the true link and have to depend altogether on that sequence in time which the poet uses, as an external device only, in proceeding from the one member of the heroic pair to the other.

The device of contrast, too, now begins to have a different look. One may well suspect, though one certainly cannot prove, that the coupling of Beowulf and Heremod, and of Hygd and Thrytho, belong to tradition and have their roots deep in Germanic story. If so, the English poet took up these characters together, not as a mere device for changing the subject, but because they went together in the songs that had come down to him, the sources he drew upon for the tale he had to tell.

What functions do the episodes have in the economy of the poem? I have already said that most of them bring out the setting in which the hero lived and died. This setting was ancient Germania; more particularly, the Scandinavia of the fifth and sixth centuries of our era. The story of Scyld, mythical founder of the Danish royal house, gives us a taste of an old legend, and the description of his funeral takes us back to pagan rites dim with antiquity. The tale of Ecgtheow's feud with the avengers of Heatholaf makes the father of the hero more than a name to us and links him with the Wulfing tribe, famous in heroic story from Iceland to the Mediterranean. When Hrothgar's scop, after singing Beowulf's praises, goes on to the exploits of Sigemund, he puts our hero side by side with a hero of Frankish legend, one of the chief figures of Germanic story. That night the scop sang once more; this time he told the tale of Finn, an ancient story very welcome at the Danish court, since it ends with a Danish victory. The tale of Ingeld the English poet puts in the mouth of Beowulf himself, as part of his report to Hygelac on the state of Denmark. All these passages serve to make our hero part and parcel of the heroic age of Germanic antiquity.

It is possible, however, to make a distinction here between these episodes which have been drawn into the narrative and those that remain external to it. Examples of the former are the passages about Scyld, Ecgtheow, and the swimming match; examples of the latter are the passages about Sigemund, Finn, and Ingeld. In part two of the poem the integration of the historical passages into the story of the dragon fight has been done in such a way as to disturb many modern readers. Thus, Klaeber says (*Beowulf,* 3d ed., p. liv),

> The facts of Geatish history, it cannot be denied, are a little too much in evidence and retard the narrative . . . rather seriously.

This verdict does less than justice to the narrative art of the poet, who in part two tells the story of his hero's tribe: past, present and future. The attack of the dragon on that tribe, and Beowulf's counter-attack, ending in the death both of the hero and of his monstrous antagonist, make part of the tribal story, a part which we may call the present crisis (present, that is, from the point of view of the hero). The poet gives us his account of this crisis, not continuously but in sections, sections which alternate with accounts of earlier crises in the tribe's history. The death of the dragon ends the present crisis, but the messenger of Wiglaf foresees disaster for the tribe in the future, now that they have lost their great king. He justifies his forebodings by reminding his hearers of certain events of the past, events which in due course will lead to ruin, want, and exile. The poet himself adds that the messenger's fears are fully justified. The poem ends in the present, with the funeral of the hero.

It will be seen that the author of *Beowulf* in part two of his poem uses a technic of alternation between events of the present and events of the past. He restricts himself throughout to his hero's own tribe, in marked contrast to his procedure in part one, where he ranges widely over Germania. The unity of part two, in theme and form alike, is noteworthy. As for the technic of alternation which the poet uses to drive home this unity, it is a technic very familiar today, especially in the narrative art of screen and novel. Many recent screen plays follow this method of shifting repeatedly from present to past. In Hollywood they have a name for the shift backwards in time: they call it a flashback. A novel of the present year (1948), *Raintree County,* by Ross Lockridge, makes systematic use of the flashback technic. In the novel, just as in part two of *Beowulf,* the action is restricted to one day, but the flashbacks take us deep into the past. It is not likely that the novelists and scenario writers of today learned this technic by studying *Beowulf,* but theirs is the technic of the *Beowulf* poet none the less.

The shift from present to past occurs three times in the narrative of part two. The poet makes the transition in a different way each time. In all three cases he manages the shift with great skill. The second transition is of special interest, as an example of the poet's craftsmanship. Beowulf and his little band of men had reached the immediate neighborhood of the dragon's lair. Beowulf was to go forward alone from that point. He sat down on the headland, and bade his followers goodbye. The aged king fell to thinking about his childhood and youth, and began to talk. His reminiscences take up nearly 100 lines of verse. The technic seems almost realistic here. What could be more natural than for an old man to talk about old times?

One may now ask whether the three long passages on the history of the Geatas incorporated in part two should really be looked upon as episodic. Without them the story of the dragon fight would remain, but would lose greatly in spiritual quality, since we should not know as we do the people for whom Beowulf was giving his life. As the poem stands, the fate of the hero and the fate of the tribe are bound together in such a way that each lends weight and worth to the other. We mourn for the Geatas as well as for their king, and this double mourning deepens as well as widens the sweep of the tragic march of events. One cannot doubt that the poet meant it so. For him, Beowulf would not have been a hero if he had not had a people to die for. The *Beowulf* poet was above all a patriotic poet.

We end as we began, with a look at the poem taken in the large. As we have seen, *Beowulf* falls into two parts, devoted respectively to the hero in young manhood and the hero in old age. Part one is predominantly cheerful in tone, as befits a period of youth. When one reads the Sigemund episode, for instance, one feels that it is good to be alive in a world made for heroic adventure. Even the Finn episode has a happy ending if one sides with the Danes, as our poet does. Now and then the shadows of feuds that are to come darken the picture of the Danish court, and the aged Hrothgar is fond of talking about his own troubles and those of others, but the hero takes all this in his stride and goes home in triumph, leaving a cleansed and happy Heorot behind him.

Utterly different is the tone of part two. Old age has come, and death is near at hand from the start. No longer does the hero leave home, to fight the good fight in other lands. He stands strictly on the defensive. He is sad at heart; his breast surges with dark thoughts. But there is one thought which he does not have. It does not occur to him to give up. Great though the odds against him, he takes the field and fights to the last. In this world defeat and death are sure to come in the end. The hero is he who, like Beowulf, faces the worst without flinching and dies that others may live.

7

BEOWULF AND CHRISTIAN ALLEGORY: AN INTERPRETATION OF UNFERTH*

Morton W. Bloomfield

IN THE DISCUSSION OF THE CHRISTIAN ELEMENTS IN BEOWULF, it seems to have escaped the notice of scholars that the character of Unferth may provide an example of Christian allegory consciously employed by the poet. If the name Unferth means mar-peace or strife, an important clue to his significance in the poem is being ignored. I wish to suggest that the author of *Beowulf* is employing, or least thinking of, Unferth as an abstract personification in the manner of Prudentius, Martianus Capella or Sedulius, and that the poem has even closer connections with the Christian tradition than has hitherto been perceived. If we can accept Unferth as, say, *Discordia,* we shall find how well this interpretation fits in with the suggestion Schücking made some years ago that the character of Beowulf has been molded, to some extent at least, by the Christian ideal of the perfect ruler, the *rex justus* [just king], as set forth by St. Augustine, Gregory the Great and others, and that the ethical ideal set up by the epic is that of *ordinata concordia* [ordered concord] or *mensura* [measure].[1]

* Reprinted, by permission of the author, and the Fordham University Press, from *Traditio,* VII (1949-1951), 410-415.

[1] 'Das Königsideal im *Beowulf,' Englische Studien,* 67 (1932-33), 1-14. See also E. Otto, *Typische Schilderungen von Lebewesen, Gegenständlichem u. Vorgängen im weltlichen Epos der Angelsachsen* (Inaugural-Dissertation, Berlin, 1901) and A. Pirkhofer, *Figurengestaltung im Beowulf-Epos* (Anglistische Forschungen 87; Heidelberg 1940) for somewhat similar approaches to the poem.

First, however, the meaning of the word *Unferth* must be discussed. Can we accept the traditional etymology and assume that the word is a combination of *un* (not) plus *ferth* or *frith* (peace), forming not-peace? Although this meaning is almost universally accepted, it must at least be pointed out that there are several alternate possibilities.

The name appears in the MS four times and always as Hunferð. It has been emended to Unferth, following Rieger's suggestion,[2] because it consistently alliterates with other vowels. The fact that the name is always misspelled by the Cotton Vitellius scribe or his model testifies to its unusual nature. He or one of his forbears simply did not understand the name and changed it to a more familiar form.[3]

It has been assumed by most scholars that the first theme in the name, *un,* is the negative particle. There is a possibility, however, that it may be an intensive as in the OE. *unhar* (very old).[4] It may even be a form of the ON. *húnn* (bear).[5] Germanic names do not, at least in historic times, have to mean anything.[6]

About the second theme, *-ferth,* there can be little room for disagreement. It is obviously a metathesized form of *frith* (peace) which occurs in many Germanic names both as a first and second name element.

[2] See *Zeitschrift für deutsche Philologie,* 3 (1871), 414. It should also be noted that the use of *h* before *i* and *u* is especially common among late Latin and Celtic scribes merely to indicate the vowel quality of these letters, for *i* and *u* could also be consonants (*j* and *v*). Anglo-Saxon palaeography is much indebted to Celtic scribal habits.

[3] Hunfrid, and variants, was a fairly common Anglo-Saxon and early Middle English name. See T. Forssner, *Continental-Germanic Personal Names in England, in Old and Middle English Times* (Uppsala, 1916), 158-9.

[4] See Forssner, *op. cit.,* 236 and W. Bruckner, *Die Sprache der Langobarden* (Quellen und Forschungen 25; Strassburg 1895), 84.

[5] See Forssner, *op. cit.,* 158-9 and Bruckner, *op. cit.,* 314.

[6] See H. B. Woolf, *The Old Germanic Principles of Name-Giving* (Dissertation submitted to . . . The Johns Hopkins University . . . Baltimore 1939), 263-4.

It must also be recorded that forms similar to Unferth turn up among Continental Germanic peoples. There are no Scandinavian parallels to the name,[7] but we do find a Lombard *Unifridus*[8] and various German forms — Unfrid, Unfrit, Umfrid.[9] Because of the various possible etymologies, however, these Continental parallels may not be true cognates.

Professor Kemp Malone has suggested another possibility for the etymology of Unferth.[10] But even he has to fall back in the last analysis upon the influence of 'mar-peace'. In an endeavor to equate Unferth etymologically with the name of the villain Ívarr in the Hrethric story as told in the Icelandic *Sögubrot,* Professor Malone assumes, as a cognate form of Ívarr, an OE. *Infere which the *Beowulf*-poet touched up to Unferth, 'trouble-maker', in the interests of poetry. Whether this rather unconvincing argument is acceptable or not, Professor Malone at least recognizes the influence of the accepted meaning of the name in shaping its final form.

The strongest argument, however, for the traditional view that Unferth means 'mar-peace' is the role Unferth plays in the epic, at least in the beginning. The fact, too, that this name is an onomastic *hapax legomenon* in English or Scandinavian documents must also argue for its special and invented character. It occurs nowhere else in Old English or Old Norse records. Taking everything known so far into consideration, we may

[7] Its ON. form would be *Ufriðr. See E. Björkmann, *Studien über die Eigennamen im Beowulf* (Studien zur Englischen Philologie, ed. L. Morsbach 58; Halle a. S. 1920), 112-3.

[8] See Bruckner, *op. cit.,* 269. The ending *-us* here is, of course, from the Latin documentary source.

[9] See E. Förstemann, *Altdeutsches Namenbuch,* Vol. I, *Personennamen* (Nordhausen etc., 1856), 1214. The later edition of Förstemann is not available to me, but we find sufficient examples here to show that the name was known. Förstemann suggests another possible etymology for *un*: from OHG. *unnan,* to give (see *ibid.,* I, 1212). Hunfrid is very common in German records. Unfrid occurs, however, only eight times in those which Förstemann examined.

[10] *PMLA* 42 (1927), 300 ff.

say that the name in *Beowulf* has an unusual character and must have the special significance suggested by its accepted meaning.

Unferth's part in the epic may be summarized as follows. After Beowulf has been welcomed at the Court of Hrothgar and speeches have been exchanged between the hero and the king, Unferth, a courtier, pricked on, the poet tells us, by jealousy, accuses Beowulf of foolhardy conduct in a swimming match with Breca years before and points out that he had been worsted by his opponent. It is obvious, Unferth says, that Beowulf will not be able to defeat Grendel. In his answer, Beowulf accuses his antagonist of having drunk too much beer and corrects his false story. He tells Unferth and the whole court that the swimming contest was the result of a youthful boast and that both he and Breca covered themselves with honor. Further, he taunts Unferth with having failed to destroy Grendel himself and of having killed his own brother. Unferth, son of Ecglaf, is thereupon silenced.

Later, after the victory over Grendel, there is rejoicing in the hall, and a scop relates the Finn episode. After the lay has been recited, Unferth, now called a *thyle,* is again mentioned. Wealhtheow, Hrothgar's queen, approaches the throne where Unferth is sitting at the feet of Hrothgar. Both she and the king, the poet tells us, trust him and his courage, even though he did kill his kinsman. Then the queen addresses Hrothgar and, after praising Beowulf, speaks of her worries about her young children. She lauds Hrothulf, the king's nephew. This speech has been rightly interpreted as referring to Hrothulf's ambition to seize the throne (which, as Scandinavian sources indicate, he actually did upon Hrothgar's death) and as an appeal to Beowulf for aid in that eventuality. From this allusion, it has been assumed that Unferth played an important role in the later dynastic quarrel and that he is really unessential in the Beowulf story and only a necessary 'figure in the origin of the Scylding feud.'[11] Olrik believes he instigated the quarrel between Hrothulf and Hrothgar's sons, supporting the latter.[12] The evidence for this is highly conjectural.

Unferth makes his final appearance in the poem just before Beowulf plunges into the fearsome mere for his struggle with Grendel's mother. He presents the hero with his own special sword, Hrunting, as a sign of reconciliation and submission. He had apparently, the poet says, forgotten his scornful words when drunk.

This, then, is the story of Unferth's activities. He first pours scorn upon Beowulf to discredit him and then finally is brought to recognize a superior being. A brief allusion before the reconciliation scene may hint at Unferth's participation in the dynastic quarrels of the Scyldings. He held the office of *thyle* and had earlier slain a brother.

Various explanations of Unferth have been put forth, most of them concerned with the origin of the figure, but my purpose is not really to refute any theory except perhaps that which Olrik has urged, that he is not essential to the Beowulf story. My concern here is not with the genesis of the figure. Unferth may have originally been an essential element of the Bear Son's folktale.[13] He may have had an historical role in the Scylding dynastic quarrels.[14] He may even have been influenced by the

[11] See A. Olrik, *The Heroic Legends of Denmark,* trans. Lee M. Hollander (Scandinavian Monographs 4; New York, 1919), 58. Olrik seems to be somewhat confused in his discussion of Unferth. He appears to be saying that he was and was not invented by the *Beowulf*-poet. It is possible that he is making a distinction between Unferth's name and role. It is clear, however, that Olrik believes that he belongs originally to the Scylding rather than the Beowulf episodes. 'Therefore the figure of Unferth cannot have been created for the purposes of a Beowulf epic but is a necessity in the economy of the Scylding story'; *ibid.,* 58.

[12] *Ibid.,* 60.

[13] See F. Panzer, *Studien zur Germanischen Sagengeschichte,* I: *Beowulf* (Munich, 1910), 279 ff.

[14] As Olrik, *op. cit.,* suggests. See also H. Munro Chadwick, *The Heroic Age* (Cambridge, 1912), 159-60.

character of Bricriu in the Irish *Fled Bricrend.*[15] These suggestions are all really concerned with the question of the *genesis* of the figure, but I am concerned with what the *Beowulf*-poet did with Unferth, no matter where he came from — from folklore, history, Irish or Scandinavian sagas, or from the poet's own subconscious. To the author, Unferth had a function in his epic. What did he conceive of his character, wherever he may have come from? And if Unferth did come from some source other than the imagination of the poet, he, as we have seen, was given a new name, probably to indicate his role in the work.

It is my contention that the author of *Beowulf* consciously patterned the figure of Unferth after the personified abstractions currently used in the Christian Latin poetry with which he was familiar. I am not concerned with any particular identification, but I do suggest that he did think of Unferth as *Discordia,* as his name indicates. Perhaps the most famous figure of that name which could have been known to him occurs in Prudentius' *Psychomachia* where *Discordia* (heresy) is the antagonist of *Concordia.* The *Beowulf*-poet may have used Unferth as *Discordia,* however, without especially modeling him on the Prudentian character. I do urge, however, that he was consciously using the allegorical method in shaping Unferth and that this method is a legacy of the Christian tradition brought to England after 597.

Beowulf was written, as most commentators agree, around 700 in England, possibly in Northumbria. It is also agreed, as is quite obvious, that *Beowulf* contains Christian elements or 'coloring' in spite of its pagan story. The Christianity of the poem is so deeply embedded in the texture of the epic that it could not have been interpolated. The poet was a Christian and, as such, was indebted to the Christian tradition as it mani-

[15] See M. Deutschbein, 'Die sagenhistorischen und literarischen Grundlagen des Beowulfepos,' *Germanisch-Romanische Monatsschrift,* 1 (1909) 114-5. Deutschbein has been effectively answered by O. L. Olson, '*Beowulf* and *The Feast of Bricriu,*' *Modern Philology,* 11 (1913-14), 418 ff.

fested itself in England at the end of the seventh or beginning of the eighth century. His point of view, his references to Biblical story, his ethical standards, even if we do not accept Schücking's *mensura* [measure], and his eschatology are all Christian. If we grant these elements — and we must — why cannot we accept allegory, which was introduced into England as part of Christian culture? The lives of Aldhelm and Bede were at least partially contemporary with that of our poet. Prudentius was referred to and drawn upon by both.[16] Sedulius and Paulinus of Nola, both of whom employed allegory, were known to Aldhelm at least.[17] Nor were pagan Latin allegorists, such as Claudian, unknown in England. Aldhelm used the allegorical method extensively in his own poetry and prose.

In contradiction to Girvan's statement that 'it [the personification of a sentiment] is a recognized method of Germanic poetry,'[18] we may say that personification is a recognized method of Christian Latin poetry. When allegory is used in Germanic poetry,[19] it is a Christian element. In fact, it is a sign of Christian influence.

I do not wish to over-emphasize the role of allegory in *Beowulf*. The poet was telling a concrete story about historical or semi-historical people. It is primarily a narrative poem, not a *Romance of the Rose*. Yet if we recognize allegory in the work as an element in the whole, we can only enrich and deepen our appreciation of it. The *Beowulf*-poet is struggling with various types of material and endeavoring to work them into a whole. He is relating a story, moralizing upon that story, endeavoring to weld together the concepts of pagan *wyrd* and Christian grace, and employing pagan folklore. Together with all these

[16] See J. D. A. Ogilvy, *Books Known to Anglo-Latin Writers from Aldhelm to Alcuin (670-804)* (The Mediaeval Academy of America, Studies and Documents 2; Cambridge, Mass., 1936), 76-7.

[17] *Ibid.*, 79-80 and 70.

[18] *Beowulf and the Seventh Century, Language and Content* (London, 1935), 67-8.

[19] Girvan's examples of 'Germanic' allegory are simply not to the point.

elements, he introduces in the figure of Unferth, Christian allegory. If he conceived of Beowulf as the *rex justus* or ideal king, the defeat of discord in the person of Unferth is demanded. If the ethic of the poem is based on *ordinata concordia* [ordered concord], *discordia* [discord] must be overthrown. Prudentius tells the story of how Discord wounds Concord and is killed by Faith. Beowulf, however, defeats his antagonist, not by force, but by example, and Unferth hands over his sword, the symbol of his might. Without trying to reduce the relation of Beowulf to Unferth to the purely allegorical level of Faith or Concord versus Discord, I do urge that such concepts were in the poet's mind as he dealt with what was perhaps a well-known story and that by giving the enemy the name of Unferth he wished to suggest this overhanging meaning (not necessarily as in Prudentius) to his readers. The story was colored by the allegorical pattern.

Several other possible abstractions appear in the poem. Wonred, father of Wulf and Eofor,[20] it has already been pointed out by Weyhe,[21] may well be 'void of advice' or 'void of power'; terms which could well indicate the fate the Geats were to undergo. Hygd, Hygelac's queen, is 'thought'. Unferth is not unique in the epic. In the contemporary *Widsith,* Unwen may be 'hopelessness', 'despair', rather than 'the unexpected one'.[22] True allegory is the personification of an abstract quality. On the other hand, a descriptive name such as Widsith (the far-traveller) is not allegorical. Widsith is rather a nickname. This distinction between quality and descriptive names must be maintained.

One further point. Unferth is called a *thyle,* a word which is usually translated as 'orator' or 'spokesman', on the basis of later Latin glosses. This office has been assumed to be an

[20] Line 2971.

[21] See 'König Ongentheows Fall,' *Englische Studien,* 39 (1908), 36.

[22] Line 114. See K. Malone, *Widsith* (London, 1936), 193.

official court position.[23] It has been suggested, however, that a *thyle* (cognate with ON. *þulr*) may have been a pagan priest.[24] If such is the case, would it not be appropriate for the Christian *rex justus* to bring about the submission of paganism in the person of Unferth, discord-heresy?[25] Not all the pagan priests would be as obliging as Coifi, who, seventy-five years before *Beowulf* was written, profaned his own heathen altars after hearing Paulinus preach.[26] The obscurity of the word *thyle,* however, prevents us from pushing this interpretation too far.

Nineteenth-century romantic and nationalistic scholarship, often German, to which we owe much of both good and evil, over-emphasized the pagan aspects of the oldest known Germanic epic. It has been difficult to shed this point of view and to see the essential Christianity of *Beowulf*.[27] It belongs to the Christian tradition, not only in mood and ideals, and in occasional Biblical references, but, at least partially and tentatively, in literary technique. An old Scandinavian tale has been changed into a Christian poem. Viewing Unferth as colored by the alle-

[23] Recently it has been suggested that Unferth is the 'Urbild des Hofnarren'; see R. Stumpfl, *Kultspiele der Germanen als Ursprung des mittelalterlichen Dramas* (Berlin, 1936), 397.

[24] See B. S. Phillpotts, *The Elder Edda and Ancient Scandinavian Drama* (Cambridge, 1920), 181 ff. and H. Munro & N. Kershaw Chadwick, *The Growth of Literature,* I: *The Ancient Literatures of Europe* (Cambridge, 1932), 618 ff. The murder of Unferth's brother may have had a ritual significance. See also Professor Kemp Malone's review of W. H. Vogt's *Stilgeschichte der eddischen Wissensdichtung* in *Modern Language Notes,* 44 (1929), 129-30.

[25] The word 'heresy' was used in a loose sense in the early Middle Ages. Any enemy of the Holy Catholic faith could be termed heretical.

[26] Bede, *Historia ecclesiastica gentis Anglorum* 2, 13.

[27] 'For the essential Christianity of *Beowulf* impresses me more and more with each re-reading of the poem' (from a private letter to me from Professor Henry Bosley Woolf dated 7 January 1948). See Professor Woolf's recent article, 'Unferth,' *Modern Language Quarterly,* 10 (1949), 45-52, published since this paper was written, for an acute analysis of the role of Unferth in the structure of *Beowulf,* which supplements and reinforces my arguments.

gorical figure *Discordia,* enables us to join *Beowulf* with the Christian Middle Ages in a way not hitherto possible. It is the work of a poet who was close to the new religion which was transforming Britain in his time, as it had earlier transformed the Roman Empire, and was later, by the help of his fellow-countrymen and others, to be carried beyond its borders into Germany and Eastern Europe. The character of Unferth is an integral part of *Beowulf*. He is the opponent and the foil of the hero; he enhances his might; he is proof of his moderation, faith and glory.

8

THE DOCTRINE OF CHARITY IN MEDIAEVAL LITERARY GARDENS: A TOPICAL APPROACH THROUGH SYMBOLISM AND ALLEGORY*

D. W. Robertson, Jr.

AT THE HEART OF MEDIAEVAL CHRISTIANITY IS THE DOCTRINE of Charity, the New Law which Christ brought to fulfill the Old Law so that mankind might be saved. Since this doctrine has extremely broad implications, it cannot be expressed satisfactorily in a few words, but for convenience we may use the classic formulation included in the *De doctrina Christiana* of St. Augustine: 'Charitatem voco motum animi ad fruendum Deo propter ipsum, et se atque proximo propter Deum: cupiditatem autem, motum animi ad fruendum se et proximo et quolibet corpore non propter Deum.'[1] [By charity I mean the soul's movement toward delight in God for Himself, and in himself and his neighbor for God's sake; but by cupidity, the soul's movement toward enjoying himself and his neighbor and any bodily thing other than for God's sake.] The opposite of Charity, as St Augustine describes it, is cupidity, the love of any creature, including one's self, for its own sake. These two loves, Charity and cupidity, are the two poles of the mediaeval Christian scale of values. For St. Augustine and for his successors among mediaeval exegetes, the whole aim of Scripture is to promote Charity and to condemn cupidity: 'Non autem praecipit Scriptura nisi charitatem, nec culpat nisi cupidi-

* Reprinted, by permission of the author, and the editor of *Speculum*, from that journal, XXVI (1951).

[1] III, 16 (10).

tatem.'[2] [Scripture inculcates only charity, finds fault only with cupidity.] Where this aim is not apparent in the letter of the Bible, one must seek it in the spirit beneath the veil of the letter. In the *De doctrina* there is developed a theory of literary interpretation by means of which one may remove the veil and effect the necessary discovery.

The obscurity of Scripture is useful, for it serves to exercise the intellect so that the truth may come to the reader in a pleasant and memorable way: 'Nunc tamen nemo ambigit, et per similitudines libentius quaeque cognosci, et cum aliqua difficultate quaesita multo gratius inveniri.'[3] [But no one doubts now either that some things are more readily known through likenesses, or that things sought with some difficulty are found with much more gratification.] The pleasure accompanying the search for and the discovery of Charity in the Bible is thus, as H.-I. Marrou has said, a pleasure 'd'ordre littéraire,'[4] so that reading the Bible confers aesthetic as well as spiritual rewards. To obtain these rewards, one must not only be familiar with purely rhetorical devices but also with the meanings of objects in the physical world: 'Rerum autem ignorantia facit obscuras figuratas locutiones, cum ignoramus vel animantium, vel lapidum, vel herbarum naturas, aliarumve rerum, quae plerumque in Scripturis similitudinis alicujus gratia ponuntur.'[5] [But ignorance of things makes figurative passages obscure, when we do not know the natures of animals, or stones, or herbs, or other things, which are put everywhere in the Scriptures for the sake of some comparison.]

[2] *Loc. cit.*

[3] II, 8 (6). Cf. Hugh of St Victor, *Didascalicon* (ed. Buttimer), p. 55, where the principle is applied to non-Scriptural literature. The argument was still being used as a defense of poetic obscurity by Petrarch and Boccaccio. See C. G. Osgood, *Boccaccio on Poetry* (Princeton, 1930), pp. 61-62, 170, note 10, 171, note 16.

[4] *Saint Augustine et la fin de la culture antique* (Paris, 1938), p. 489. I am indebted to Professor B. F. Huppé for calling my attention to this work and for many other helpful suggestions.

[5] *De doctrina*, II, 24 (16).

In other words, one must be able to read the Book of God's Work in order to understand His Word. In the later Middle Ages, the *trivium* was devoted to studies facilitating the literal reading of the Bible. It was for this purpose that one studied rhetoric. The *quadrivium* furnished the necessary information about creation to enable one to discover allegorical and tropological values, 'in quibus constat cognito veritatis et amor virtutis: et haec est vera reparatio hominis.'[6] [in which consist the knowledge of truth and the love of virtue; and these are man's true restoration.]

The techniques of reading developed by St. Augustine were not confined to the study of the Bible. Thus, Rabanus Maurus prefaces his transcript of part of the *De doctrina* in the *De clericorum institutione* with an indication that the methods described apply to the reading of profane as well as sacred letters.[7] And in the *Didascalicon,* which is basically an elaboration of the *De doctrina,* Hugh of St. Victor describes a procedure for arriving at the underlying meaning of literature of any kind. One begins with the *letter,* or grammatical structure, turns next to the *sense,* or obvious meaning, and finally to the *sentence,* or doctrinal content, which furnishes the desired allegorical and tropological values.[8] Profane letters were thought of as being allegorical in much the same way as the Bible is allegorical. To quote Professor Charles G. Osgood, 'This allegorical theory of poetry, deriving from the Ancients, and sustained in early mediaeval times by a naturally strong inclination to symbolism and allegory, supports the allegorical quality of literature and art from Prudentius to Spenser. Nor is it confined only to formal allegory such as the *Divine Comedy,* but suspects and seeks ulterior mean-

[6] G. Paré, A. Brunet, and P. Tremblay, *La renaissance du XIIe siècle* (Paris and Ottawa, 1933), pp. 233-237. The quotation is from Hugh of St Victor, *ibid.,* p. 234, note 1.

[7] *PL,* CVII, 296. Cf. C. Spicq, *Esquisse d'une histoire de l'exégèse latine au moyen âge* (Paris, 1944), p. 41.

[8] *Didascalicon,* p. 125.

ing in all art and poetry worthy of the name.'[9] In this paper I wish to examine first some of the more obvious meanings of gardens and garden materials as they are explained in mediaeval commentaries and encyclopedias. The selection of this particular chapter from the Book of God's Work is purely arbitrary; similar studies might be made of names, numbers, animals, stones, or other things. When a sufficient background of meanings, presumably of the kind studied in the *quadrivium*, has been presented, I wish to show that the conventionally established meanings are relevant to the interpretation of natural and artificial gardens in mediaeval literature. When these conventional meanings are applied in 'art and poetry worthy of the name' it becomes apparent, I believe, that mediaeval literary authors frequently share the primary aim of Scripture, to promote Charity and to condemn its opposite, cupidity. Not all mediaeval literary gardens may be included in a preliminary study of this kind, so that I have selected a few typical gardens from a wide range of literary types. At the same time, I have used illustrations which cover a very long period, from the early Middle Ages to the second half of the fourteenth century.

Many gardens are little more than groves of trees, and still others have a tree as a central feature. Some notion of the significance of the tree is still familiar, since it occupies a very important position in the story of the Fall, which involves the Tree of Knowledge of Good and Evil; and the Redemption involves another tree, the Tree of Life, or the Cross. In the Middle Ages, the very important position of these trees in Biblical narrative gave rise to an enormous complex of associations. Any tree may be considered as an aspect of one of the trees just mentioned, or as a transitional growth between the two extremes. A tree *per se* without further qualification suggests both of them. Any tree may have implications for the individual, for society, or for the afterlife. Thus the Tree of Life variously represents *sapientia* [wis-

[9] *Op. cit.*, pp. xxxviii-xxxix.

dom], the Cross, Christ, or the good Christian.[10] The Tree of Knowledge of Good and Evil was not evil in itself, since God put nothing evil in Paradise; but eating the fruit of the tree represents turning away from God in pride. When man suffered the consequences, he knew 'quid intersit inter bonum quod deseruit, et malum quod cecidet.'[11] [what was the difference between the good he had abandoned and the evil he had fallen upon.] After they had eaten the fruit Adam and Eve concealed themselves 'in medio ligni paradisi' [in the garden, among the trees] (Gen. 3.8). St. Augustine comments: 'Quis se abscondit a conspectu Dei, nisi qui deserto ipso incipit jam amare quod suum est? Jam enim habebant cooperimenta mendacii: qui autem loquitur mendacium, de suo loquitur (Jo. 8.44). Et ideo ad arborem se dicitur abscondere, quae erat in medio paradisi, id est ad seipsos, qui in medio rerum infra Deum et supra corpora ordinati erant.'[12] [Who hides himself from the sight of God, except he who, having deserted him, has already begun to love his own nature? For they have already cooperated in a lie; but he who utters falsehood is uttering what is natural to him (John 8.44). And therefore it is said that they hid themselves by the tree, which was in the midst of Eden, i.e. by themselves, who were made properly for the midst of beings, below God and above bodies.] To hide within the tree is to hide within oneself in self-love or cupidity. In one sense, the tree represents free will, and the eating of the fruit is the corruption of the will that follows abandonment of reason.[13] Theoretically, the reason is made up of three parts: memory, intellect, and will. When these parts are preserved in their proper hierarchy, with the will subservient to the other two,

[10] St. Augustine, *De Gen. contra Manich., PL,* xxxiv, 203; St. Gregory, *Moralia, PL,* 75, 988; St. Bede, *Comm. in Gen., PL,* xci, 203, *Expl. Apoc., PL,* xciii, 204; Bruno Astensis, *PL,* clxv, 87; St. Martin, *PL,* ccix, 413; etc.

[11] St. Augustine, *De Gen. contra Manich., PL,* xxxiv, 203.

[12] *Ibid.,* 208.

[13] Cf. the *Quaest. in Gen.* attributed to Bede, where Isidore is quoted to this effect, *PL,* xciii, 269-270.

they reflect the Trinity and constitute the Image of God in man.[14] But when the will dominates in disobedience, the Image is corrupted. To eat the fruit of the Tree of Knowledge of Good and Evil is to corrupt the Image of God, and to hide under the tree is to seek protection in lying rationalization.

The shade of the tree where Adam and Eve sought refuge is frequently associated with *scientia* (as opposed to *sapientia*), for worldly wisdom is conducive to a false sense of security. This shade is vividly and eloquently described in a sermon by Hugh of St. Victor:

> Cave ergo ne et tu dum sub umbra, foliorum requiem quaeris, incipias pati caliginem. Nec possis in umbra positus clare discernere; quia imago quae apparet umbra, sola est, non veritas. Hanc ergo umbram foliorum suspectam habe, ne decipiaris. Quae sunt folia? Species rerum visibilium folia sunt; quae modo quidem pulchra et virentia apparent, sed cadent subito cum turbo exierit. Quae sunt folia? Domus, vineae, horti, piscinae, sylva lignorum, germinantium, familiae, possessiones, aurum, argentum, substantiae regum et provinciarum: lyrae, citharae, tibiae, organa, scyphi, et urcei, et vasa pretiosa divitiae et pompae, et gloria: omnia haec folia sunt. Quare folia? Quia vana, quia caduca, quia transitoria: ideo folia. Virent quidem modico tempore, sed cito arescunt et cadunt. Sed tamen dum stant, umbram faciunt et habent refrigerium suum; sed est obscura umbra et inimica lumini. . . . Ideo dixi ut suspectam habeas umbram, qui te sub foliis positum confiteris. Sub foliis es, in umbra es, et sapientiam juxta te vides. Vide diligenter ne forte non sit sapientia, sed aliud aliquid latens sub specie illius. Quae est enim sapientia in umbra foliorum? Nam umbram foliorum dilectio est et jocunditas in specie et pulchritudine rerum transitoriarum. Et habet ista sapientiam suam. Sic enim homines vacant sapientiam qua ista requies, et tranquilitas ista carnis callide et astute queritur, et prudenter conservatur . . . et lumen verae sapientiae, apud quam stultitia est sapientia ista, videre non possunt.[15] [Take care, therefore, lest you too, while you seek rest under the shadow of the leaves, begin to suffer darkness. You cannot see clearly when you stand in shadow, because what appears in the shadow is only image, not truth. So hold that shadow of the leaves suspect, do not be deceived by it. What are the leaves? The leaves are the kinds of visible things, which now indeed appear beautiful and flourishing, but they will fall suddenly when trouble comes upon them. What are the leaves? Houses, vines, gardens, fishing pools, the forest trees and buds, families, possessions, gold, silver, kings' and provinces' substance; lyres, harps,

[14] See St. Augustine, *De Trinitate,* XIV.

[15] Hom. IX in Eccles., *PL,* CLXXV, 171-172.

flutes, organs, goblets, and pitchers, and precious vases, riches and pomps and glory; all these things are the leaves. Why leaves? Because they are vain, because they are frail, because they are transitory; leaves, therefore. They flourish indeed for a little while, but quickly they dry up and fall. But still while they stand they make a shadow and they have its coolness; but it is a dark shadow and unfriendly to the light. . . . So I said that you should hold the shadow suspect, you who admit that you stand under the leaves. You are under the leaves, you are in the shadow, and you see wisdom near you. See to it diligently lest perhaps it should not be wisdom, but something else hiding under that appearance. For what is wisdom in the shadow of the leaves? For the shadow of the leaves is affection for and pleasure in the appearance and beauty of transitory things. And that has its own wisdom. For thus men have time for the wisdom by which that rest and fleshly tranquility is sought shrewdly and astutely, and is prudently preserved, . . . and they cannot see the light of true wisdom, beside which that wisdom is stupidity.]

Here the leaves of the tree are the objects of worldly vanity — wealth, physical beauty, music, and so on — and the shade is the deceitful comfort which things of this kind afford, a comfort fortified by a *scientia* which excludes true wisdom or *sapientia*. In the shade the image we see 'sola est,' ['is alone'] without the higher meaning of Divine truth. But the leaves ultimately fall, leaving the person seeking shelter fully exposed to the heat and light from which he sought to escape. As we shall see, this light is the sunshine of God's justice. These transitory leaves should be contrasted sharply with the evergreen leaves of the Tree of Life, which represent the unfading and eternal Word of God. They offer true protection to those who seek solace beneath them.[16]

[16] See St. Augustine on Ps. 1, *PL,* XXXVI, 68 (partly quoted below); St. Bruno of the Carthusians, *PL,* CLII, 641; or St. Martin on Apoc. 22.2, *PL,* CCIX, 413: *'Et folia ligni,* scilicet praecepta Christi quae tegunt et ornant fructum, id est verba praedicationis ejus sunt *ad sanitatem gentium,* gentilium videlicet conversorum si implentur. Christus ergo reddet fructum, et apostoli eorumque successores post eos praedicando, per universum mundum spargent folia, id est praecepta ipsius Christi.' [And the tree's leaves, namely Christ's teachings which bear and supply fruit, i.e. the words of his preaching are for the health of the gentiles — of the converted gentiles, if they will fulfill his word. Christ therefore brings forth fruit, and the apostles and their successors after them, by preaching; they scatter leaves, i.e. the precepts of Christ himself, through the whole world.]

Tropological elaborations of the two trees as trees of the virtues and vices were extremely popular in the Middle Ages. Unusually fine specimens appear in the *De fructibus carnis et spiritus* printed by Migne among the works of Hugh of St. Victor. The edition in the *Patrologia* contains a schematic reproduction of the manuscript illustration which shows some of the wider implications of the trees very clearly. The evil tree on the left appears under the rubric *Vetus Adam,* or man unredeemed. The tree is rooted in *superbia* and its crowning fruit is *luxuria.* On branches which droop toward the ground are six other vices depicted as fruits surrounded by vicious leaves. The tree is prominently marked *Babylonia* [Babylon]. The good tree on the right appears under the rubric *Novus Adam* to indicate man redeemed and in a state of grace. It is rooted in *humilitas* and its crowning fruit is *caritas.* On ascending branches hang the other two theological virtues and the cardinal virtues surrounded by virtuous leaves. It is marked *Hierosolyma*[17] [Jerusalem]. Other fruits for these trees appear when they are considered on other levels. For example, when the good tree is the Cross, its fruit is Christ.[18] When the tree is Christ, its fruits are the Apostles and their successors;[19] when the tree is an individual its fruits may be good works.[20] Anagogically, the fruit is eternal life.[21] In any event, the symbolic act of eating the fruit confers salvation on the individual. The fruit of the evil tree has corresponding and opposite values.

Some of this material may be clarified by a reference to a simple example of the use of these meanings in art. The Ruthwell Cross, a stone monument probably dating from the first half of the eighth century, shows on its sides two panels covered with

[17] The root of the good tree (rather than its crowning fruit) is sometimes *caritas,* and, conversely, the root of the evil tree is sometimes *cupiditas,* the *radix malorum.*

[18] Honorius, *In Cant., PL,* CLXXII, 425.

[19] St. Martin, *PL,* CCIX, 413.

[20] Bruno Astensis, *PL,* CLXV, 87; cf. *ibid.,* 131-132, 180, etc.

[21] St. Bruno of the Carthusians, *PL,* CLII, 641.

foliage. In the foliage are birds and beasts eating the fruit.[22] In the light of what has been said above, it is clear that the carvings are not merely decorative. The foliage is made up of the unfading leaves of the Tree of Life, and the birds and beasts are those who in the shelter of the Word of God eat the fruit of eternal life. Monuments such as this undoubtedly suggest to their creators various levels of significance. Thus in the Old English poem, *The Dream of the Rood,* part of which appears on the Ruthwell Cross, there is a clear reference to the tropological level of meaning. Referring to the Day of Judgment, the poet observes: 'Ne þearf ðær þonne ænig unforht wesan/þe him ær in breostum bereð beacna selest.' No one who has borne the Tree within him need fear at the Last Judgment. To live righteously is to live in the image of the Tree of Life, or in imitation of Christ. Then one bears the fruit of good works which assures the fruit of the anagogical tree and a place before it.

The author of the *De fructibus,* as we have seen, associates the two trees with Jerusalem and Babylon. To see the full implications of the trees, we must examine these concepts briefly. Jerusalem (*visio pacis* [the vision of peace]) implies tropologically virtue and spiritual peace, allegorically the Church of the faithful, and anagogically the Celestial City. Babylon (*confusio* [confusion]) implies the opposites of these things. The two cities, as St. Augustine explains in the *De civitate Dei,* spring from two loves, Charity and cupidity. Properly, all Christians are strangers and pilgrims in the world: 'Carissimi, obsecro vos tanquam advenas et peregrinos abstinere vos a carnalibus desideriis' [Beloved, I call upon you to be like strangers and exiles, to resist those natural appetites which besiege the soul. (Knox)] (I Pet. 2.11). The manner of the voyage from Babylon to Jerusalem is succinctly described by Peter Lombard:

Sciendum itaque est duas esse spirituales civitates in praesenti: unam malorum quae incoepit a Cain, et dicitur Babylonia; alteram bonorum,

[22] This account is based on the description in B. Dickens and A. C. Ross, *The Dream of Rood* (London, 1945), pp. 1-13.

quae coepit ab Abel, et dicitur Jerusalem. Illius cives facit cupiditas, Jerusalem cives facit charitas. Quae licet sint mistae corpore, separatae sunt mente, quarum una peregrinatur in altera, et captiva tenetur. Quandiu enim sumus in hoc corpore, peregrinamur a Domino, qui de Babylonia ad Jerusalem suspiramus, id est de saeculo et corpore peccati ad coelum . . . . De hac tamen captivitate incipit redire, qui incipit amare. Charitas enim ad reditum movet pedem.[23] [Therefore one must know that there are two spiritual cities at present: one of evil men, which began from Cain, and is called Babylon; one of good men, which began from Abel, and is called Jerusalem. Cupidity makes men citizens of the former, charity makes them citizens of Jerusalem. Although they are physically mixed, spiritually they are distinct. Of them, one is on pilgrimage to another place, and is held captive. For as long as we are in the body, we are sent on pilgrimage by the Lord, we who sigh from Babylon for Jerusalem, i.e. from the world and the body of sin for heaven. . . . However, he has begun to return from this captivity who has begun to love. For charity moves his feet to return.]

The direction of man's journey is thus dependent on the kind of love which moves in his will. Cupidity, which is the source of all of man's sins and hence of his discontents, makes a Babylon of the individual mind, a Babylon of society, and leads to an ultimate Babylon in eternal damnation. Charity brings the peace of Jerusalem to the mind, to society, and to the Celestial City where its radiance is all-pervasive. With these loves go two fears. Cupidity is accompanied by the fear of earthly misfortune, and Charity is accompanied by the fear of God which leads to wisdom. The supreme importance of this concept in Christian doctrine may be indicated with a brief quotation from Peter Lombard, who here reflects a traditional Augustinian position: 'Omnia ergo peccata, duae res faciunt in homine, scilicet cupiditas et timor: sic econtra amor Dei et timor ejus ducunt ad omnem bonum. Amas enim ut bene sit tibi; times ne male sit tibi. Hoc age in Deo, non in saeculo. Uterque amor incendit, uterque timor

[23] In Ps. 64, *PL,* CXCI, 581. Cf. St. Augustine, *De civitate Dei,* XIV, 28. The references to Cain and Abel are not, of course, historical. Abel begins the generation of the just, to which all faithful Christians belong, regardless of physical parenthood. Cain begins the generation of the wicked, among whom must be included all those who love in cupidity.

himiliat.'[24] [Therefore two things make all sins in man, namely cupidity and fear; so, on the other hand, the love and fear of God lead to all good. For you love to enjoy good and you fear to suffer evil. Do this in God, not in the world. Both loves inflame, both fears humiliate.] Both loves inflame, and both fears humiliate, but the two loves produce radically opposite results. These loves and fears are the key to the behavior of any individual, and the key to his destiny.

The fact that the word love (*amor*) could be used for either Charity or cupidity opened enormous possibilities for literary word-play. It is also, I believe, responsible for the manifest preoccupation with 'love' in mediaeval literature. A certain very significant discrepancy between the scheme represented in the traditional Augustinian position just outlined and the scheme of the trees in the *De fructibus* is relevant in this connection. The crowning fruits of the trees are *caritas* and *luxuria* rather than *caritas* and *cupiditas*. Again, if we look in St. Bonaventura's magnificent account of the two cities in the Prologue to his comment on Ecclesiastes, we find the word *libido* used where we should expect *cupiditas*.[25] And in the treatise on the two loves written by Gérard of Liège the contrast is obviously one between the love of God and sexual love.[26] But this tradition is also Augustinian, for

[24] Comm. in Ps. 79, *PL*, CXCI, 765-766. Cf. St. Augustine, *PL*, XXXVI, 1026; or the *Summa sententiarum* (authorship disputed), *PL*, CLXXVI, 113, where Isidore is quoted.

[25] *Opera* (Quaracchi, 1882 et seq.), VI, 4.

[26] Ed. Wilmart, *Analecta reginensia* (Vatican, 1933), p. 183: 'Et [quia] uere nullus tantus labor, nulla tanta miseria est in praesenti uita quam illicito et carnali amore capi et superari, et eius imperiis deseruire, quia aufert deum, aufert animam, cor et corpus a deo, idest in tantum ut non permittat hominem et mulierem sui iuris et sue potestatis esse; sed in seruitute miserabili detinentur, nec se de tali iugo possunt excutere, quando uolunt, sicut sciunt experti. At uero econtra, nichil dulcius, nil iocundius nichilque fructuosius est quam deum toto corde diligere et amoris eius obsequiis se assidue mancipare . . . . Ad contra, amor carnalis tam nobilium quam rusticorum, tam diuitum quam pauperum in immundicia terminatur et consummatur. . . . Sic seruiunt carnales amatores

St. Augustine interpreted the word *fornicatio* in the Scriptures to mean not only illicit conjunction of the sexes, but also idolatry or any aspect of love of the world as opposed to the love of God.[27] When *luxuria* or *fornicatio* is used symbolically, either one well describes the sin of Adam and Eve and may be justly placed as the crowning fruit of the Tree of Babylon. The evil tree thus suggests idolatrous sexual love, an extreme form of cupidity and a reflection of the Fall.

Trees exist in various stages of development, and there are many widely different types of trees. For example, a tree appears with budding leaves at the approach of summer in Matt. 24.32: 'Ab arbore et folia nata, scitis quia prope est aestas; ita et vos, cum videritis haec omnia, scitote quia prope est in ianuis.' [The fig-tree will teach you a parable; when its branch grows supple,

---

et amatrices in immunditia miserabili, et idcirco debemus ut possumus amorem carnalem et illicitum fugere et contempnere, et deo per perfectum amorem totaliter adherere.' [And there is no labor or misery in this life so great as being seized and overcome by fleshly love, and being subject to its commands; for it takes God away, it takes soul, heart and body away from God, i.e. inasmuch as it does not permit a man and woman to be under their own law and in their own power; but they are confined in unhappy slavery, nor can they get themselves out when they will from such a yoke, as experienced persons know. But on the other hand nothing is sweeter, nothing more delightful and nothing more fruitful than to love God with the whole heart and to submit oneself assiduously to the requirements of his love. . . . On the contrary fleshly love — nobles' or rustics', rich men's or poor men's — is ended and consummated in uncleanness. . . . So they enslave fleshly lovers, men and women, in miserable uncleanness, and therefore we should, as we can, fly from and despise fleshly and lawless love and cling wholly to God by perfect love.]

[27] Sermo CLXII, *PL*, XXXVIII, 887: 'Non solum fornicatio in sacris Litteris specialiter, sed etiam generaliter arguitur et nominatur . . . advertamus, illam esse generalem fornicationem animae humanae, quae non adhaerens quisque Deo, adhaeret mundo.' [Fornication is both particularly and generally condemned and blamed in holy scripture . . . we note that this is a general fornication of the human soul, which clings to the world rather than to God.] Cf. *De sermone Domini in monte*, 36.

and begins to put out leaves, you know that summer is near; so you, when you see all this come about, are to know that it is near, at your very doors. (Knox)] The context shows that the budding tree is a promise of the second coming, which implies the Resurrection of the Just. The *Glossa ordinaria* contains the observation that the dry tree is revivified with faith and charity, and that the new leaves are the 'verba praedicationis' which announce the summer of 'aeterna serenitas'[28] [words of proclamation . . . eternal peace]. On the other hand, in Ju. 12 there are some 'arbores autumnales, bis mortuae, eradicatae' [autumn trees that bear no fruit, given over anew to death, plucked up by the roots]. Bede explains that the autumnal trees bear either no fruit or evil fruit. They are individuals who perform no good works and who live in despair of salvation.[29] Among trees of various species, the palm has a prominent place. It is a symbol of the just, since its flowers of hope do not fall but produce the fruit of eternal reward. In contrast to the flower of the flesh, Bede explains, the palm flourishes in the sunshine of God's justice.[30] Generally, the good tree is a green tree. Thus, in Luc. 23.31 Christ exclaims: 'Quia si in viridi ligno haec faciunt, in arido quid fiet?' [If it goes so hard with the tree that is still green, what will become of the tree that is already dried up?] The *Glossa ordinaria,* following Bede, identified the green tree with Christ and His elect, the dry tree with sinners.[31] Hence the willow, because of its persistent green foliage is sometimes identified with the just.[32] But much more commonly it represents those sterile in good works, since it bears no fruit, and it

[28] *PL,* CXIV, 162.

[29] *PL,* XCIII, 127.

[30] *PL,* XCIII, 12. Cf. St. Augustine, *PL,* XXXVII, 1179; *Glos. ord., PL,* CXIV, 671.

[31] *PL,* CXIV, 346-347; cf. Bede, *PL,* XCII, 615.

[32] Alanus de Insulis, *Distinctiones, PL,* CCX, 932; cf. *Allegoriae in sacram scripturam* (twelfth century, authorship unknown), *PL,* CXI, 1545.

is associated with the waters of cupidity. In this sense, its green leaves are words of false piety.[33] An especially interesting variant of the Tree of Life is afforded by the sycamore. Its peculiarity arises from the story of Zacchaeus, who in Luc. 19.4 climbs a sycamore in order to see Jesus. The sycamore's leaf resembles that of the fig, but its fruit is not attractive, so that it came to be called 'ficus fatua' [the foolish fig]. In the commentaries, however, it represents foolishness in the eyes of the world and wisdom in the eyes of God. Extending this concept, commentators associate it with faith or with the Cross, and they sometimes point out that the faithful will, like Zacchaeus, climb the sycamore.[34] Conversely, the sycamore may represent 'vana scientia' [useless knowledge], but this meaning is rare.[35] St. Bernard divides evil trees into three classes: those which do not bear fruit, like the elm; those hypocritical trees which bear fruit that is not their own; and those trees which bear fruit too early so that it is destroyed before it ripens.[36]

. . . Gardens frequently contain wells or streams by means of which the trees and flowers are watered. Thus in Ps. 1, the Tree of Life grows 'secus decursus aquarum' [by running water] and in Apoc. 22.1-2 it stands on either side of a 'fluvium aquae vitae splendidum tanquam crystallum' [a river clear as a crystal,

[33] See the references in note 32 and St. Gregory, *Moralia, PL,* LXXVI, 671-676; *Gregorianum, PL,* CXCIII, 298. Isidore of Seville, *Etymologiae,* XVII, vii, 47 (ed. Lindsay), associates the willow with sterility on other grounds.

[34] See St. Gregory, *Moralia, PL,* LXXVI, 444-446; Bede, *PL,* XCII, 559-560; *Allegoriae, PL,* CXII, 1053; Alanus, *Distinctiones, PL,* CCX, 964. Cf. Urban T. Holmes, Jr, *A New Interpretation of Chretien's "Conte Del Graal"* (Chapel Hill, 1948), p. 22, note 12, and p. 32.

[35] Rabanus Maurus, *De universo, PL,* CXI, 513. This work not only contains a useful general discussion of the tree but a list of trees of various kinds together with their higher meanings. See also Rabanus on Ecclus. 24, *PL,* CIX, 929-931.

[36] *Sermones, PL,* CLXXXIII, 378-379.

whose waters give life].[37] Again, in Genesis, the Tree is associated with a river which flows away in four streams, usually said to be the cardinal virtues. The Water of Life, which either flows by the tree or emanates from it,[38] is variously interpreted as baptism, wisdom, true doctrine, *Christus irrigans* [Christ who makes the water flow], Charity, or the Holy Spirit.[39] This water is contrasted with the temporal water of cupidity offered by the Samaritan woman in Jo. 4.13-14, which has opposite values. Either tree may be depicted beside a river or shading a well or fountain. As we have already seen, the willow grows beside evil waters. In the later Middle Ages, the well beside the good tree also suggests the Blessed Virgin Mary, who was called 'Well of Grace.' Representations of the Cross standing beside a well were common in late mediaeval art. St. Augustine associates the Rock whence flow the Living Waters, a common Scriptural designation of Christ, with the Tree of Life.[40] The fountain or well under either tree may be thought of as coming from a rock or stone basin.

Many gardens offer protection to singing birds. The *De universo* of Rabanus supplies a list of various species with their higher meanings. Although the birds in Scripture frequently

[37] St. Martin, *PL,* CCIX, 413, explains the somewhat puzzling location of the tree here as follows: 'Vel citra fluvium, id est in hac vita, habemus lignum vitae, scilicet corpus et sanguinem Christi in quibus reficimur, et ultra flumen, videlicet in futuro habebemus ipsum praesentem.' [Either on this side of the stream, i.e. in this life, we have the tree of life, namely the body and blood of Christ on which we are fed, and beyond the river, namely in the future, we shall have his presence.]

[38] For a suggestion that the river in Paradise flows from the tree, see St. Augustine, *De Gen. ad litt., PL,* XXXIV, 375. Cf. Bruno Astensis, *Expos. Apoc., PL,* CLXV, 730.

[39] Bede, *Comm. in Gen., PL,* XCI, 203; Rupert, *PL,* CLXVII, 274; Strabo, *PL,* CXIV, 754. This water also appears in Ecclus. 24.40 ff. Rabanus, *PL,* CIX, 943, comments: 'Ego sapientia Dei effudit in mundum flumina doctrinae evangelicae, quae abundantissime reficiunt et satiant avidas mentes electorum.' [I, the wisdom of God, poured out into the whole world rivers of the gospel's doctrine, which abundantly fill and satisfy the eager souls of the elect.] Cf. note 44, below.

[40] *De Gen. ad Litt., PL,* XXXIV, 375.

tend to have an evil significance, representing evil spirits, vices, and so on,[41] St. Ambrose describes the birds in the garden of Eden at some length, showing that the song they sing is an inspiration to Charity. St. Gregory finds good birds in the parable of the Grain of Mustard Seed. The very small seed grows into a very large tree, in which the birds of the air find shelter. The seed is the seed of doctrine planted by Christ, the branches of the tree are holy preachers who have spread the doctrine throughout the world, and the birds who rest in the shade are pious spirits who desire to abandon terrestrial things and fly to celestial realms.[42] A more elaborate development of these ideas appears in Bede's comment on Matthew.[43] The tree itself is an aspect of the Tree of Life.

Having considered the most important elements which combine to form gardens, we may now examine complete gardens very briefly. To begin with, the Tree of Life stands in a *hortus deliciarum* [garden of delights]. The garden surrounding the Tree and irrigated by its waters is interpreted in various ways. Usually, it symbolizes either the Church allegorically or the individual tropologically. Anagogically it is the New Jerusalem.[44]

[41] E.g., see Bede on Iac. 3.7, *PL*, XCIII, 28.

[42] *Moralia, PL*, LXXVI, 97. For the birds of St. Ambrose, see *PL*, XIV, 237 f.

[43] *PL*, XCII, 173-174.

[44] Bede, *PL*, XCI, 203, gives several alternative interpretations of the garden. Cf. Richard of St. Victor, *In Cant., PL*, CXCVI, 490. The river of wisdom in Ecclus. 24.42 also waters a garden: 'Dixi: Rigabo hortum meum plantationum et inebriabo prato mei fructum.' [I said, I will water my garden of plants and I will take my fill of fruit in the meadow.] Rabanus, *PL*, CIX, 944, comments: 'Hortus enim plantationum sapientia sancto est Ecclesia, quam ipso Veritas [sc. Christus] suo dogmate semper irrigat et inebriat, ut fructum pratus spiritalis quotidie proferat, in doctrina videlicet catholica et sacris virtutibus, et merito, quia illuminata a vera luce *quae illuminat omnem hominem venientem in hunc mundum* (Jo. 1.9), a sole justitiae ipsoque oriente . . . .' [For the garden of plants, wisely, is for the holy man the Church, which the Truth himself by his own teaching always irrigates and gives its fill, so that the spiritual meadow might daily bring forth fruit, namely in catholic doctrine and the holy virtues; and properly, because it is given light by the true light which illuminates every man coming into this world, by the sun of justice, the day-star himself.]

A garden with a *fons signatus* [sealed fountain], this time called a *hortus conclusus* [closed garden], also appears in the *Canticum;* and the commentators, in accordance with their usual practice, relate the two gardens. Like the Paradise of Genesis, the garden of the *Canticum* represents the Church or the individual, although it is sometimes used in praise of the Blessed Virgin Mary. The commentaries on it yield a wealth of values for trees and flowers.[45] An especially valuable tropological description of the garden may be found in Richard of St. Victor's sermons. We are shown in some detail how one may prevent or eradicate weedy vices and encourage the desirable plants. In this discussion the *fons* is the 'anima devota' [devoted soul], and the *puteus*

[45] A concise but detailed summary of both allegorical and tropological meanings for this garden appears in a sermon by Hugh of St. Victor. I quote part of it, *PL,* CLXXVII, 1086, as an illustration: 'Habet ergo sancta mater Ecclesia hortum conversationem bonam, clausam per disciplinam, fontem per sapientiam, signatum per figuram. Habet paradisum malorum punicorum in passis martyribus, cyperos in praelatis rectoribus, nardum in subjectis humilibus, crocum in eruditis doctoribus, fistulam in conpunctis poenitentibus . . . . Et istae sunt spiritales sanctae matris Ecclesiae divitiae . . . . Matrem Ecclesiam, charissimi, nobis in his omnibus imitemur, ut cum ipsasponsum in decore suo videre mereamur, et cum sponsa in coelis gloriemur. Habeamus et nos paradisum malorum punicorum, adversa pro Christo saepius patiendo, et oppressis quotidie compatiendo; cyperos, discrete nos regendo; nardum, nostris praelatis humiliter nos subdendo; crocum, luce sapientiae effulgendo . . . .' [Holy Mother Church therefore has a garden through good behavior, enclosed by discipline, a fountain by wisdom, sealed by its imagery. She has a paradise of deep red apples in the martyrs' sufferings, cypresses in the prelates who rule her, nard in her humble subjects, the crocus in her learned doctors, an ulcer in the compunction of her penitents . . . and these are the spiritual riches of holy mother Church . . . Dearly beloved, let us imitate mother Church in all these, so that we may deserve with her to see the Spouse in his beauty, and with the Bride be glorified in heaven. Let us too have a paradise of deep red apples, by often suffering adversities for Christ, and by daily enduring our burdens; cypresses, by governing ourselves discreetly; nard, by subjecting ourselves humbly to our prelates; crocus, by shining with the light of wisdom.] Although the various commentaries on the *Canticum* differ in detail, for the most part they are not actually inconsistent.

aquarum viventium [well of living waters] is the Holy Spirit.[46] The *fons* is to be associated with the well or fountain under the Tree of Life, but the appearance of the well here without the tree makes possible the literary or artistic use of wells and streams independently of the two trees. The meaning of the garden is general enough so that it may represent an individual, the world of men or the Church, or the next world. These meanings have considerably more force when we remember that Christ is described at one point in Scripture as a *Hortulanus*. The nature of any garden, that is, of any individual, any society of men, or any ultimate afterlife, is determined, in a given instance, upon whether Christ, or *sapientia,* is the gardener. When Christ is the gardener, the garden is ruled by wisdom and suffused with the warmth of Charity. Otherwise it is ruled by worldly wisdom or *scientia* and suffused with cupidity. To the mediaeval mind, cupidity or self-love can lead only to the discomfort and disaster of an unweeded garden.

We may conclude that the various meanings of trees, flowers, streams, and other features of gardens have a very wide scope, and that they suggest what were regarded in the Middle Ages as the most important doctrines of Christianity. In fact, their implications are wide enough so that it would be possible to use the two trees and their surroundings for a contrast just as fundamental and meaningful as that between the two cities which underlies St. Augustine's *De civitate Dei*. To rest comfortably in the shade of the wrong tree amounts to the same thing as to make a home in Babylon. If one wished to distinguish the two forms of expression, one might say that the garden suggests forcibly the truth as it is contained in Genesis and the *Canticum,* whereas the city suggests the truth as it is expressed in later Old Testament history and in the Psalms. Both devices appear in the Prophetic Books and in the New Testament. The garden image emphasizes the relationship between the sexes, which is apparent on the surface in both Genesis and the *Canti-*

[46] *PL*, CXCVI, 487 ff.

cum, so that it tends to be associated with idolatrous sexual love used as a symbol for extreme cupidity. The conventional associations of both the evil tree and the *flos faeni* reinforce this tendency. But, at the same time, the sexual relationship is not a necessary adjunct of the garden, since the Fall of Adam and Eve was only figuratively sexual, as is the relationship expressed in the *Canticum*. This is not to say that cities and gardens afford the only means of making the contrast between Charity and cupidity. Since all creation is meaningful in the same way, the number of ways of making the contrast is infinite. For, it should be recalled, it is not the words *tree* or *city* which are meaningful, but trees and cities themselves. Creation is an expression of God's infinite love, but to see it there, one must set aside the shell, which is in itself the object of scientific investigation, to find the kernel beneath, the food of wisdom and, in accordance with mediaeval doctrine, the source of the only true beauty human eyes may see.

II

The appearance of the higher meanings of garden materials in early vernacular poetry may be illustrated in *Beowulf*. Competent scholars now agree that the author of the poem was a man of considerable learning and that his basic intention was pious, although the 'interpolator' still lingers in the background.[47] One scene in the poem appears to utilize certain features of the materials presented above, the picture of Grendel's mere. It has already been observed that a very similar description is used in one of the Blickling Homilies to suggest Hell,[48] which is simply the evil garden taken anagogically. As the *Beowulf* poet describes the scene, its general features at once suggest commonplace Scriptural associations: a stream makes a pool in a place surrounded by overhanging trees, and beside the pool is a rock. Certain attributes of the scene are extremely significant. In the

[47] See Fr. Klaeber, *Beowulf,* pp. xlviii-li, civ, cxix, cxx-cxxiv.
[48] *Ibid.,* note to 1357 ff., pp. 182-183.

first place, the pool is the dwelling of a giant, one of the generation of Cain. In Bede's *Hexaemeron* we find that the giants of Gen. 6.4. were 'terrenis concupiscentiis adhaerentes' [men who cling to fleshly lusts] and that although they were destroyed in the Flood, they arose again thereafter.[49] Figuratively, the generation of Cain is simply the generation of the unjust to which all those governed by cupidity belong. They are monsters because they have distorted or destroyed the Image of God within themselves. Babylon, as we have seen, traditionally began with Cain, and it is maintained on earth by his generation. We may say as much for the evil garden. Thus Grendel is the type of the militant heretic or worldly man, and his dwelling is appropriately in the waters which are the opposite of those which spring from the Rock of Christ. It is pertinent also that Beowulf should find under these waters a sword which is a relic of the struggle between the giants and the just in the days before the Flood (ll. 1687-1693). The poet could hardly refer more specifically to the character of the pool and of its inhabitants. The relationship between the stream and the rock is not entirely clear in the poem, but the rock is a part of the traditional scenery, one of the elements associated with either garden. The trees overhang the pool in a manner suggesting that they shade it, excluding from it, or seeming to exclude from it, the sunshine of God's justice. This impression is reinforced by the fact that the pool suddenly becomes light when Beowulf kills Grendel's mother, who may be taken as the source of the evil which her offspring spreads throughout the world:

1570 Lixte se leoma, leoht inne stod,
efne swa of hefene hadre scineð
rodores candel.[50]

[A gleam flashed forth, a light arose within, even as the candle of the sky shines brightly from heaven.]

[49] *PL*, XCI, 84 f.

[50] This light should not be confused with the *fyrleoht* of the monster's den (l. 1516), which comes from the flame of the wrong love.

The trees are covered with frost, a feature which Professor Klaeber recognizes as being symbolic. On the word *hrinde* [frost] (l. 1363) he comments: 'The epithet is eminently suitable symbolically. . . . It is not to be imagined that Beowulf found the trees covered with hoar-frost. He would not have sailed for Denmark in winter.'[51] Implicit in these observations is the excellent principle that when a work by an obviously accomplished mediaeval poet does not seem to make sense on the surface, one must look beneath the surface for the meaning. Frost and ice are traditional symbols of Satan, whom God permits to tempt the human spirit to fall in cupidity.[52] Moreover, the chill of cupidity may be considered characteristic of the evil garden as opposed to the warmth of Charity in the good garden. The trees, the rock, and the pool all point strongly to the theory that what the poet had in mind was the evil garden of the Scriptures.

Grendel's mere has other attributes which tend to reinforce this interpretation. We are told that the hart pursued by hounds chooses rather to give up its life than to hide its head in the grove surrounding the pool. Literally, this description makes little sense, since a hart could hardly fear a fate worse than death. But the associations of Ps. 42 lead us to recognize in the hart the faithful Christian who seeks his Lord in the Living Waters. Thus Bede wrote in his poem on this Psalm:

> cervus ut ad fontes sitiens festinat aquarum,
> sic mea mens ardet te, conditor alme, requirens
> viventemque sitit te cernere libera lucem.

> [As the thirsty deer makes haste to the fountains, so my soul pants for you, loved creator, searching for you, and thirsts for the freedom to see you, the living light.]

But the hart in *Beowulf* carefully avoids Grendel's waters, which he knows will not assuage his thirst. The example of Adam and Eve has warned him that this is not an effective hiding place. He prefers death to the eternal damnation which results from

[51] *Beowulf,* p. 183.
[52] See St. Gregory, *Moralia, PL,* LXXVI, 510.

hiding under the wrong trees. We may see the opposite of the hart in the monsters which swim about in the pool or rest on its banks. The poet says somewhat cryptically of them,

ða on undernmæl oft bewitigað
sorhfulne sið on seglrade,
1430 wyrmas ond wildeor.
[Those who in the morning often carry out a sorrowful journey on the sail road, serpents and wild beasts.]

Professor Klaeber's note on this passage has a tone of despair: "In any case, consistency is not to be postulated in the descriptions of the scenery."[53] However, if we see in these monsters those who allow their spirits to be killed by Grendel, the sea voyage they make does not involve an actual sea, somehow contiguous with the pool, but is merely the last journey which leads, in this instance, to damnation. In so far as the epic as a whole is concerned, the interpretation of Grendel's mere as a reflection of the evil garden is consistent with the attitude toward the poem expressed in the introduction to Klaeber's most recent edition. The suggestion of Christ which Klaeber sees in Beowulf should lead us to expect further suggestions of the same kind consistently and thematically interwoven in the poem. Although it is obvious that Beowulf is not Christ historically, every true Christian lives in imitation of Christ, and there are certain virtues and abilities which a ruler must exhibit in the course of this imitation. In the Grendel episode Beowulf shows himself capable of purifying a society of men from the forces of cupidity. The fact that neither Christ nor the Tree of Knowledge of Good and Evil is mentioned in the poem is in keeping with the principles of Augustinian literary interpretation. An intellectual effort is necessary to discern Divine truth in the arrangement of materials in the poem, and it is from the fruitful pursuit of this effort, not from the decoration on the outer shell, that the poem's aesthetic value arises.

In *Beowulf* the evil garden is repulsive on the surface. But the shade of the tree undoubtedly seemed attractive to Adam and

[53] *Beowulf,* p. 185.

Eve, and, moreover, we who succeed them are also tempted by it. There is, thus, no reason why the evil garden should not be made to appear superficially attractive. A picture of a more attractive evil garden appears at the beginning of the Old English 'Doomsday' based on the *De die judicii* attributed to Bede:

> Hwæt! Ic ana sæt innan bearwe,
> mid helme beþeht, holte tomiddes,
> þær þa wæterburnan swegdon and urnon
> on middan gehæge eal swa ic secge.
> Eac þær wynwyrta weoxon and bleowon
> innon þæm gemonge on ænlicum wonge,
> and þa wudubeamas wagedon and swegdon;
> þurh winda gryre wolcn wæs gehrered
> and min earme mod eal wæs gedrefed.

[Lo! I sat alone within a grove, protected by the foliage, in the midst of a wood, where the water-stream sounded and ran in the midst of a meadow, even as I say. Pleasant plants also grew and bloomed there amid the throng in the glorious field, and the forest trees tossed and sounded. The heavens were troubled by a terrible wind and my wretched spirit was all in distress.]

The poem goes on to express the speaker's fears concerning his state of sin and the coming of Doomsday, when the world and its garden will be no more. It should be noticed that the wood is 'helme beþeht' [protected by the foliage], indicating that the speaker is hiding from the sun of God's justice. He sits 'holte tomiddes,' *in medio ligni*. Beneath the trees in this 'gehæge' [meadow] bloom the flowers of the flesh watered by the streams of worldly wisdom. But a storm arises. That is, the wood where Adam and Eve sought protection, even though its flowers and rippling streams may seem attractive, will soon pass in the storm of God's wrath.[54] In spite of the flowers and murmuring streams,

[54] Bede's comment on Gen. 3.8 may furnish the basis for the description in the poem, *PL,* XCI, 214: 'Deambulat Deus in illis, non stabat, quia in praecepto illius non stabant. Et bene ad auram post meridiem, quia ab illis auferebatur lux illa ferventior veritatis, appropinquantibus errorem tenebris. *Absconderunt se,* et reliqua. In medio namque ligni se abscondit, qui versus a Deo, in erroris sui atque arbitrii voluntatibus vivit.' [God walks about among them, he does not stand still, because they did not stand firm in his commandment; and rightly for the after-

the speaker is not altogether comfortable. A famous successor to this poet also found himself uneasy in this grove:

> Nel mezzo del cammin di nostra vita
> mi retrovai per una selva oscura
> che la diritta via era smarrita. . . .
>
> [In the middle of the journey of our life I came to myself in a dark wood where the straight way was lost.]

---

noon air, because the more fervent light of truth was taken from them, when the darkness brought them near error. *They hid themselves*, etc. For he has hidden himself in the midst of a tree who has turned away from God, and lives in his own errors and self-willed judgment.] Cf. Gregory, *Moralia, PL*, LXXVI, 671-676. This poem is examined more thoroughly in a study of Caedmonian poetry by Professor B. F. Huppé, now in the course of preparation.

9

THE ORAL-FORMULAIC CHARACTER OF ANGLO-SAXON NARRATIVE POETRY*

Francis P. Magoun, Jr.

IN THE COURSE OF THE LAST QUARTER-CENTURY MUCH HAS BEEN discovered about the techniques employed by unlettered singers in their composition of narrative verse. Whereas a lettered poet of any time or place, composing (as he does and must) with the aid of writing materials and with deliberation, creates his own language as he proceeds, the unlettered singer, ordinarily composing rapidly and extempore before a live audience, must and does call upon ready-made language, upon a vast reservoir of formulas filling just measures of verse. These formulas develop over a long period of time; they are the creation of countless generations of singers and can express all the ideas a singer will need in order to tell his story, itself usually traditional. This progress is primarily due to the work of two men, the late Milman Parry[1] and his former pupil and successor in this field, Professor

* Reprinted, by permission of the author, and the editor of *Speculum*, from that journal, XXVIII (1953), 446-467.

[1] For a complete bibliography of the writings of Milman Parry, see A. B. Lord, 'Homer, Parry, and Huso,' *American Journal of Archaeology*, LII (1948), 43-44. Two of Parry's papers may be specially noted as representing the full development of his thought: 'Studies in the Epic Technique of Oral Verse-Making, I: Homer and Homeric Style,' *Harvard Studies in Classical Philology*, XLI (1930), 73-147, esp. pp. 118-121 for charts exposing the formulaic character of ll. 1-25 of the *Iliad* and the

Albert Bates Lord of Harvard University.[2] First in connection with Homeric language, later as a result of field-work in Yugoslavia, chiefly among unlettered Muslim singers, Parry, aided by Lord, demonstrated that the characteristic feature of all orally composed poetry is its totally formulaic character. From this a second point emerged, namely, that the recurrence in a given poem of an appreciable number of formulas or formulaic phrases brands the latter as oral, just as a lack of such repetitions marks a poem as composed in a lettered tradition. Oral poetry, it may be safely said, is composed entirely of formulas, large and small, while lettered poetry is never formulaic, though lettered poets occasionally consciously repeat themselves or quote verbatim from other poets in order to produce a specific rhetorical or literary effect. Finally, it is clear that an oral poem until written down has not and cannot have a fixed text, a concept difficult for lettered persons; its text, like the text of an orally circulating anecdote, will vary in greater or lesser degree with each telling.

Odyssey respectively; and 'II: The Homeric Language as the Language of Oral Poetry,' *ibid.*, XLIII (1932), 1-50, esp. pp. 12-17 ('The Art of Oral Poetry'). These papers are cited here as Parry I and II and by page.

[2] Parry in the summer of 1933, and Parry and Lord in the years 1934-35, studied the production of the oral epic style in Yugoslavia and collected some 12,500 texts, 'The Parry Collection of South-Slavic Texts,' now deposited in the Harvard College Library. Following Parry's lead and working with this opulent material Lord submitted in 1949 a Ph.D. thesis (Harvard, unpublished), 'The Singer of Tales: A Study in the Process of Yugoslav, Greek, and Germanic Oral Poetry.' Lord revisited Yugoslavia in 1950 and 1951; for his report on the collecting trip of 1950 see 'Yugoslav Epic Folk Poetry,' *Journal of the International Folk Music Council,* III (1951), 57-61. His thesis, revised and expanded, will be published by the Harvard University Press as *The Singer of Tales* in the series "Harvard Studies in Comparative Literature."

P.S. The work of Parry and Lord and the rich material preserved at Harvard were very familiar to Sir Cecil Maurice Bowra and utilized by him in his *Heroic Poetry* (London: Macmillan, 1952). This distinguished work appeared too late for me to use in preparing my London lectures or in preparing this paper, though I am happy to be able to add a specific reference or two in the footnotes below. For an excellent review of Sir Maurice's book see *The Times Literary Supplement*, Friday, 12 December 1952, p. 824.

The oral singer does not memorize either the songs of singers from whom he learns nor later does he memorize in our sense of the word songs of his own making. His apprenticeship involves the learning of thematic material, plots, proper names, and formulas with which he will gradually become able to compose in regular verse songs of his own. A good singer is one able to make better use of the common fund of formulas than the indifferent or poor singer, though all will be drawing upon essentially the same body of material. The length of a song or, better, the length of a given performance (since there is no fixed text) will largely depend upon the audience-factor, on how much time an audience has to give to the singer on any given occasion. A good singer can go on as long as an audience will listen to him, be it persons assembled in a Bosnian coffee-house, or in the presence of a tape-recorder or a stenographer. The analogies with musical improvisation will be evident.

The present paper is essentially an extension into the realm of Anglo-Saxon narrative poetry of the work of Parry and Lord, to whom it is indebted at every turn and in more ways than can easily be expressed. Indeed, without the stimulation of Parry's published works and the works and spoken words of Albert Lord, the present paper, or, indeed, anything like it would not have been written.

When one first reads of the existence of Anglo-Saxon poetry in the seventh century in Bede's account of Cædmon (*H.E.*, IV, 22 [24]), there is every reason to believe that already behind this lay a long tradition, running back to the Continental homeland and into a distant common Germanic heritage, a tradition of at least seven centuries and probably more. Toward the end of the first century A.D. Cornelius Tacitus comments on the art of poetry among the Germanic peoples of his day, and from that time on there are allusions by authors from late antiquity to the singing of songs among various Germanic tribes. Since these ancient Germanic singers were unlettered, their poetry must have been oral, and its diction, accordingly, must have been formulaic and traditional. The birth of this diction must have taken place in a very distant past and, like the birth of any diction, is beyond observation. As Parry observes of Homeric language:

> A single man or even a whole group of men who set out in the most careful way could not make even a beginning at such an oral diction. It must be the work of many poets over many generations. When one singer . . . has hit upon a phrase which is pleasing and easily used, other singers will hear it, and then, when faced at the same (metrical) point in the line with the need of expressing the same idea, they will recall it and use it. If the phrase is so good poetically and so useful metrically that it becomes in time the one best way to express a certain idea in a given length of verse, and as such is passed on from one generation of poets to another, it has won a place for itself in the oral diction as a formula. But if it does not suit in every way, or if a better way of fitting the idea into the verse and sentence is found, it is straightway forgotten or lives only for a short time, since with each new poet and with each new generation of poets it must undergo the twofold test of being found pleasing and useful. In time the needed number of such phrases is made up: each idea to be expressed in the poetry has its formula for each metrical need, and the poet, who would not think of trying to express ideas outside the traditional field of thought of poetry, can make his verses easily by means of a diction which time has proved to be the best.[3]

At this late date speculation about origins is rather idle, but one may perhaps imagine that in its earliest beginnings isochronous utterances in Old Germanic, almost surely based on the rhythmic beat of some instrument, involved short sequences of verse at first almost accidentally arrived at and consisting, say, of a maxim of a few verses or a protective charm or encomiastic song of similarly modest dimensions. By the time of Tacitus it would seem that more ambitious compositions were possible and the order of the day. In his *Germania* (ch. 2) he says of the Germanic peoples:

> In ancient songs (*carminibus antiquis*), which is the sole kind of record (*memoria*) or history (*annales*) among them, they celebrate the god Twisto, begotten of the earth, and his son Mannus, as the beginning and founder of their people. To Mannus they ascribe three sons from whose names those tribes nearest the Ocean are called Ingvaeones [North Sea Germans], the central Erminones [Elbe Germans?], and the rest Istvaeones [Western Rhine Germans?].

[3] Parry II, 7-8.

This suggests possibly rather elaborate narrative and there seems to be little reason to assume that the apparently more or less mythological or cult songs of the North Sea and Inland Germans were merely mnemonic verses on the order of the *þular* in *Widsith* or in the Old-Norse *Hervarar saga* (ch. 12, Stanza 69).[4] In the *Annales* (Book II, §88, *ad fin.*) Tacitus further reports that songs about Arminius, who had died nearly a century earlier, were still being sung by Germans of his day. These familiar statements are adduced only to emphasize the presumably high antiquity of Old-Germanic poetry and the length of tradition behind it. Furthermore, in order to suggest the antiquity not merely of the art of Germanic poetry in general but specifically the antiquity of the metrical-rhythmical forms of Anglo-Saxon poetry as we know it, one may point to the fact that Anglo-Saxon verse is cast in a form to all intents and purposes identical with all Old-Germanic poetry — Old-Norse, Old-Saxon, Old-High-German — in a word, identical with everything except the later skaldic *vísur* of Norway and Iceland. Since any theory of independent origins for the five basic metrical-rhythmical patterns, the 'Sievers Five Types,' is so exceedingly unlikely, one is forced to assume that something very close to the later preserved forms and patterns had been established and was in good running order before the Anglo-Saxons began to colonize Britain.

In the nature of the case we do not have and cannot have any record of Anglo Saxon poetry before the introduction of the art of reading and writing by Christian missionaries from Rome and from Iona in the Hebrides; indeed, we have no poetical text which can in exactly the form preserved be thought of as having been put together very early at all. Consequently, it has been natural to think of the preserved poems as composed as we compose poetry, i.e., by lettered persons making use of writing materials, and until the time of Parry and Lord there was no available technique permitting one to decide on the basis of internal

[4] E.g., Rudolf Much, *Die Germania des Tacitus* (Heidelberg, 1937), pp. 21-22.

evidence alone to which tradition a given text might belong — to the oral or to the lettered. The recurrence of verses and verse-pairs in Anglo-Saxon poetry, the 'Parallelstellen' of German scholars, has been much noted and commented upon, and cross-references accumulated and often cited by editors of individual poems, with the main conclusion drawn from this phenomenon being that those parallels might constitute evidence of the direct influence of one poem upon another (see p. 213, below). But with the discovery of the dominant rôle of the formula in the composition of oral poetry and of the non-existence of metrical formulas in the poetry of lettered authors, we have suddenly acquired a touchstone with which it is now possible to determine to which of the two great categories of poetry a recorded text belongs — to the oral or to the lettered tradition.

As a first test I have analyzed the first twenty-five lines or, better, the first fifty verses or twenty-five typographical lines of *Béowulf,* chosen because they deal with highly specialized thematic material not represented elsewhere in the poetry, for the presentation of which in verse one might suppose that a poet would need to create his own language if he would ever have to do so. The formulaic character of the verse is demonstrated by Chart I (pp. 216-219, below).[5] A word-group of any size or importance which appears elsewhere in *Béowulf* or other Anglo-Saxon poems unchanged or virtually unchanged is marked with solid underlining and is a formula according to Parry's definition that a formula is 'a group of words which is regularly employed under the same metrical conditions to express a given essential idea.'[6] A word-group marked with solid and broken

[5] Quotations and line-references from *Béowulf* are based on Fr. Klaeber's third edition with First and Second Supplements (Boston, 1950), those from *Judith* on the edition of Benno J. Timmer (London: Methuen, 1952); all others on *The Anglo-Saxon Poetic Records* (New York: Columbia University Press, 1931-42). Spellings are normalized on the basis of early W.S. as set forth in *Les Langues modernes,* XLV (1951), 63-69. Title-abbreviations, coded in three letters, are based on the titles used in *The Anglo-Saxon Poetic Records.*

[6] Parry I, 80.

underlining, or with broken underlining only, may be called a formulaic phrase or system; such groups are of the same type and conform to the same verbal and grammatical pattern as the various other verses associated with them and cited in the supporting evidence. For verses which are unmarked I have found no supporting evidence. Following the marked text on the chart comes the supporting evidence assembled under numbers answering to the *a* and *b* parts of the respective typographical lines.

Looking at Chart I one notes first that of the fifty verses only some thirteen, or twenty-six per cent, are not matched wholly or in part elsewhere in Anglo-Saxon poetry. In a word, despite the relatively limited corpus of some 30,000 lines — a little more than the two Homeric poems — in which to find corresponding phrases, some seventy per cent of the text of this passage does occur elsewhere. Were the surviving corpus, say, twice as big and if, above all, we had other songs of any extent dealing with anything like the same thematic material, there well might be almost nothing in the language here used that could not be demonstrated as traditional.

Though usefulness rather than mere repetition, is what makes a formula, it is instructive to look at the repeated formulas first, since it is easier to recognize a formula as such when it occurs a second or third time,[7] and from this regular use in various songs one readily sees how it helps this and that singer to compose his verses. Verses 1b, 3a, 3b, 4b, 5a, 5b, 8a, 10b, 11b, 13a, 14a, 15a, 16a, 17a, 23a, and 25a are of this sort. They occur exactly the same elsewhere or with only some insignificant change in inflection about which a singer would scarcely have to devote conscious thought in order to fit them into some different context or slightly different grammatical situation. The very fact of their recurrence in and/or outside of this poem bears witness to their usefulness not only to the singer of *Béowulf* but to singers of many other songs dealing with quite different themes.

A number of these formulas are something more than mere re-

[7] Parry I, 122.

peats and form part of larger formulaic systems used to express the same, or almost the same, idea or used to fit some larger rhythmical-grammatical pattern. As Parry observes of such formulas in Homer, 'any group of two or more such like formulas makes up a system, and the system may be defined in turn as a group of phrases which have the same metrical value and which are enough alike in thought and words to leave no doubt that the poet who used them knew them not only as a single formula, but also as formulas of a certain type.'[8] Here belong verses 1b, 6b, 11b, 16a, and 19a.

1b. *on géar-dagum* is one phase of a system *on* x-*dagum* used to express the idea 'long ago' and occurs twice elsewhere in *Béowulf* and in other poems as well. Either alone or with one or two preceding unstressed words it forms a complete C-verse. With the substitution for *géar,* with the sense 'of yore,' of *ǽr, eald,* or *fyrn,* the formula remains unchanged in meaning and meter, though the variant first elements of the compound are patently more than useful in meeting the exigencies of alliteration, a restrictive and technical problem with which neither Homeric nor Yugoslav verse, for instance, have to contend. The degree of thrift that marks the use of formulas in Homeric verse[9] is scarcely conceivable in the construction of the much more restrictive alliterative Germanic verse.

6b. *siþþan ǽrest wearþ* shows us three words repeated as a formula in *Béowulf* where it serves to express the general idea 'after something or other has happened'; it must have often been used by singers to express this same idea in a complete D-verse. But *siþþan ǽrest* (or *furðum*) can be followed by any monosyllabic verb-form in the past tense and in the recorded instance with *wéox* expresses a closely related idea.

11b. *þæt wæs gód cyning!* is a formula that may well have come into being in connection with encomiastic verse, of which we hear so much and have so little. Stylistically this and related

[8] Parry I, 85 and ff.

[9] Parry I, 86.

formulas stop the narrative for a moment and thus serve as a kind of emphatic punctuation. It is used twice in *Béowulf,* and elsewhere with unfavorable adjectives it serves as a parallel phrase of disapprobation. The system is *þæt wæs* (is) x *cyning.* There are other more distantly related formulas noted in the supporting evidence, all referring to persons.

16a. *lange hwíle* is part of a large system expressing the idea 'for a long time' and is closely related to a similar system with *þráge,* equally popular with the *Beowulf* singer. This formula or formulaic system occurs with *ealle, góde,* and *mićele* substituting for *lange,* alternates which affect neither sense nor meter; here alliteration must dictate the singer's choice. Whether he uses *hwíle* or *þráge* is surely a matter of accident or indifference, since both words fill the same measure of verse and here will not enter into the alliteration.

19a. *Scieldes eafora* is not repeated elsewhere in the poetic corpus, for nowhere else does the need exist to use this particular patronymic. The value of this system, whereby an A-verse can be constructed with the genitive of any monosyllabic personal name, is obvious from the supporting evidence. For patronymics involving the numerous dithematic names it may be observed that *sunu* is the favorite keyword and automatically forms a D- or E-verse, as do the somewhat less common *maga* and *magu.*

The present passage includes three nominal compounds which I have underlined as formulas not merely because they are repeated elsewhere to make up whole verses but because their second elements constitute the core of many small systems of formulas. These are *þéod-cyninges* (2a), *ymbsittendra* (9b), and *willgesíðas* (23a).[10] If these words did not make up entire

[10] For further instances of words of similar structure, and thus with similar rhythmical patterns, in *Béowulf* see John Collins Pope, *The Rhythm of Béowulf* (New Haven, Conn., 1942), pp. 300, 358 (type D1, No. 1) and 248 (type A1, No. 2a). Examples from other poems and with other first elements can be found in Christian W. M. Grein — Ferd. Holthausen — J. J. Köhler, *Sprachschatz der angelsächsischen Dichter* (Heidelberg, 1912).

verses, one might perhaps be inclined to view them merely as repeated words, and just as formulas need not be mere repetitions, so mere repetitions need not constitute a formula.

þéod-cyninga (2a) is one of a large number of compounds with inflected forms of *cyning,* usually in the genitive singular, which express the idea 'king' within the limits of a D3-verse. In most cases the first element merely emphasizes in one way or another the importance of the king or kings in question, as here where the Danish *þéod-cyningas* are tacitly opposed, as it were, to *smákonungar* 'roitelets' of ancient Scandinavia. Occasionally the first element will be more functional and will define or locate a king. In the on-verse position *Beowulf* 2795 has *Wuldor-cyninge* and in the off-verse position *eorþ-, héah-, þéod-cyninges,* also *Frís-cyninge* and *sǽ-cyninga;* of the same general order is *weorold-cyninga.* Except for *Frís-,* used to place geographically Dæghræfn's overlord, the first elements add little to the thought and were presumably chosen for alliterative convenience.[11]

ymbsittendra (9b), a compound present participle forming a D1-verse, presents a quite similar situation; it handily expresses the idea of 'persons residing round about.' Very close is *ymbstandendra.* In a broader way *ymbsittendra* is to be associated with a large number of verses consisting of a compound present participle, of which there are many in *Béowulf,* which tend in turn to break down into various semantic systems such as the idea of 'sea-farer' expressed by *brim-* and *sǽ-líðende* in *Béowulf,* and in other songs with the substitution of *éa-, mere-, and wǽg-* as the first element but with no change in thought.

will-gesíðas (23a) is but one of a largish formulaic system centering on *gesíþ* to express in a complete A-verse the idea of 'follower(s)' 'retainer(s)' the large variety of available first elements being highly useful to the singers in connection with alliteration. Thus are found compounds with *dryht-, eald-, folc-, wéa-,* and *wynn-.*[12]

[11] See further *ibid.,* p. 106, col. 1, under *cyning.*
[12] *Ibid.,* p. 608, under *gesíþ.*

Within the first fifty verses of *Béowulf* occur three so-called kennings, two Christian: *Líf-fréa* (16b), varied by *wuldres Wealdend* (17a), and one non-Christian: *hran-ráde* (10a). Reserving the Christian formulas for later discussion in connection with the special diction of the Christian songs (pp. 205 ff. below), we may examine here the formulaic character of the C-verse *ofer hran-ráde* and some closely related expressions by the aid of which the singers were able to place people on the sea or to get them over it. Much has been written about Anglo-Saxon kennings by themselves and as part of Old-Germanic poetical technique, but there is one particular aspect of this problem which can probably support further thought and investigation, namely, the formulaic character of the kenning. Like the rest of the language of oral poetry kennings must have developed over a long period of time and must be traditional and formulaic. An examination of the phrase *ofer hran-ráde* will tend to bear out this view. The feminine accusative singular *hran-ráde,* combined with the prepositions *geond, ofer,* and *on,* forms a complete C-verse, whose repeated use marks it as formulaic. Yet it is more than that, in that it is also one phrase of a formulaic system *on* (*ofer, geond*) x-*ráde,* where for *x* one can substitute any appropriate monosyllabic first element. With the substitution of *swan* one finds *ofer swan-ráde* in *Béowulf* and *Elene, on swan-ráde* in *Juliana,* while *on segl-ráde* appears in *Béowulf* with little or no real difference in meaning, and none in meter, from the other combinations. The singers are presumably concerned not primarily with some refinement of imagery produced by varying the first elements *hran, segl,* and *swan* — something for which an oral singer could scarcely have time — but with recalling a formula expressing the fundamental idea in question with availability for different alliterative situations. It is hard to believe that they had much concern with possible connotative effects produced by passing mention of sails, swans, or whales.

There is another aspect of this general problem that semantically at least is related to the *ofer hran-ráde* verse in *Béowulf.*

Now this particular formula and related formulaic systems were obviously useful to Anglo-Saxon singers and provided them with a C-verse with the aid of which they could get their characters onto or across the sea. Nevertheless, this system imposed certain limitations, including the fact that a verse based on this formula cannot well contain a verb; yet the need for composing such verses was felt and was met in more than one way. A fair example centers on a parallel to *rád,* f., namely, *weg,* m. In the accusative singular of *weg* there will be no ending; hence any compound of *weg* in this grammatical case, where ending a verse, must be fitted into a metrical pattern other than C, one in which there will be place for a verb or some other important alliterating word at the beginning. The pertinent compounds of *weg* are *bæþ-, flód-, flot-,* and *hwæl-,* of which *bæþ-weg* is the most frequent combination. *Ofer bæþ-weg* occurs three times, always with some form of *brecan* in the sense 'pressing on across the sea': thus, *brecan ofer bæþ-weg* (*And* 223, *Ele* 244) and *brecaþ ofer bæþ-weg* (*And* 513), where the phrase *ofer bæþ-weg* combines with the alliterating verb to make a formula. The two *f*-compounds, *flód-* and *flot-weg,* serve their purpose in combination with *faran. Flód-weg* appears in an instrumental construction *fóron flód-wege* (*Exo* 106) '[the sailors] journeyed on or over the sea'; while in the accusative plural there is *Fór flód-wegas* (*Rid* 36, 9) '[it, probably a ship] traversed the seas.' With *on* the combination *flot-weg* appears in *faran on flot-weg* (*HbM* 42 '[was fated] to journey on the sea.' Finally comes *hwæl-weg,* in meaning identical with *hran-rád* of *Bwf* 10a and occurring in *hweteþ on hwæl-weg* (*Sea* 63a) 'impels on [to?] the whale's route.' Beside offering various alliterative alternates this cluster of *weg*-formulas permits the inclusion of a verb in a single D-verse, an opportunity of which the singers were obviously glad to avail themselves.

I shall conclude this discussion of the formulaic character of the first 50 verses of *Béowulf* with a brief word on the first five verses (1a-3a) of the poem, where the singer appears to have adjusted, combined, and recombined a number of formulas. He begins with a formula much used to start songs or to introduce an important new section of a song, a formula built around the weakly exclamatory *hwæt* plus a personal pronoun. This is in effect a sort of filler-in, something to let the singer get going; the phrase, ordinarily metrically unstressed, opens the way to a B- or C-verse. The total system, embracing all personal pronouns in the nominative and a few in oblique cases, cannot be presented here, but looking at all instances of the subvariety *Hwæt, wé* (1a), collected on Chart I, one is struck by two points: (1) that in each case the singer includes his audience in assuming familiarity with the thematic material of his song,[13] and (2), more important, the fact that he is saying 'we have all heard or learned about something or other,' at times adding that the events took place long ago. *Híeran* is the verb favored in preserved song, with *frignan* of *Béowulf* running (perhaps by chance), a poor second. It will be noticed that the singers ordinarily work in the important verbal idea 'hearing about,' 'learning about' in the course of the first two verses, but the *Béowulf* singer introduced mention of the Spear-Danes (*Gár-Dena*) before proceeding farther. This apparently spoiled his chance of getting in a verb in what appears to be the favored or ordinary position in the first verse. Comparable to Cynewulf in *Ele* 397b, he might in some fashion have worked in a suitable verb in 1b, had there been such a one capable of *g*-alliteration, but at all events he next called upon one of the several available formulas expressing the idea 'long ago,' already discussed (p. 196, above) under *on géar-dagum* (1b). Thus *gefrugnon* is put off to the fourth verse (2b), while the *hú* of the total phrase *wé gefrugnon hú* has to wait for the fifth (3a). The basic formula is all there and the

[13] See Dorothy Whitelock, *The Audience of Béowulf* (Oxford University Press, 1950), pp. 34-44 and ff. *passim* on audience-familiarity in gross and detail with the *Béowulf* stories and substories introduced for purposes of embellishment; the latter are not in any ordinary sense 'digressions.'

singer has used every scrap of it, though not in what would appear to be the usual way. One might interpret this exceptional treatment as an example of a first-rate singer coping quickly and deftly with an almost awkward situation into which he had got himself, even though the resulting order of words is perhaps not quite natural. To suggest that this order of words is any sense 'literary' is virtually to deny oral technique in the composition of the poem, a technique demonstrated in the preceding analysis of the first fifty verses of the poem. The traditional character of the recorded text is further borne out by the fact that at least fifteen per cent of the verses of the poem are to all intents and purposes repeated within the poem,[14] a phenomenon unthinkable in lettered tradition.

In the opening lines of *Béowulf* are two formulas which must be called Christian: *Líf-fréa* (16b) and *wuldres Wealdend* (17a). Neither of these so-called kennings could well refer to anything but the Deity and hence could not have formed part of the traditional language of pre-Christian poetry. They must be relatively young and their presence in *Béowulf* raises the general question of the relation of the language of Christian narrative poetry — by far the largest genre in the corpus — to the older traditional poetic language. There are no means of knowing when first a singer or singers started making songs based on such novel thematic material as that found in the Old Testament, Apocrypha, saints' lives, and homilies, but it cannot well have been before the arrival of Augustine in Kent in 597 and of Paulinus in York in 625, an influence fortified by the settlement of Aidan on Lindisfarne (Holy Island) off the Northumberland coast in 635. Yet somewhere in the neighborhood of 675 St. Aldhelm was quite possibly singing religious verse, interspersed among diverting secular songs, in public at Malmesbury in Wiltshire in order to get the local populace to stay on after mass for

[14] Communicated orally by Mr. Robert P. Creed of Smith College, who is presently studying the oral style in *Béowulf*.

the sermon,[15] and sometime between 658 and 680, the years during which Hild ruled as abbess of Whitby in the North Riding, the unlettered Cædmon, farm-hand on the monastic estate, is said on first-rate authority[16] to have been successfully composing all

[15] Reported by William of Malmesbury (d. 1125) in his *De Gestis Pontificum Anglorum* (ed. N. E. S. A. Hamilton, Rolls Ser. No. 52, London, 1870), Bk. V. Pt. 1 ('Life of Aldhelm'), p. 336, based on Alfred the Great's lost *Handbóc* (William's *Manuale, ed. cit.*, pp. 332-333):

'Litteris itaque ad plenum instructus nativae quoque linguae non negligebat carmina, adeo ut, teste libro Elfredi de quo superius dixi, nulla umquam aetate par ei fuerit quisquam. Poesim Anglicam posse facere, cantum componere, eadem apposite vel canere vel dicere. Denique commemorat Elfredus carmen triviale adhuc vulgo canitatur Aldelmum fecisse . . . Populum eo tempore semibarbarum, parum divinis sermonibus intentum, statim cantatis missis domos cursitare solitum. Ideo sanctum virum super pontem qui rura et urbem continuat abeuntibus se opposuisse obicem quasi artem cantandi professum. Eo plus quam semel favorem et concursum emeritum. Hoc commento, sensim inter ludicra verbis Scripturarum insertis, cives ad sanitatem reduxisse.'

'And thus fully instructed in [Latin] literature he also did not neglect the songs of his native tongue, so that, according to Alfred's book of which I spoke above, at no time was anybody ever his equal. He was able to make English poetry, compose a melody, and properly sing or recite the same. Finally, Alfred remarks that Aldhelm composed a light song which was still [i.e., in Alfred's day] being commonly sung . . . The people, at that time [about 675] semibarbarous and too little intent on divine discourses, were in the habit of hurrying to their homes after masses had been sung. Therefore, the holy man stationed himself on a bridge [over the Avon] which connects the town [of Malmesbury] and the countryside as an obstacle to those going away, as though professing the art of song. After he had done this several times [lit. 'more than once'] he gained the good-will and the attendance of the common people. By this device, gradually working in words of the Scriptures among entertaining words, he led the people back to right reason.'

It may be remarked that the Scriptural words introduced in the course of the recitation of secular poems need not have been in verse, though this is a reasonable inference. It should also be noted that nothing is said about writing despite the rendering '*write* a poem' (*Poesim . . . facere*) of George F. Browne, *St. Aldhelm: His Life and Times* (London, 1903), p. 79.

[16] I refer not merely to Bede himself but to the tradition of the Whitby community on which Bede drew, surely completely reliable in this local matter, unless one assumes a monstrous conspiracy of falsification.

sorts of songs based on Christian story. There is no way of learning more about Aldhelm's compositions but, as I hope to show elsewhere, Cædmon was probably the father of nothing but his own songs and composed these against the background of a developed tradition.

In talking or thinking about the chronology, real or relative, of Anglo-Saxon poems one is notoriously treading on very swampy ground, but if one adopts the conservative view that a *Béowulf* song in form fairly close to the preserved performance had come into being not far from, say, 730 or even somewhat later, it is clear that by that time Christian poetry was a commonplace and that its recitation was a familiar form of entertainment not only in monasteries but in lay circles. Were this not the case, the recitation in Heorot of a song about the Creation (*Bwf* 90-98) would, as Dr Whitelock has recently pointed out, 'surely have been incongruous, or even ludicrous, if minstrels never sang on such themes to lay audiences.'[17] As it is, the Creation song seems to enjoy a status no different from that of songs sung about Sigemund and Fitela or the tragedy of Finn's stronghold in the same hall on another occasion. Indeed, apart from this, the entire fabric of *Béowulf* is shot through with the language and thought of Christianity and must be viewed as a Christian poem though of an unusual sort.[18]

Now, as Parry emphasizes, the traditional language of unlettered singers develops very, very slowly and over a long period of time and is created to deal only with traditional themes with which singers and audiences are in the main familiar. On his visits to Yugoslavia in 1950 and 1951 Professor Lord noted that the traditional singers were proving unable to cope with such radically new themes of a social-political nature as Marxism and related matters, for the simple reason that they lacked formulas necessary to express these new ideas in just measures of verse.

[17] Whitelock, *op. cit.*, p. 9; on pp. 9-11 Whitelock is on the verge of suggesting what I suggest here.

[18] *Idem*, pp. 3-4; Klaeber, *ed. cit.*, p xlix, *ad fin.*

Except for rather obvious substitutions of key-words in an old formula (e.g. *enǵla Dryhten* for *eorla dryhten*), no one singer ever creates many new formulas and most of them never create any at all. Thus, standing on the threshold, so to speak, of the year 600, one might well have wondered whether and how Anglo-Saxon singers would be able to meet the challenge of adapting their traditional verses to the needs of singing about themes so different as Christian material would seem to be. In actual fact they did rise to this occasion and often magnificently.

A glance of Chart II (pp. 219-21) analyzing ll. 512-535 of *Christ and Satan,* a poem of appreciably later date than *Béowulf* and mainly telling a story of Christ's harrowing of hell, exhibits plainly the formulaic character of the language. If not as many verses are underlined as in Chart I, this can, in the case of the unmarked verses, only mean that the surviving corpus of Anglo-Saxon poetry does not happen to contain verses which furnish supporting evidence, that is, either exactly similar verses or, equally significant, verses constructed on closely similar formulaic patterns.

It will be unnecessary to take up the text of this chart in detail, for the supporting evidence will now be telling its own story. There are, however, two matters, quite different from one another, which the present passage brings to one's attention. The first concerns the 'Christianity' of the language of this and perhaps any other Christian poem, while the second concerns the possibility of occasionally making use of an understanding of the nature and function of the formula in textual criticism.

The prime point of interest in the sample of verse analyzed on Chart II lies in the fact that it is from a Christian poem. It is a passage treating a most central event in Christian belief, the Ascension of Jesus Christ, and in that sense at least could scarcely be more Christian as opposed to the opening verses of *Béowulf*. What, as far as the language is concerned, is Christian about it? Very largely references to God, specifically Jesus Christ. This passage of forty-six verses includes thirteen such references, more than one for every four verses: *wuldres Weard* (512a), *Meotod mann-cynnes* (513a), *Dryhten God* (514a), *enǵla Dryhten* (518b), *God* (522b), *Godes Sunu* (526b), *Sunu Meotodes* (527b), *se Éća* (530b), *Þéodne* (532a), *Scieppend enǵla* (533b), and *Dryhten* (535a). These are all in one way or another different from one another. In addition there are ten other 'Christian' words, that is, words which would normally only appear in a Christian context: Galilee is mentioned twice (522a, 529a), Simon called Peter twice (521b, 536b); there is one reference to the Holy Spirit (525b), two to the disciples (520b, 529b), and three to angels (518b, 520a, 533b), of which two occur as parts of kennings designating the Deity. In all these forty-six verses include twenty-three Christian words, or words used in a Christian way; thus there is one Christian word for every other verse or one for each typographical line. It might be hard to find a more 'Christian' passage, and for these words and formulas used in a Christian way only *giengran* lacks supporting evidence. This is no doubt due to the limits of the surviving corpus and, had the singer happened to have preferred formulas with the much more frequent equivalent of 'disciple,' namely *þegn*, it would probably be possible to collect no little supporting evidence.

In this so very Christian passage there may be a hint and more as to how Anglo-Saxon singers were able, apparently from early on, to sing in a slightly adjusted traditional language songs based on these novel and untraditional themes. In the first place and stated in most general terms, the Christian themes that the singers apparently liked best to sing about are in the main stories involving extraordinary and exciting adventures and events, such as the stories on which center *Andreas, Azarias, Daniel, Elene, Exodus, Judith,* and *Juliana*. To the ear of Anglo-Saxons not yet fully initiated in this new development most immediately striking and strange were no doubt the presence of non-Germanic proper nouns, names of persons such as Simon Peter and places such as Galilee. These could be and were, however, readily fitted into older formulas created to embody Germanic proper names, and since these strange new names were all but invariably accented on the first syllable, regardless of the stress in the original tongues, they offered few, if any, metrical problems to the singer. Some of them must have been awkwardly long and more than queer sounding, such as *Nabochodonossar,* used five times in *Daniel* (48, 411, 497, 618, 663) and once in *Azarias* (183) to form a complete A-type on-verse, yet the singers made do with them. Aside from the pre-Christian word *God* and elsewhere *Críst,* to be viewed as ordinary personal names, the singers had available from pre-Christian tradition, already evidently rich in words and kennings to express the idea of 'ruler,' a large number of expressions ready to take off the rack, available as substitutory epithets for the Deity. As a result of new formations on the analogy of the old, e.g., the weaving into compounds of such characteristically Christian word-elements as *heofon* and *wuldor,* the number of epithets for the Deity was increased to a point where this is by all odds the largest single group of kennings in the poetical corpus.[19] The frequency and hence importance of this group can scarcely be overestimated. The concept 'angel' is new as is the loan-word *enǵel,* an idea also capable of being expressed by the old word *gást*. The Latin titles *Sanctus* and *Beatus* were easily handled by the old words *hálig* (originally 'inviolate') and *éadig* ('favored by fortune,' 'prosperous'). Expression of general conceptions of theology, dogma, and Christian doctrine is notably rare in the Christian songs,[20] as it is in *Béowulf,* where action predominates, and even in that most beautiful song of meditation or devotion, *The Dream of the Rood*. This lack is surely due neither to mere accident nor to ignorance or indiffer-

[19] See Hendrik van der Merwe Scholtz, *The Kenning in Anglo-Saxon and Old-Norse Poetry* (Utrecht-Nijmegen, 1929), pp. 92-98, and Hertha Marquardt, *Die altenglischen Kenningar,* etc. (Schriften der Königsberger gelehrten Gesellschaft, XIV, 3, Halle, 1938), pp. 269-292, and cp. *ibid.*, pp. 266 ff. *passim* (§D 'Christliche Begriffe').

[20] Cp. Klaeber, *ed. cit.*, p. xlix, *ad init.*

ence, but to a lack of formulas capable of adaptation to such ideas. The lyrically keyed poem on the Advent (*Christ I*) and the song on the Ascension (*Christ II*), based on the latter part of Pope Gregory the Great's Ascension homily, are both traditional in diction and adhere pretty strictly to narrative.[21]

It would be wrong to suggest that the adaptation of the traditional language of the ancient poetry to this new and different thematic material did not take doing on the part of the singers or to withhold from them full credit for the successful exercise of what at the outset particularly must have called for skill and ingenuity. It is, however, fair to point out, in view of the obviously traditional language of the Christian poems — a matter that in essence has long since been noticed and stressed — that the singers did not make things unnecessarily hard for themselves by attempting to sing about matters for the expression of which the old diction would have been inadequate. As it was singers and audience probably felt little difference between the general style and narrative technique of, say, *Béowulf* and *Christ and Satan,* to mention two poems of very different thematic backgrounds. This marked uniformness or unity of style is largely to be accounted for by the continuity of the traditional formulaic language of the Anglo-Saxon singers, a continuity that seems to live until the Norman Conquest.

Many factors, political and social as well as linguistic, probably contributed to the death of the traditional poetry after the Conquest, and one must also reckon with the difficulties, prob-

[21] P.S. Mr. Robert E. Diamond, presently engaged in the study of 'The Diction of the Signed Poems of Cynewulf' (Harvard thesis in preparation) tells me (30 April 1953) that 20 per cent of the 5194 verses (i.e., 2598 numbered typographic lines of the editions) in the signed poems of Cynewulf are repeated in the signed poems themselves. A series of samples, amounting to 581 verses (including the entire *Fates of the Apostles,* the runic passages in the other three poems, and several 15-20 line samples chosen at random from the other three poems), checked against the entire Anglo-Saxon poetical corpus, shows 30.8 per cent of repeated verses, and 61.1 per cent of verses, of which parts, by virtue of recurrence elsewhere, demonstrate themselves to be formulaic.

ably insuperable, which the relatively swift introduction of ideas and activities incidental to the advent of the feudal age brought in their train, ideas which could not easily be sidestepped by singers trying to sing in the old tradition and for which they had no formulas.

Quite by chance the present passage from *Christ and Satan* offers an opportunity to consider the general possibility of the use of an understanding of the role of the formula in occasional matters of textual criticism. Verse 513b, with the manuscript reading *ǽr on morgen* (A), 'early in the morning,' technically violates a basic principle of alliteration in that the first down-beat or ictus in the off-verse does not here alliterate with the preceding on-verse where the alliteration is *m*. Acting on a suggestion of Professor Holthausen, Professor M. D. Clubb emended this verse in his edition of 1925 to read *on morgen ǽr,* thus producing which he rightly described as a normal (B) verse. Nevertheless, in the light of the supporting evidence which demonstrates the existence of a formula *ǽr on morgen,* taken together with the phrase *on ǽr-morgen,* with which may also be compared *mid ǽr-dœge* of similar meaning, one may wonder whether the singer did not himself violate the usual procedures of alliteration in order to make use of a formula that he needed, a formula or system in which *ǽr* preceded the word it modified. Consequently, one might do well, not only here but in other similar situations, to test such alliteratively defective verses for their formulaic character before embarking on a course of emendation, however much better emendation may make, or may seem to make, matters. If given time to think his verse over, in a word to compose at a more leisurely pace, a singer might well agree with what a modern editor was proposing to do; on the other hand, such an emendation might produce a sequence of words which would strike him as stranger than the technical defect in versification.

If this discussion of manuscript *ǽr on morgen* suggests that it should be left regardless of the technical imperfection that its use and retention produces, the case of manuscript *on þæm fæstenne* (519a) would seem to speak in favor of emendation to *of þæm fæstenne,* 'from, out of the tomb,' an emendation adopted by certain earlier editors, though not by Clubb or Krapp, last to edit the poem. The supporting evidence on Chart II exhibits two expressions, one with *fram* or *of,* meaning 'from or out of the prison, stronghold or tomb,' the other with *on,* always except here with the obvious meaning 'in the prison, stronghold or tomb.' Now it is true that Old-English uses expressions with *on* which are convenient to render by 'from,' generally in connection with removing something from a surface on which the object in question is lying or reposing (see B.T. *s.v.* 'on,' III, 2). From the Anglo-Saxon point of view *on* is in these cases entirely appropriate, though the approach to the act is different from ours. It is as if one said 'he took the pencil *on* the table,' that is, 'he took the pencil which was lying on the table,' in the sense that he took it *from* the table. When Grendel assails Béowulf, it is said that the troll *nam . . . rinc on ræste* (ll. 746-47), 'took the warrior from his resting place.' This is, however, far from saying that OE *on* means 'from'; it is simply to say that the image of the action is different. In the verse in *Christ and Satan* such an image would in the nature of things be highly unlikely if not out of the question altogether. The singer must be trying to say that Our Lord went out of the tomb and thus it is all but certain that the manuscript *on* does not go back to the words of the singer or to anybody who was giving attention to the thought but to a miscopying by a scribe somewhere along the line of written transmission. If this is so, then in the small verbal matter of the preposition, manuscript *on,* the supporting evidence involving *on's* does not support the manuscript reading, but rejects it rather.

The future is full of many problems involving a reappraisal of certain aspects of Anglo-Saxon poetical style and compositional technique and what these are, or at present seem likely to be, can here be merely adumbrated. First of all let it be said that, if further study of the formulaic character of the poetry is to be conducted in a thoroughgoing way, the first and most crying need is the construction of a concordance of the entire poetical corpus; without this the collecting of supporting evidence to test the formulaic character of a given verse or group of verses will prove to be incredibly laborious and often uncertain.[22]

More sample analyses of narrative verse are certainly desirable, though it seems doubtful that any narrative poem will be found to be non-traditional in language. Particularly interesting will be a study from this point of view of the diction of the rather small body of lyrical-elegaic poetry. One might suspect that lyrical composition would call for formulas not elsewhere used and that for many of the verses there would be little or no supporting evidence of their formulaic character, due to the limited size of the body of lyric-elegiac verse. The same may be said of the literary *Riddles* of the *Exeter Book*, a genre new to the Anglo-Saxons and a direct imitation of Latin enigmas, specifically those 685-705? of Aldhelm, of which two are translated into Old English. At least some of the language of the *Riddles* is traditional, since verses from these appear in the support-evidence in the charts above, but it may turn out that many riddles, often very short compositions, were composed word by word. And what of the verses that embody runes other

[22] For any comparative study of Old-Germanic formulaic diction concordances are equally needed for the Old-Norse Edda-type verse (*Eddukvæði* of Mod. Icel. parlance) and for the Old-Saxon corpus (see n. 26, below).

Efficient techniques for concordance-making have been worked out by Professor Emeritus Lane Cooper of Cornell University and are set forth in considerable detail in 'The Making and the Use of a Verbal Concordance,' *Sewanee Review*, XXVII (1919), 188-206, esp. pp. 191-195, reprinted in his *Evolution and Repentance* (Ithaca, N. Y., 1935), esp. pp. 24-33. See also his 'Instructions for preparing the Slips,' three pages, inserted in *A Concordance to the Works of Horace* (Washington, D. C., 1916). No concordance should ever be attempted without consulting these writings.

than isolated logograms (e.g., *éðel* and *mann*), notably Cynewulf's signature passages?[23]

Mention of Cynewulf raises a question concerning the relation between lettered persons and orally composed poetry. Not all Anglo-Saxon Christian poetry needs to have been composed by lettered singers — witness the story of Cædmon. Any good unlettered singer who had translated for, or expounded to, him the *Apocryphal Gospel of St. Matthew and St. Andrew* could easily have composed *Andreas*. But Cynewulf was surely a lettered person, else how could he have conceived a plan to assure mention of his name in prayers by means of runic signatures which depend on a knowledge of spelling and reading for their efficacy?[24] If, however, the narrative parts of his poems prove on testing to be formulaic, one must assume that those parts at least he composed in the traditional way. That he subsequently got them written down, whether dictating to himself, as it were, or to another person — possibly a more convenient procedure — is beside the point. In any event there would be no conflict with, or contradiction to, tradition.[25]

A different view will, I think, have to be taken of the significance or lack of significance of phrasal similarities between

[23] P.S. Mr. Diamond further informs me that the four verse paragraphs which include the runic signatures (72 typographic lines in all), checked against the entire Anglo-Saxon poetical corpus, show 25.6 per cent of repeated verses and 52.7 per cent of verses, of which parts, by virtue of recurrence elsewhere, show themselves to be formulaic.

[24] From *Juliana* 718b-22 it is clear that the poem was intended for recitation (*þe þis giedd wrece*) and that a prayer was hoped for from a singer rather than some indefinite reading public. Does this suggest that Anglo-Saxon poems got put on record primarily for memorization by a class of later, memorizing entertainers, answering somewhat to the Greek rhapsodes of post-oral times? One thinks here of Asser's familiar ch. 23 (ed. W. H. Stevenson, p. 20, notes on p. 221) where we are told that Alfred learned by heart native poems read aloud to him by his mother.

[25] On oral-formulaic verse making by lettered persons see Parry II, 29, and Bowra, *op. cit.*, esp. pp. 370-372.

this and that poem and poems than has prevailed up to now.[26] Certain verbal similarities among poems may in a sense represent borrowing from one poem to another, for traditional singers perforce learn from other singers. But one verbal similarity or even a number of verbal similarities in themselves prove nothing beyond suggesting that given singers have found the same formulas useful to express a certain idea in a similar measure of verse. To quote Parry, 'Plagiarism is not possible in traditional literature. One oral poet is better than another not because he has by himself found a more striking way of expressing his thought, but because he has been better able to make use of the tradition.'[27] When by the aid of a concordance we gradually get to know what the Anglo-Saxon formulas are and what, indeed, constitute their dimensions[28] and the like, it will perhaps be possible to begin to detect individual styles. Apart from general over-all organization of material, the broad architectonics of a given poem, a singer's individuality will, as in other traditional poetry, presumably emerge in rather small matters,[29]

[26] E.g., Klaeber, *ed. cit.*, pp. cx-cxiii. For a competent survey of thought on 'the testimony of the parallels' see Claes Schaar, *Critical Studies in the Cynewulf Group* (Lund Studies in English, XVII, Lund, 1949), pp. 235 ff. Over sixty years ago J. Kail, 'Über die Parallelstellen in der angelsächsischen Poesie,' *Anglia*, XII (1889-90), 21-40, was clearly nearer right than he lived to know. In the case of Old-Saxon poetry a start was made by Eduard Sievers in his ed. of the *Hêliand* (Halle, 1878) through his very comprehensive though inconveniently arranged 'Formelverzeichnis,' pp. 391-463, a reference for which I am most grateful to Professor Fernand Mossé of the Collège de France.

[27] Parry II, 13.

[28] Parry I, 84-85, n. 3, would for Homeric verse regard as a formula or a possible formula nothing less than four words or five syllables, a restriction that could not be applied to Anglo-Saxon verse.

[29] I am thinking of such small points as the *þe* of the formula *þe hit riht ne wæs* (*Mal* 190) contrasted to the *swá*'s of the parallel formula in *Gen* 901, *Vainglory* 61, with *gerisne* (*Gen* 1564) *gedéfe* (*PPs* 105, 22; *Met* 26, 90), *geþíewe* (*Bwf* 2331), references for which I am grateful to Dr. Randolph Quirk of University College, London. Without the negative cp. *Bwf* 561,1670 (with *gedéfe*).

verbal and stylistic, and will not be revealed by the large and rather obvious components known to all or almost all singers.

Lack of truly early material will preclude our ever knowing much about the relative age of the formulas encountered in the preserved poems, but perhaps something can be done with verses containing words which in earlier times had suffered contraction, either from the simple contraction of two vowels (as *dón*<*dó-an*) or as a secondary result of the loss of intervocalic *h* (as *héan*<*héahan*).[30] The poetry abounds in such verses as *héan landes* (*Gen* 2854b) which, if pronounced as they almost surely were pronounced in later times, were metrically deficient though at the time created they formed metrically regular verses: *héahan landes* (A). The becoming unmetrical of such a verse would have been a gradual process and singers would naturally have hung on to it as long as possible, down, in fact, to the time when the contraction-process had long since been completed. This

[30] For a somewhat analogous phenomenon see Parry II, 10, 30-31, and *idem*, 'Traces of the Digamma in Ionic and Lesbian Greek,' *Language*, x (1934), 130-144, esp. 131 and n. 6, for reference to *Béowulf*. See also Whitelock, *op. cit.*, p. 27 and n. 1, for general observations on intervocalic *h* and for references. Since the formulas in which contracted forms occur are, like the rest of the diction, traditional, their occurrence can tell us little about the age of a text in which they appear.

P.S. In his splendid and welcome edition *Béowulf with the Finnesburg Fragment* (Boston: Heath, 1953); 2d ed., London: Harrap, 1958, Professor C. L. Wrenn has taken the revolutionary step of decontracting the various contracted forms over which previous editors have placed a circumflex (see pp. 31-32), e.g., *fré* [*ge*]*a* (16b) for manuscript *fréa*, *dó*[*a*]*n* (1116b) for manuscript *dón*. Were there any evidence that such words (discussed in Luick, §§ 242-249, pp. 218-226) were pronounced as if uncontracted at the time when the text was first committed to writing, one would welcome such a procedure, however daring, as restoring the meter of otherwise metrically deficient verses (for literature see Luick § 242, nn. 2-3, p. 219). But the phenomenon of contraction had almost surely quite run its course by, say, 650. (See Luick, § 249, pp. 225-226: after the working of *i*-umlaut; for a few exceptional survivals of sorts see Sievers-Brunner, 2d ed., § 218, 3, p. 197; Northumbrian *dóan*'s and the like are late and are analogical restorations comparable to Mod. Icel. *smáum* for *smám* of the old language and do not help here.)

would suggest that later-day singers and their audiences became habituated to such metrical irregularities and accepted these 'deficient' verses as traditional.[31] This matter might profitably be further explored.

Just as the half-hexameter is the basis of most Homeric formulas, so is the single verse that of Old-Germanic poetry. But in the Homeric poems there are also whole-line formulas[32] answering in a sense apparently to such Anglo-Saxon verse-pair formulas as *on þǽm dæge þisses lífes* (*Bwf* 197, 790, 806), *þæs oferéode: þisses swá mæg* (*Déo* 7, 13, 17, 20, 42), and *siþþan of líc-haman lǽded wǽre* (*Vercelli SlB* 21) with which cp. *Bwf* 3177, where *of líc-haman lǽded weorðan* is almost surely the right reading (cp. *Jul* 670a).

Oral singers are often faced with situations where enjambement is required,[33] and the Anglo-Saxon singers appear to be no exception. *Béowulf* offers at least one interesting example where enjambement is accomplished with the aid of a two-verse formula: *ende gebídan / weorolde lífes* (*Bwf* 1386b-87a, 2342b-43a); Dr. Whitelock has already pointed out how the formula *God éaðe mæg* (*Bwf* 478b, *And* 425b. *Chr* 173b) operates in this situation.[34]

There is perhaps much that will never be known about the origin and special function, if any, of the expanded or hypermetric verses, but a casual survey suggests that, whereas the second measure of each such verse seems to be formulaic and

[31] See Parry II, 22-23, n. 1, for instances in Homeric verse where the retention of a formula leads to a violation of meter.

[32] Parry, 'Whole Formulaic Verses in Greek and Southslavic Heroic Song,' *Transactions of the American Philological Association,* LXIV (1933), 179-197.

[33] See Lord, 'Homer and Huso III: Enjambement in Greek and Southslavic Song,' *ibid.,* LXXXIX (1948), 113-124.

[34] *Op. cit.,* p. 10. This formula is a phase of the system *x éaðe mæg;* cp. *B* 2764 *sinc éaðe mæg*. There are other systems with forms of *magan* to express the idea of the possibility of something happening or being done.

out of its context would form a complete verse, the organization of the first measure would appear to be somewhat different, perhaps somewhat less rigid in structure, thus perhaps allowing the singer certain freedoms not available in a normal verse. Here, too, a concordance will be necessary for further study of the character of these first measures.[35]

At the end of these rather miscellaneous remarks on possible problems of the future, problems which will require the thought of many persons to test and solve, I should like to comment on the possible relation of one aspect of the physical preservation of our Anglo-Saxon poems that may reflect their oral background, namely, the fact of their all being written out as prose. It is a not uncommon view that this method was employed as a measure of economy, that the vernacular poetry was perhaps felt not quite worth, or worthy of, as much parchment as writing the poetry out as we today print it would require. I find it hard to believe this to be the case and suspect it was written as prose merely because neither scribes nor singers understood in a formal sense the metrics of the verse, even when they may have had an understanding of Latin verse studied in monastic schools. That tenth-eleventh century scribes at times separate verses (not our typographical lines) by dots may merely reflect a feeling for the basic rhythm, the onset of a down-beat, comparable to a musically unschooled person's tapping time with foot or finger though knowing nothing of the writing of music or of musical composition.

CHART I

(Béowulf, ll. 1-25)

Hwæt, wé Gár-Dena on géar-dagum
þéod-cyninga þrymm gefrugnon,
hú þá æðelingas ellen fremedon.
Oft Scield Scéafing sceaðena þréatum,

[35] An impetus to a revaluation of the expanded verses has recently been given by Benno J. Timmer, 'Expanded Lines in Old-English Poetry,' *Neophilologus,* xxxv (1951), 226-230.

5 manigum mægðum medu-setla oftéah,
egesode Eorle, siþþan ærest wearþ
féasceaft funden; hé þæs frófre gebád,
wéox under wolcnum, weorþ-myndum þáh,
oþ-þæt him ǽghwelć ymbsittendra
10 ofer hran-ráde híeran scolde,
gamban gieldan; þæt wæs gód cyning!
Þǽm eafora wæs æfter cenned
geong on geardum, þone God sende
folce to frófre; firen-þearfe ongeat
15 þe híe ǽr drugon ealdorléase
lange hwíle; him þæs Líf-fréâ,
wuldres Wealdend weorold-áre forgeaf
Béow wæs bréme — blǽd wíde sprang —
Scieldes eafora Sceden-landum on.
20 Swá sceal geong guma góde gewyrćan
framum feoh-giftum on fæder bearme
þæt hine on ielde eft gewunien
will-gesíðas þanne wíg cume,
léode gelǽsten; lof-dǽdum sceal
25 on mǽgða gehwǽm man geþêon.

SUPPORTING EVIDENCE

1a-2b Hwæt, wé feorr and néah / gefrigen habbaþ (*Exo* 1); Hwæt, wé gefrugnon / on fyrn dagum (*And* 1); Hwæt, wé þæt gehíerdon / þurh hálge béć (*FAp* 63, *Ele* 364, 852); Hwæt, wé éac gehíerdon / be Ióhanne (*FAp* 23); Hwæt, wé nú gehíerdon / hú þæt Hǽlubearn (*Chr* 586, *with whose* gehíerdon *cp. Bwf* 2b-3a gefrugnon hú); Hwæt, wé hierdon oft / þæt se hálige wer (*Glc* 108); Hwæt, wé þæt gehíerdon / hæleþ eahtian (*Jul* 1); Hwæt, wé Ebréisce æ leornodon / þá on fyrn-dagum fæderas cúðon (*Ele* 397-98). **1b** *XSt* 367, *Wan* 44. Cp. *Chr* 251 þe on géar-dagum; *Bwf* 1354 þone on géar-dagum, 2233 swá híe on géar-dagum. *Note also instrum. use without* on: *And* 1519 giefum géar-dagum; *Ele* 290 þæt gé géar-dagum, 834 swá hie géar-dagum (*also Bwf* 2233). *Note closely related formulas:* on fyrn-dagum, on ǽr-dagum, *and* on eald-dagum (*Chr* 303, *SFt* 1). **2a** *Nom. pl. Gen* 1965 þéod-cyningas / þrymme mićele; *gen. sg. Bwf* 2694 þá ić æt þearfe gefrægn / þéod-cyninges; *FAp* 18 Ne þréodode hé fore þrymme / þéod-cyninges; *Edw* 34 þæs-þe þearf wæs / þæs þéod-cyninges. **2b** *See* 1-2 *above for combination of formulas to express the idea of 'having heard or learned long ago.'* **3a** *FAp* 3 hú þá æðelingas / ellen cýðdon, 85 þus þá æðelingas; *Rid* 49, 7 þá æðelingas. *Cp. without def. art. but with a preceding word, usually of light stress Gen* 1059 þára-þe æðelingas, 1647 þá nú æðelingas, 1868 ellor æðelingas;

Dan 689, *And* 805 þær æðelingas, 857 Him þá æðelingas. **3b** *And* 1208 Scealt þú, Andréas, / ellen fremman. **4b** *Jul* 672 sceaðena þréate; *cp. Glc* 902 féonda þréatum.

5a *Bwf* 75 manigre mǽgðe, 1771 manigum mǽgða. **6b** *Bwf* 1947; cp. 1775 siþþan Grendel wearþ; *Ele* 913 siþþan furðum wéox. *Note the more general metrical scheme involving* siþþan *plus a two- or three-syllable word plus verb: And* 1223 siþþan ge-ypped wæs; *Ele* 18 siþþan wǽpen ahóf, 841 siþþan béacen geseah; *Bwf* 1077, 2124 siþþan morgen (mergen) cóm, 1233 siþþan ǽfen cóm, 1689 siþþan flód ofslóg. **7a** Cp. *And* 181 onfindap féasceaftne. **8a** *Gen* 1702 wéox þá under wolcnum; cp. *Bwf* 714 Wód under wolcnum; *Phx* 27 wrídaþ under wolcnum; *Gen* 1438 wǽre under wolcnum; *Phx* 247 awierde under wolcnum. **8b** *Exo* 258 weorþ-myndum spræc. **9a** *Ele* 865 oþ-þæt him gecýðde, 885 oþ-þæt him uppan. **9b** *Bwf* 2734, *Ele* 33. *Cp. other inflections: dat. pl.* ymbsittendum *PPs* 78, 4; 88, 35; *fem. acc. pl. Met* 35, 14 ymbsittenda. *Cp. closely related Gen* 2490 ymbstandendra; *PPs* 140, 4 ymbstandende.

10a *Gen* 205 geond hran-ráde; *And* 266, 821 on hran-ráde. *Cp. Bwf* 200, *Ele* 996 ofer swan-ráde; *Jul* 675 on swan-ráde; *Bwf* 1429 on segl-ráde. **10b** *Dan* 135; *Ele* 367; *Met* 9, 45; *Met* 1, 31 híeran scoldon. **11a** *Gen* 1977b-78a níede scoldon, / gamban gieldan. **11b** *Bwf* 863, 2390. *Cp. Bwf* 1885 þæt wæs án cyning; *Jul* 224 þæt is sóþ cyning; *Déo* 23 þæt wæs grimm cyning; *Wíd* 67 Næs þæt sǽne cyning, *and further Bwf* 1075 þæt wæs geómru ides, 1812 þæt wæs módig secg; *Met* 26, 35 (?) þæt wæs geó cyning, *etc.* **12a** *Gen* 1188 Se eafora wæs / Énoc háten. *Note and cp. Bwf* 12a-b eafora . . . cenned *with Gen* 1159 þá wearþ on éðle / eafora féded, 2394 of idese biþ / eafora wæcned. **12b** *Cp. Cæd* 8 æfter téode; *Rid* 40, 44 and ić giestran geong cenned. **13a** *Phx* 355, 647; *Chr* 201 geongre on geardum. *Cp. Jul* 35 geong on gáste; *Bwf* 2446 geong on gealgan. **13b** *Dan* 525 þe þider God sende; *cp. Gen* 1371 Dryhten sende. **14a** *Exo* 88; *And* 606; *Ele* 1142; *Men* 228 folcum to frófre; *Ele* 502 folca to frófre; *Rid* 39, 19 manigum to frófre; *Men* 57, *Ps 50* 148 mannum to frófre.

15a *Bwf* 831, 1875; *Chr* 615 þe wé ǽr drugon; *Jud* 158 þe gé lange drugon. **15b** *Cp. Bwf* 2935; *And* 405 hláfordléase. *Ealdorléas* is ordinarily used in the sense 'lifeless.' **16a** *Bwf* 2159, 2780; *Dan* 660; *DrR* 24; *Jul* 674; *Rid* 28, 9; *Met* 4, 46. *For numerous formulas to express a 'long' or 'short time' cp. DrR* 70 góde hwíle, *also* mićele, lýtle, sume hwíle, *and with* þráge: *ealle, lýtle, lange, sume, also* ǽnige stunde. **16b** *Cp. Exo* 271 and éow Líf-fréa; *Chr* 27 hwanne ís Líf-fréa. **17a** *Bwf* 183, 1752; *Dan* 14; *And* 193, 539. **18a** *Sol* 182 Saloman wæs brémra; *Dan* 104 Þá wæs bréme; *Sol* 238 béć sind bréme. **18b** *FAp* 6 Lof wíde sprang; *cp. Bwf* 1588 hráw wíde sprang; *Jul* Léad wíde sprang; *also Max I* 194 wíde gesprungen. **19a** *Bwf* 897 Wælses eafora; 1847 Hréðles eaforan; *Gen* 1133 Séthes eafora, 2054 Þáres eafora; *Met* 26, 36 Ióbes (*Jove's*) eafora; *Men* 136 Zebedes eafora. *Cp. also Gen* 1578 eafora Nóes, 2834 eafora Þáres. **19b** *Bwf* 2357 Frís-landum on; *Gen* 1052 éast-landum on. *Cp. Jul* 83 wín-(wynn?) burgum on.

20a *Bwf* 1172, 1534 Swá sceal man dôn; *cp.* 2066 Swá sceal mǽg dôn, 2590 swá sceal ǽghwelć mann. **21b** *Cp. Bwf* 35, *Exo* 375 on bearm scipes, 896 bær on bearm scipes, 214 on bearm nacan. *Note related formula with* fæðm: *Bwf* 188 and to Fæder fæðmum; *Max II* 661 on Fæder fæðm; *And* 616 on banan fæðme; *Ele* 765 on dracan fæðme. **22a-b** *Cp. FoM* 60 and on ielde eft / éadig weorðan. **22b** *See* 22a-b, *also Phx* 481 lang gewunien. **23a** *Gen* 2003. **25a** *Pre* 74 þá-þe hér on mǽgðe gehwǽm.

CHART II

(Christ and Satan, ll. 512-35)

Swá wuldres Weard wordum sægde,
Meotod mann-cynnes, ǽr on morgen,
þæs-þe Dryhten God of déaðe arás.
515 Næs nán þæs stranglića stán gefæstnod,
þéah hé wǽre mid írne eall ymbfangen
þæt meahte þǽm mićelan mægene wiþhabban,
ac Hé út éode, enǵla Dryhten
on þǽm fæstenne. And gefetian hét
520 enǵlas eall-beorhte endleofan giengran,
and húru secgan hét Símon Pétre
þæt hé móste on Galiléam God scéawian,
éćne and trumme, swá hé ǽr dyde.
Þá ić gangan gefrægn giengran ætsamme
525 ealle to Galiléam; hæfdon Gástes blǽd,
(ongéaton) háligne Godes Sunu
swá híe gesáwon, hwǽr Sunu Meotodes
þá on upp (a-?) stód, éće Dryhten
God on Galiléam. To þæs giengran þider
530 ealle urnon, þær se Éća wæs.
Féollon on foldan, to fótum hnigon;
þancodon Þeodne þæt hit þus gelamp
þæt híe scéawodon Scieppend enǵla.
Þá sóna spræc Símon Pétrus:
"Eart þú þis, Dryhten, dómes geweorðod?"

SUPPORTING EVIDENCE

512a *XSt* 659. Cp. *Gen* 941 Híe þá wuldres Weard; *And* 596 hú ús wuldres Weard; *Ele* 84 (beseoh) on wuldres Weard; *Chr* 527 þá wæs wuldres Weard. **512b** *Gen* 707, 2053, 2704, *Glc* 451. Cp. *Exo* 377, *Phx* 425 wordum secgaþ; *And* 624 wordum gesecgan; *Chr* 64 wordum sægdon;

Bwf wordum secge. **513a** *Sat* 457, *Gen* 459, *And* 172, 357, 446. **513b** *Frag. Ps* 5, 3; *also cp. PPs* 107, 2, 118, 148 on ǽrmergen, *PPs* 62, 7 and on ǽrmergen; *Met* 28, 37; *PPs* 56, 10 and ić on ǽrmergene. **514a** *XSt* 313 mid Dryhtne Gode; *And* 1281 Geseoh nú Dryhten God, 1462 Þá cóm Dryhten God; *Pan* 55 Swá is Dryhten God; *Bwf* 181 ne wisson híe Dryhten God; *Jud* 300 him féng Dryhten God; *LPr* 3 18 Críst, Dryhten God. *Cp.* God Dryhten *in And* 897 Nú ić God Dryhten, *Ele* 759 Þæs þú, God Dryhten; *also* Dryhten Críst *in Glc* 592 gief éow Dryhten Críst; *Sol* 337 Dryhtne Críste. **514b** *Ele* 187; *FAp* 56 þæt hé of déaðe arás; *Chr* 467 fram déaðe arás.

515a *Cp. Chr* 241 for-þon n'is ǽnig þæs horsc; *GfM* 8 Ne biþ ǽnig þæs / earfoþ-sǽlig; *Sea* 39 For-þon n'is þæs mód-wlanc. **515b** *Cp. Jul* 499 folde (*subj.*) gefæstnod. **516b** *XSt* 143b (*cp.* 145a selfe mid sange); *cp. Bwf* 2691 heals eallne ymbeféng. **518b** *Exo* 559; *XSt* 395; *Sol* 462. **519a** *Wha* 71; *And* 1034 fram þǽm fæstenne, 1177 of fæstenne; *cp. Gen* 2536, *And* 1068 to þǽm fæstenne; *Sol.* 320 on fæstenne; *Met* 1, 79 né on þǽm fæstenne. **519b** *Gen* 525 and meć hér standan hét; *XSt* 521 and húru secgan hét; *And* 330 and ús féran hét, 587 and wendan hét; *Bwf* 3095 and éowić grétan hét. *Cp. with subordination: Gen* 1865 oþ-þæt hé lǽdan hét; *And* 823 Þá gelǽdan hét, 931 swá ić þeć féran hét; *Ele* 863 ǽr hé asettan hét, *also* 129 arǽran hét. *With finite verb first: Gen* 2667 hét him fetian tó; *Ele* 1160, *Jul* 60 hét þá gefetian; *Bwf* 2190a-b hét . . . inn fetian.

520a *Chr* 880; *Aza* 52 enġel ealle-beorhta; *Dan* 336 enġel eall-beorht. *For this formula used to connect a verse-pair of consecutive off- and on-verses see Chr* 506 Gesáwon híe eall-beorhte / enġlas twégen, 548 þæt him eall-beorhte / enġlas togéanes. **521a** *see* 519b, *above.* **521b** *XSt* 534b Símon Pétrus. **522a-b** *Cp.* 529a. **522b** *For* scéawian *with preceding object entering into the alliteration: see Gen* 979 (tíber), 1679 (weorc), 1780, 1920 (land), 2595 (wíć), *Chr* 1136 (weorod), 1206 (dolg), *Rid* 59, 2 (menn); *Bwf* 840, 3032 (wundor), 1391 (gang), 1413 (wang), 2402 (dracan), 2744 (hord). **523a** *Cp. Chr* 1071 éće and edgeong. **523b** *Gen* 1840; *XSt* 116, 278. *Cp. Chr* 1233 swá híe geworhton ǽr, 161 þá þú geworhtest ǽr. **524a** *Gen* 2060 þá ić néðan gefrægn; *And* 1706 Þá ić lǽdan gefrægn; cp. *Sol* 179 Hwæt, ić flítan gefrægn.

525b *Cp. Phx* 549 þurh gástes blǽd; *XSt* 644 gemunan Gástes blǽd; **526b** *Gen* 1163 Enoses sunu; *XSt* 118 Wealdendes Sunu; *Bwf* 1009 Healf-Denes sunu; 2602, 2862, 3076 Wéoh-stánes sunu; *Wal I,* 11 Ælf-heres sunu. *For the closely parallel and more common patronymic formula* sunu X's *see* 527b. **527b** *XSt* 142 þær Sunu Meotodes, 172 Sunu Meotodes; *And* 881 Swelće wé gesáwon / for Sunu Meotodes; *Ele* 1318 and to Suna Meotodes, 461, 564 sóþ Sunu Meotodes, 474 hú híe Sunu Meotodes, 686 þurh Sunu Meotodes. *Cp. XSt* Sunu Wealdendes. *With the substitution of various personal names cp.: Gen* 1064 (Enoses), 1081, 1086 (Lámeches), 1240 (Nóes), 2465 (Arones); *Bwf* 524 (Béan-stánes),

590 (Ecg-láfes), 645, 1040 (Healf-Denes), *etc. For a patronymic formula centering on* eafora *see Chart 1,* 19b. **528a** *Cp. And* 443 Hwílum upp astód, *and note other combinations of* upp *and* astandan *in Grein-Holthausen-Köhler, suggesting the XSt* 530a *Ms.* stod *should, perhaps be emended to* astód *vs.* gestód *of the editors.* **528b** *Frag. Ps.* 5, 1, 3; *PPs* 53, 4; 70, 18, 20; 71, 19; 73, 17; 78, 1, etc.; *Cæd* 4; *and in inflected cases as follows: gen. sg. Bru* 16 *Men* 12 éćes Dryhtnes; *Gen* 7, 1885; *Chr* 396, 711; *Phx* 600; *PPs* 67, 3, 9; 68, 29 éćan Dryhtnes; *dat. sg. Bwf* 2796 éćum Dryhtne, 1779, 2330 éćan Dryhtne; *acc. sg. PPs* 55, 9; 65, 1, 3, 7 éćne Dryhten; *Bwf* 1692 éćan Dryhten.

530a *Cp. PPs* 61, 4 wíde urnon. **531a** *XSt* 544 féolon to foldan, *And* 918 Féoll þá to foldan; *Bwf* 2975 féoll on foldan. *Cp. Phx* 74 Ne feallaþ þǽr on foldan; *Sol.* 298 afielleþ hine on foldan. **531b** *Cp. Gen* 2441 þá to fótum [féoll / on foldan] Loth; *Mal* 119 þæt him æt fótum féoll. **532a** *Glc* 778, *and cp. with object (usually God) first: Dan* 86, *And* 1011, *Ele* 1138, *Bwf* 1397 Gode þancode; *Bwf* 227, 1626 Gode þancodon. *Note the combined formulas of Ele* 961-62, *Bwf* 625-26 Gode þancode . . . þæs(-þe) hire se willa gelamp (*see* 532b, *below*). **532b** *XSt* 568 þá hit þus gelamp, *and cp. Ele* 961-62 *and Bwf* 625-26 *under* 532a, *above.* **533b** *And* 434; *And* 119, *XSt* 562 enǵla Scieppend. **534a** *Cp. Gen* 862 þá sóna ongann, 1589 and þá sóna ongeat; *Chr* 233 And þá sóna gelamp; *Bwf* 1280 þá þǽr sóna warþ; *Fin* 46 þá hine sóna frægn. **534b** *XSt* 522 Símon Pétre. **535a** *Bwf* 506 Eart þú sé Béo-wulf.

10

BEOWULF AND THE LITURGY*

Allen Cabaniss

TO APPROACH *Beowulf* FROM THE STANDPOINT OF THE ANTIQUE Christian tradition is to be unavoidably impressed with its Christian coloration—and this despite the non-appearance of specific doctrinal references.[1] Although the story itself is certainly a composite of heathen tales of the early Northland, yet as a finished product by the hand of a courtly and Christian Anglo-Saxon poet in the era of Bede it falls within a "golden age" of Old English learning derived from both Graeco-Roman and ecclesiastical sources. More particularly as one reads the middle section, the account of the struggle with Grendel's mother, he observes a rather strange suggestion of Patristic theological speculation about Christ's "harrowing of hell."[2] Indeed this is adumbrated

* Reprinted, by permission of the author, and the University of Illinois Press, publishers of the *Journal of English and Germanic Philology,* from that journal, LIV (April 1955), 195-201.

[1] Fr. Klaeber, "Die christlichen Elemente im Beowulf," *Anglia* xxxv (1912; Neue Folge Band xxxiii), iii-36, 249-70, 453-82; xxxvi (1912; Neue Folge Band xxiv), 169-99. See also R. W. Chambers *Beowulf: An Introduction,* 2nd ed. (Cambridge: University Press, 1932), pp. 121-28; W. W. Lawrence, *Beowulf and Epic Tradition* (Cambridge, Mass.: Harvard University Press, 1930), pp. 281-84; Ritchie Girvan, *Beowulf and the Seventh Century* (London: Methuen, 1935).

[2] For brief bibliographical references on this topic, consult my note, "The Harrowing of Hell, Psalm 24, and Pliny the Younger," *Vigiliae Christianae,* vii, No. 2 (April, 1953), 65-74.

by Klaeber in his remark that "we need not hesitate to recognize features of the Christian Savior in the destroyer of hellish fiends, the warrior gentle and brave, blameless in thought and deed, the king that dies for his people. Nor is the possibility of discovering direct allusions to the person of the Savior to be ignored."[3]

We may notice the following points in the section about Grendel's mother. First, the mere in which Grendel and his mother lived and into which Beowulf plunged is identified by the poet as hell (lines 852, 1274), an identification which is perhaps strengthened by the statements that it is a water weirdly aflame (1365 f.), reminiscent of the Apocalyptic "lake which burneth with fire and brimstone: which is the second death" (Rev. 21:8; 19:20, etc.); and that it is a habitation of sea-monsters and sea-worms (1425-30, 1510-12; cf. Mark 9:44, 46, 48; Isa. 66:24). Secondly, Beowulf prepares for his descent as though for death. As he girds himself, the hero mourns not at all for life (1442); as he addresses Hrothgar, he gives directions in the event of his dying (1477 f.). The parallel with Christ is even more striking as Beowulf magnanimously forgives his enemy Unferth just before the plunge into the fen-depths (1488-90; cf. Luke 23:34). Third, the descent itself is depicted as a victorious military campaign against the powers below (1441-71; cf. Col. 2:15; I Cor. 2:8; Rev. 1:18; 19:15; Ps. 24:7-10). Fourth, at the moment of victory a beam of preternatural light penetrates the dismal scene beneath the waters and brightens it (1570-2; cf. Isa. 4:2; Luke 1:78 f.)[4] Fifth, in the meanwhile back on the edge of the mere, all the onlookers, except Beowulf's own faithful Geats, supposing that the hero has been killed, give up the vigil

[3] Fr. Klaeber, *Beowulf and the Fight at Finnsburg,* 1st ed. (New York: Heath, 1922), p. li. I have employed Klaeber's edition for all references to the poem. Most of the references are given in parentheses in the body of the paper.

[4] And especially the "Gospel of Nicodemus," 18:1 f., as given in M. R. James, *The Apocryphal New Testament* (Oxford: Clarendon, 1950), 124 f.

at the ninth hour of the day (1594-1602).[5] It will be recalled immediately and inevitably that it was at the very same hour that Christ, abandoned by all but the most faithful few, died on the cross (Matt. 27:46; Mark 15:34, 37; Luke 23:44-46). Sixth, the returning champion brings with him trophies of his victory (1612-15; cf. Col. 2:15). Finally, there is a suggestion of winter's end and springtime's burgeoning as Beowulf comes up in triumph (1608-11), which, although not strictly Biblical, is one of the most ancient of Easter themes.

Thus, in succession of ideas and motifs, there is a significant parallel between Beowulf's adventure and Christ's death, harrowing of hell, and resurrection. Closer examination, however, reveals that the apparent similarities to the "harrowing" are enveloped, as within widening concentric circles, by allusions to the deluge and creation. For instance, the sword-hilt, one of the trophies brought up from the struggle by Beowulf, was the work of the giants who lived before the flood. On it were runes telling of their ancient battles (1677-98), presumably against God (113 f.; cf. Gen. 4:22; 6:3 f., 17). The mention of Cain's fratricide, outlawry, exile, and begetting of ancestors of Grendel (1261-67) recalls the more elaborate treatment earlier in the poem where one of the scops in Heorot sings a song of creation, of beauty-bright land wrought by the Almighty in the midst of encompassing waters, of sun and moon set as light to land-dwellers, of leafy woods adorning regions of earth, and of human life shaped by the same Eternal (90-114).[6] It was this song uttered to the music of the harp which incited Grendel, of the evil brood of Cain, to his depredations (99-114).

We have therefore, in the account of Beowulf's encounter with Grendel's mother, a strong central reminiscence of Christ's harrowing of hell which widens to include recollections, next, of the deluge, and then of creation. We may now inquire where else we have the same complex of ideas. The answer is to be found in

[5] Note the very liturgical term, *nōn*, for "ninth hour."
[6] Here one is, of course, reminded of Caedmon.

the rites associated with Christian baptism. In the ancient church these were exceedingly prolonged, occupying the entire period of Lent and culminating in the actual ceremony on Holy Saturday.[7] By the sixth and seventh centuries, however, they had been somewhat curtailed; and, although they were no longer reserved for the Lenten and Paschal seasons, and although the catechumenate had fallen into virtual desuetude, the traditional teaching concerning baptism was preserved in the liturgy of Holy Saturday.

Originally the candidate for baptism was examined at the beginning of Lent concerning his character, disposition, and intention by the bishop who then enrolled his name in the register. The allegoresis of ancient theologians interpreted the questioning as recalling the temptation (trying, testing) of Christ, thus a conflict with Satan, hence similar to the temptation of Adam; and the registering of the name as an anticipation of the recording of the name in the book of life. Lent itself was one long preparation for baptism with frequent exorcisms of the candidate because Satan (serpent, dragon) was barring the road to salvation at every turn.[8]

[7] The ritual of Holy Saturday persists with little change today and may be consulted in any edition of *Missale Romanum*. The baptismal rite may be read in *Rituale Romanum*. See also Adrian Fortescue, *The Ceremonies of the Roman Rite Described,* 8th ed., rev. and aug. J. C. O'Connell (Westminster, Md.: Newman Press, 1949), *ad loc.* For historical considerations, consult L. Duchesne, *Christian Worship: Its Origin and Evolution,* trans. M. L. McClure, 5th ed. reprinted (London: Society for the Propagation of Christian Knowledge, 1949), pp. 250-57, 292-338; A. Fortescue, *The Mass,* 9th impression (London: Longmans, Green, 1950); Gregory Dix, *The Shape of the Liturgy,* 2nd ed., 3rd impression (Westminster: Dacre, 1947). Although it belongs to the tenth century, the *Regularis Concordia* has an interesting description of English usage concerning the "new fire," especially the employment of a dragon-shaped candlestick; see Thomas Symons (ed. and trans.), *Regularis Concordia* (New York: Oxford University Press, 1953), p. 39.

[8] For an excellent discussion of ancient baptismal symbolism, see Jean Daniélou, *Bible et Liturgie* (Paris: Les Éditions du Cerf, 1951), a rewarding study of the Biblical theology of the sacraments and ecclesiastical festivals as it is expressed in the Church Fathers. Since it is replete with detailed citations of the Patristic sources, I shall not attempt to reiterate

The grand climax came on Holy Saturday. The ceremonies began with the blessing of the new fire, the readying and lighting of the Paschal candle accompanied by the singing of the *Exultet,* the solemn reading of the twelve "prophecies," and the blessing of the font. Then came the administration of baptism. In the baptistery (usually an octagonal structure), often embellished with a portrayal of the Good Shepherd and His sheep amid beautiful trees and flowers, a fountain nearby where harts slaked their thirst, directly opposite a representation of the fall and expulsion of Adam and Eve from Paradise, the candidate, facing westward, renounced the devil and all his pomps; then, facing eastward, professed allegiance to Christ. Anointed with holy oil, like an athlete made ready for a struggle, and signed with the proprietary and protective *sphragis* (seal) of the cross, thus rendered redoubtable against demons, the neophyte entered the baptismal pool. Saint Cyril of Jerusalem referred to this particular act as a descent into the waters of death, into the habitat of the sea-dragon, just as Christ went down into Jordan where dwelled the monster Behemoth (Job 40:15, 23). The font is therefore both the burial place of the old Adam and the maternal womb of the New Adam. After the baptism there followed the litany and the first Mass of Easter.

It is of special importance to scrutinize more closely the content of the *Exultet* and the twelve prophecies, for they are the proximate source of the Patristic teachings about the symbolism of baptism. Sung in the grave tone of the Gospel, the *Exultet* blesses Christ who paid for us the debt of Adam's transgression; commemorates the passage of Israel dry-shod through the Red Sea led by the pillar of fire; adverts to the triumphant harrowing

---

its documentation. The reader is urged to use this very essential work; I rely heavily on it in this paper. This type of interpretation is by no means outmoded; for an illuminating contemporary presentation of it, see L. Bouyer, *The Paschal Mystery,* trans. Sister Mary Benoit (Chicago: Henry Regnery, 1950), a series of appealing meditations on the last three days of Holy Week. Bouyer's approach is essentially Patristic.

of hell; and exults over the moment of resurrection by which "the night shall shine as the day." When the officiant has inserted into the Paschal candle the grains of incense, the chant is resumed begging God to accept this "work of the bees." The same thought follows the lighting of the candle, which is "nourished by the melting wax which the bee as a mother has brought forth for the substance of this precious light." Thereupon ensued a curious Virgilian digression (later deleted by the Church) which is here presented in full.[9]

> The bee excels the other living creatures which have been made subject to man. Although it is least in bodily size, it cherishes great thoughts within its small breast; it is weak in strength but strong in talent. When the round of the seasons has been completed, when frosty winters have laid aside their hoariness and springtime's mildness has supplanted icy decay, immediately to it [the bee] comes zeal for advancing to labor. Scattered through the fields, wings poised delicately, legs uncertain, they settle suddenly with mouth to suck the blossoms. Laden with their nourishment, they wander back to the hive. And there some with incredible art build little cells with firm glue, some compress the flowing honey, some turn flowers into wax, others form offspring with the mouth, still others envelope the nectar with leaves gathered together. O truly blessed and marvelous bee! The males never violate the other sex, they do not shatter the embryo, nor do births destroy chastity! Thus the holy Virgin Mary conceived: as a Virgin she brought forth and as a Virgin she remained.

After the conclusion of the *Exultet,* there begins the reading of a series of twelve lessons, each "explained" by a brief collect. The first reading (Gen. 1:1-31; 2:1-2) sets forth the majestic

[9] The Latin of the passage here translated is given in Duchesne, *op. cit.,* p. 255, where it is dated late eighth century and earlier. Both Duchesne, *op. cit.,* p. 255, n. *2,* and Bouyer, *op. cit.,* p. 271, describe the digression as "Virgilian." That characterization may indeed be correct, but I wonder if it may be ultimately Scriptural. In the Septuagint version of Prov. 6:8, following the familiar passage beginning, "Go to the ant, thou sluggard; consider her ways, and be wise," there is an expansion which reads (my translation): "Or go to the bee, and learn what a worker she is, and her work how respectfully she does it, whose labors kings and commoners use for their health. Desired is she and praised by all; although weak in strength, she is preferred because she has honored wisdom." Some of the Old Latin versions, following the LXX, also have this addition.

story of creation; the second (Gen. 5, 6, 7, 8), the account of the deluge, the saving of Noah's family in the ark, and the new covenant; the third (Gen. 22:1-19), the sacrifice of Isaac; the fourth (Ex. 14:24-31; 15-1), the crossing of the Red Sea and the destruction of Pharaoh's host (this is followed by the singing of the canticle of Moses, Ex. 15:1, 2); the fifth (Isa. 54:17; 55:1-11), a veiled oracular promise of baptism and Eucharist; the sixth (Baruch 3:9-38), a contrast between the deceitful wisdom of the world and the supernatural character of Divine wisdom; the seventh (Ezek. 37:1-14), the vision of the valley of dry bones; the eighth (Isa. 4:1-6), a vision of the ultimate purification and glory of Zion (followed by the canticle of the vineyard, Isa. 5:1-2, 7); the ninth (Ex. 12:1-11), an account of the institution of the Passover; the tenth (Jon. 3:1-10), Jonah's preaching to Nineveh and the repentance of that city; the eleventh (Deut. 31:22-30), Moses' exhortation to fidelity (followed by the canticle of Deut. 32:1-4); and the twelfth (Dan. 3:1-24), the story of the Three Children in the fiery furnace.

It is worthy of note that the succession of theological allusions in *Beowulf* (creation, deluge, harrowing of hell, resurrection) finds interesting parallels in the *Exultet* (where the catalogue is Adam's guilt, passage of the Red Sea, harrowing of hell, resurrection) and in the prophecies (where the catalogue is creation, deluge, sacrifice of Isaac, passage of the Red Sea, a vague prophecy, a Wisdom reference, the valley of dry bones, another prophecy, the Paschal institution, Jonah's preaching, an exhortation, and the fiery furnace). All of the allusions, Biblical and Beowulfian, were used by the Church Fathers as types or symbols of Christian baptism. It seems therefore that the middle section of *Beowulf* is quite heavily laden with a complex of ideas which presuppose familiarity with the baptismal liturgy. It is of added significance that the ancient *Exultet* which the author of *Beowulf* may have known contained that strange and irrelevant eulogy of the bee, indeed it is suggestive if the name Beowulf is correctly interpreted as "Bee-wolf" or "Bee-foe" (that is, "Bear").[10]

However heathen the original story was, it is surely reasonable to suppose that the account of Beowulf's descent into the grim fen, his encounter with the demon-brood staining the water with blood, and his triumphant emergence from it into joyous springtime is, at the least, a reflection of the liturgy of baptism; at the most, an allegory of it.[11] That this view is not on a priori grounds impossible is evident from the quite elaborate Christian allegories of Cynewulf and of the Caedmonian *Exodus,* both approximately contemporary with the *Beowulf*-poet. Indeed the *Exodus* shows precisely the influence of the same twelve Holy Saturday prophecies.[12] And, interestingly enough, it reflects a knowledge of just that portion of *Beowulf* with which we are here concerned.[13] Since it has been demonstrated that the *Exodus* shows the effect of the ancient liturgy of baptism and Holy Saturday, one goes not too far afield in presuming that a similar relationship exists in reference to *Beowulf.*

If we can place the compilation of *Beowulf* within the generous period A.D. 650-825, it is worth recalling that the rite of

[10] On the etymology, see Chambers, *op. cit.,* 365-69. It is by no means far-fetched or improbable to suppose that the mention of one thing may evoke a train of thought dealing with the precise opposite.

[11] On the general plane of the relation of *Beowulf* to allegory, see J. R. R. Tolkien, "Beowulf: The Monsters and the Critics," *Proceedings of the British Academy,* XXII (1936), 245-95; T. M. Gang, "Approaches to *Beowulf,*" *Review of English Studies,* III n.s., No. 9 (January, 1952), 1-12; Adrien Bonjour, "Monsters Crouching and Critics Rampant," *Publications of the Modern Language Association* (*PMLA*), LXVIII, No. 1 (March, 1953), 304-12; A. G. Brodeur, "The Structure and the Unity of *Beowulf,*" *PMLA,* LXVIII, No. 5 (December, 1953), 1183-95.

[12] Bright, J. W., "The Relation of the Caedmonian *Exodus* to the Liturgy," *Modern Language Notes,* XXVII, No. 4 (April, 1912), 97-103; C. W. Kennedy, *The Earliest English Poetry: A Critical Survey* (New York: Oxford University Press, 1943), pp. 175-83.

[13] Cf. Kennedy, *op. cit.,* pp. 181 f.; G. K. Anderson, *The Literature of the Anglo-Saxons* (Princeton: Princeton University Press, 1949), pp. 122 f.

baptism was of peculiar importance. First, during the seventh century it was being very frequently performed in England, often under impressive circumstances and often upon massed numbers of converts.[14] Second, during the eighth century there was a like situation among the Continental kinsmen of the Anglo-Saxons.[15] Third, near the end of the eighth century and beginning of the ninth, it even became an instrument of policy in the political, military, and diplomatic exploits of Charlemagne. Moreover, the Frankish ruler evoked from many of his prelates detailed discussions of the ceremonies of the rite.[16] We may therefore add *Beowulf* to the *Exodus* and the *Christ* as evidence of the debt to the liturgy, for, as Bright has said, "doctrine and rite had control of the popular consciousness and were . . . available for artistic treatment."[17] Lawrence has made an equally significant observation which is pertinent: "the audience obviously waited with no less eagerness for reminiscences of old historic tradition. Almost every page of *Beowulf* gives evidence of how completely

[14] The Venerable Bede (died 735) does not supply any notable occasions of the administration of baptism, but he does afford record of some remarkable conversions which apparently imply the use of the full ritual and ceremonial; see particularly his *Historia ecclesiastica Anglorum gentis,* II, 13 (the famous case of King Edwin).

[15] Nor do we find in the record of St. Boniface's life (died 754) any actual accounts of baptism, but we do find instances of dramatic conversion which were presumably followed by impressive baptismal ceremonies; see Willibald, *Vita Bonifatii,* 6, 9.

[16] Charlemagne's query (*ca.* 810) is given in J. M. Hanssens (ed.), *Amalarii Episcopi Opera Liturgica Omnia,* I (*Studi e Testi,* 138; Città del Vaticano: Biblioteca Apostolica Vaticana, 1948), 235 f., and the reply of Amalarius, bishop of Treves, in *ibid.,* pp. 236-51. A few of the other answers: Leidrad, bishop of Lyons, *De Sacramento Baptismi* and *Epistola II* [Migne, *Patrologia Latina* (*PL*), XCIX, 853-72, 873-84]; Jesse of Amiens, *De Baptismo* (*PL,* CV, 781-96); Maxentius of Aquileia, *De Significatu Rituum Baptismi* (*PL,* CVI, 51-54). It may be worth while to call attention to the elaborate portrayal of the baptism of a Danish king and queen as depicted in Book IV of Ermoldus Nigellus, *De Rebus Gestis Ludovici Pii* (*PL,* CV, 569-640), written about 826. Note especially the description of the scene of the ritual, the chapel at Ingelheim.

[17] Bright, *op. cit.,* p. 103.

this filled their minds. The poet had only to suggest, in order to evoke vivid recollections."[18] This remark could apply just as well for the liturgical element in the Christian tradition, which is surely evoked in the account of Beowulf's encounter with Grendel's mother.

[18] Lawrence, *op. cit.*, p. 22.

11

BEOWULF'S THREE GREAT FIGHTS*

H. L. Rogers

IN THIS ARTICLE ON THE OLD ENGLISH *Beowulf*[1] I SHALL EXamine the poet's attitude towards the material he used, in order to gain a better appreciation of why and how he made his poem as he did. Most of the subject-matter was not invented by him; a good deal of it was probably in metrical form already.[2] The poet fashioned this material to his own purpose, placing his personal emphasis upon it.

The definition of the 'poet' I adopt is that given by Dr. Whitelock: 'the Christian author who was responsible for giving the poem the general shape and tone in which it has survived'.[3] The present text of *Beowulf* is no doubt substantially as he left it; there may have been additions or alterations, but these cannot have been extensive.

The poet saw the heroic past of the Danes and the Geats through the eyes of a Christian Anglo-Saxon. In his poem heroic, material, and worldly things all fail: joy in the hall is the prelude

* Reprinted, by permission of The Clarendon Press, Oxford, England, publishers of *Review of English Studies,* from that journal, VI (October 1955), 339-355.

[1] All references to the poem are, unless otherwise stated, to the edn. of F. Klaeber, *Beowulf and the Fight at Finnsburg* (3rd edn. with two supplements, London and New York, 1951).

[2] Klaeber, edn., p. ciii.

[3] D. Whitelock, *The Audience of Beowulf* (Oxford, 1951), p 3.

to disaster. He was no pessimist, but a Christian who believed in the vanity of all earthly things.[4] The past fascinated him, but his faith told him that God ruled over the race of men in those days, as He still does (1057 f.). In every way he gives the impression of being a secure, even a complacent Christian; he is far enough from living paganism to be interested in it and tolerant of those customs not directly connected with devil-worship. Hence his acceptance of the idea that man is mortal and that the things of this world are transitory — that *lif is læne*[5] [life is transitory] — has no more than a formal similarity to the belief of his heathen forefathers in that same universal truth.

Among the traditional elements of Germanic heroic story that play a large part in *Beowulf* are the motives of weapons, treasure, and society. Their traditional nature is indicated roughly in the following brief analysis of common plots in early Germanic literature.

At the centre of the story is the hero himself,[6] classically, an heroic spirit in a narrow place against odds, undaunted even in death. Potent in their effect on the hero, who is never wholly independent, are the externals of the heroic world. These may be conveniently grouped under the headings of 'superhuman', 'human', and 'material'.

The superhuman forces are Fate, the heathen gods, or the Christian God; conflicts between them and the hero's character are frequently found. The human forces are those generated by the bonds of kindred, or by contractual ties between lord and retainer or husband and wife. Material things, like weapons, treasure, horses, and ships form the 'realistic background'[7] to the story, but in many plots they play an active part. The most comprehensive example which can be cited is perhaps the story

[4] *Ibid.*, p. 98.

[5] Cf. J. R. R. Tolkien, 'Beowulf: The Monsters and the Critics', *Proceedings of the British Academy,* xxii (1936), 245-95.

[6] See, for example, A. Heusler, *Die altgermanische Dichtung* (Berlin, 1923), pp. 147, 156-7.

[7] C. M. Bowra, *Heroic Poetry* (London, 1952), pp. 132-78.

of Sigurðr as told by Snorri Sturluson in his *Edda*. Here can be seen the workings of Fate, and the social conflicts between Sigurðr, Guðrún, Brynhildr, and Gunnarr. Sigurðr gains treasure (by killing a dragon), and has a sword Gramr, a ring Andvaranautr, and a faithful horse Grani. The ring is the ultimate cause of Sigurðr's death, for it touches off Brynhildr's jealous anger and sets in motion the plot to kill the hero.

Such motives are known to and used by the *Beowulf* poet, but they are emphasized differently, for he sees them in the perspective of Christian eternity. In other literature, a hero may do great deeds with a sword; in *Beowulf* the only sword with which the hero does a great deed melts away in his hand afterwards. In other literature, treasure may perhaps bring no good to him who possesses it; in *Beowulf* the treasure is positively evil. Other literature shows the strengths and weaknesses of heroic society; *Beowulf* shows only its weaknesses.

The truly heroic, as it might be exemplified in the motives of weapons, treasure, and society, is suppressed; the tragedy is made so inevitable that it ceases to be tragic in terms of the heroic world. For instance, the stories of Finn and Ingeld are not tragic as they are told in *Beowulf*. The poet had the opportunity of bringing out the love of Hildeburh for Finn, the loyalty of Hengest to Hnæf, or the delight of Ingeld in his bride: but he rejected it. The interplay of human passions did not interest him; he only knew that in the end no good came of them. To him, all the world was vanity, and these old tales merely gave additional proof of what he believed.

A consistent pattern emerges in the accounts of Beowulf's three great fights.[8] As regards the treatment of the motives of weapons, treasure, and society the fights form a progression, the second fight standing half-way between the first and the last. In each, the measure of the hero's success is in inverse proportion

[8] Cf. L. L. Schücking, 'Beowulfs Rückkehr', *Studien zur englischen Philologie*, xxi (1905), 11.

to the extent of his use of weapons and armour, his acquisition of treasure, and his need of help from his companions.

Against Grendel Beowulf used neither weapons nor armour; he did not fight to gain treasure; he placed no reliance on his companions and needed no help from them, though they were all faithful to him. He trusted in God's help and in the strength (*mægen*) that God had given him. Grendel was God's adversary; Beowulf, His champion, was easily victorious.

Against Grendel's mother Beowulf wore full armour and used a borrowed sword. There was treasure in the monster's cave, and Hroðgar had promised gold as a reward for success. Although the female monster was weaker than her son, Beowulf had a more desperate struggle to overcome her; his armour protected him but the borrowed sword was useless. The Danes gave Beowulf up for lost and left the mere, while the Geats remained hopelessly. Finally Beowulf killed the monster with an *ealdsweord eotenisc* [old giant sword] (a weapon different in its very nature from the useless Hrunting). He took the precious hilt of this sword and Grendel's head back with him as trophies.

Against the Dragon Beowulf's armour failed to protect him; his sword broke; he needed help from his companions, but all except one were faithless to him. The treasure he won by his death was buried again with him:

þær hit nu gen lifað
eldum swa unnyt, swa hit æror wæs. (3167 f.)
[where it still exists as useless to men as it was before.]

In spite of this pattern, I do not believe that *Beowulf* can be regarded as an artistic unity in the modern sense, or that the poem has a higher theme than the life and death of its hero. Indeed it may be doubted whether modern conceptions about artistic unity are relevant to a long Old English poem like *Beowulf*. That the three fights form a progression does not favour Professor Tolkien's view that its structure is

essentially a balance, an opposition of ends and beginnings. In its simplest terms it is a contrasted description of two moments in a great life, rising and setting; an elaboration of the ancient and intensely moving contrast between youth and age, first achievement and final death.[9]

Beowulf, though old when he fights the Dragon, is not weaker: his arm still has strength enough to break his sword.

Unless the poem can be shown to possess a definite artistic unity, it is not permissible to assume that everything in it has a purpose or an ulterior significance. On the other hand, when a well-defined pattern has been identified, it cannot be dismissed as the product of a series of coincidences. The pattern as a whole must somehow reflect the mind of the poet.

The treatment in the three great fights of the motives of weapons, treasure, and society implies a moral idea in which the poet believed: that a man should not trust in the things of this world, for they will fail him. Another aspect of this idea comes out clearly in the account of the first fight: that a man should trust rather in God and in the natural powers God gives him, for these will not fail him. The *Beowulf* poet understood the distinction between physical and spiritual weapons.[10]

The poet does in fact express his moral idea fully only in the earlier part of the poem; particularly, in the account of the Grendel fight. In that of the second fight, his idea and the subject-matter are on somewhat strained terms; in that of the third fight, they are fundamentally at variance. In the narrative passages and recapitulations which connect the Danish and Dragon parts, his idea is hardly realized at all, and the subject-matter does not always harmonize with it. In many of the episodes and digressions, however, the idea is quite clearly presented; some of them seem to have been written in their existing form especially for the purpose, so that one might reasonably surmise that the poet intended to mix instruction with his entertainment.[11] Yet the didactic element in *Beowulf* could have been produced simply by the poet's natural taste for moral reflection.

[9] Tolkien, *loc. cit.*, p. 271.

[10] See Whitelock, *op. cit.*, p. 80, on Felix's *Life of St. Guthlac*.

[11] L. L. Schücking, 'Wann entstand der Beowulf?', *Beiträge zur Geschichte der deutschen Sprache und Literatur*, xlii (1917), 347-410.

The variations of treatment and emphasis, which become more marked as the poem proceeds, make it impossible to accept the opinion that *Beowulf* is a self-evident unity, and hence must be entirely the creative work of one man. But 'unity of authorship' has established itself in the canon of modern dogma about *Beowulf,* and a recent editor was able to dismiss the question as one with which

> it is no longer necessary to deal, because almost all scholars have come to agree that the contrast in style and tone between the two main parts of the poem, which formerly suggested disunity of authorship, is artistically right. . . .[12]

In a limited sense *Beowulf* is a homogeneous poem, and there was rightly a reaction against attempts to dissect it, but homogeneity and complete unity of authorship are not exactly synonymous terms. The *Beowulf* poet is responsible for the present form of the poem; nevertheless the numerous attempts to dissect his work are testimony to the strong feeling of many scholars that his sources lie, as it were, not far beneath the surface.

While the pre-history of *Beowulf* cannot be certainly reconstructed without new evidence, it is inherently probable that the poem had a long and complex development, not all necessarily oral. Consequently, there is nothing unlikely in the assumption that the poet has access to some sort of archetype, in which the story of a hero's adventures in Denmark was already joined to that of his fight with a dragon. I suppose that there was such an archetype, and that a Christian poet — not a mere redactor — set about the task of reshaping it in his own words, and in his own way. It might be expected that he would betray his model by keeping too close to it sometimes; he would naturally follow its general plan. He would concentrate most on the essential features, that is, on the hero's three fights. He might also fill out the plot by the insertion of episodic matter.

[12] C. L. Wrenn, *Beowulf* (*London,* 1953), p. 67.

Many features of the extant *Beowulf* — features which cannot comfortably be accommodated by the theory of complete unity of authorship — may be plausibly explained in this way. Klaeber, who appreciates the difficulties involved, suggests the possibility that 'the author had no complete plan of the poem in his head' when he began, 'and perhaps did not finish it until a considerably later date'. He detects 'signs of weariness' in the Dragon part, the 'grave structural defects' of which he is inclined to attribute 'primarily to the nature of the material used by the poet.[13] But if the poet were free from the influence of a model he could write his poem to any length he wished; and if he were composing independently as he went along his work would hardly show so many wide divergences of treatment and emphasis: at least, not of the sort to be seen in *Beowulf*.

My hypothesis (not in itself new, for something similar has necessarily been assumed by earlier dissectors from Müllenhoff to Berendsohn) is more consistent with the evidence which the text of the poem affords, and is not itself improbable. The observations which have led me to propose it I shall now set out in more detail, in order to show that the poet expressed himself best in his account of Beowulf's fight with Grendel, but found his hero's second and third fights less congenial — as though he found as he went on that the material he was obliged to use would not conform to his design.

Beowulf's possession of *mægen* was particularly noticed by Professor Tolkien.[14] The hero's *mægen*, equal to that of thirty normal men, is his outstanding quality.

From inspection of the relevant material[15] I have reached some negative conclusions: that the word is not relatively more common in *Beowulf* than in other Old English verse, and that

[13] Klaeber, p. cvi and n. 3.

[14] Tolkien, *loc. cit.*, pp. 270, 287.

[15] See Grein-Köhler, *Sprachschatz der angelsächsischen Dichter* (Heidelberg, 1912), s.v. *mægen* and compounds; M. K. Mincoff, *Die Bedeutungsentwicklung der ags. Ausdrücke für 'Kraft' und 'Macht'* (*Palaestra* 188, Leipzig, 1933).

no significance can be attached to the distribution of its occurrences in the poem. It is true that *mægen* is attributed to Beowulf more times than to anyone else in the poem, and that it is found with comparatively greater frequency in the Danish part than in the Dragon part: but the poem is about Beowulf, and naturally more attention is paid to his characteristics in that portion of the work where he is first introduced.

One striking fact, however, is that *mægen* is never attributed to Grendel's mother, to the Dragon, or to any of the worldly heroes like Finn, Hengest, or Ingeld: it is credited to Heremod (1716) only for the purpose of comparison with Beowulf. There is one glaring exception: the description of Grendel as *mægnes rof* [famous of might] in 2084, that is, in Beowulf's Return (1888-2199). This exception is the more notable because *mægen* means more than brute strength.

Both *mægen* and *miht* are derived from *magan* 'to be able', and their basic meaning was 'power, ability'.[16] In West Saxon *miht* is a higher form of *mægen,* more suitable to the expression of 'divine power', whereas *mægen* is rather 'human power' and is often used to mean 'physical strength'. But the circles of meaning of the two words overlap. In Anglian a similar distinction in their use is observed rather more clearly.[17]

Among the connotations of *mægen* are 'virtue' and 'divine power';[18] in translations from the Latin, the word corresponds to 'vis', 'virtus'.[19] Phrases in religious verse like *þurh Metodes mægen* [through the strength of the Lord] (*Daniel,* 4) are noteworthy.

As used of Beowulf in the earlier part of the poem, *mægen* has a distinctly Christian flavour. It is his innate power; it has its most decisive victory over Grendel, the foe of God. It is God's liberal gift to him (1270 f.; cf. 2181 ff.), and it is diffi-

[16] Mincoff, *op. cit.*, p. 107.
[17] *Ibid.*, p. 124.
[18] *Ibid.*, pp. 42-52.
[19] *Ibid.*, pp. 124-35.

cult to separate it from his mental virtues of courage and resolution, balanced by restraint and discretion.[20] There is a close connexion between *mægen* and *mod* [courage] generally in Old English,[21] and particularly in *Beowulf*, as 1055 ff. make clear. Both qualities are, as a rule, denied to Beowulf's enemies, for example to Unferð (593 ff., 1166-8) and to Grendel, who became afraid as soon as he felt Beowulf's grip (753 f.).

Hence the attribution in 2084 to Grendel of *mægen* is wholly unexpected. It is perhaps a small point, but one which combines with other points in Beowulf's Return to raise doubts about the original authorship of that section of the poem.

From the beginning of *Beowulf* the material success and glory of the Danes is emphasized, so that their failure to defeat Grendel is brought into sharper relief. The Danish power was founded on force of arms (4 ff.), on the receipt of tribute (11), and on diplomatic marriages (possibly 62 f.; certainly 2020 ff.). Hroðgar was successful in war, and built Heorot (64 ff.). But the great hall was ultimately useless: it was unable to protect the Danes against the foes of God, and it was doomed to destruction by fire as a result of the *ecghete* [sword hate] between Danes and Heaðobards (81 ff.). This course of events Hroðgar vainly tried to avert by giving his daughter in marriage to Ingeld.

In all this the poet's attitude to the heroic world of the Danes is clear: the hall is doomed, Hroðgar's dispensing of treasure in it (80 f.) will not avail, the sword will have deadly work to do, peaceful contracts will be broken. Through this atmosphere of heroic futility strides Grendel, God's foe, whom only Beowulf's *mægen* will vanquish.

Grendel is descended from the first fratricide; and the poet later adds that Cain killed Abel with a sword — he was his *ecgbana* [sword-slayer] (1262). This detail is not in the Bible,

[20] Cf. L. L. Schücking, 'Das Königsideal im *Beowulf*', *Englische Studien*, lxvii (1932-3), 1-14.

[21] Mincoff, *op. cit.*, p. 144: 'Seelische und leibliche Kraft vereinigen sich zu dem vollkommensten Ausdruck der menschlichen Fähigkeit'.

nor in the Old English Genesis; I have not been able to trace it elsewhere. It may be an innovation by the poet, and would be quite consistent with his representation of the sword as useless on the supernatural level, but capable of causing human woe.

Beowulf is introduced, not by name, but by allusion to his main characteristic:

> se wæs moncynnes mægenes strengest
> on þæm dæge þysses lifes,
> æþele ond eacen. (196 ff.)
> [He was greatest of strength of mankind in that day of this life, noble and mighty.]

Klaeber has shown that the line *on þæm dæge þysses lifes* has a Christian flavour,[22] and I have already suggested that Beowulf's *mægen* implies something of Christian virtue as well as physical strength.

The frequent descriptions of weapons and armour in this part of the poem provide further contrasts between Beowulf's *mægen* and the material things of the heroic world. All these warlike trappings, carefully enumerated in a way that seems ironical, are soon to fail against the monsters. The Danish coastguard holds the shores of Denmark against hostile invaders (240 ff.), but not all the Danes can hold Heorot against Grendel.

When Hroðgar is told of Beowulf's arrival he talks first of his lineage, then of his *mægen,* then of the mercy of God in sending him to deal with Grendel (372 ff.). Hroðgar says he will offer Beowulf treasure *for his modþræce* [for his dashing courage] (385), but he does not say this to Beowulf himself: to him his only direct promise is *Ne bið þe wilna gad* [You will have no lack of good things ("of wishes")] (660). Hence the treasure-motive is much less conspicuous in the account of Beowulf's first fight than it is in that of the second, before which Hroðgar's promises are extensive and specific.

[22] F. Klaeber, 'Die christlichen Elemente im Beowulf', *Anglia,* XXXV (1911), 461-2.

In his first address to Hroðgar Beowulf takes some pains to establish his reputation for *mægen*: he says his people advised him to visit Denmark *forþan hie mægenes cræft minne cuþon* [because they knew the strength of my might] (418). Again, Klaeber has noted the Christian flavour of the expression *mægenes cræft*.[23] Beowulf's insistence on his reputation (of which Hroðgar is already aware) no doubt indicates the poet's desire to impress the importance of *mægen* upon his audience.

Beowulf says he will fight Grendel without weapons, and adds that God will decide the issue between them (435 ff.). He explains that he will meet Grendel on equal terms so as to win Hygelac's approval.

Hroðgar's next speech underlines the contrast between *mægen* and weapons: he tells of how his men waited for Grendel *mid gryrum ecga* [with the terror of swords] (480 ff.), and of how in the morning the hall was stained with blood. Abruptly Hroðgar ends his speech by inviting Beowulf to sit down and take part in the feast: the change from thoughts of death in the hall to the description of joy in the hall is sudden and pointed.

An argument follows between Beowulf and Unferð. Their dispute concerns Beowulf's *mægen*. Unferð asserts that Breca *hæfde mare mægen* [had greater strength] (518); Beowulf immediately refutes this (532 ff.), reproaches Unferð for his lack of courage (593 f.), and says that Grendel does not dread the *atol ecgþracu . . . Sige-Scyldinga* [terrible fight with swords . . . of the Victory-Scieldings] (596 ff.).

In the swimming-contest, swords were used and armour was worn: they were effective against sea-monsters. As Beowulf tells the story, it was all a youthful escapade, not to be compared with the present graver struggle. It provides many contrasts: between sea-monsters vulnerable to weapons and enemies of God who are not; between Beowulf's swimming in the sea and his later descent into the mere; between Beowulf, who used his sword

[23] *Anglia,* xxxv (1911), 468.

to kill sea-monsters, and Unferð, who used his (Hrunting?) to kill his brothers (587). It is notable that Unferð, like Cain, was a fratricide.

Beowulf is appointed by God to be the guardian of the hall; he trusts in his *mægen* and in God's favour, then takes off his armour and hands it, with his sword, to a servant (665-74). Professor Tolkien thought that *modgan mægnes, Metodes hyldo* [in his proud might (and), the favor of the Creator] (670) were two parallel expressions for the same thing, and that no 'and' should appear between them in translation: 'the favour of God *was* the possession of *mægen*.'[24] But as Klaeber remarks, *ond* need not be in the text where 'and' is necessary in translation.[25] From 1270-4 it is clear that Beowulf trusted in (i) his *mægen,* which came to him from God; (ii) God's favour: thus he overcame Grendel.

Beowulf does not himself say that he trusts in God: this is a comment of the poet's. Yet to conclude, as Professor Tolkien does,[26] that the poet was deliberately differentiating between his own language and that employed by his characters is hazardous. Such differentiation as there is in the poem arises naturally and inevitably. The poet had made Grendel the foe of God, while Beowulf was on God's side, and so could hardly be represented as a pagan. Yet he could not, without grave risk of incongruity apparent to both poet and audience, be represented too dogmatically as a practising, believing Christian. Besides, I doubt whether the poet ever faced the question squarely, or was sharply conscious of the difference between direct and indirect speech.

That a Christian Anglo-Saxon poet would wish to 'repaganize' his language seems neither possible nor probable. When Beowulf speaks of *witig God* [wise God] and *halig Dryhten* [holy Lord] (685 f.) he is talking of God, not of Fate, to whom the adjectives are not applicable. When he tells Unferð he shall

[24] *Loc. cit.,* p. 287.
[25] Edn., p. 454.
[26] *Loc. cit.,* pp. 284-6.

suffer punishment in hell (588 f.) he is talking about the Christian hell; when he uses the word *scrifan* [sentence] in 979 he is using it in a Christian sense. To both poet and audience words like *Metod* [measurer of fate, God] (whatever their etymologies, and in spite of such fossils as *meotudsceaft* [decree of fate, doom] and *meotudwang* [battlefield]) surely meant the Christian God, and none other.[27] Such words were firmly established in the Christian usage, as the diction of Cædmon's *Hymn* shows. Some confusion between God and Fate is quite natural and need not be specially explained.

Beowulf's decision to fight Grendel without weapons and without armour is right; but not, as it were, for the right reasons. In fact a sword would not have harmed the monster, for Hrunting was useless against Grendel's mother, and Beowulf's companions had no more success when they attacked Grendel with their swords (794 ff.). But in the reasons given by Beowulf for his renunciation of weapons (I take *forswerian* ["make useless by a spell" (Klaeber)] in 804 in this sense) the poet's struggle with his source can be traced. He had to contrast Beowulf's trust in his *mægen* and in God with his rejection of weapons, for the stage had to be set for the second fight, in which swords play an important role; yet he could not allow Beowulf to be conscious that his *mægen* would win where a sword would fail, for then his courage would seem less and his later use of Hrunting would be inconsistent. The poet's way out of the dilemma was to make Beowulf appear chivalrous in wishing to meet Grendel on equal terms (677-87; cf. 433-41).[28]

Beowulf's final words before the fight are that God shall award the victory as He thinks fit (685 ff.). The poet goes on to comment that God granted success to the Geats, and that they defeated their enemy *ðurh anes cræft* [through the power of one man]; he adds then a general observation:

[27] Grein-Köhler, *Sprachschatz*, p. 461 b.

[28] Cf. R. C. Boer, *Die altenglische Heldendichtung. I. Beowulf* (Halle, 1912), p. 60.

Soð is gecyþed,
þæt mihtig God manna cynnes
weold wideferhð. (700 ff.)
[The truth is well known, that God Almighty
has always ruled over the race of men.]

Here the poet's own attitude to the story is revealed: it is an exemplum from which valid morals may be drawn, for the wisdom of God and his sovereignty over men are eternal.

Beowulf's *mægen* and mortality are stressed in 789-90, echoing 196-7; the further repetition of *on ðæm dæge þysses lifes* [in that day of this life] (806) emphasizes the mortality of his foe, Grendel. The texture of the poem throughout the account of Beowulf's first fight is close-knit; nowhere else in *Beowulf* is the poet's Christianity so fully expressed.

After Beowulf's victory the poet creates again an atmosphere of worldly glory, and introduces various episodes: of Sigemund, Heremod, Finn, and Hama. It will be more convenient to deal with these together later: in all, the treatment of the motives of weapons, treasure, and society is similar.

The essential weakness of material strength is again exposed by the coming of Grendel's mother to the hall. The futility of the Danes' martial customs is demonstrated: in 1242 ff. these are described in detail, and then they fail to prevent Grendel's mother from carrying off Æschere. In martial terms, the female monster is said to be weaker than her son:

Wæs se gryre læssa
efne swa micle, swa bið mægþa cræft,
wiggryre wifes be wæpnedmen. (1282 ff.)
[The terror was less by even so much as is the strength
of maidens, the terrible power in war of a woman in
comparison with a weaponed-man.]

Because Beowulf has a more difficult fight against Grendel's weaker mother, some commentators have found these lines troublesome. Klaeber thinks they are 'to discredit the unbiblical notion of a woman's superiority',[29] while Chambers saw in them

[29] Edn., p. 181.

an attempt to avoid an anti-climax.[30] Of course, there is no anti-climax, for the circumstances of the second fight are themselves more difficult than those of the first. Also, in the second fight Beowulf uses a sword, whereas in the first he trusted in his *mægen* and in God; this contributes to his difficulties.

The air of folk-tale is stronger; Grendel's mother is not so clearly the foe of God, and she did not attack without provocation; Beowulf is more of a Germanic hero and less of a Christian knight. He speaks now of revenge and glory, not of God's judgment. This time Hroðgar has offered him gold as a reward for success, and Beowulf accepts the loan of Hrunting.

The excellence of Hrunting is stressed (1455 ff.; 1525 ff.; 1810 ff.) so that its subsequent failure is made to seem more remarkable. Beowulf's final words before diving into the mere are that he will win glory with Hrunting or die; but this is a boast that cannot be fulfilled. His last words before his fight with Grendel were very different.

In the account of the fight proper the poet's endeavour to reconcile his source and his ideas about swords and *mægen* is again apparent. Hrunting fails, though it is a fine weapon and Beowulf wields it with all his strength (1519); he throws it aside and trusts again in his *mægen* (1533 ff.). The poet adds an approving comment: so should a man do. This is admirably explicit, but rather laboured; for of course Beowulf would have been a fool to persist further with a useless weapon.

The magic sword hanging on the wall must have been in the poet's source.[31] He adapted it to his purpose by making it a special sword: it is *ealdsweord eotenisc, gigȧnta geweorc* [old giant sword, the work of giants] (1558 ff.). Germanic belief was in the dwarfs as makers of swords, but 'in conformity with the pedigree imposed upon the Grendel race, the good sword of

[30] R. W. Chambers, *Beowulf: An Introduction* (Cambridge, 1921), p. 50.

[31] Cf. F. Panzer, *Studien zur germanischen Sagengeschichte. I. Beowulf* (München, 1910), pp. 153 ff.

tradition is converted into a *giganta geweorc'*.[32] This is no ordinary worldly weapon; it has associations with Tubalcain.[33] It was the sight of its inscribed hilt that provoked Hroðgar's homily, and the melting away of its blade is described in a Christian simile (1605 ff.).

Since the poet had decided to treat the sword in this way, the motive of *mægen* would necessarily prove something of an embarrassment. If it were emphasized too much, there would inevitably be a subtraction from the importance of the sword on the wall. Hence the vagueness in the narrative. Even when Beowulf trusts in his *mægen* he gains only temporary advantage, for the poet, reasonably enough, makes him *werigmod* [weary at heart] (1543). The text does not make clear how Beowulf managed to get to his feet again, though presumably he exerted his *mægen* in standing up.

Dr. Whitelock observes that there are no actual discrepancies in the account of the fight, and suggests that God directed Beowulf's attention to the sword on the wall (1557 ff.; 1661 ff.) as the hero lay at the monster's mercy.[34] The sight of the sword would then give him new strength to rise to his feet. However, this is not the order of events in the text; and it cannot be denied that the narrative lacks clarity.

It is notable that in the account of the second fight there is much less reference to the Almighty than there was in that of the first. From 1398 until 1553 God is not mentioned at all. Beowulf does not refer to God until the fight is over (1658); the Geats thank God for his safe return in 1626. In its context the Christian simile used to describe the melting away of the sword (1605 ff.) is remarkable: it compares this to God's unbinding of the fetters of winter, and implies the final release of the Danes from the terrors of the monsters. While the simile is

[32] Klaeber, edn., p. 187.

[33] Klaeber, *Anglia,* xxxv (1911), 260-1; O. F. Emerson, 'Legends of Cain', *P.M.L.A.*, xxi (1906), 929.

[34] *Op. cit.,* pp. 68-69.

clearly the work of the *Beowulf* poet, the rationalizing comment that it was the monster's hot blood that melted the sword-blade (1615 ff.) is more the sort of thing to be expected in his source.

Although there was much treasure in the cave, Beowulf left it all there (1612 ff.); his *mægenbyrþen* [mighty burden] as he returned was the hilt of the marvellous sword and Grendel's head (1623 ff.). In the treatment of the treasure-motive, the second fight again stands half-way between the first and the third. The society-motive is similarly treated: there is a hint of desertion on the part of the Danes in leaving the mere.

To Beowulf's fights with the monsters Hroðgar's homily (1700 ff.) is a key: not a well-cut key to a precision lock, but it serves. It is essentially on the proper use of the natural powers and advantages God gives to man: on Beowulf's rightful and Heremod's wrongful use of great *mægen;* on man's spiritual weapons and armour; on the sins of pride and miserliness; and on the uselessness of swords and spears against such as Grendel. There is no need to dismiss any of this as interpolated.

Whether the homily was intended to apply directly to Beowulf is impossible to decide, but it may have been. Beowulf was over-proud when he dived into the mere saying he would win glory with Hrunting; it was not until he threw this sword aside that victory appeared within his reach. The homily would certainly drive home to the audience that man's victories are God's victories — that God gives *mægen,* but man is fallible and mortal.

Much of the inconsistency that critics have seen in the obviously Christian passages of *Beowulf* disappears if the poet's point of view is properly understood. It is impossible to believe that he was a self-conscious antiquary, 'einer art altgermanischen Walter Scott.'[35] He was not reconstructing the sort of speech which he imagined a pagan king might have made in a Danish hall: he was merely expressing his own views through the mouth of one of his characters, Hroðgar. The poet stood back from

[35] Schücking, 'Wann entstand der Beowulf?', p. 393.

the story he told, and interpreted it in the light of his own times. If he were forced seriously to consider the question whether Hroðgar was Christian or pagan he would be forced next to the conclusion that the story about Beowulf was not worth telling. As it was, however, his justification for his poem lay in his treatment of it as matter which was entertaining but from which moral instruction could be derived. Essentially, his answer to Alcuin's rhetorical question 'Quid Hinieldus cum Christo?' was 'Nihil' [What has Ingeld to do with Christ? . . . Nothing]; yet from this there was a moral to be drawn, and he drew it. The poet's background was not confused semi-paganism, but established — long-established — Christianity. Consequently I doubt whether even 175-88 are not his work; and it would not be astonishing if his knowledge of heathen worship in temples came from Bede's *Ecclesiastical History*.

Hroðgar's homily marks, in some ways, the end of the Danish part of *Beowulf*: what follows is largely tidying-up. Schücking took Beowulf's Return to begin at 1. 1888.[36]

However, the first signs of a change of emphasis on the motives of *mægen,* weapons, treasure, and society occur before that: to take an arbitrary point, after 1816. After this, also, the Christian tone is less marked. Beowulf, for instance, promises Hroðgar *mægenes fultum* [the support of strength] (1835), but this is now purely military help. In 1881-2 Beowulf is *guðrinc goldwlanc, since hremig* [a warrior brave with gold, exulting in his treasure]. By 2146, where treasure is called *mægnes med* [the reward of strength], the shift is complete. At the end of Beowulf's Return, Hygelac honours the hero with a precious sword and an extensive grant of land (2190 ff.). Beowulf, who was God's champion, is now a powerful temporal lord; and the duality of the Danish and the Dragon parts of the poem is apparent.

It is in Beowulf's speech to Hygelac telling of his adventures that the change is most evident. Beowulf nowhere makes

[36] 'Beowulfs Rückkehr', p. 14.

acknowledgement of God's help, and his Danish expedition seems like mere worldly heroism. Grendel, with his glove, now appears as a creature of folk-tale, not as a foe of God. That a detail like this should have been 'purposely reserved'[37] until now is very hard to believe. The account Beowulf gives of his fight with Grendel's mother (2135 ff.) contains no actual inconsistencies, but is hardly an adequate condensed version of events.

Schücking's minute syntactical study of Beowulf's Return led him to conclude that the peculiarities of this section were due to the poet who first connected the Danish and the Dragon parts together.[38] My hypothesis is that the peculiarities are there because the *Beowulf* poet did not rework his material thoroughly enough at this point to remove them: that by now the poet was tiring of his task and becoming aware that what he had done earlier with Grendel and his mother could not be done with the Dragon.

Grendel was God's foe; the Dragon is not, even though he may have been 'the recognized symbol of the archfiend'[39] in ecclesiastical tradition. The Dragon's rage is not unjust, for he was provoked by theft from the hoard.[40] The poet did perhaps make the Dragon into Beowulf's final and inevitable foe, and thus raised more problems for himself. For how could Beowulf use his *mægen* and not a sword against the Dragon?

The poet seems to try, rather clumsily, to make out that Beowulf had always used his *mægen*: he avoids reference to any use of swords in his accounts of the Geats and their wars. Beowulf took no part in the battle of Ravenswood. After his return from Denmark, the only part of his doings described in detail is that connected with Hygelac's expedition to Frisia. On that occasion Beowulf performed feats reminiscent of his swimming-contest with Breca and his fight against Grendel. He killed

[37] Klaeber, edn., p. cvi.
[38] 'Beowulfs Rückkehr', pp. 73-74.
[39] Klaeber, edn., p. 1.
[40] T. M. Gang, 'Approaches to Beowulf', *R.E.S.*, N.S. iii (1952), 1-12.

Dæghrefn with his bare hands, as he killed Grendel; he swam home, as he swam against Breca. It seems that when he had killed Dæghrefn (2501 ff.) he took from him the sword Nægling (2680), and he says himself that this sword helped him many times (2500). Yet the poet does not explain what Beowulf was doing on occasions when we might expect to have news of him: when Heardred was killed, and when Onela was killed.[41] Then, after the mention of Dæghrefn, Beowulf says he will fight with the sword for the Dragon's hoard of treasure (2508 f.) but adds that he would fight without it, bare-handed as he fought Grendel, if he knew how (2518 ff.). There is something most awkward and strained about this: the poet is trying to force his ideas about swords and *mægen* upon his story, with unhappy results. Again, my hypothesis is that he kept too close to his model: it needed radical adaptation before it would suit his purpose.

The poet comments that no sword was ever much use to Beowulf in battle: Nægling broke in his hand (2680 ff.). The passage ends with words similar to those applied to the Dragon's possession of the hoard of treasure: *næs him wihte ðe sel* [it was none the better for him]. Yet the Dragon, as well as Beowulf, had to die; and to help accomplish this the poet produces another *ealdsweord etonisc* (2616), wielded by Wiglaf, Beowulf's kinsman and his one faithful companion. This is a reminiscence of Beowulf's fight with Grendel's mother; but Wiglaf's sword, a family heirloom that has been involved in deadly feud,[42] bears no real resemblance to the sword that hung on the wall of the monster's cave. And in the end Beowulf slew the Dragon with his knife.

The treasure-motive is also handled without much skill. It dominates the Dragon part, dominates the Dragon, and comes near to dominating Beowulf himself. To the poet treasure was evil: he says in 2764 ff. that gold in the earth may over-

[41] Cf. Whitelock, *op. cit.*, pp. 96-98.

[42] Cf. A. Bonjour, *The Digressions in Beowulf* (Oxford, 1950), p. 39.

power every man. The Dragon is no better off for his possession of the hoard (2277; cf. 2687).

Beowulf's exact position as regards the treasure is not made clear. Before he fights the Dragon he says he will win the gold or die in the attempt (2535 ff.), and when he lies dying he asks Wiglaf to carry the hoard out to him (2747 ff.). When he sees it he thanks God for it, and rejoices that he has gained it for his people (2794 ff.). Yet it is buried with him (3163 ff.).[43]

It is usually understood that Beowulf, in acquiring the treasure, thereby became involved in the curse on it. The curse on the gold is certain (3052), but from its effects Beowulf seems to be exempted, for 3053 ff. apparently mean that God allowed Beowulf to open the hoard. Great eagerness to win the treasure would be wrong, in the light of the poem in general and of Hroðgar's homily in particular. Yet the poet never makes it quite clear whether Beowulf is condemned or exonerated.

No doubt Dr. Whitelock is right when she says: 'Beowulf has taken Hrothgar's advice and chosen the *ece rædas*'[44] [eternal help, counsel]. That at least seems to be the underlying intention of the poem. Yet why is it not expressed more clearly, either in the general narrative, or in one of the moralizing asides of which the poet is so fond?

I have suggested reasons. First, that the poet found difficulty in imposing his moral ideas on his source. Secondly, that he did not think of Beowulf as definitely either Christian or pagan, but was to some extent detached from the story and the characters, using it and them as far as he could to convey his Christian philosophy.

The validity of these reasons may be tested against the episodes in *Beowulf*. The allusive way in which these are presented is frequently taken to indicate that the audience had minds stocked with Germanic legend, and that they were ready to respond at the mention of a hero's name. Doubts about the strength

[43] Cf. Klaeber, edn., p. li, n. 2.
[44] *Op. cit.*, p. 98.

of tradition in Anglo-Saxon times have recently been expressed in another connexion,[45] but as far as *Beowulf* is concerned, all the information required for the understanding of allusions is given by the poet. He does not give more because he does not want to give more.

For instance, the poet drew a detailed comparison between Beowulf and Sigemund (875-97). The basis of the comparison is that both heroes killed monsters and a dragon. But then the poet pointed out the differences between Beowulf and Sigemund, relating these differences to his ideas about the motives of weapons, treasure, and society. Beowulf killed Grendel with his bare hands: Sigemund killed giants with his sword (883 f.). When Sigemund fought his dragon he was alone, and killed it with his sword (890 ff.); Beowulf was not alone when he killed his dragon, and his sword broke in his hand. Sigemund carried off the treasure (895 ff.); Beowulf's treasure was buried uselessly with him.

Hence the Sigemund episode in *Beowulf* is, in microcosm, the whole poem and the poet's attitude to it. The heroic deeds of Sigemund did not interest the Christian author of the Old English poem any further. The Heremod episode provides a foil to set off Beowulf's rightful use of his *mægen*. The point of the allusion to Hama (1198-1209) is that Hama carried off the *Brosinga mene . . . to þære byrhtan byrig* [the necklace of the Brosings . . . to the glorious fortress] and *geceas ecne ræd* [he chose eternal counsel]; while Hygelac wore his precious torque 'when he went raiding a peaceful people, and thus lost it to his enemies'.[46] And Hygelac *under rand gecranc* [fell under his shield]. Whether 'the bright city' really means a monastery or not hardly affects the general sense of the reference: *beorht* sometimes means 'holy' and is applied to Christ, while the noun *burg* is sometimes ap-

[45] K. Sisam, 'Anglo-Saxon Royal Genealogies', *Proceedings of the British Academy*, xxxix (1953), 345-6.

[46] Whitelock, *op. cit.*, p. 56.

plied to the dwellings of Heaven.[47] The phrase 'chose eternal counsel' probably 'implies that Hama became a good Christian and that he died as such'.[48] The poet uses the whole allusion to present the moral of Hygelac and his undue pride (1206).

The Finn and Ingeld episodes have much in common. The poet tells the stories allusively because he does not wish to exploit their possibilities of psychological tragedy. In both episodes, marriage fails to bring lasting peace to tribes in a state of feud; in both it is a sword which touches off the last deadly act of the drama (1142 ff.; 2047 ff.). The handling of the motives of weapons, treasure, and society is consistent; each story is adapted so that it conforms with the poet's moral ideas. The adjective 'heroic' is strictly inapplicable to these episodes; and it is of course pointless to try to reconstruct the exact course of events which the poet has done his best to obscure.

In one episode only is the handling of material and human motives different: in the episode of Offa and his queen.

If Dr. Sisam is right in thinking that manuscript *mod þryðo wæg* (1931) means 'she was proud' and that a line or so has been omitted from the text,[49] the episode reads like another warning on the sin of pride, suitably reinforcing the admonitions of Hroðgar's homily; and the transition from the subject of Hygd does not seem unduly violent. Certainly there would be no good reason to regard the passage as an interpolation, or to doubt that it is the work of the *Beowulf* poet.

In the episode, as Dr. Whitelock has remarked, Offa is praised in unusually glowing terms.[50] There are other features which point to her conclusion that the poet was here going out of his way to praise the Anglian king. Elsewhere in the poem praise of a hero is always balanced in some way, but the praise

[47] Grein-Köhler, *Sprachschatz,* s.vv. *beorht, burg.*

[48] Klaeber, edn., p. 179.

[49] *Studies in the History of Old English Literature* (Oxford, 1953), p. 41 n.

[50] *Op. cit.*, p. 60.

of Offa is unqualified by prophecies of future woe. Offa's marriage is the only one referred to at length which does not end badly; Offa is the only king in *Beowulf* whose warlike deeds do not bring about his own downfall. Here the *Beowulf* poet for once frankly admires the heroic, but whether this is an indication that he was a Mercian cannot of course be decided without other evidence.

There is no doubt that the 'episode poet', as critics of the dissecting school called him, was also the *Beowulf* poet. On the other hand, I have given reasons for doubting that this Christian author was entirely responsible for the whole of *Beowulf,* and for supposing that he followed some sort of model which already contained the story, at least in outline. What form this took cannot be reconstructed, nor is it possible to guess at the author's other sources. My hypothesis concerns only the final stage of composition.

When and where *Beowulf* was written in its present form are open questions, full of paradox. Northumbria in the age of Bede; Mercia later in the eighth century? Yet there is some justification for Schücking's dating about 900.[51] It is precisely in the Viking Age that Christian Anglo-Saxons might derive consolation from reflecting upon their spiritual superiority over Scandinavians enjoying material success in this world; it is precisely in the Viking Age that detailed traditions about Danes and Geats may have come to England to fill out vaguer memories from an earlier period. And yet again, the poem is apparently pre-Cynewulf.

To questions like these the answers cannot be simple, because *Beowulf* is not a simple poem. Whether my partial solution of the problem of its authorship proves acceptable or not, it is clearly time to face the fact that the problem is there. It may never be solved, but it cannot be ignored.

[51] 'Wann entstand der Beowulf?', p. 407.

12

GOOD AND EVIL; LIGHT AND DARKNESS; JOY AND SORROW IN *BEOWULF**

Herbert G. Wright

THESE CONTRASTING OPPOSITES ARE, OF COURSE, BY NO MEANS peculiar to *Beowulf*. They are part of the stuff of everyday life, and so it is not surprising to find that two of these groups appear in the gnomic verses in Cotton MS. Tiberius BI,[1] where various truisms are assembled. Yet even though these groups in themselves may appear trite, if we examine *Beowulf* from the point of view of each, the three, taken together, may help in the interpretation of the whole work.

. . . Corresponding to the clash between good and evil is that between light and darkness. A people like the Old English, largely concerned with agriculture and scantily provided with artificial light, watched sunrise and sunset with an interest less common in a complex, urban society. J. L. Lowes has emphasized the separation of the medieval from the modern world in respect of the calculation of time, with the result that 'unless we are mariners or woodsmen or astronomers or simple folk in lonely places, we never any longer reckon with the *sky*.'[2] If that

* Reprinted, by permission of The Clarendon Press, Oxford, England, publishers of *Review of English Studies,* from that journal, VIII (1957), 1-11.

[1] Cf. *Maxims,* ii. 50-51, in *The Anglo-Saxon Minor Poems,* ed. E. V. K. Dobbie (New York, 1942), p. 57.
[2] *Geoffrey Chaucer* (London, 1934), p. 7.

was true in Chaucer's time, it was even truer of the observation of waxing and waning light in the eighth century, when the fear of darkness and of solitary, waste lands induced a willing acceptance of tales of giants lurking in the fens. Grendel is such a giant — a demon, an *ellengæst* [bold demon] (86) and *scynscaþa* [demon foe] (707) — who roams about moors and fens and haunts remote places. Enveloped in darkness, he is irritated by the erection of Heorot, and the poet heightens the general impression of blackness by calling him a *feond on helle* [hellish fiend] (101) and *deorc deaþscua* [dark death-shadow] (160) who *sinnihte heold mistige moras* [in the endless night held the misty moors.] (161-2). It is precisely because Grendel is a monster of darkness that the author of *Beowulf*, choosing his words with all care, says that Hrothgar's councillors could not expect a '*bright* remedy' from the slayer.[3] He lies in wait and finally raids the hall. On the black nights *nihtbealwa mæst* [the greatest of evils in the night] descends on the *sincfage sel* [richly decorated hall] (167, 193). The description of the Creation, with its picture of the *wlitebeorhtne wang* [plain fair (bright) to look upon] (93) and the sun and moon, has already been used as a contrast to the murky haunts of Grendel, and the landing of Beowulf and his followers in Denmark is the signal for the irradiation of the scene with a flood of brilliant light.

When the Geats end their voyage, they see the gleaming cliffs of Denmark. Their shields and armour are bright; the boar-images on their helmets, adorned with gold, shine resplendent. As they approach Heorot, it offers a spectacle even more radiant. It too is adorned with gold, a bright abode, a luminary that

[3] 157-8. It is interesting to see how the image of brightness is applied to the sound of mirth in the hall, after the tragic episode of Finn and Hengest is over:

Gamen eft astah,
beorhtode bencsweg. (1160-1)

[Mirth rose high again, the noise along the benches sounded loudly.]

flashes over many lands. But the author is not yet content to leave this dazzling vision. Once more, when the travellers reach their destination, he dwells on their bright and shining armour, and when Beowulf stands before Hrothgar to announce his errand, his coat of mail becomes associated with the evening light that precedes the coming of darkness. At the banquet the mead is as bright as the voice of the bard is clear, and Beowulf confidently looks forward to the return next day of the sun clothed in radiance.[4] For the moment the terrors of night are in abeyance.

With the introduction of the Breca episode, however, the poet begins to prepare the listener for a change. Beowulf's grim struggle with the sea-beasts takes place by night; only the coming of morning reveals the deadliness of the encounter, when they are seen lying dead along the shore. This is a prelude to the fight with Grendel, and the very fact that Beowulf has dealt so successfully with nocturnal foes inspires confidence, not only in the hero, but also in the wise Geat councillors who urged him to undertake the voyage to relieve Hrothgar. At the end of the episode the King commits Heorot to the keeping of Beowulf. Soon the *sceadugenga* [walker in darkness] (703) is drawing near from the misty hillsides. He knows full well the *goldsele gumena . . . fættum fahne* [the gold hall of men . . . gleaming with plated gold] (715-16). Within the building all is dark; nothing is visible except the hideous light that flashes from the eyes of the monster. But the quality of this light differs from that which illumined the scene a little earlier. It is like fire and is contrasted with the glory of God, the *scir Metod* [the bright Lord] (979).

The next day is one of cheerful normality. The giant has fled into the darkness, leaving his hand behind him. In the morning light the roof of Heorot shines resplendent, and again and again the rich, warm glow of gold is seen. As Grendel's attacks are made only on the *sweartum nihtum* [on dark nights] (166-7), the moon can play no part as a background to the first half of the

'sunne sweglwered' (606) [the sun clothed in radiance].

poem. Light, therefore, is predominantly that of the sun or of the metal which approaches most closely to it in the appeal to the eye. Certainly, after Grendel has vanished, there is a repeated emphasis on gold — in the tapestry hanging on the walls, in the weapons, the banner, and the trappings of the steeds presented to Beowulf by Hrothgar, and in the armour, arm-rings, and collar handed to the hero by Wealhtheow, as she moves through the hall, wearing her golden crown. But all this radiance is eclipsed when under cover of darkness Grendel's mother carries off Æschere to her retreat below the mere.

The passage that describes this spot is remarkable as a creation of the poetic imagination, and it would be futile to seek in it any close correspondence with reality. The atmosphere is the main thing, with its vague suggestion of the eerie and mysterious. The frost-covered trees strike chill, and even in broad daylight the wood overshadows the dark pool. The nocturnal fire on the flood provides light of a sort, but it bodes ill, like the fiery light of Grendel's eyes. Nevertheless, Beowulf plunges into the turbid water in full armor, his shining helmet standing out against the surrounding gloom. Once he is in the cave, the circumstances of the narrative require that he shall be able to look around. He is enabled to see, but again it is a fiery light that shines forth, revealing first one monster of darkness, then the other.

The same dramatic sense of contrast is displayed after Beowulf has assured Hrothgar of the death of both Grendel and his mother. Heorot, which they had so long menaced, towers up in its golden splendour, and next morning the black raven announces the return of the sun. This function is so unusual for a bird normally associated with death that one is tempted to regard it as another example of the employment of a symbol for the triumph of light and life over darkness and death. However that may be, the sun continues to irradiate the landscape when Beowulf and his men land on the coast of Geatland, bringing the news of victory over the monsters.

Just as Hrothgar, after protecting the Danes for fifty years (1769), in his old age has to endure the attacks of Grendel, so Beowulf, worn by time, after ruling the Geats for exactly the same period, is called upon to face a struggle with yet another monster, the most fearsome of all, the fiery dragon. He, too, is a creature of darkness and lurks in his barrow like Grendel in his den, awaiting impatiently the waning of daylight, and hastening back as dawn approaches. But in the interval he vomits fire and sets the homes of men ablaze. This fiery glow associates him with the earlier passages in which the light of Grendel's eyes and the light on the mere and in the cave are mentioned. Thus the *bryneleoma* [gleam of fire], which flashes out as the dragon flies through the air at midnight, becomes a symbol of danger, and it is this angry glare that inevitably predominates in the latter part of the poem.

By contrast darkness in a metaphorical sense is transferred to the mind of Beowulf (2331-2). The light that shone so freely in the narration of his youthful exploits has vanished; so, too, has the glittering splendour which united men and precious metal in happier times. The treasures of the dragon's hoard are committed to the darkness of the earth, and gold is no longer associated with human pleasure but with a deadly curse or the misery of captivity (2931, 3018). The only joy is that of the wolf and the raven, now restored to his wonted role, as they feast on the slain. The bright coats of mail shine momentarily, but soon they are lost in the roaring flame of the funeral pyre, while the black smoke climbs upward and is engulfed by the sky, on this still day when the tumult of the winds is silent.

Closely related to the coming and going of light and darkness are the fluctuations of joy and sorrow in *Beowulf*. The joy is intermingled with the social life of rulers and warriors. The erection of Heorot provides a setting for the conviviality of Hrothgar and his nobles, and the clear song of the bard is accompanied by the music of the harp. The banqueting scene on Beowulf's arrival at the Danish court again shows the *scop* singing to his instrument. Queen Wealhtheow and her daughter Freawaru move through the hall, handing round drinking-cups, and the laughter of the warriors is heard. The banqueting-scene on the following day is similar. The bard appears once more, and a lay is often sung. On this occasion, when Grendel's death is celebrated, wine as well as mead is served. As before, Wealhtheow passes through the hall, goblet in hand, but there are also cupbearers. At intervals, for the sake of variety, the poet describes the presentations to Beowulf and his men by Hrothgar, and to Beowulf by the Queen. Possibly he felt that a third banquet on the lines of the first two would be tedious: he imposes strict limits on the conviviality after the hero's triumphant return from the slaying of Grendel's mother. Hrothgar bids him partake of the banquet, and Beowulf, who has been promised rewards next morning, joyfully takes his seat. Then, after a few lines, the poet records that both Hrothgar and Beowulf retire to bed. Thus the problem of the narrator is solved in a realist manner.

For the same reason, no doubt, the author does not dwell at any length on the emotions aroused by Hrothgar's gifts. Nor does he delay his narrative to tell of the delight of Beowulf and his men on reaching their native land. It may be that the adjective *cuþe* [well-known] in the lines:

> hie Geata clifu ongitan meahton,
> cuþe næssas (1911-12)
> [they might see the Geatish cliffs, the
> well-known headlands]

was intended to convey their pleasure at the sight of familiar landmarks. The mention of the *hyðweard* [harbor-guardian], who for a long time had been looking for the 'beloved men' and was now quickly down by the sea, discloses a little more of the gladness with which the Geat warriors were awaited. But on the whole the joy has to be divined. This is even truer of the scene at Hygelac's hall. Inevitably, after three banquets the poet was somewhat handicapped. He tells how Hygd carried round mead-cups as Wealhtheow had done, and from time to time there are presentations — Beowulf to Hygelac and Hygd, Hygelac to Beowulf. But the treatment is somewhat perfunctory. Here is no word of welcome, and emotions are left undefined. For the mirth and conviviality we must hark back to the earlier part of the poem.

Joy and sorrow are often contrasted in *Beowulf,* sometimes with striking effect. This applies to the monsters, as when Grendel laughs in his heart at the prospect of devouring the sleeping Geats, only to lament his defeat, wail over his pain, and seek his *wynleas wic* [joyless dwelling] after Beowulf had wrenched his arm away at Heorot. However, such fluctuations of emotion are naturally most prominent in the human figures of the poem. The grief of Hrothgar and his people on account of Grendel's ravages gives place to relief and confidence on the arrival of Beowulf, and they shed no tears over the death of the giant who has plagued them so long. With typical understatement the poet declares:

No his lifgedal
sarlic þuhte secga ænegum. (841-2)
[His parting from life did not seem painful to any of the men.]

But the distress of the Danes is renewed by the loss of the peerless Æschere on the very night of the banquet to celebrate Beowulf's victory. The sorrow is prolonged in the scene at the mere, when the Danes despair of his success in the encounter with Grendel's mother and set out for Heorot. On the other hand, the Geats, bound by the ties of loyalty to their lord, remain gazing at the water without much hope and sick at heart. On the unexpected emergence of Beowulf they rejoice to see him safe and sound, and with Grendel's head on a pole, *ferhðum fægne* [glad in their hearts], they enter Hrothgar's hall. Quite apart from such contrasts in the story proper, the poet achieves a similar result by the introduction of episodes. Thus amid the revelry at the banquet after Grendel's overthrow Hrothgar's bard sings the lay of Finn and Hengest, a theme of feud and sorrow. Again in the scene at Hygelac's hall, when Beowulf and his men have returned in triumph, the mood changes while the story of Ingeld, with all its bitter enmity and vengeance, is related.

The sombre mood recurs most frequently in the relationship of Hrothgar and Beowulf to the people over whom they rule. Grief weighs heavily on the aged Danish king when, in spite of his warlike prowess, he can do nothing to keep Grendel at bay. The poem dwells on his suffering, anxiety, and despair: 'unbliðe sæt' [sat unhappy], 'þegnsorge dreah' [endured sorrow for his followers] (130-1),

> torn geþolode
> . . . weana gehwelcne,
> sidra sorga; (147-9)
>
> [endured trouble, each of woes, of deep sorrows]

'wræc micel' [great distress], 'modes brecða' [sorrow(s) of the heart] (170-1), 'bealuwa bisigu' [torment of afflictions], 'cearwylmas' [surging of grief] (281-2). The death of Æschere, his old comrade-in-arms, was a cause of peculiar sorrow to Hrothgar.[5] He felt this the more acutely because he was seventy or more.[6] Hence it is not surprising that at the last banquet at Heorot he should let his mind travel back to all that he had undergone, *gyrn æfter gomene* [grief after joy] (1775), and that at the second banquet, in the very moment of rejoicing at the victory over Grendel, he should introduce a note of melancholy by lamenting his old age and failing strength:

> hwilum eft ongan eldo gebunden,
> gomel guðwiga gioguðe cwiðan
> hildestrengo; hreðer inne weoll,
> þonne he wintrum frod worn gemunde. (2111-14)
>
> [At times, in turn, the aged warrior, bound by age, began to mourn for his youth, his battle-strength; his breast surged within, when he, old in years, remembered many things.]

The poet went out of his way to emphasize Hrothgar's great age and physical weakness by making the Geats on the way from

[5] Cf. 1322-9 and 2129.

[6] Cf. 1769-70, where we learn that he had ruled the Danes for fifty years before Grendel's hostility began.

Heorot to their ship speak of this. To them he seemed a faultless king until old age deprived him of the joys of strength.

By the time that the dragon began his nocturnal raids, Beowulf was in much the same position as Hrothgar. He, too, had held sway for fifty years and was advanced in age (2208-10). The moment had come which Hrothgar had foreseen on the occasion of the third banquet at Heorot. It was with personal knowledge that he uttered his warning to Beowulf that the glory of his strength was but for a time and that the ways of losing it were manifold. Among these was the grasp of fire or dire old age, and he summed up with an anticipation of Beowulf's death:

semninga bið
þæt ðec, dryhtguma, deað oferswyðeð. (1767-8)
[Very soon it is that death will overcome you, warrior.]

In the second part of *Beowulf* there is a constant preoccupation with death. The hero himself meditates on the past and turns his thoughts to Hrethel, who brooded so much over the accidental slaying of his son that he died.[7] Arising out of this tragic theme is yet another grief-laden story, that of the old man whose son is hanged on the gallows. The passage (2455-62) culminates in Beowulf's comment, so poignant in its reticence: 'þuhte him eall to rum, wongas ond wicstede' [the fields and the dwelling place now seemed to him all too large]. The father is the only survivor and so his home and his lands seem far too spacious. Beowulf's insight is appropriate, for he, too, is heirless, and shortly after, when he lies dying, he regrets that he has no son to whom he can bequeath his armour (2729-32).

The mood of these later passages is anticipated in the poet's relation of the burial of the hoard which the dragon afterwards guarded so jealously. All the owners but one have been carried off by their death; their abode is deserted. Soon death overtakes the last of the race when he has committed the treasure to the earth (2236-70).

[7] This appears to be the meaning of 2469: 'gumdream ofgeaf, godes leoht geceas' [he gave up the joys of men, he chose God's light].

From the moment that Beowulf hears that his hall has been burnt down, he is overcome by a melancholy that contrasts notably with his youthful confidence at Heorot. He is filled with gloomy thoughts, as was not his wont. He takes leave of his followers, and the poet leaves no doubt that the aged Beowulf's forebodings will soon come to pass:

> Him wæs geomor sefa,
> wæfre ond wælfus, wyrd ungemete neah,
> se ðone gomelan gretan sceolde,
> secean sawle hord, sundur gedælan
> lif wið lice. (2419-23)

[His heart was sad, restless and ready for death, fate was exceedingly near, which was to greet the old man, seek the treasure of his soul, to part asunder life from the body.]

Fate, as he tells Wiglaf after the fight with the dragon, has swept away his kinsmen to their death, and he must follow (2814-16).

The scenes which thus prepare the way for Beowulf's death contain some of the noblest lines in the poem. They are specially intended to throw light on the hero. Indirectly this is done also by the attitude of his followers. Even before the fray Wiglaf's mind is sad (2632), and the force of warriors that sits awaiting news of the struggle is mournful at heart (2894). After the report has reached them, they set off sorrowfully and with welling tears (3031-2). When the pyre has been raised, the King is placed in the middle by the lamenting warriors, and as the smoke ascends, 'Higum unrote modceare mændon mondryhtnes cwealm' [Sad in soul, they complained with sorrow of heart, the death of their lord] (3148-9). Ten days later, when the mound has been completed, the solemn procession of Beowulf's retainers rides round it, bewailing their grief (3169-71). More is involved than the loss of a great ruler. Beowulf's death is a national disaster, and the messenger who carries the bad tidings is quick to foretell what they portend — invasion from abroad, captivity for the women, death in battle for the men (3016-27).

It is evident that the author of *Beowulf* constructed his poem in such a way that the end should recall the beginning, which tells how the other great hero, Scyld, passed away. At his own request Scyld is carried *to brimes faroðe* [to the current of the sea] (28); at his own request Beowulf is placed in the mound *æt brimes nosan* [on the promontory of the sea] (2803). The mourning of the followers of the Danish king is echoed by the dirge of those of the Geat. Yet there is a difference. Scyld, whose origin is enveloped in mystery, drifts away across the sea to a destination equally strange. But there is no such powerful impression as with Beowulf of national calamity and of dynastic extinction. Neither the story of Scyld nor that of Beowulf is just an illustration of the path of glory leading to the grave. Yet the issues at stake are wider in scope and deeper in effect in the one than in the other, and the poet has endeavoured by various devices to impart a peculiar force and poignancy to the exploits and death of Beowulf.

He has no meticulous design, worked out with mathematical precision from start to finish. The three groups of opposites that have been examined are seen to intersect but not to coincide; and though they contribute to a fundamental unity, as the poem advances, with the deepening of the elegiac strain sorrow gets the upper hand, and all else is subordinate. It is significant that the lament of Hrothgar over his old age and growing weakness, though spoken on the occasion of the second banquet at Heorot, is introduced only in the latter half of *Beowulf*. Here is a notable diminution of festivity, and joy gives place to melancholy. The hero broods darkly over the misfortunes that have befallen him and his people. One last survivor after the other passes in sombre procession, and Fate hangs more and more heavily over all mankind. The word *geomor* [sad] and its derivatives echo at intervals[8] like a mournful bell, and the whole culminates in the dirge for the fall of a great king.

[8] *geomor* (2419, 2632, 3150); *geomorlic* [sad] (2444); *geomormod* [sad of heart] (2044, 2267, 3018).

13

SAPIENTIA ET FORTITUDO AS THE CONTROLLING THEME OF *BEOWULF**

R. E. Kaske

I

IT SEEMS GENERALLY AGREED THAT *Beowulf* IS A POEM ESSENTIALLY about a hero and heroism. I believe that the elaboration of these important concepts in the poem is based on the old, widely-recognized heroic ideal of *sapientia et fortitudo,* which so far has received only incidental attention in *Beowulf* studies;[1] and that the *sapientia et fortitudo* ideal is accordingly the most basic theme in the poem, around which the other major themes are arranged and to which they relate in various ways. So far as I can see, this interpretation generally complements rather than opposes the most important *Beowulf* criticism of the past twenty-odd years. While it is perhaps no great novelty in the literature of any age or race to find an epic hero wise and brave, the formulary use of the *sapientia et fortitudo* ideal in *Beowulf,* as I hope to show it, seems to me to speak for a high degree of conscious-

* Reprinted, by permission of the author, and the editor of *Studies in Philology,* from that journal, LV (July 1958), 423-457.

[1] Most from Anton Pirkhofer, *Figurengestaltung im Beowulf-Epos* (Anglistische Forschungen, 87; Heidelberg, 1940), pp. 101-2, 114-5, 118, 125. Ernst Otto, *Typische Motive in dem weltlichen Epos der Angelsächsen* (Berlin, 1902), pp. 11-2, and Friedrich Klaeber, "Die christlichen Elemente im *Beowulf,* III," *Anglia,* XXXV (1912), 457, both consider it as part of a Thought-Word-Deed formula. Frederick Tupper, *Types of Society in Medieval Literature* (New York, 1926), p. 37, mentions one obvious example.

ness in its employment. For the sake of clarity I will adhere generally to the Latin formulation of the ideal, whatever the poet's own version of it may have been.

Ernst Curtius[2] has sketched the development of the *sapientia et fortitudo* ideal in the Græco-Latin-Christian tradition: its supposed origin in Homer and adaptation by Vergil, and its subsequent decline to a rhetorical *topos* ["commonplace"], expressing sometimes a combination of the two heroic virtues in a single hero, sometimes a separation of them anticipating the later tragedy of

> Rodlanz est proz ed Oliviers est sages.
> [Roland is brave and Oliver is wise.]

The value of Curtius' study for my present purpose lies in his examples of the use of the *sapientia et fortitudo* formula in literature possibly contributing to or reflecting aspects of the culture that produced *Beowulf.* It is variously employed, for example, by Statius; by "Dares" and "Dictys"; by the sixth-century Fulgentius Mythographus in interpreting the opening line of the *Aeneid;* in a poem of Alcuin and a number of other Carolingian pieces in the *Monumenta Germaniae Historica;* and in the *Waltharius* (103-5).[3] As a possible suggestion of theme for *Beowulf,* the most promising reference cited by Curtius seems to me to be that in the enormously popular *Etymologiæ* of Isidore of Seville: "Heroicum enim carmen dictum, quod eo virorum fortium res et facta narrantur. Nam heroes appellantur viri quasi aerii et caelo digni propter sapientiam et fortitudinem."[4] [For a song is called heroic because in it the affairs and doings of brave men are narrated. For men are called "heroes" (*heroes*) as if to say

[2] Zur Literarästhetik des Mittelalters, II," *ZfrPh,* LVIII (1938), 200-15. More briefly but with some additions in *Europäische Literatur und lateinisches Mittelalter* (Bern, 1948), pp. 177-83.

[3] Curtius, "Literarästhetik," pp. 203 ff.; *Europ. Lit.,* pp. 181-3.

[4] Ed. W. M. Lindsay (Oxford, 1911), Bk. I, 39, 9. Also VIII, 11, 98; and X, 2, "Aeros, vir fortis et sapiens." On the probable availability of the *Etymologiæ,* see J. D. A. Ogilvy, *Books Known to Anglo-Latin Writers from Aldhelm to Alcuin (670-804)* (Cambridge, 1936), p. 47.

that they are "aerial" (*aerii*), and worthy of heaven on account of wisdom and fortitude.] The same dichotomy, though hardly to be thought of as a heroic ideal, is frequent in the Old Testament, particularly in the Sapiential Books and the Book of Job.[5] Similar expressions occur in the *Disticha Catonis*[6] and the Irish *Instructions of Cormac.*[7]

In the Germanic tradition as we have it, the *sapientia et fortitudo* ideal appears in the poems of the *Edda,* as for example in the *Hávamál*:

þagalt ok hugalt skyli þióðans barn
ok vígdiarft vera; . . . [8]

[Silent and thoughtful shall a king's son be, and daring in battle.]

It is also frequent in Old English poetry. One finds, for example, clear expository references embedded in the *Gifts of Men* (39-43, 76-7)[9] and at the end of *Widsiþ* (138-41). As a basic formula for describing a hero, *sapientia et fortitudo* occurs in many of the religious-heroic poems.[10] In the *Descent into Hell* it is em-

[5] I Par. 22:12-3; Job 9:4; 12:12-3, 16; 36:22, 26; 37: 23-4; 38 ff., passim; Ps. 89:11-2; Prov. 8:14; 16:32; 21:22; 24:5-6; Eccle. 9:18; Sap. 6:1; 8:15; 10:12; Ecclus. 15:19; 22:20; Jer. 9:23; 51:15; Dan. 2:20, 23; Ezek. 28:4-5. Some of these references, and those in the *Disticha Catonis,* are noted by Curtius, "Literarästhetik," p. 206.

[6] Ed. Marcus Boas, completed by H. J. Botschuyver (Amsterdam, 1952), p. 208 (IV, 12); p. 109 (II, 9).

[7] Ed. and transl. Kuno Meyer (Royal Irish Academy, Todd Lecture Series, XV; Dublin, 1909), pp. 26-7.

[8] Str. #15, 1-2, ed. Gustav Neckel, *Edda: Die Lieder des Codex Regius nebst verwandten Denkmälern* (Germanische Bibliothek, 2nd Abt., IX; 2nd ed., Heidelberg, 1927), I, 18. See also #64, 1-2, p. 26; #131, 4, p. 37; *Vafþrúðnismál,* #1, 3-4, and #2, 3-4, p. 44; *Gripísspá,* #7, 1-4, p. 161; *Sigrdrífomál,* #36, 3-4, p. 192; *Atlakviða,* #9, 2, p. 235; *Hamðismál,* #27, 1-2, p. 267.

[9] All references to OE poetry, including *Beowulf,* are from *The Anglo-Saxon Poetic Records,* 6 vols., ed. G. P. Krapp and E. v. K. Dobbie (New York, 1931-53), by line numbers.

[10] *Andreas,* 624-5; 919; 1495-7; 1577-9; *Guthlac,* 156-8; 184; 1109; *Judith,* 145-6; 333-4 (no corresponding expressions in Vulgate); *Juliana,* 431-2; 547-51 (no corresponding expressions in *Acta S. Julianae;* see William Strunk's ed. (Boston, 1904), pp. 41, 43); *Elene,* 934-5; *Genesis,* 1151-2; *Exodus,* 12-4; *Daniel,* 666.

ployed in a heroic description of the risen Christ (21-3). Alfred seems to give evidence of a similar pattern of thought in his preface to the *Liber Pastoralis*.[11]

There seems hardly any room for doubt, then, that *sapientia et fortitudo* as a heroic ideal was familiar in the literature and the ways of thought most likely to have been available to the poet of *Beowulf,* and that there is no *a priori* unlikelihood about his having known and used the theme. But if so, what did it mean to him? As the quality of a hero, *fortitudo* implies physical might and courage consistently enough. With regard to *sapientia,* we seem to have in *Beowulf* a general, eclectic concept including such diverse qualities as practical cleverness, skill in words and works, knowledge of the past, ability to predict accurately, prudence, understanding, and the ability to choose and direct one's conduct rightly;[12] in this respect it contrasts noticeably with the *sapientia* of the religious-heroic poems, which seems more strictly Augustinian. But there is a further, partly overlapping problem: Christian *sapientia* or pagan Germanic *sapientia?* Statements of "Christian" *sapientia,* possibly available to the poet of *Beowulf,* are prominent in the Sapiential and other books of the Old Testament and the various references in the New; the mountainous works of the Fathers and lesser early Christian writers; the *De Consolatione* of Boethius; predominantly Christian gnomic utterances like the *Precepts* of the Exeter Book; popular hangers-on of questionable orthodoxy like the *Disticha Catonis;*

[11] Ed. Henry Sweet (EETS, OS 45, 1871), p. 2: ". . . & hu him ða speow ægðer ge mid wige ge mid wisdome. . . [and how they prospered both with war and with wisdom]."

[12] So comparatively naturalistic a view of *sapientia* may seem unlikely in a Christian writer of the eighth century. All these aspects, however, may be found in the *sapientia* of the Vulgate Old Testament; for a good many of them in combination, see Sap. 8:7-8. Comparable views of *sapientia* can also be found among early Christian writers. See Ambrose, *PL* 14, 492, with some dependence on Sap. 8:8; the dedication of St. Martin of Braga's *Formula Vitæ Honestæ, PL* 72, 22-3; Isidore on "sapiens," *Etymologiæ,* X, 241; and the anonymous seventh-century *Testimonia Divinæ Scripturæ et Patrum, PL* 83, 1207.

and so on. Pagan Germanic wisdom — in whatever form it may have been known to the *Beowulf* poet — reaches us through collections of basically pagan gnomes more or less interlarded with Christian sentiments; the belated evidence of the sagas; and the reconstructions of Germanic scholars.[13] Which body of "*sapientia*" is pertinent for interpreting *Beowulf?*

I believe that in the *sapientia et fortitudo* theme itself we may find "the precise point at which an imagination, pondering old and new, was kindled" [14] — that the poet has used this old ideal as an area of synthesis between Christianity and Germanic paganism. In a broad way, he seems first to draw on both traditions primarily as they relate to *sapientia et fortitudo;* and secondly, within this circumscribed area he seems to emphasize those aspects of each tradition that can be made reasonably compatible with the viewpoint of the other — somewhat like Dante's more complex synthesis of classical and Christian morality in the *Inferno*.[15] Hence, from the Christian point of view, the strangely Old Testament tone of the poem, since the *sapientia* of the Old Law is more nearly compatible with the wisdom of Germanic paganism than is the *sapientia* of the New. And hence from the Germanic point of view the almost chivalric character of Beowulf as compared with, say, Sigmundr, since uses of "wisdom" open to Sigmundr will not be open to Beowulf. I do not mean of course that the poet has preserved so equivocal a principle of selection uniformly throughout. The *sapientia* of Hroðgar's sermon is certainly more Christian than Germanic (though I think not so much as is usually assumed); the wisdom of Hengest — if I may illustrate by an example I do not intend to discuss — is peculiarly Germanic, and that of Wiglaf is Germanic at least in

[13] A convenient brief account is Andreas Heusler, "Altgermanische Sittenlehre und Lebensweisheit," in *Germanische Wiedererstehung,* ed. Hermann Nollau (Heidelberg, 1926), pp. 156-204.

[14] The expression is that of J. R. R. Tolkien, "*Beowulf*: The Monsters and the Critics," *Proc. Brit. Acad.,* XXII (1936), 269.

[15] W. H. V. Reade, *The Moral System of Dante's Inferno* (Oxford, 1909), especially Ch. 20 and 22-5.

its emphasis. In Beowulf himself, however, the equivocation seems to me to be generally maintained. We may notice in passing that a core of this kind in the poem helps account for some of its apparent large ambiguities, like the co-existence of eternal salvation and earthly glory as the goals of human life. If Beowulf is deliberately made to behave wisely and bravely according to both codes, then the very ambiguity of both the *soðfæstra dom* [judgment of the righteous] and earthly *lof* [praise, fame, glory] is not only relevant but in a way demanded. This same principle may perhaps help account for the roles of God and Wyrd in the poem, with emphasis on Beowulf's wise acknowledgement of the power of each.

Convenience dictates that we approach the poem by way of the major characters, in the following order: Beowulf in Part I (1-2199); Hroðgar and the Danes; the Grendel family; Hygelac and the Geats; Beowulf and the dragon; and finally the "over-theme" of God's *Sapientia et Fortitudo.* In the hope of proportion and clarity, I will make no attempt to deal with a number of episodes and passages which are not necessary to establish the main lines of my interpretation, and which would require an unwieldy amount of additional explanation — the Finn Episode, the Sigemund-Heremod and Hama-Hygelac passages, the passage on Weohstan's sword, and others. All of them, I believe, can be firmly attached to my interpretation; but the very nature of the problems they present makes it more convenient to take them up in individual studies.[15a]

II

In Part I, we find five key allusions to the *sapientia et fortitudo* of Beowulf, arranged symmetrically within the poem and themselves following a pattern of increasing elaborateness. The first, climactically withheld until after Beowulf's first definite victory,

[15a] Two of these studies have subsequently appeared, as "The Sigemund-Heremod and Hama-Hygelac Passages in *Beowulf,*" *PMLA,* LXXIV (1959), 489-94; and "Weohstan's Sword," *MLN,* LXXV (1960), 465-8.

is the poet's summarizing description of him immediately following the defeat of Grendel:

> Hæfde þa gefælsod se þe ær feorran com,
> snotor ond swyðferhð, sele Hroðgares. (825-6)

[He who had come previously from afar, wise and stout-hearted, had cleansed Hrothgar's hall.]

The second is Wealhþeow's admonition to Beowulf near the end of the festivities following the Grendel fight:

> cen þec mid cræfte ond þyssum cnyhtum wes
> lara liðe. (1219-20)

[Show yourself with valor, and be kind of counsel to these boys.]

The third is Hroðgar's remark to Beowulf following the defeat of Grendel's mother:

> Eal þu hit geþyldum healdest,
> mægen mid modes snyttrum. (1705-6)

[You hold it all with patience, strength with wisdom of mind.]

The fourth is Hroðgar's similar comment near the end of the festivities following her defeat:

> ne hyrde ic snotorlicor
> on swa geongum feore guman þingian.
> Þu eart mægenes strang ond on mode frod,
> wis wordcwida. (1841-5)

[Never heard I a man speak more wisely, so young in years. You are strong of might and wise in mind, wise of speech.]

So far, I trust the symmetry is clear: a reference to Beowulf's *sapientia et fortitudo* as the thematic climax of each battle and of each celebration following his battles. The fifth and most elaborate statement occurs at the end of Beowulf's reception at the court of Hygelac, and seems to serve as the thematic climax of Part I as a whole. The poet first alludes to Beowulf's *fortitudo* (2177-8) and then summarizes the *sapientia* of his career — his pursuit of glory and his avoidance of Germanic crime (2178-80). The passage concludes:

> næs him hreoh sefa,
> ac he mancynnes mæste cræfte
> ginfæstan gife, þe him god sealde,
> heold hildedeor. (2180-3)

[His heart was not fierce, but he, brave in battle, guarded by means of the highest power the noble gift which God gave to him.]

Mæste cræfte I translate as "by means of the highest power," that is, *sapientia* — though Klaeber's "ability" or "self-control" would carry much the same force, as a product of *sapientia.*[16] So interpreted, the passage takes on added point as an exact confirmation, by the poet, of Hroðgar's comment following the fall of Grendel's mother (1705-6). *Hreoh sefa* [fierce heart] I take to be a description of *malitia,* an interpretation that will become clear as we proceed.

These five important passages[17] are supported by Beowulf's speeches and actions in Part I. His *fortitudo* is obvious. As for his *sapientia,* he has at the simplest level the skill and quickness of invention that go to make an effective warrior. He is wise in the ways of violence — both "philosophically," in his manner of accepting it (440-55, 1384-9), and practically, in his ability to plan against it. His skill in using words and his accurate appraisal of men, together with his other gifts of mind, make him an effective and persuasive speaker in a variety of situations;[18] and these same gifts — plus, apparently, a subtle grasp of situation and innuendo (1836-9) and some skill in intertribal affairs (1826-35) — make him a competent diplomat. His wise foresight is shown by his preparations for combat, his arrangements for the management of his affairs in case of his death (1474-91), his clear realization of the possible outcome of his own actions (440-55),

[16] Ed. *Beowulf* (3rd ed.; Boston, 1936), pp. 207, 313. Johannes Hoops' strenuous objection to the traditional construction of these lines, *Beowulfstudien* (Heidelberg, 1932), pp. 76-8, is apparently based on nothing but the belief that it makes no sense in context; but this objection seems eliminated by my interpretation.

[17] Other lesser or doubtful statements: (1) ll. 669-70, with Beowulf's trust in God as *sapientia;* (2) ll. 860-1, if one is willing to understand *rices wyrðra* [more worthy of a kingdom] as synecdoche for *sapientia;* (3) ll. 1270-3, same comment as on (1).

[18] Probably Beowulf's tendency to speak in "Lebensregeln," noted by Pirkhofer, *Figurengestaltung,* p. 127 and note 1, is to be considered further evidence of his *sapientia.*

and his ability to predict accurately in the affairs of others (974-7, 1674-6, 2029-69). He knows his own worth, but he also knows the value of controlling himself and is aware of other possible limiting or controlling factors, like the counsels of wise men (415-7) and the dependence of human affairs on Wyrd (455) and on God (1272-3, 1657-64). Finally, he places an appropriately high value on glory, and apparently holds other good things, like wealth, as properly subordinate to it.

As a specific example, we may notice Beowulf's successive speeches with the coastwarden, Wulfgar, Hroðgar, and Unferþ, which form a series of confrontations designed to illustrate the *sapientia* of Beowulf in handling different types of questioners, and a broad parallel to the test of his *fortitudo* in the monster-fights. The initial challenge of the coastwarden contains a more or less open imputation of recklessness — *fortitudo* without *sapientia* (244-7). The success of Beowulf's answer (260-85) in removing this impression is indicated by the coastwarden's response, particularly the difficult gnomic passage with which he begins:

Æghwæþres sceal
scearp scyldwiga gescad witan,
worda ond worca, se þe wel þenceð. (287-9)

[The keen shield-warrior who thinks well must know the difference between these two — words and deeds.]

We can see here, I think, a double appeal to the *sapientia et fortitudo* ideal. The coastwarden, seeing the Geats land, had formed an impression of their audacity; he now learns from Beowulf's speech that they are wisely led, and remarks that it is best to judge by words as well as deeds — words as the means of judging *sapientia,* as deeds are the means of judging *fortitudo.* His *scearp scyldwiga . . . se þe wel þenceð* appears to be a further appeal to the ideal, meaning in effect, "the hero equal to all occasions through his *fortitudo* and *sapientia.*" The success of Beowulf's two quite different replies to Wulfgar, himself an exemplar of the same ideal (349-50), and to Hroðgar — two worthy but strongly contrasting questioners — is evident.

The last questioner, Unferþ, provides a hostile test of Beowulf's *sapientia*. If, as seems likely, the office of *þyle* implies some professional command of wisdom or knowledge,[19] I would interpret Unferþ himself in accordance with Gregorian psychology, as the speaker of *sapientia* who because of arrogance is himself no longer *sapiens*.[20] His taunt accuses Beowulf of recklessness — a lack of *sapientia* — and of a *fortitudo* inferior to Breca's. Beowulf defends his *sapientia* by emphasizing the formal *beot* [promise, vow] (536) with its implicit purpose of attaining glory; the fitness of this venture for boys (535-7); and their prudence in carrying weapons (539-41). To the reflection on his *fortitudo* he replies that he was not overcome; and that for him — unlike Breca — the exploit turned into an adventure

[19] Laurence Marcellus Larson, *The King's Household in England Before the Norman Conquest* (Bulletin of the University of Wisconsin, No. 100, 1904), pp. 120-1; Walther Heinrich Vogt, *Stilgeschichte der eddischen Wissensdichtung,* I: *Der Kultredner* (Breslau, 1927), rev. Kemp Malone, *MLN*, XLIV (1929), 129-30; D. E. Martin Clarke, "The Office of Thyle in *Beowulf*," *RES,* XII (1936), 61-6.

[20] *Moralia in Job, PL* 76, 442: "Viri namque arrogantes et docti cum recte non vivunt, sed tamen recta dicere doctrinæ impulsionibus compelluntur, ipsi damnationis suæ aliquomodo præcones fiunt, quia dum ea quæ agere respuunt prædicantes insinuant, suis se vocibus damnatos clamant. . . . Unde summa cura providendum est ne accepta sapientia, cum ignorantiæ tenebras illuminat, lumen humilitatis tollat, et jam sapientia esse nequeat. Quæ etsi virtute locutionis fulgeat, elationis tamen velamine cor loquentis obscurat." ["For proud and learned men, when they do not live properly but are forced to speak properly by the pressures of doctrine, are made in a certain sense the heralds of their own damnation, because while as preachers they demand what they abhor doing, they proclaim that they are damned with their own voices. . . . Therefore the greatest care must be taken lest the wisdom received, when it enlightens the darkness of ignorance, should put out the light of humility, and already wisdom could not exist. Wisdom, although it shines by virtue of speech, still darkens the heart of the speaker with a shade of vainglory."] See also cols. 269-70. All citations from Gregory are from the *Moralia in Job* unless otherwise noted.

worthy of a grown warrior: a fight against monsters, representing like Grendel the forces of external violence.

III

With this suggestion of how the ideal applies to Beowulf in Part I, I turn to Hroðgar. Like Nestor or Latinus, he is a model of kingly *sapientia* no longer supported by *fortitudo*.[21] This fact is stated unambiguously in Beowulf's description of him to Hygelac (2111-4), a passage which in turn clarifies the time-reference in other descriptions of his age (especially 1885-7). There are, to be sure, along with the many remarks characterizing Hroðgar as *sapiens*, a number that seem to characterize him as *fortis;* but I think they can all be interpreted without violence as references to something other than the literal present.[22] The majority referring to Hroðgar's *fortitudo* in the past probably carry overtones besides of a kind of "predicamental irony" — a melancholy comment on the fact that things are as they are, and in this world must be so. Moreover, with two possible and

[21] Gregory, *PL* 75, 674: ". . . mentis virtute crescente, oportet procul dubio ut carnis fortitudo torpescat." ["When the mind's power grows, it must undoubtedly happen that the body's fortitude declines."]

[22] Ll. 64-5 avowedly refer to the past; *guðcyning* [warrior king] (199) occurs in a report of Beowulf's speech and is interpretable as courtesy; *guðrof* [brave in battle] (608) can refer to his fame from the past, and the emphasis seems thrown in that direction by *gamolfeax* [grey-haired]; *sigerof* [renowned for victory] (619), same explanation; *wigfruma* [war chief] (664) seems firmly established as melancholy irony by the very situation; ll. 1039-42 are established as a reference to the past by the saddle's now being given to Beowulf; *Healfdenes hildewisan* [the battle-leader of Healfdene] (1064) is clearly a title out of the past (see Klaeber's note, *Beowulf*, p. 170); *rice* [the mighty (one)] (1237) refers rather to his power of rule; *hilderinc* [battle warrior] (1307) seems thrown into the past by *frod* [wise, old] and *har* [gray], and by the contrasting epithets for Hroðgar and Beowulf which immediately follow (1310-19); *modige on meþle* [brave men in council] (1876) seems to aim at describing the atmosphere of the council rather than Hroðgar.

weak exceptions,[23] the expressions indicating *sapientia* in Hroðgar are never joined with those indicating *fortitudo*, as they are for Beowulf — one more sign, apparently, that in Hroðgar the two qualities are temporally distinct.

Hroðgar's *sapientia* is of course different from that of Beowulf — a contemplative wisdom primarily of inner cultivation of self, rather than of external proficiency and accomplishment. It receives its greatest expression in his "sermon," introduced as a sort of typical case-history to explain the phenomenon of such a king as Heremod (1709-22). This explanation is simply a psychological analysis — in terms of patristic psychology, chiefly that of Augustine and Gregory — of the progressive loss of *sapientia* in the human mind. A detailed interpretation of the sermon will be presented in a separate article; a summary will best serve my purpose here.

Sapientia is bestowed by God (1724-7), in accordance with the continual assertions of the Scriptures[24] and the teachings of the Fathers.[25] This patristic *sapientia* is the *bonorum operum magistra* [the teacher of good works], and man's greatest defense against evildoing; it is lost through evildoing itself but increased through righteous living.[26] In Hroðgar's sermon, the beginning of the man's downfall occurs *for his unsnyttrum* [be-

[23] Ll. 1306-7, *frod cyning, har hilderinc* [wise king, gray battle warrior], would involve reading the equivocal *frod* with emphasis on *sapientia*, plus the considerations mentioned in note 22. L. 190, *snotor hæleð* [wise man], would necessitate reading *hæleð* as an indication of present *fortitudo*. Though such a reading would be likely enough in itself (see my interpretation of ll. 50-2 below), it is not demanded; and everything here seems against it. John R. Clark Hall (transl.), *Beowulf*, rev. C. L. Wrenn and J. R. R. Tolkien (London, 1950), p. 30, translates, "the wise prince."

[24] I Reg. 3:29; Prov. 2:6; Eccle. 2:26; Ecclus. 43:27; Jer. 9:23; Dan. 2:21-3; Acts 7:10; James 1:5-6. And see the account of the king of Tyre, Ezek. 28:1-19, which in a general way parallels the story of Hroðgar's sermon.

[25] For example Augustine, *De Libero Arbitrio* (hereafter *LA*), III, 24, 72, *PL* 32, 1306; and *De Gratia et Libero Arbitrio, PL* 44, 912.

[26] Gregory, *PL* 76, 243-4; Augustine, *LA*, III, 24, 72-3, *PL* 32, 1306-7.

cause of his folly] (1734), to which he has been brought by worldly prosperity (1727-39).[27] His decisive turn from *sapientia* comes with the sin of pride —

oðþæt him on innan   oferhygda dæl
weaxeð ond wridað.   (1740-1)

[until a measure of overbearing pride waxes and grows within him.]

— firmly established by Augustine as the beginning of all sin;[28] the opposition between *sapientia* and pride is obvious.[29] For reasons that would lead too far from the present subject, I prefer to interpret the *weard . . . sawele hyrde* [the guardian . . . guardian of the soul] (1741-2) as *sapientia* itself put to sleep by pride; but even if this guardian is to be thought of as "conscience," "intellect," or "reason,"[30] its sleep represents a turning away from *sapientia* coincident with the growth of pride.[31]

Passing over the *bona* [slayer] and his arrows, we encounter the lines,

þinceð him to lytel   þæt he lange heold,
gytsað gromhydig,   nallas on gylp seleð
fædde beagas. . . .   (1748-50)

[What he has held for a long time seems to him too little; he covets wrathful-minded, not at all does he, exuberantly, give gold rings.]

Their dominating theme is *avaritia*, which even in early Christian thought is sometimes considered the root of all sin, in accordance with the well known I Tim. 6:10.[32] Augustine, confronted by the scriptural designations of both *superbia* and *avaritia* as

[27] On the opposition between material prosperity and *sapientia*, see especially Gregory, *PL* 76, 75-6.

[28] William M. Green, *Initium Omnis Peccati Superbia: Augustine on Pride as the First Sin* (Berkeley, 1949).

[29] "Superbia enim avertit a sapientia" [For pride turns one away from wisdom], Augustine, *LA* III, 24, 73, *PL* 32, 1307. See also Gregory, *PL* 76, 98. Also Prov. 8:13; 11:2; 13:10; 14:3; 21:4; Ecclus. 15:7; Ezek. 28:5-7, 17. In OE poetry, see especially *Daniel*, 593-611.

[30] Klaeber, *Beowulf*, p. 191; "Christliche Elemente," pp. 131-2.

[31] The opposition between *sapientia* and the worldly cares implicit in *bisgum gebunden* [hedged in with cares] (1743) is well stated by Gregory, *PL* 76, 76-80, and in the OE *Elene*, 1239-46.

[32] For example Gregory, *PL* 76, 150; *PL* 75, 1073-4.

the source of evil, explains that the two have a necessary mutual connection, since *superbia* is really the dominating principle of *avaritia* in its larger sense, including not only *amor pecuniæ* [love of money] but a desire for more than is sufficient in all things.[33]

This part of the sermon presents primarily,[34] then, a pattern of pride and Augustinian avarice as the two great sources of spiritual ruin. The account concludes with an allusion to the final absence of *sapientia*:[35]

. . . ond he þa forðgesceaft
forgyteð ond forgymeð, þæs þe him ær god sealde,
wuldres waldend, weorðmynda dæl. (1750-2)

[and he forgets and neglects the future because God, the Ruler of Heaven, gave him earlier his share of honors (glory).]

The state of the man at this point may be described as one of *malitia,* used among early Christian writers with the general meaning, "peccatum gravius, peccandi studium" [quite serious sin, eagerness to commit sin],[36] though it is still used also with varying degrees of its classical meanings: deceitful wickedness, or the will to harm or love of harming.[37] Gregory considers it the *vitiorum mater* [mother of the vices][38] (as *sapientia* is the *bonorum operum magistra* [the teacher of good works]), and elsewhere describes it as one of the marks of a *mens perversa*

[33] *De Genesi ad Litteram,* XI, 15, 19, *PL* 34, 436-7; also *LA* III, 17, 48, *PL* 32, 1294-5.

[34] A complementary pattern, based on Gregory's analysis of the interdependence of the capital vices, will be examined in the article mentioned above.

[35] The thought is paralleled, along with a more specific reference to *sapientia,* in *Christ* III, 1549-54.

[36] *Thesaurus Linguae Latinae,* VIII, 188.

[37] Ibid., VIII, 187. See for example Augustine, Sermon 353, *PL* 39, 1560-1: "Quid est malitia nisi nocendi amor?" [What is *malitia* but a love of doing harm?]

[38] *Reg. Past. Lib.,* III, 9, *PL* 77, 61. See also *PL* 75, 923; also St. Peter Chrysologus, *PL* 52, 287: "Bonitas virtutum mater, malitia origo vitiorum." [Goodness is the virtues' mother, *malitia* is the origin of the vices.]

[perverse mind], the result of guilt being added to guilt.[39] St. Boniface makes it the underlying principle in a list of *capitalia peccata* [capital sins].[40] Isidore stresses the element of habitual evil: "Malitiosus, deterior malo, quia frequenter malus" [*Malitiosus,* worse in evil because often evil].[41]. All these aspects, except deceit, are of course prominent both in Heremod and in the man of the sermon. And *malitia* is naturally enough opposed to *sapientia*:

Pauci sunt, qui calcatis vitiis tramitem teneant veritatis, dum malitia innumeris nocendi utitur artibus, et vinci non potest, nisi sapientiæ desuper fulciamur auxilio. . . . Sapientia quippe in nobis operatur bonum: postquam ei mundum cordis præbuerimus habitaculum, et cogitationes in opera verterimus. [So long as *malitia* employs its countless means of doing harm and cannot be overcome, few there are who — trampling down their vices — would hold to the path of truth, unless we were supported by the help of wisdom from above. . . . Wisdom assuredly works good in us, as soon as we have offered it the pure habitation of the heart and have turned our thoughts into deeds.][42]

After a familiar sapiential reflection[43] on the frequent fate of unwisely cherished wealth (1753-7), Hroðgar applies the lesson of his sermon directly to Beowulf:

Bebeorh þe ðone bealonið, Beowulf leofa,
secg betsta, ond þe þæt selre geceos,
ece rædas; oferhyda ne gym,
mære cempa. (1758-61)

[Protect yourself, dear Beowulf, against evil rancor, best of men, and choose the better course, eternal counsels; heed not pride, famous warrior.]

He is to keep himself from *bealonið* [evil rancor], which I understand to mean those final, overt aspects of *malitia*[44] that de-

[39] *PL* 75, 786.
[40] *PL* 89, 855.
[41] *Etymologiæ,* X, 176.
[42] Jerome, *PL* 22, 815. See also Augustine, *LA* III, 24, 72, *PL* 32, 1306. Note Sap. 1:4, 7:30.
[43] For example Ps. 38:7; Prov. 28:8; Eccle. 6:2-3; Ecclus. 14:4. Cp. Exeter Gnomes (Maxims I), 154-5.
[44] C. W. M. Grein, *Sprachschatz der angelsächsischen Dichter,* rev. J. J. Köhler (Heidelberg, 1912), p. 39, defines *bealunið* as "studium pravum vel perniciosum" [perverse or destructive zeal].

stroyed Heremod as a king. He is to do this by nipping the evil in the bud, by not letting his prosperity betray him to pride, the first inner step in a man's spiritual ruin. As opposed to pride, he is to choose *þæt selre . . . ece rædas* [the better course . . . eternal counsels] — the lasting counsels of *sapientia*.[45]

The remainder of the sermon may be briefly summarized. *Fortitudo* soon fades through death or age (1761-8). When it does, even the king who has cultivated *sapientia* — Hroðgar himself — must expect great afflictions; but afflictions of this sort, to a wise man who trusts in God, may be only temporary (1769-81). By implication, the king who does not cultivate *sapientia* — Heremod — inevitably loses all. Before leaving the sermon, however, let us notice that its apparent univocal "Christianity" is in part deceptive. The poet bases his psychological explanation intensively on patristic analysis, presumably because it was the only tool at his disposal for dealing in a concrete way with man's inner consciousness. But the *sapientia* of the sermon, while psychologically it behaves like that of the Fathers, is seen in relation to an inner and an outer world that for the most part are as Germanic as they are Christian. Hroðgar's explicit aim is not eternal salvation, but wise kingship. The only basically Christian references in the sermon are the general ones to God as distributor and ruler of all, and the psychologically useful ones to pride. With these observations, I return to Hroðgar.

[45] A clear use of *ece ræd* with the meaning *sapientia* occurs in the OE *Daniel*, where God sends the Israelites prophets,

> þa þam werude   wisdom budon.
> Hie þære snytro   soð gelyfdon
> lytle hwile,   oðþæt hie langung beswac
> eorðan dreamas   eces rædes. . . .   (27-30)

[who declared wisdom to the throng. For a little while they held that wisdom as truth until desire of earthly delights deceived them of eternal counsels.]
Note also the parallel between Hroðgar's "þæt selre geceos" [choose the better course] (1759) and the statement in the *Elene* that Judas "þæt betere geceas" [chose the better course] (1038)—together with the emphasis on his reception of *sapientia* (934-8, 958-66) leading to the choice.

If Hroðgar is a model of kingly *sapientia,* how does he make such mistakes as the marriage of Freawaru to Ingeld and, apparently, the unwise toleration of Hroþulf at the Danish court? I believe that his perfection in the *sapientia* of his sermon — that most befitting rulership and old age — has obscured certain features of heroic, youthful *sapientia* still accompanied by *fortitudo.* There are situations in which wise decision itself must include a reliance on physical courage and prowess; and Hroðgar's very *sapientia* has been circumscribed by his decline in *fortitudo.*[45a] As we meet him in the poem, he is no longer at his best when facing decisions involving violence or the prospect of it. With the waning of his own *fortitudo,* violence no longer compels his attention as a force to be foreseen, guarded against where possible, and sometimes fought directly. He now relies chiefly on counsel, kingly munificence, diplomacy, and wise endurance — all valuable means in themselves, but indifferent substitutes for *fortitudo* as a defense against the forces of naked violence. Hence, primarily, Hroðgar's failure to provide adequately against the threats of violence represented by Ingeld and Hroþulf. Hence also perhaps certain lesser but parallel signs in him: his failure to foresee the likelihood of vengeance for Grendel, though he had known that there were a pair of monsters (1345-57); the dramatically aimless and ineffectual — though richly poetic — quality of his long speech to Beowulf after the fresh violence (1322-82), followed by Beowulf's brief and purposeful reply (1384-96); and just possibly his leadership of the *witan* [coun-

[45a] See Fulgentius, *Expositio Virgilianae continentiae,* ed. Rudolf Helm, *Fabii Planciadis Fulgentii V. C. Opera . . .* (Bibliotheca Teubneriana; Leipzig, 1898), p. 88, in an extended application of "virtus et sapientia" to the opening line of the *Aeneid*: "Defectus enim uirtutis egritudo est sapientiae hoc uidelicet pacto, quia quidquid sapientiae consultatio agendum inuenerit, si ad subrogandum posse uirtus deficiat, curtata in suis effectibus sapientiae plenitudo torpescit." [For a defect of bravery is an illness for wisdom in this sense, that whatever wisdom's reflection has found must be done, if bravery cannot get the job done, the fullness of wisdom, curtailed of its proper effects, grows feeble.]

cillors] who form the mistaken judgment about the violent action beneath the mere (1591-1602).

This development in Hroðgar is paralleled in the Danish nation. *Sapientia* is there in great variety: the noble precept of Hroðgar himself; cultivated knowledge of the past and of the arts of song in Hroðgar (2105-14) and the scop; the tact and insight of Wealhþeow; warrior-wisdom in the coastwarden and Wulfgar; professional "wisdom" turned back upon itself in Unferþ; and the general impression of gray-headed wisdom contributed by the frequent mention of the *witan* and Beowulf's description of Æschere (2122-3). But except for the early references to the coastwarden and Wulfgar, who play no further part in the story, we hear nothing about present Danish *fortitudo* and a good deal about its absence;[46] and *sapientia* alone is at a loss against the brute violence of Grendel, as is shown dramatically in the Danes' futile search for an effective *ræd* [good counsel, wise plan] (171-4). Hroðgar sums up the situation perfectly in his speech after the combat:

Nu scealc hafað
þurh drihtnes miht dæd gefremede
ðe we ealle ær ne meahton
snyttrum besyrwan. (939-42)

[Now through the might of the Lord, a warrior has performed a deed which we could not earlier contrive by skill.]

The introduction concerning Scyld and his successor seems to form a composite presentation of the *sapientia et fortitudo*

[46] Particularly 138-43; 595-601; and *atelic egesa* [horrible fear] (784) by contrast with the behavior of the Geats. I assume that the poet would not admit the beer-courage of 480-3 as true *fortitudo* (Ecclus. 31:30-42; *Hávamál,* ed. Neckel, #12, #13, 1-2, p. 18; OE *Fortunes of Men,* 48-57; and the interpretations of *dolsceaðan* [foolish foe] (479) by S. O. Andrew, *Postscript on Beowulf* (Cambridge, 1948), p. 93, and Norman E. Eliason, "Beowulf Notes," *Anglia,* LXXI (1953), 446-7). The Danes' behavior at the attack of Grendel's mother seems courageous enough, yet even here the poet manages to imply a mistaken basis for it (1282-4). References like *scealc monig swiðhicgende* [many a strong-minded retainer] (918-9) seem plausible as irony in the light of the total situation; or perhaps simply as means to the development of an impressive scene.

ideal, with strong initial emphasis on the latter quality (1-3) by contrast with the Danes' present situation. Scyld himself is described as a model of kingly *fortitudo* (4-11); his son is distinguished for munificence (20-4), an apt enough synecdoche for kingly *sapientia* and paralleled of course in Hroðgar; and the fulfillment of the whole ideal in each of them seems implied by a summary attribution of excellence to each: *þæt wæs god cyning!* [that was a good king] (11); *Beowulf wæs breme* [Beowulf was famous] (18).[47] The whole account of Scyld closes with what may be a reference, rather like that of the coastwarden, to the *sapientes et fortes* as embodying the highest virtues of heroic society (italics mine):

Men ne cunnon
secgan to soðe, *selerædende,*
hæleð under heofenum, hwa þam hlæste onfeng. (50-2)

[Men, the counselors in the hall, men beneath the heavens, knew not how to say truly who received that burden.]

IV

As the product of the present Danish situation comes Grendel, whom I take to be an embodiment of external evil, or violence — a perversion of *fortitudo,* completely freed from the restraints of *sapientia* and directed instead by *malitia.* This interpretation of Grendel is supported not only by his reckless savagery, but also by his relationship to Cain and the giants of the Old Testament — traditionally creatures of strife and vio-

[47] This pattern is paralleled fairly closely in Saxo, I, III, 1-2; IV, 1, ed. J. Olrik & H. Ræder, *Saxonis Gesta Danorum* (Copenhagen, 1931), I, 11-3. Skiold is clearly praised for both heroic qualities (III, 1), and for munificence in particular (III, 2); he is then said to have had a son exactly like him (IV, 1). One cannot of course build too confidently on the existence of such parallels in Saxo, particularly since by his time the *sapientia et fortitudo* formula seems to have become even more popular.

lence, lacking in *sapientia*.[48] The violence of Grendel's actions speaks for itself. Let us pause only to notice that just as Beowulf is first mentioned with a comment on his *fortitudo* (196-8), Grendel is introduced as *se ellengæst* [the bold demon] (86); and that the succeeding epithets and brief descriptions of him and his actions seem to lay particular stress on violent brutality.[49]

Grendel's lack of *sapientia* also seems supported by the entire presentation of him, though there are details worth noticing. For example, such descriptions as *dreamum bedæled* [deprived of joys] (721), *ond no mearn fore; . . . wæs to fæst on þam* [and he had no regret for that; . . . he was too confirmed in them] (136-7), and *godes yrre bær* [he bore God's anger] (711) imply an absence of *sapientia* in Augustinian terms.[50] The *"giefstol"* [gift-throne] passage (166-9) I reserve for fuller treatment elsewhere; but briefly, I find the central point of the lines in the antithesis between *sincfage sel* [richly adorned hall] (167) as the worldly treasure which Grendel's might enables him to hold, and *maþðum* [treasure] (169) as the treasure of *sapientia* from which he is cut off by his own continuing *malitia*. His lack of

[48] Their strife and violence is referred to twice in *Beowulf* (113-4, 1688-90), and in the OE *Genesis* (1268-9); for further examples see Oliver F. Emerson, "Legends of Cain, Especially in Old and Middle English," *PMLA*, XXI (1906), particularly 916-26. The classic reference to the giants' lack of *sapientia* is Baruch 3:26-8, prominently cited by Augustine in the *De Civitate Dei*, XV, 23, 4, PL 41, 471. Emerson, p. 923, cites also Sap. 10:3-4 as often applied to Cain; and, p. 907, the reference in the Alfredian *Boethius*, III, pr. 12, to "'dysig Nefrod se gigant [foolish Nefrod, the giant]."

[49] Ll. 121-2, 127, 133, 136, 152-4, 156, 174, 191-3, 275-7, 737-8, 766, 2077, 2079, 2082.

[50] For l. 721, see *LA* III, 15, 44, *PL* 32, 1292-3. Also Marie Padgett Hamilton, "The Religious Principle in *Beowulf*," *PMLA, LXI* (1946), 320; as in several other places (for example my reading of ll. 166-9, below; Hamilton, p. 321), I differ only in substituting *sapientia* for her "grace"—a difference rather of emphasis than of basic meaning. For ll. 136-7, *LA* III, 15, 52, *PL* 32, 1296. *Godes yrre bær* is of course biblical and common (Klaeber, "Christliche Elemente," p. 121; Hamilton, p. 320, note 76); but the many references in Augustine (like *Civ. Dei,* XV, 21, *PL* 41, 467) probably make it in effect a negation of Augustinian *sapientia* as well.

sapientia is further alluded to in Beowulf's *for his wonhydum* [in his lack of thought] (434) and possibly also in the later variant explanation that Grendel does not know how to use weapons (681-2). His rash approach (723-6, 739-40) seems contrasted with the circumspection of Beowulf (736-8). And there is a continual contrast between what Grendel hopes or expects and what actually happens, a sort of ὕβρις [hubris] in him that contributes to poetic effect even if, logically, he could not be expected to foresee the outcome.[51]

There is, then, the strongest of contrasts between Grendel, who is all action and no reflection, and Hroðgar and his Danes, who reflect a good deal more than they act. And the tragedy of the Danish situation lies in this very spectacle of a rich and varied *sapientia* — in broad terms, a culture — so completely at the mercy of the mindless force which in a sense it has invited into being, and the sole remedy for which is an extraordinary *fortitudo*:

Swa ða mælceare maga Healfdenes
singala seað, ne mihte snotor hæleð
wean onwendan; wæs þæt gewin to swyð
laþ ond longsum. (189-92)

[Thus the son of Healfdene (Hrothgar) continually brooded over the care; the wise man was unable to put aside his woe; that strife was too strong, too hateful, and too long-lasting.]

Ealdgewinna [old adversary] (1776) is Hroðgar's final word for Grendel, and for the strife, *ofer ealdgewin* [after the old strife] (1781). He is the outer evil that waits forever on a diminishing *fortitudo*.

For the miscellaneous monsters who swim through Part I, as well as for Grendel's mother, I would suggest this same general significance. For the apparent major duplication of motif created by the introduction of Grendel's mother — analogues and possible sources apart — there are several possible expla-

[51] Ll. 712-3 *vs* 718-9; 730-4 *vs* 734-6; 745-8 *vs* 750-4; perhaps 763-5 *vs* 805-8; 967-73 *vs* 974-9; 2081-91 *vs* 2091-2.

nations. Most important, I believe, are the fact that she represents violence motivated by the duty of vengeance as against the purely malicious violence of Grendel, and so provides an important comment on the power of even defeated violence to spawn further violence; the fact that the undertaking against her develops the presentation of Beowulf's *sapientia et fortitudo* by confronting him with a number of new situations — particularly by making him much more directly dependent on the help of God (1550-6) and allowing him to illustrate his *sapientia* by acknowledging the dependence later (1657-64); and perhaps also the fact that she provides a sort of negative pattern of feminine behavior contrasting with that of Wealhþeow and Hygd and to some extent paralleled by that of "Þryð" in the same way that Grendel's violence and lack of *sapientia* contrast absolutely with the qualities of Hroðgar, are largely paralleled by those of Heremod, and so on.

V

I turn now to Hygelac and the Geats. Hygelac himself is presented as a king of unblemished *fortitudo,* but lacking in the developed *sapientia* of an ideal hero-king. The failing is shown most prominently in the repeated mentions of his Frankish raid, first introduced with a direct mention of his recklessness:

hyne wyrd fornam,
syþðan he for wlenco wean ahsode,
fæhðde to Frysum. (1205-7)

[Fate took him off when he for pride asked for woe, feud with the Frisians.]

But I think this judgment of Hygelac is also tacitly supported by such things as his previous underestimation of Beowulf (2185-8); his evident opposition to the judgment of the *snotere ceorlas* [wise men] who encouraged Beowulf's exploit (202-4, 415-20, 1987-98); and the absence of a single epithet for him expressing a variant of *sapiens,* though he is described repeatedly as *fortis*. Hygelac, then, forms a basic contrast to Hroðgar, and the contrast is sharpened by the typical motifs of vigorous youth and wise old age.[52] Together, the two constitute a melancholy presentation of the ideal almost inevitably divided; rarely does there come a Hroðgar-Hygelac, a man apt for all occasions, a Beowulf.

Hygelac is also implicitly contrasted with his wise young queen, Hygd (1926-8) — a contrast that provides a new basis for interpreting the "Þryð-Offa" episode which follows it. Offa is distinguished by the *sapientia et fortitudo* ideal:[52a]

Forðam Offa wæs
geofum ond guðum, garcene man,
wide geweorðod, wisdome heold
eðel sinne; . . . (1957-60)

[Because Offa was a spear-bold man, was honored far and wide for gifts and warfare, he ruled with wisdom his native land.]

His queen behaved unwisely (1940-1) before her marriage but changed under Offa's rule. Of the Geatish royal pair it is the queen who is wise and the king who is evidently less so; and Hygelac is not brought to kingly *sapientia* but dies through his own audacity, leaving Hygd in straits which even her woman's *sapientia* (lacking its complementary *fortitudo*) can deal with only imperfectly. The point of the contrast seems to be that while a wise and powerful king can control unwise tendencies in his queen, a wise queen in heroic times — even Hygd or Wealhþeow — can do little to offset the results of a fatal lack in her lord. The really successful ruler must combine *sapientia et fortitudo* within himself.

Just as the Danish nation reflects Hroðgar, so the Geats — particularly the Geat rulers — share in various ways the failing

[52] Otto, *Typische Motive*, pp. 22, 45; Levin L. Schücking, "Heldenstolz und Würde im Angelsächsischen," *Abhandlungen der philologisch-historischen Klasse der sächsischen Akademie der Wissenschaften*, XLII, Nr. 5 (Leipzig, 1933), pp. 31 ff.; Pirkhofer, *Figurengestaltung*, pp. 1-28.

[52a] The description reappears of Uffo in Saxo, IV, III, 1, ed. Olrik and Raeder, p. 92: "et quantum inertiae spectaculum fuit, tantum prudentiae et fortitudinis exemplum evasit" ["and as great a marvel of inertia as he had been, so great an example of prudence and fortitude did he leave behind him"].

of Hygelac. The Geatish *fortitudo* may be sufficiently illustrated by the conduct of Beowulf's troop in Part I in comparison with that of the Danes (783-801); Beowulf's offer of military support to Hroðgar (1826-35); and the battle of Ravenswood.[53] Geatish lack of *sapientia* is elaborated most fully in the historical accounts of Part II, which I interpret as a sort of catalogue of persistent unwisdom in the Geatish royal house. Its chronological beginning is artfully presented under the guise of a long reminiscence by Beowulf of his own career (2426-2508); the real organization of the speech, however, is around four great crises of Geatish history.

For the first, the shooting of Herebeald by Hæðcyn, there is admittedly no positive evidence of unwisdom in the poem, though it is not difficult to imagine the incident being regarded as an example of heedlessness; or it may be simply the unfortunate accident that sets up a situation in which a lack of *sapientia* becomes fatal. The second crisis is the death of Hreþel, and its theme — grief for which there is no remedy, a problem obviously related to the exercise of *sapientia* — is pointed by the comparison to the plight of a man whose son has died on the gallows.[54] Perhaps we are to see both a parallel and a contrast with the *apparently* remediless grief of Hroðgar (191-4, 932-9); Hroðgar wisely endures (146-9, 929-30, 1777-8), and God eventually sends him relief (930-1, 1778-81). In any event, this fatal grief of Hreþel is in Christian terms an improper or unwise *tristitia*. According to the Fathers generally, *tristitia* over having offended God is the part of *sapientia; tristitia* over having of-

[53] The trait—perhaps together with the Geatish rashness—is supported historically by Jordanes, *De Origine Actibusque Getarum*, III, 22, ed. Theodor Mommsen (*MGH, Auctores antiquissimi,* V, 1; Berlin, 1882), p. 59: "post hos . . . Gauthigoth, acre hominum genus et at bella prumtissimum." [After them . . . the Gauthigoths, a fierce tribe of men, very ready to make war.] See also Isidore, *Etymologiæ*, IX, 2, 89.

[54] Dorothy Whitelock, "*Beowulf* 2444-2471," *Medium Ævum,* VIII (1939), 198-204.

fended men, or over the loss of things of this world, is not.[55] And in every other tradition likely to have been available to the poet, one finds comments on the unwisdom of excessive grief.[56] The fact that Hreþel is a king gives the failing a significance beyond himself, in the attacks that are apparently the result of his death (2472 ff.).

The third crisis is the battle of Ravenswood. As told by Beowulf (2472-89), it is the story of a heroic and justified defense by the Geats, with nothing in it to suggest lack of *sapientia;* but I believe we must understand this as reticence on the part of Beowulf himself, consistent with both his general character and the dramatic situation. In the later and fuller review of the same events by the messenger — a commentary that has the explicit approval of the poet (3028-30)—the emphasis is unmistakable:

þa for onmedlan   ærest gesohton
Geata leode   Guðscilfingas. (2926-7)

[when for arrogance, the people of the Geats first attacked the Battle-Scylfings.]

The expedition, for all its momentary glory, results in the loss of Hæðcyn and the killing of Ongenþeow — which in turn sows the

[55] Augustine, Serm. 254, *PL* 38, 1183-4; St. John Cassian, *PL* 49, 627; Gregory, *PL* 75, 1103.

[56] In the Vulgate OT, Ecclus. 30:22-5; 38:17-24. *Disticha Catonis,* II, 25, Boas p. 132. If, as has been maintained, there is a strong Stoic or Stoic-Christian current in *Beowulf* (Schücking, "Das Königsideal im *Beowulf," MHRA Bulletin,* III (1929), 143-54), the pertinence of Senecan or Boethian *sapientia* is obvious; see also the *Libellus de Moribus,* doubtfully attributed to St. Martin of Braga, *PL* 72, 29. In OE poetry, see especially *Solomon and Saturn,* 351-2. Also perhaps *Wanderer,* 65-91, 111-5; and *Beowulf,* 1059-62. The *Fates of Men* is rather close in its emphasis on parental love and the uncertain fate of the child (1-9); its mention of death by the spear and on the gallows as possibilities (16, 33-43); and its emphasis on God's ordering (64-6, 93-8) and the implicit wisdom of acceptance. The *Hávamál* contains a characteristically shrewd observation, ed. Neckel, #23, p. 19. And in the psychologically close parallel in the *Egilssaga,* Ch. 78, ed. Sigurður Nordal, *Egils Saga Skalla-Grímssonar* (Íslenzk Fornrit, II; Reykjavik, 1933), pp. 244-5, Egil's abandonment of his first purpose is surely represented as the wiser course.

seeds of further enmity (2922-3, 2999-3001) and creates the situation leading finally to the death of Heardred.[57]

The fourth crisis in the speech of Beowulf is his oblique allusion to the fall of Hygelac (2501-8), again with no immediate imputation of unwisdom. But we have already noticed the accusation of recklessness with which the story of his raid is first introduced (1205-7); and the messenger's later foreboding remarks about it (2910-21) once again read like a necessary completion of Beowulf's tactful allusion.

We leave the speech of Beowulf now to consider the last Geatish crisis, the royal hospitality of Heardred and his resulting death (2202-6, 2379-88). That his action is to be thought of as unwise, seems probable on two counts. First, the poet appears to be at some pains to imply that Heardred's sympathies were not on the side whose claim was soundest. Eanmund and Eadgils are *wræcmæcgas* [banished men] (2379) who had rebelled against Onela (2381); and the description of Onela himself (2381-4) is an unlikely one for a usurper.[58] Secondly, the Swedes are consistently described as an enemy to be feared; Onela is presented as a strong king; and it seems reasonable to suppose that the reception of Eanmund and Eadgils might be expected to call forth an already latent hostility.[59]

In Part I, we do at first hear of *snotere ceorlas* among the Geats (202, 416), just as we are at first shown Wulfgar and the coastwarden as apparent exceptions among the Danes. There are, however, some hints pointing in the opposite direction: Beo-

[57] The suggestion of Morton W. Bloomfield, "*Beowulf* and Christian Allegory," *Traditio,* VII (1949-51), 414, that the name *Wonred* (2965, 2971) may signify "void of advice," would be a supporting detail.

[58] See Kemp Malone, *The Literary History of Hamlet* (Anglistische Forschungen, 59; Heidelberg, 1923), pp. 62-3, slightly modified in *Speculum,* XXVI (1951), 150; also R. W. Chambers, *Beowulf: An Introduction* (2nd ed. rev.; Cambridge, 1932), pp. 412-3.

[59] Beowulf's subsequent support of Eadgils (2391-6) is no objection. A course entered on unwisely may later be continued wisely, if only as the lesser evil (see *Disticha Catonis,* I, 7, Boas p. 39); and in any case, he presumably had the duty of avenging Heardred.

wulf's parenthetical *wean ahsodon* [they asked for woe] (423), which I would interpret as a reference to the Geats themselves;[60] possibly Hroðgar's barely told tale of Ecgþeow, which seems to imply a degree of rashness (459-62) though it is far from decisive;[61] and the statement that Hygelac was not alone in his early underestimation of Beowulf (2183-4).[62]

If one can assume that in Part I the Geats already have some reputation for *fortitudo* without *sapientia* and that Beowulf and his Danish interrogators are conscious of it, the motivation of many of their speeches will take on added sharpness. In the larger design of the poem, just as Danish lack of *fortitudo* invites Grendel, so Geatish lack of *sapientia* — as we shall see — partly accounts for the dragon. And as the Danish lack of *fortitudo* circumscribes *sapientia* and results finally in disaster to the Scyldings, so Geatish lack of *sapientia* exhausts *fortitudo*, and at the end leaves the Geat nation helpless before the enemies made in earlier days through lack of *sapientia*. And finally, we may perhaps see in this very failure of *sapientia* the trigger that sets in motion both great national calamities. The treaty concluded between Beowulf and Hroðgar (1826-35) has effected something like a balance of *sapientia* and *fortitudo* on an intertribal basis — Danish cultivation and Geatish military might. If we

[60] It has more usually been applied to the monsters (Hoops, *Kommentar zum Beowulf* [Heidelberg, 1932], pp. 66-7; Klaeber, *Beowulf*, p. 143). But this is syntactically more awkward, and seems supported only by the belief that the expression would not be applicable to the Geats. Hall, *Beowulf*, rev. Wrenn and Tolkien, p. 41, makes it refer to the Geats. Note the same expression used of Hygelac, 1206.

[61] This suggestion is complicated—though not necessarily disproved—by Beowulf's earlier reference to Ecgþeow's fame and long life (262-6), which in the world of *Beowulf* do not seem the likely results of rashness of character; and by Kemp Malone's arguments, "Ecgtheow," *MLQ*, I (1940), 37-44, that Ecgþeow was not a Geat but a Wylfing.

[62] Possibly also the falling asleep of Beowulf's troop in the face of imminent danger (703-5) bespeaks an unwise excess of *fortitudo*—in contrast to his retainers in Part II, who err by a lack of *fortitudo*.

may accept Professor Brodeur's opinion[63] that Hygelac's fall gave the deathblow to the Danish royal house as well as to the Geatish by making it impossible for the Geats to come to the aid of Hreðric against Hroþulf, we begin to discern in and beyond the poem a failure of *sapientia* as terrifying in its causality as that of Lear: two great dynasties brought low through a single reckless foray on the Frankish coast.

VI

We are now confronted by the difficult second part of the poem. Like Part I it is governed by the *sapientia et fortitudo* ideal, though less obviously and with one important difference: Beowulf has progressed from hero to hero-king; and the ideal, accordingly, is related to a different set of responsibilities and goals.[64] Again, however, we find a somewhat symmetrical pattern of three major statements of the theme, all more elaborate than those in Part I, and all bearing a direct relation to Beowulf's kingship.

The first occurs at Beowulf's real entry into Part II, following the announcement that his own hall has been burned (2324-7). His *sapientia,* particularly his freedom from the pride warned against by Hroðgar, is illustrated by his personal, inner response:

Þæt ðam godan wæs
hreow on hreðre, hygesorga mæst;
wende se wisa þæt he wealdende
ofer ealde riht, ecean dryhtne,
bitre gebulge. Breost innan weoll
þeostrum geþoncum, swa him geþywe ne wæs. (2327-32)

[That was distress in the breast, the greatest of heart sorrows for the good man. The wise man thought that he, contrary to ancient law, had

[63] "The Structure and the Unity of *Beowulf,*" *PMLA, LXVIII* (1953), 1191.

[64] Clearly sketched by Schücking, "Königsideal." On the adaptation of the *sapientia et fortitudo* ideal to the praise of kings, see Curtius, "Literarästhetik," pp. 207-10; *Europ. Lit.,* pp. 183-4. Possibly the concluding lines of Part I (2198-9), which otherwise seem an unlikely note on which to end, are to be taken as foreshadowing this important distinction?

bitterly offended the Almighty, the everlasting Lord. His breast was troubled within with gloomy thoughts, as was not customary for him.]

Whatever the meaning behind *ealde riht* [ancient law] (I read it as an ambiguity embracing both pagan and Christian morality), Beowulf's gloom here seems evidence of a proper and wise *tristitia*.[65] Further, the attitude implied in him by the passage inevitably suggests the common biblical connection between *timor Dei* [fear of the Lord] and *sapientia*.[66] Augustine's comment on Ps. 2:11, "Servite Domino in timore, et exultate ei cum tremore" [Serve the Lord in fear, and exult in Him tremblingly,"] elaborates the need of this wise fear among kings.[67]

After a brief reminder of the dragon's ravages against the Geat nation (2333-5), Beowulf's *fortitudo* is emphasized in his external response to the situation, as king (2335-6, 2345 ff.) — along with an illustration of warrior's *sapientia* in his provision for the iron shield (2337-41). This first appearance of Beowulf in Part II, then, is organized as a dramatic presentation of the *sapientia et fortitudo* ideal; and the dichotomy is sharpened by the introductory epithets *se wisa* [the wise man] (2329) for the first part and *guðkyning* [war-king] (2335) for the second.

The second major statement of the ideal is Beowulf's own summary, following the fatal battle, of his career as king. It begins with a description of his kingly *fortitudo* reminiscent of Scyld or the early Hroðgar (2732-6), and illustrates his *sapientia* by his avoidance of the major forms of Germanic wrongdoing (2736-43), all of them Christian sins as well.

[65] Gregory, *PL* 75, 1103: "Qui autem aut hominibus placens Deo displicet, aut simul Deo et hominibus displicere se credit, si hunc tristitia non afficit, a virtute sapientiæ alienus existit." [Whoever displeases God while pleasing men, or believes that he is displeasing God and men at the same time, lives a stranger to the virtue of wisdom if *tristitia* does not afflict him.] See also note 56 above.

[66] Job 28:28; Prov. 2:3-6; 3:7; 9:10; 14:16; 15:33; 28:14; Eccle. 9:1-2; Ecclus. 1:20-5, 34; 18:27; 19:21; 21:13. See also Prov. 18:17 and the well known Philipp. 2:12. Also Gregory, *PL* 76, 139-40. In OE, *Seafarer,* 103-6; *Guthlac,* 162-9.

[67] *PL* 36, 71-2. See also Gregory, *PL* 76, 376-8.

The third statement is in the concluding fourteen lines of the poem, where Beowulf is first praised for *fortitudo* (3169-74), and finally said to have been

. . . wyruldcyninga
manna mildust ond mon[ðw]ærust,
leodum liðost ond lofgeornost. (3180-2)

[. . . of earthly kings the mildest of men and the gentlest, kindest to his people and most eager for praise (glory).]

The first three adjectives describe in a general way traits traditionally associated with *sapientia* in the Vulgate Old Testament: "Est enim in [sapientia] spiritus intelligentiæ . . . benefaciens, humanus, benignus" [For there is in [wisdom] the spirit of understanding . . . beneficent, kindly, gracious] (Sap. 7:22-3). And such qualities are essential to the ideal of kingly *sapientia* found in Augustine, Gregory, and other early Christian writers.[68] *Lofgeornost* [most eager for praise (glory)] I would interpret as the highest manifestation of Germanic wisdom — the quest for the highest possible good, roughly corresponding to Christian salvation — preserving a final and meaningful balance between Christian and pagan as well as between kingly and individual *sapientia*.

Passing over several lesser or doubtful statements of the theme,[69] I approach the interpretation of Part II with one im-

[68] Schücking, "Königsideal," pp. 146-52. St. Martin of Braga in the *Formula Vitæ Honestæ*, *PL* 72, 26, admonishes the wise king: "Cunctis esto benignus, nemini blandus, paucis familiaris, omnibus æquus. Severior esto in judicio quam sermone, vita quam vultu: cultor clementiæ, detestator sævitiæ, bonæ famæ neque tuæ seminator, neque alienæ invidus. . . . Ad iram tardus, ad misericordiam pronus." [Be gracious to all, flattering to no one, familiar to few, just to all. Be more severe in your judgment than in your speech, in your way of life than in your appearance: one who fosters clemency, detests fierceness, is not one to sow his own good fame or to envy another's . . . slow to anger, inclined to mercy.] See also Augustine, *Civ. Dei*, V, 24, *PL* 41, 171.

[69] (1) 2369-72 as *fortitudo;* 2377 as *sapientia.* (2) *niðheard cyning* [king brave in battle] (2417) and *goldwine Geata* [gold friend of the Geats] (2419), the latter conceivably an allusion to kingly *sapientia* though it is extremely conventional. (3) The equivocal *frod* [wise, old]

portant assumption: that in view of the prominence given to Hroðgar's sermon in Part I, and the fact that it is addressed specifically to Beowulf, we may expect Part II to be in some way an account of how Beowulf does or does not live up to its precepts. The latter possibility is hardly worth considering. Now Hroðgar's advice consisted, briefly, of the admonition to cultivate *sapientia* and to combat its opposite, *malitia,* by checking the initial inner growth of pride and avarice. Or course the career of Beowulf between Parts I and II, as we pick it up piecemeal from the allusions and reminiscences, provides some evidence that he has fulfilled Hroðgar's hopes; in the long catalogue of Geatish unwisdom, in fact, the ideal conduct of Beowulf seems to be inserted at least partly by way of deliberate contrast. Again, his refusal of the Geatish throne (2373-6) is the antithesis of avarice, just as his fear of having offended God is the antithesis of pride. But these things are not the central action of Part II, and it remains for us to discover a connection between the thought of Hroðgar's sermon and the dragon fight.

One notorious incitement to both pride and avarice is of course wealth; and the dragon's hoard is literally wealth, fought for by Beowulf. Of this menacing fact the poet takes care to remind us:

> Sinc eaðe mæg,
> gold on grund[e], gumcynnes gehwone
> oferhigian, hyde se ðe wylle. (2764-6)

[Treasure, gold in the earth, may easily delude any man, hide it who will.]

(2513); and 2513-14. (4) Beowulf's explanation of his shield and corslet (2522-4) and his resignation to the decree of Wyrd (2525-7), both evidences of *sapientia;* and between them his proclamation of courage (2524-5). (5) The *ellen* [courage] of Beowulf and Wiglaf (2706) and Beowulf's past victorious deeds (2710-1); and *wishycgende* [wise in thought] (2716). (6) 3003-4 and 3007 as *fortitudo;* 3006 as *sapientia.* (7) *wis ond gewittig.* 3094 (which I would render as "still possessing his customary wisdom and prudence"; Klaeber's objections, *Anglia,* XXIX (1906), 381-2, seem eliminated by my interpretation); and 3098-9.

To one who has the principles of Hroðgar's sermon in mind, there is even a certain amount of suspense connected with Beowulf's attitude toward the treasure — particularly if we recall the traditional view of avarice as the besetting vice of old age. His first mention of the gold (2535-6) is completely ambiguous in motive, and his second (2747-51) might even be thought to show a last pathetic gleam of avarice. Not until he is at the point of death does Beowulf reveal his motive fully (2794-2801): As a wise king, he has desired not the gold itself but the good of his people to which it may contribute; just as in Part I, as a heroic retainer, he wisely exults over treasures not for themselves but for the glory of which they are the token. And this maintenance of a right attitude toward the gold, with the resulting preservation of his spirit from avarice and pride, is by definition *sapientia* — itself traditionally a treasure, and more precious than all earthly treasures.[70]

One is tempted at this point to go a bit further, and, in view of the prominence of *sapientia* as a theme in the poem, the traditional association of *sapientia* with treasure, and Gregory's warnings that the inordinate pursuit of *sapientia* itself is a beginning of pride,[71] to see in the hoard also a symbol of worldly *sapientia,* which Beowulf again pursues only in just measure and for the good of his people. His preservation of true *sapientia,* then, would have two aspects: his avoidance of avarice and pride by maintaining a right attitude toward the hoard literally as wealth, and his avoidance of pride by maintaining a right attitude toward it symbolically as *sapientia* itself. There are a few details that gain in attractiveness from such a reading; for example, *hæðen gold* (2276) might be a particularly telling description for the pagan *sapientia* that gave the Fathers so many uneasy moments. But this whole suggestion is one I would not

[70] Job 28:12; Prov. 2:3-4; 3:13-6; 8:10-1, 18-9; 16:16; 17:16; Sap. 7:8-9, 14; 8:5; Ecclus. 1:21, 26, 31; 40:25; Col. 2:3.
[71] *PL* 75, 621-2, 1124, 1160; *PL* 76, 23.

want to press, and the rest of my interpretation in no way depends on it.[72]

This will be a convenient place to discuss the "curse" on the treasure. I am not convinced that it is to be taken as causing Beowulf's death;[73] but even if it is, that aspect of it (3066-70) is essentially part of the machinery of the literal narrative and has little directly to do with our theme — except perhaps as a comment on the limitations and the transience of even peerless *sapientia et fortitudo* (3035-7, 3067-8). That aspect of the curse involving sin and Christian damnation (3069-73), however, and the spell that prevents the treasure-chamber from being touched by any man except one whom God considers fitting (3051-7), are a different matter. Certainly *soðfæstra dom* [the judgment of the righteous] (2820) tells us that Beowulf has escaped the sin and damnation. I believe that in this element of the curse we are to see a reflection of the "curse" that in Christian terms (and apparently to some degree in pagan Germanic terms)[74] does permanently rest on wealth/wisdom, as the raw material of avarice and pride. By maintaining a right attitude toward wealth/wisdom and so avoiding the temptations to avarice and pride, Beowulf escapes as a matter of course. The passage ends with the much disputed pair of lines,

> næs he goldhwæte gearwor hæfde
> agendes est ær gesceawod. (3074-5)

One must not rest any interpretation too heavily on such sore spots of course; but it seems safe to observe that practically all

[72] Hereafter "wealth/wisdom" will be used to mean "wealth, and worldly wisdom also if the suggestion is worth entertaining."

[73] It has also been doubted by Hamilton, "Religious Principle," p. 328, note 101.

[74] See for example the "Gullveig" strophe (#21) in the *Völuspá, ed.* Sigurður Nordal (Reykjavík, 1952), and Nordal's note, pp. 79-80; also G. Turville-Petre, *Origins of Icelandic Literature* (Oxford, 1953), p. 57. Even if such ideas should not be Germanic in their origin (Heusler, "Sittenlehre," p. 179), they might well be part of the *Beowulf* poet's "Germanic" heritage. On wisdom, see the *Hávamál,* ed. Neckel, #54-56, p. 24.

of the translations that have been proposed fit my interpretation of the curse at least fairly well, as is illustrated by Klaeber's cautious summary: "In its general intent the statement seems to be a declaration of Beowulf's virtual innocence."[75]

This freedom of Beowulf from the motives leading to avarice and pride explains also why he is the man who has seemed to God *gemet* (3057) for the undertaking: as his *fortitudo* makes him the right man to face the physical terror of the dragon, so his *sapientia* makes him the right man to face the spiritual dangers of acquiring the hoard. And this observation explains in turn why the messenger speaks of burning the gold with Beowulf (3010-5), and especially why it is finally buried with him,

þær hit nu gen lifað
eldum swa unnyt swa h[it ær]or wæs. (3167-8)
[where it still exists as useless to men as it was before.]

Thematically, I interpret this as a final recognition of Beowulf's unrivalled and irreplaceable *sapientia et fortitudo*. The Geats, sadder and wiser by the death of their king — and, as we shall see, by the quelling of the dragon — realize that just as there has been no one but Beowulf strong enough to win the treasure and wise enough to avoid its dangers, so there is no one left among them with the *fortitudo* to hold it and the *sapientia* to use it blamelessly and well. The treasure is *unnyt* [useless] because the rare ability to wield it has perished.

And now at last, what of the dragon? First of all he is a real dragon, by defending his people against whom Beowulf gives final proof of kingly *fortitudo*. But there is more. Just as Grendel is an embodiment of external evil, or violence, so the

[75] *Beowulf*, p. 227. Of the proposed translations, I prefer either Wrenn's, of the unemended reading, "Yet by no means too eagerly had he before gazed upon its owner's treasure abounding in gold" (*Beowulf*, p. 227); or Tinker's, defended by Hamilton, "Religious Principle," pp. 327-8: "But Beowulf was not greedy for gold; rather had he looked for the grace of the Almighty"—except that I would translate *est* as "gift" and interpret it as a reference to *sapientia*, with the traditional antithesis between *sapientia* and worldly treasure.

dragon represents the greatest of internal evils, the perversion of the mind and will, *malitia*. Grendel and the other perpetrators of evil in the poem must of course be thought of as themselves inwardly ridden by *malitia;* this I take to be the significance of Grendel's *glof* made of dragonskins (2085-8). The dragon by contrast represents *malitia* itself, as a universal, and so comes a long step nearer to allegory than any other figure in the poem.[76] As violence is the perversion of *fortitudo* and is combatted primarily by *fortitudo,* so *malitia* is a perversion or abandonment of *sapientia* and is combatted by it, as in Hroðgar's sermon. That some such idea of external violence and internal *malitia* as two great poles of evil did exist in the poet's scheme of things, seems evident from their mention by Hroðgar —

ne him inwitsorh[77]
on sefan sweorceð, ne gesacu ohwær
ecghete eoweð. (1736-8)

[Nor does grief caused by malice become grievous to his heart, nor does enmity anywhere show itself in sword hate.]

The association of *malitia* with dragons is made several times by Gregory. One instance follows an account of how the various sins open the way for one another, much as in Hroðgar's sermon:

Sed cum culpa culpæ adjungitur, quid aliud quam involutis semitis atque innodatis vinculis pravorum gressus ligantur? Unde bene contra perversam mentem sub Judææ specie per Isaiam dicitur: *Erit cubile draconum, et pascua struthionum, et occurrent doemonia onocentauris, et pilosus clamabit alter ad alterum* (*Isai.* XXXIV, 13). Quid namque per dracones nisi

[76] Tolkien, "Monsters and Critics," p. 259, makes the same judgment in saying that the conception of him approaches *draconitas* [dragon-ness] rather than *draco* [dragon]; and it is reassuring to find "malice" among the qualities he takes to be personified in the dragon.

[77] I take *inwitsorh* [evil care, grievous sorrow] to mean the suffering caused by one's own state of *malitia.* See Gregory, *Hom. in Ezek., PL* 76, 800: "cor pessimum ex sua malitia tabescit." [The wickedest heart wastes away from its own *malitia.*] The citation in the *Sententiæ* in *PL* 83, 1171, adds after *sua,* "et non aliena." [its own, and not from another's.] Space forbids a detailed defense here; note Hoops' translation "boshafte Sorge," *Kommentar,* p. 191.

malitia . . . designatur? . . . In perversa igitur mente draco cubat . . . quia et latens malitia callide tegitur.[78] [But when fault is joined to fault, what else are our steps bound by except by the intricate paths and tangled chains of bad deeds? Therefore Isaias speaks well, under the semblance of Judea, against the perverse mind: "It will be the house of dragons, and the pasture of ostriches, and demons and monsters shall meet, and the hairy ones shall cry out one to another" (Is. 34:13). For what is designated by the dragons except *malitia*. . . ? For this reason the dragon lies in the perverse mind . . . that secret *malitia* is skillfully concealed.]

In view of the continual emphasis on the dragon's fire in *Beowulf,* it is worth noticing that Gregory also allows *ignis* to signify *mentis malitia.*[79]

As Grendel is *se ellengæst* [bold demon] (86), so the dragon is an *atol inwitgæst* [terrible malicious spirit] (2670).[80] The roof of his lair is an *inwithrof* [*malitia*-roof, enmity-roof] (3123), a detail so slenderly related to reality as to suggest allegorical intent. His connection with avarice is suggested by his traditional occupation itself and perhaps by *unrihte . . . gehydde* [wrongfully hid] (3059). He is posthumously given characteristics of pride (2832-4). And in a very real sense *malitia* does "sit on guard" over worldly wealth/wisdom, in that the pursuer or possessor of them is subject to the constant dangers of avarice and pride.

The dragon fight, then, is a brilliant device for presenting in a single action not only Beowulf's final display of kingly *fortitudo,* but also his development and his ultimate preservation

[78] *PL* 75, 786. See also his comment on Job 30:29, with a particular reference to pride, *PL* 76, 183; also col. 578. The dragon in the stories Gregory tells in his *Homilies, PL* 76, 1158-9, and in the *Dialogues, PL* 77, 389-93, is not identified, though in two of the three stories the monks he attacks seem far gone in *malitia.*

[79] *Hom. in Ezek., PL* 76, 800-1. Augustine makes the same association, *Enarr. in Ps.* (34:7-8), *PL* 36, 329-30. Gregory also equates *avaritia* with fire, *PL* 75, 1016, 1093.

[80] If we may read *inwitgǽst* [spirit of *malitia*], the description becomes particularly apt. In any case, this seems to be the only clear use of an *inwit-* compound as personal epithet in OE poetry (Grein, *Sprachschatz,* p. 391); but see Hoops on *inwitþancum* [hostile intent] (749), *Beowulfstudien,* pp. 102-3, *Kommentar,* pp. 94-5.

of personal and kingly *sapientia*: first in combatting the ever-present danger of *malitia* in himself as a human being, and so fulfilling the theme announced in Hroðgar's sermon; and secondly, as king, in combatting an apparent spread of *malitia* among his people. This last proposal will require a digression from the dragon.

A spread of *malitia* among the Geats would of course be consistent with the great theme of Geatish lack of *sapientia*. How the Geats are supposed to have fallen prey to widespread *malitia* under the presumably wise fifty-year rule of Beowulf is a difficulty to add to the other difficulties surrounding Beowulf's reign; perhaps a growing *malitia* is being represented as the fruit of peace among an unwise people, as it is the fruit of individual prosperity in Hroðgar's sermon. At any rate, the theme enters with the goblet-stealer, who is explicitly called *secg synbysig* [man troubled by sin] (2226). This description makes it possible to see in the conjectured *þ[eow]* [slave] (2223) and the later *hæft hygegiomor* [slave sad in mind] (2408) the meaning of slavery to sin, whether as the literal meaning or as an additional significance — with *hygegiomor* as possible evidence of a wicked *tristitia* paralleling that of Heremod (1720).[81] Like the man of Hroðgar's sermon, the goblet-stealer is *bisgum gebunden* [hedged in with cares] (1743), even though through need rather than opulence (2221-5); it is this that leads to his action. I would interpret him as one possessing traits that are to be considered somehow typical among the Geats — perhaps emphasized by *nathwylces hæleða bearna* [of someone or other of the sons of men] (2223-4) — and his taking of the goblet as a twofold failure in *sapientia*: literally as a rash action, resulting in the literal devastation; symbolically as some violation of a right attitude toward wealth/wisdom, a growth of avarice and pride leading to the inner ravages of *malitia* represented by the dragon and his fire.

[81] For a pertinent analysis of the role of *tristitia* in the psychology of sin, see Gregory, *PL* 76, 621-2.

The default of Beowulf's retainers is surely evidence of a decline in Geatish *fortitudo,* contrasting with the conduct of his retainers in Part I, and probably paralleling the general failure of *sapientia* as shown through the goblet-stealer. The point seems to be that the inordinate valuation of self implicit in avarice and pride and the consequent descent to *malitia,* exhausts *fortitudo;* true *sapientia* here would of course prescribe the duty of loyal support and the pursuit of glory for themselves and their lord, with whatever exercise of *fortitudo* might be called for. Just as the goblet-stealer seems to lack *fortitudo* as well as *sapientia* (2227, 2230), so the retainers' failure in right decision is emphasized as well as their mere cowardice, both by Wiglaf's words to them (2633-60, 2864-91) and by the poet's comment on Wiglaf's return to battle:

sibb æfre ne mæg
wiht onwendan þam ðe wel þenceð. (2600-1)
[Nothing may ever put aside kinship for him who thinks well.]

And if Beowulf displays both heroic qualities by opposing the dragon, the retainers by turning from him must show a lack of both: by refusing to fight the literal dragon they fail in *fortitudo;* by refusing to fight the dragon of *malitia* they turn away from *sapientia.*

Are we then to follow this theme of *malitia* consistently, and conclude that by killing the dragon Beowulf has slain the growing evil among his people? I believe so. It is difficult to avoid the impression that in the concluding three hundred-odd lines of the poem we are being shown a people sadder and wiser, though realistically not transfigured out of the weakness and vulnerability that are the legacy of past folly. The ten cowards are duly ashamed (2850-2); Wiglaf predicts that their action will be judged justly and severely (2884-91); for the first time in Part II we hear of Beowulf's *duguð* [band of (experienced) retainers] as *eorlweorod . . . bordhæbbende* [troop of warriors . . . shield bearers] (2893, 2895), as well as of their concern about him (2894-7); the messenger delivers a clear account and an obviously wise comment (2900-3030); the dignified sorrow of the *dugud* is emphasized (3031-2); there are a distinct competence and dignity about the funeral preparations and the funeral itself (3110-9, 3135-72); and the final lament is a recognition of the worth of the *sapientia et fortitudo* ideal, besides being discriminating praise of Beowulf. Not all these things can be defended logically as the results of sudden reformation of course; but in terms of poetic emphasis it is remarkable how the picture changes with the death of the dragon. A final contribution to the effect is the emergence of Wiglaf, to whom our circular course has finally led.

Wiglaf is himself an embodiment of the *sapientia et fortitudo* ideal, as shown both by his own speeches and actions and by two clearly parallel descriptions of him: *byre Wihstanes, hæle hildedior* [son of Weohstan, the hero bold in battle] (3110-1), introducing his orders for constructing the pyre; and *se snotra sunu Wihstanes* [the wise son of Weohstan] (3120), introducing his direction of the disposal of the treasure. That he is not comparable to Beowulf in these respects is of course shown conclusively by the fate predicted now for the Geat nation, even if it were shown by nothing else. The difference is essentially that between Beowulf himself in Parts I and II — between hero and hero-king. Wiglaf's *sapientia et fortitudo* is that of a heroic young retainer; Beowulf's in Part II, that of an experienced and responsible ruler who must expend himself in the guidance and defense of his people. The prominent part played by Wiglaf helps to emphasize the vast difference in complexity between these two forms of the ideal, and to remind us how far Beowulf himself has come since Part I. There are even possible signs that Beowulf, through age and concentration on the higher aspects of *sapientia* illustrated by Hroðgar, has inevitably declined in some points of warrior-*sapientia,* in which Wiglaf now excels him; witness Wiglaf's ignoring the head which has been Beowulf's downfall (2677-82), to strike the dragon *nioðor hwene* [somewhat lower] (2699) where the sword will sink in.[82]

To return finally to Beowulf and the dragon, there remains a last possible question: if Part II is to be interpreted in this way, why is the dragon of *malitia* allowed to kill Beowulf? I think the answer lies less in any one compelling reason than in an overall fitness of this ending. One important consideration is that the dragon fight as I have interpreted it represents not only Beowulf's victory over potential *malitia* in himself, but also his battle against *malitia* in his people and his defense of them against a literal monster; and these last two themes certainly gain by Beowulf's not only facing death but undergoing it, bravely and willingly for his people's sake. Again, in both Germanic and Christian terms the fact of death, of final physical defeat, is inevitable and relatively unimportant; what *is* of desperate importance is having fought the good fight. And the dragon fight is not only the climax, but also the summary of Beowulf's kingship and of his life — in a sense, he has always fought the dragon. Besides, one may reflect that an ending in which Beowulf won a final victory over the dragon of *malitia* and remained alive, would leave him in a condition rather like that of Adam before the Fall. For man, the permanent victory over evil can be realized only through death. And finally, there is about Beowulf's death an air of inevitability that tends to remove it from the cause-and-effect of even symbolic dragon's tusks. Poetically, it is perhaps less accurate to say that the dragon kills Beowulf, than that Beowulf dies fighting the dragon. He dies because he has reached his *endedæg* [final day].

VII

There remains for our consideration one great theme hovering over the poem rather than active in it: that of the infinite

[82] Gustav Neckel, "Sigmunds Drachenkampf," *Edda,* XIII (1920), 131, believes that in earlier forms of the story this action was performed by the wise advice of a god.

Sapientia et Fortitudo of God, as the source of all finite human *sapientia et fortitudo* — an idea familiar in the Old Testament, particularly the Book of Job:

> In antiquis est sapientia
> et in multo tempore prudentia.
> Apud ipsum est sapientia et fortitudo. . . .[83]

[In ancient (men) is wisdom, and in length of days prudence. With Him (God) is wisdom and fortitude.]

The frequency of similar brief allusions in *Beowulf* is obvious.[84] Against this greater ideal the limited *sapientia et fortitudo* of the people in the poem are continually being projected, in a variety of ways. There are for example more or less explicit references, like the poet's remarks on the Danes' idol worship (175-88) or the complex passage just before the Finn Episode (1055-62) — both of which I reserve for fuller treatment elsewhere, but which do seem to carry at least the general force I am suggesting here. By way of less explicit comparison, there is the whole texture of allusion to the giants and their works, the scop's unusual knowledge of the distant past, the forgotten past of which the treasure is a dim reminder, and so on, all suggesting the limitations of individual human *sapientia*. Its limitations are expressed again in what might be called the "men know not —" theme, usually though not always applied to the forces of evil.[85] Still subtler contributions are the repeated mentions of the awe with which the people in the poem behold evidences of a mysterious evil imperfectly comprehended.[86]

[83] Job 12:12-3. See also Job 9:4; 12:16; 36:22-6; 37:23-4; 38 ff., passim; Ps. 89:11-2; Ecclus. 15:19; Jer. 51:15; Dan. 2:20. On *sapientia et fortitudo* bestowed by God, Jer. 9:23; Dan. 2:23.

[84] For example ll. 180-3; perhaps 685-7 and 700-2; 1056-8; 1553-6; 1725-6; perhaps 2857-9; 3054-7.

[85] Ll. 50-2; 162-3; 798 ff.; 876, 878; 1331-3; 1355-7; 1366-7; 1410; 2214; 3062-8. Cp. *Hávamál,* ed. Neckel, #53, p. 24.

[86] Ll. 980-90; Hroðgar's description of the mere; *folc to sægon* [the people gazed on it] (1422); 1440-1; perhaps 1603; 1607; 1647-50; 1677-98; 2085-8; 2227-30 (conveyed even by the imperfect lines); 3038-46.

Finally, there is an even broader way in which the action of *Beowulf* is projected against this higher *Sapientia et Fortitudo*. Vital as human *sapientia et fortitudo* is for the very survival of peoples in the heroic age, the total impression left by the poem is that it is a rare enough combination in a world full of possibilities for error and weakness. Even the infrequent combinations of the two heroic virtues are not guaranteed to last; Hroðgar's decline in *fortitudo* invites Grendel, and Heremod's decay in *sapientia* brings on his own destruction and the dreaded lordless time. And finally, beyond his own control, man himself is mortal, as the elegy of the Last Survivor emphasizes to good purpose; even Beowulf, the persevering combination of both virtues, must die at last, leaving to his people the unlikely chance of finding the ideal embodied in a new ruler. And above the imperfection, the mutability, and in any case the final impermanence of human *sapientia et fortitudo* — and heightening its poignancy — there towers the *Sapientia et Fortitudo* of God, perfect, unchanging, everlasting. In that contrast lies, at its deepest and most inclusive, the tragedy of *Beowulf*.[87]

[87] The essence of this study was presented as a brief paper, under the same title, at the 1955 MLA meeting. In its present form, it has benefited from the criticism of the late Professor Vladimer Jelinek of Washington University and Professor Norman E. Eliason of the University of North Carolina.

14

SUTTON HOO AND BEOWULF*

C. L. Wrenn

IN THE 18 YEARS SINCE THE DISCOVERY OF THE SUTTON HOO ship-cenotaph a quite considerable literature of descriptive material and various discussion has been published. This is conveniently listed up to 1954 in F. P. Magoun Jr.'s *Chronological Bibliography* in *Speculum,* vol. XXIX of that year. Since then, in three successive years, the fullest cultural and historical background has been provided in the monumental *Herrschaftszeichen und Staatssymbolik* of P. E. Schramm and his contributors in the 3 parts of vol. XIII of the *Schriften der Monumenta Germaniae Historica.*[1] An admirable popular account of the actual course of the findings by C. W. Phillips has appeared in Bruce-Mitford's *Recent Archaeological Excavations in Britain* (London, 1956). Miss Evison's study of *Early Anglo-Saxon Inlaid Metalwork* in the *Antiquaries' Journal* for 1955 provides a useful addition to the background for the study of the traces of silver wire-work discernible on the Sutton Hoo helmet, and makes clearer indirectly the remarkable parallel between the

* Reprinted, by permission of the author, and the publisher of *Mélanges de Linguistique et de Philologie* (Fernand Mossé in Memoriam) (Paris: Didier, 1959), pp. 495-507.

[1] *Herrschaftszeichen und Staatssymbolik, Beiträge zu ihrer Geschichte vom dritten bis zum sechzehnten Jahrhundert,* von Percy Ernst Schramm mit Beiträgen verschiedener Verfasser (Stuttgart: Band 1 1954, Band 2 1955, Band 3 1956.)

helmet of *Beowulf* 1030-31 with its *walu wirum bewunden,* and that of Sutton Hoo.

Two articles, however, among recent work, are of very special significance for the subject of this paper. First that treating of the meanings of the Sutton Hoo 'standard' and whetstone 'Sceptre' contributed by Wilhelm Berges and Adolf Gauert to Schramm's *Herrschaftszeichen und Staatssymbolik* mentioned above, entitled *Die eiserne 'Standarte' und das steinerne 'Szepter' aus dem Grabe eines angelsächsischen Königs bei Sutton Hoo.*[2] Secondly, an article prompted by the last-named by Karl Hauck in the *Festgabe Anton Ernstberger*[3] which is *Jahrbuch* 14 *für fränkische Landesforschung* of 1954, which discusses very fully the 'Wodenistic' significances of the Sutton Hoo standard, shield and helmet. For Hauck's further linking of the Sutton Hoo finds here with the cult of Woden, while showing that the decorations and accessories of the standard and armour might have at the same time a Wodenistic and a Christian significance, is of obvious importance for the study of *Beowulf.*

Yet the full significance and implications of the Sutton Hoo finds for the study of *Beowulf* and of the light which the poem and Sutton Hoo may throw on each other, have not yet by any means been thoroughly explored.

On Aug. 14th, 1939, a Coroner's jury of good Suffolk citizens, meeting in the village hall of Sutton, were called to decide whether the finds of the previous month were legally 'Treasure-trove' and therefore the property of the Crown, or that of the 'finders' (the land concerned then belonged to the late Mrs. Pretty.) If the artefacts could be shown to have been publicly buried with no intention of ever being resumed, they were, according to British law, not Treasure-trove: but if it should appear that they had been hidden with intent to recover and in

[2] Band 1, pp. 238-280.

[3] *Herrschaftszeichen eines Wodanistischen Königtums* in *Festgabe Anton Ernstberger herausgegeben vom Institut für fränkische Landesforschung der Universität Erlangen,* pp. 9-65.

secret, then they would become Crown property. The Coroner's Inquest easily decided that the Sutton Hoo treasures had been buried at a public ceremony and had been meant to remain for ever undisturbed. This decision was reached after the jurymen had listened to an exposition of the account of the ship-passing of Scyld Scefing in *Beowulf*[4] with its astonishing parallels to the Sutton Hoo ship-cenotaph: and the matter was clinched by the reading of the story of the final disposal of the Dragon's hoard in ll. 3156-68:

Geworhton ða Wedra leode
hleo on hoe, se wæs heah ond brad,
weg-liðendum wide gesyne,
ond betimbredon on tyn dagum
beadu-rofes becn; bronda lafe
wealle beworhton, swa hyt weorðlicost
fore-snotre men findan mihton.
Hi on beorg dydon beg ond siglu,
eall swylce hyrsta, swylce on horde ær
nið-hedige men genumen hæfdon;
forleton eorla gestreon eorðan healdan,
gold on greote, þær hit nu gen lifað
eldum swa unnyt, swa hit æror wæs.[5]

[Then the people of the Geats made a place of shelter on a headland, which was high and broad, widely visible to seafarers, and they built in ten days the monument of the man bold in battle. They built a wall around the leavings of the flames — i.e. the ashes, as wise men might most nobly devise it. Into the barrow they put the rings and jewels, all such adornments such as men hostile in mind had taken from the hoard earlier. They left the wealth of nobles to the earth to hold, gold in the earth, where it still exists as useless to men as it was before.]

I have italicized the all-important words in the above passage. It is perhaps worth adding that, if my reading is right, Beowulf's barrow (his *hleo on hoe*) may have been built on a *hoh* (heel of land, or promontory), the same OE word from which the second element of Sutton Hoo is derived. So the Sutton Hoo treasures were declared to be the property of the finders: and Mrs. Pretty then magnificently donated them all to the British

[4] *Beowulf* 26-52.
[5] All citations are from *Beowulf,* ed. C. L. Wrenn (London, 1953).

Museum, the place which would almost certainly have received them had they been found to be treasure-trove. There, in the King Edward VII Gallery, they are exhibited with exquisite skill and showmanship.

Nine years later, Sune Lindqvist ended the article *Sutton Hoo and Beowulf* (translated by Bruce-Mitford in *Antiquity* for 1948) with these words: — 'It is obvious that the *rapprochement* that was at once made between the Sutton Hoo burial and the substance of Beowulf was fully warranted, and rich with possibilities. Everything seems to show that these two documents complement one another admirably. Both become the clearer by the comparison.'

The rich variety and assimilative creativeness of Anglo-Saxon culture with its progressive adaptation of pagan elements into Christian contexts, have often been remarked: and these features are well illustrated by both the Sutton Hoo cenotaph and by *Beowulf*. In the famous description of the ship-passing of Scyld Scefing which so amazingly seems to remember Sutton Hoo, the poet says:

þær wæs madma fela
of feor-wegum, frætwa, gelæded.
(36-7)

[There were brought many treasures, adornments from distant parts.]

At Sutton Hoo were found expressions of pagan symbolism along with some clearly Christian artefacts, just as in *Beowulf* the pagan sentiment and Christian thinking go together. For there can be no doubt about the specifically Christian character of the two silver spoons of Sutton Hoo, with their Greek charactering of the names respectively Paul and Saul. They must have been a Baptismal gift to the East-Anglian King symbolizing his passing from pagan to Christian, remembering the miracle on the road to Damascus by which the Jew Saul became the Christian St. Paul. And the cruciform work on the silver bowls must likewise be capable of Christian interpretation, though such decorations were not entirely confined to Christianity. It is equally certain that the whole idea of the ship-cenotaph is pre-Christian: and the cult of Woden, the 'principalis deus Anglorum' is apparent in such things as the shield-decorations, the winged figure projecting from the shield· of victory ready to carry the hero to Valhalla, the scenes of sword-dancing graven on the helmet, and much else. Again there is variety in the ages of the artefacts. The large silver dish has the hall-mark of the Byzantine Emperor Anastasius I who died in the year 518; and the shield and helmet were some hundred years old when buried. Some of the jewelry, on the other hand, may well have been quite recent when placed in the cenotaph. The stag which surmounts the iron standard-frame, which reminds us of the wondrous hall *Heorot* in *Beowulf,* suggests magic perhaps, as well as being another possible link with the cult of Woden.

Another aspect of variety is seen in the heterogeneity of place of origin of the artefacts. While most of the goldsmiths' and gem-cutters' work seems to have been native English, the gold coins found as having fallen from the royal purse, are Merovingian Frankish, as probably is some indirect influence in the garnet-setting and cloisonné-work. Byzantine is the large silver dish of Anastasius I, and probably the spoons with the Greek names; though the fact that the Greek *L* (lambda) is cut the wrong way round in the name *Saulos* might lead one to think of English craftsmen imitating the work of Byzantine artists.[6] Celtic influence is seen in the hanging bowls and in some of the animal figure-work on the jewelry, which reminds me of the illuminated figures of Irish-Latin Gospel-books, especially that at St. Gall in Switzerland. Swedish are most of the weapons — the shield, helmet, and sword-trappings.

That loving connoisseurship of treasures of aesthetic appeal which is so characteristic in the artefacts of Sutton Hoo, is equally strongly felt in *Beowulf,* where there is the same suggestion of sheer joy in the contemplation and possession of

[6] On Byzantine influence throughout OE culture, see Talbot Rice, vol. 2 of *The Oxford History of English Art, passim.*

treasures of the art of the goldsmith and the gem-cutter. That love of ordered ceremony and ornament which is so marked a characteristic of Anglo-Saxon culture, is apparent alike in the Sutton Hoo cenotaph and in *Beowulf*. Though there is much blending of authentic tradition from pre-Christian times with ideas drawn from contemporary practice in the poet's accounts of the passing of Scyld Scefing, of the funeral rites of the slain in the fight between Hnæf's men and those of Finn,[7] and in Beowulf's own funeral ceremonies at the end of the poem, all three suggest reminiscences of Sutton Hoo. Let us look a little more narrowly at some of these features in which the Sutton Hoo cenotaph and *Beowulf* seem to parallel, explain and illustrate one another.

The Standard.

It has been shown by Karl Hauck (*op. cit.*) that the iron standard-frame surmounted by the figure of a stag, the winged creature on the shield together with some of its accessories, and the scenes of sword-dancing on the helmet, are in origin ritually significant pagan elements, *signa sacra* in fact which may at the same time be susceptible of pagan or of Christian symbolic interpretation. The cult of Woden is thus linked with transitional Christian art. For instance, the royal stag suggests a memory of the ancestral cult of that Woden from whom the East-Anglian Wuffingas, like many other OE royal families, derived their origin. Yet at the same time the animal might be a Christian symbol suggested by the thirsting hart of the 42nd Psalm. In like manner one may think of *Heorot,* Hrothgar's hall in *Beowulf,* as having its origin in some such complex set of symbolic significances. Indeed the royal standard — though of course the gold embroidery of the Sutton Hoo exemplar has left no trace — with all its complicated ritual symbolizing of victory, protection, death, etc. as it waved over the king's treasure in death as in life, is a marked feature alike at Sutton Hoo

[7] *Beowulf* 1107 ff.

and in *Beowulf*. And it again merges pagan and Christian ritual and symbol. Both in the cenotaph and in the poem it always implies royalty and treasure. The standard is always embroidered in gold thread. So the treasures which went in the bosom of the ship of Scyld Scefing were waved over by such a golden standard:

> þa gyt hie him asetton *segen gyldenne*
> *heah ofer heafod.*
>
> (47-8).

[Then, besides, they set up a golden standard high over his head.]

Again, among the treasures with which Hrothgar rewarded Beowulf, there was the same type of standard:

> Forgeaf þa Beowulfe brand Healfdenes
> *segen gyldenne, sigores to leane,*
> *hroden hilde-cumbor.*
>
> (1020-22).

[Then he gave to Beowulf the sword of Healfdene, as a reward of victory, a golden standard, a decorated battle-banner.]

Then too the Dragon's hoard described at the end of the poem (2756 ff.) is waved over by just such a gold-embroidered standard as was that of Scyld:

> Swylce he siomian geseah *segn eall-gylden*
> *heah ofer horde,* hond-wundor mæst
> gelocen leoðo-cræftum.
>
> (2767-69).

[Likewise, he saw hanging high over the treasure a standard all worked in gold, greatest of marvels made by hand, woven by skill of limbs.]

If we may judge by the exquisite delicacy and beauty of the gold and inlaid purse-frame of the Sutton Hoo cenotaph, the purse itself must have been made of wondrously embroidered cloth of gold, as must also have been the actual standard whose iron frame alone survives. It is remarkable too that the standard in *Beowulf* is always described as *gylden* or *eall-gylden*. Throughout their history the Anglo-Saxons were famed for their *opus Anglicanum,* as witness from a later time the Stole of St. Cuthbert and the Bayeux Tapestries. One may compare the mention of the gold-embroidered tapestry in Hrothgar's Heorot:

gold-fag scinon
web æfter wagum, wundor-siona fela
secga gehwylcum þara þe on swylc starað.
(994-6).

[The tapestries shone gold-adorned along the walls, many wondrous sights for those among men who gaze upon such things.]

That the standard of the Dragon's hoard, like that of Sutton Hoo, was already ancient when buried, is suggested by the words of the poet describing the treasures which were waved over by the standard as including 'vessels of men of old' and helmets 'ancient and rust-covered.'

Geseah ða sige-hreðig, . . .
mago-þegn modig maððum-sigla fealo,
gold glitinian grunde getenge,
wundor on wealle, ond þæs wyrmes denn,
ealdes uht-flogan, *orcas* stondan,
fyrn-manna fatu, feormend-lease,
hyrstum behrorene, þær wæs *helm monig,*
eald ond omig, earm-beaga fela,
searwum gesæled.
(2756-64).

[Then the brave young retainer, triumphing in victory, saw many precious jewels, shining gold near the earth, marvels on the wall, and the lair of the serpent, of the old twilight flyer, — beakers standing, vessels of men of old, without polishers, deprived of their adornments. There was many a helmet, ancient and rust-covered, many armrings, twisted with skill.]

The Shield and the Helmet.

It is generally agreed that the shield and helmet are of Swedish manufacture, probably from the neighbourhood of old Uppsala, and that they were from 100 to 150 years old when placed in the Sutton Hoo cenotaph. It seems that the helmet, like those in the Dragon's hoard in *Beowulf,* was already rusty when buried, and that both it and the shield had undergone necessary repairs with material inferior to the original before the burial. They and the Anastasius silver dish were apparently ancestral family heirlooms — or possibly booty won in war — carefully cherished as in some way links with the founder of the royal house of the Wuffingas who, according to Bede, were the first Anglo-

Saxon rulers of East-Anglia. When time came for the funeral of the King, they, together with other treasures and symbols, were placed in a ship-cenotaph in the pagan manner. For, it would seem, a public ceremonial funeral with all the traditional pagan rites, was required by family sentiment: and while the now Christian King would have been buried privately with proper religious rites, intense traditional regard for ancestral practice demanded that there should be a public ship-cenotaph in a manner holding vivid memories of that Woden and his cult to whom the King looked back as his ultimate ancestor. So all the treasures were placed in the centre of the funeral ship just as described in the *Beowulf* account of the passing of Scyld Scefing, and in a way too, much resembling the placing of the originally royal treasure in the Dragon's hoard in the poem. This East-Anglian king, descendent of the formerly Woden-worshipping Wuffingas and of the lineage of that god, would have cherished his weapons and personal adornments.

Turning now to the Sutton Hoo helmet, mention was made at the beginning of this paper of the traces of silver wire-work discernible on its face, which find a clear parallel in the helmet given to Beowulf by Hrothgar:

> Ymb þæs helmes hrof heafod-beorge
> *wirum bewunden walu* utan heold.
> (1030-31).

[Around the crown of the helmet, a rounded protection, bound with wires, furnished protection for the head on the outside.]

Unfortunately Miss Vera Evison in her important article on *Early Anglo-Saxon Metalwork* noticed at the beginning of this discussion,[8] deliberately omits the Sutton Hoo wire-work after noting its importance, on the ground that 'it appears to be Swedish.' But not only does the Sutton Hoo helmet explain the meaning of the words *wirum bewunden* [bound with wires] here. We have at last learned from the reconstructed exemplar exactly what the hitherto mysterious *walu* of *Beowulf* 1031 was like.

[8] *The Antiquaries' Journal* vol. XXV, 1955, pp. 20 ff.

This can conveniently be seen at a glance from the British Museum postcard. It was a tubular metal ridge running from the nose to the middle of the top of the head, apparently intended to strengthen the protective power of the helmet. It was already rusty, like those of *Beowulf* 2763, *eald ond omig* [old and rusty]; and it was originally, like it, *wirum bewunden.*[9]

Karl Hauck (*op. cit.,* especially pp. 45 ff.) has shown the important cultural significance of the ritual sword-dance figured on the helmet's face in that religion of Woden which was common to old Sweden and pre-Christian Anglo-Saxon England: and it is significant that the figure of Woden is seen in this dance characteristically one-eyed. The traditional connotations of such warlike metaphorical phrases as *sweorda gelac* [play of swords] (1040) and *æt ecga gelacum* [at the plays of swords] (1168) of *Beowulf* at once become clear, and their poetical depth of meaning is enhanced.

Like the stag on the standard-holder, the shield and helmet could be given a Christian as well as a Wodenistic interpretation, from St. Paul's 'shield of faith' and 'helmet of salvation.' But perhaps Karl Hauck goes too far at times in seeing Wodenistic elements in *Beowulf* itself.[10] For instance, while it seems likely that the five-rayed sun-decoration on the Sutton Hoo shield symbolizes the protective power of Woden, one may hesitate to discern the origin of the OE phrase *beorht beacen Godes* [bright symbol of God] (*Beowulf* 570) as a symbol of Woden's protective shield. It is also to be remembered that the shield and helmet of Sutton Hoo, which seem to have been Swedish ancestral heirlooms of the East-Anglian Wuffingas, were already old when buried, and that their figured signa sacra belonged to the sixth rather than to the seventh century; though it is true that such symbolic decorations, like the stag on the standard, could be given a Christian interpretation while yet preserving for the Christian witness the still significantly attractive flavour

[9] Cf. H. Maryon, *The Sutton Hoo Helmet* (*Antiquity* vol. XXI, 1947).
[10] *Op. cit.,* p. 51 and footnotes.

of a half-consciously remembered ancestral pagan Germanic tradition.

The Musical Instrument.

In Beowulf (89 ff.) we read:

> þær wæs hearpan sweg,
> swutol sang scopes. Sægde se þe cuþe
> frumsceaft fira feorran reccan:

[There was the sound of the harp, the clear song of the minstrel. He spoke who knew how to tell from long ago the creation of men:]
and there follows the famous account of the scop's lay of the creation of the world which has often been thought to look back directly to Cædmon's *Hymn*. Now the date of the Sutton Hoo ship-cenotaph is fixed within fairly narrow limits by the Merovingian coins, between about the years 650 and 670, and nearer the latter point: and this corresponds almost exactly to the date when, according to Bede, the poet Cædmon miraculously received the gift of aristocratic poetic diction. For Cædmon at that time, during the reign of the Abbess St. Hilda (657 to 680) was of advanced or infirm age — *provectioris aetatis* or *gelyfedre ylde*. The Sutton Hoo musical instrument, therefore, must have been buried at almost the exact time when Cædmon and his companions were passing round the harp for the recitation of poetry in their *convivium* or gebeorscype [feast]: and it thus has a very special interest as being contemporary with the recitation of the first OE poem that has come down to us.[11] Though its reconstruction at the British Museum may not entirely satisfy, it should help us to form some idea of what kind of 'harp' it was that was used as accompaniment to the recitations of the earlier Anglo-Saxon scop. That the instrument is a harp (OE *hearpe*) can scarcely be doubted. It is, as reconstructed with the expert aid of the Dolmetsch firm, a six-stringed harp of maple-wood, about 16 inches high, with willow pegs for tuning

[11] Cf. Bede, *Historia Ecclesiastica Gentis Anglorum,* IV 24; and C. L. Wrenn, *The Poetry of Cædmon* (Proceedings of the British Academy, vol. XXXIII, 1947).

the strings: but the sounding-board at the base has had to be added in the reconstruction. It was played and recorded to the accompaniment of the recitation of Cædmon's *Hymn* by Dr. Bessinger (now of Toronto University Canada): and this blending of harp and recitation was done by Dr. Bessinger in accordance with the well-known view of Anglo-Saxon vers-rhythm developed by J. C. Pope of Yale.[12] Though of course the music could only be based on imaginative conjecture suggested by later examples, the aim was to bring out the exact relationship between harp and recitation. When, through the kindness of Mr. Bruce-Mitford of the British Museum, I was privileged to hear this record, I found it convincing as a demonstration of the integral relationship of harp and voice, and of the view based on Bede and on a number of passages in OE poetry, that at least the earlier Anglo-Saxon recitations were in fact accompanied by the harp in a manner comparable to the reciting of traditional Serbian ballads and heroic poems to the accompaniment of the *gusle*.

The most detailed account of the harp as a stringed instrument, though unfortunately expressed in difficult or corrupt language, occurs in the '*Fortunes of men*' from the *Exeter Book* (80-84):

> Sum sceal mid hearpan æt his hlafordes
> fotum sittan, feoh þicgan,
> ond a snellice *snere wræstan,*
> *lætan scralletan sceacol,* se þe hleapeþ,
> *nægl neomegende.*[13]

[Another shall sit at his lord's feet with his harp, receive treasure, and ever rapidly pluck the harpstrings. Let the plectrum, which leaps, sound loudly, the nail sound sweetly.]

In Bede's account of the *convivium* or *gebeorscype* which led to Cædmon's gift of poetry (IV 24) it is significant that the Latin *cantare* is rendered in the OE version *be hearpan singan* [to sing with a harp]. Pope (*op. cit.* pp. 88 ff.) has briefly given

[12] See *The Rhythm of Beowulf* (Yale University Press, 1942).

[13] From vol. III of *The Anglo-Saxon Poetical Records* ed. Krapp and Dobbie (London and New York, 1936).

good reasons for believing in the necessity of harp-accompaniment for OE poetry on metrical grounds; and there are a number of passages in the corpus poeticum which well bear this out.

One difficulty about the Sutton Hoo harp is its unexpected smallness. Could so apparently limited an instrument have served as an effective accompaniment or rhythm-keeper for poetical recitation in an Anglo-Saxon hall such as Heorot? Magoun, in a note to his *Chronological Bibliography* already referred to, suggests (how seriously it is not clear) that this little instrument might have been 'a sort of after-dinner harp'; and perhaps one may imagine Cædmon's companions passing round in their very simple *gebeorscype* just such a harp, as the men took it in turns to recite. I have sometimes thought it more likely that the Sutton Hoo harp was a kind of symbolic or small model instrument commemorating the fact that the royal hero in whose cenotaph it was placed, was, like other Germanic heroes, skilled in the arts of music and poesy as well as in war. Such an artefact would be a fitting companion for the King's other symbolic heirlooms and treasures, to accompany him as he was borne away to Woden's hall on his ship *fugle gelicost* [most like a bird], or by the winged creature of victory portrayed in the figure projecting from his shield. Yet after having heard the harp in action several times through Mr. Bruce-Mitford's recording, I became inclined to believe that the instrument could in fact make enough noise to serve its proper purpose for reciter and audience, at least in a moderately sized room: and we know that silence was properly observed in Germanic halls on such occasions. Or again one may think that the royal hero may have used the harp for private entertainment; and those in charge of his funeral arrangements may have selected it as a most fitting symbol of his skill as musician and scop. But here, clearly, one must for the present remain upon extremely speculative ground.[14]

[14] For a brief summary of the Sutton Hoo harp, see Bruce-Mitford's account in *Archaeological News-letter* I of 1948. Cf. the British Museum postcard of the instrument.

The King.

It seems certain that the hero of the Sutton Hoo ship-cenotaph was an East-Anglian king of the royal house of the Wuffingas, in view especially of the remains of the staff with traces of the figure of a wolf found among the artefacts. For the wolf would be the proper symbol of the Wuffingas or people of the wolf; and we know from Bede that the East-Anglian kings were (W)uffingas. Whether one might link these Wuffingas with the *Wulfingas* of *Widsith* 29, and the *Wilfingas* or *Wylfingas* of *Beowulf* 461 and 471, it is not yet possible to determine.[15] But the suggestion of Bruce-Mitford and others which would connect the *Wehha* of the royal East-Anglian genealogy in Bede and the early 9th century MS. Brit. Mus. Cotton Vespasian B VI with that *Wihstan* (*Weohstan*) who was the father of Wiglaf, Beowulf's one loyal kinsman and helper in his last fight against the dragon, is very attractive.[16] And the Wægmundingas to whom these men belonged seem to have been, as were the original founders of the East-Anglian royal house (if one may trust the clearly Swedish character of the Sutton Hoo shield and helmet) Swedes. Bruce-Mitford, in his outstanding work *The Sutton Hoo Ship-burial, Recent Theories and some Comments on General Interpretation* (Proceedings of the Suffolk Institute of Archeology, vol. 25, part I, 1949) has convincingly worked out the probable consequences of the Swedish origin of the house of the Wuffingas historically and for the explanation of the Scandinavian elements in *Beowulf,* and the special interest assumed in the audience of the poem in the Geatas of South Sweden who were the hero Beowulf's own people, and in the Swedes themselves. One might go further and even regard the poem as having been inspired as a compliment to a king or prince of the royal house of the Wuffingas, or one linked by marriage with it. For like the East-Anglian Wuffingas, the hero

[15] See *Widsith,* ed. Kemp Malone (London, 1936), pp. 199 ff. under *Wulfingas.*

[16] Cf. *op. cit.,* infra.

of *Beowulf* had come from the tribe of the Geatas then living in South Sweden: and such associations would have had a very special appeal to an Anglo-Saxon royal family and aristocracy whose ancestors had originally come from that same country.

I incline to think that the king of the Sutton Hoo ship-cenotaph was Æthelwald who died in the year 663-4, since he is the East-Anglian ruler whose death occurred nearest to the date which numismatical evidence seems to favour for the burial, which is generally held on the evidence of the Merovingian gold coins to have been nearer to 670 than 650. His brother Æthelhere, slain at the battle of Winwaed in Yorkshire and probably washed away by the sea, was suggested by some, chiefly because his disappearance in the sea would explain the at first amazing absence of any corpse in the cenotaph. Chemical tests have established, that there never was a corpse: but once it is admitted that the king honoured at Sutton Hoo was a Christian (and the Baptismal spoons leave no doubt of that), the corpse may, as already indicated, be supposed to have been given a private Christian and separate burial quite apart from the public ceremonial funeral which a still living traditional sentiment required in the third quarter of the seventh century.

Sutton Hoo and the Genesis of Beowulf.

It may now seem appropriate to ask what new light the discoveries at Sutton Hoo may throw on the still quite unsolved problems of the date and place of the composition of *Beowulf*. Sune Lindqvist, in his now famous article *Sutton Hoo and Beowulf* which originally suggested the title of this paper, looks for the explanation of the apparent confusions and anachronisms in the poet's account of the passing of Scyld Scefing and of the funeral rites of Beowulf himself in the idea that phenomena like the Sutton Hoo ship-burial were still remembered at the time when the poem was composed: — 'The Christian skald,' he says, 'imagined that lavish burials after the fashion of the one still remembered in his own day, at Sutton Hoo, and notions then current such as leaving the gravegoods unburned in the ground, were the rule in more ancient times too.'[17] He then goes on to suggest that the connexion between the Swedish elements in the subject-matter of *Beowulf* and the royal house of the Wuffingas of East-Anglia which the Sutton Hoo finds bring to mind, may be a reality. This is seen in linking the Wehha of the Wuffing genealogy with the Wiglaf son of Wihstan or Weohstan of *Beowulf* — that last of the Wægmundingas who alone stood fast by the hero in his last fight with the dragon, who was also a prince of the Scylfingas, the royal Swedish house (cf. *Beowulf* 2603, 2907 and 2813 ff.) This Wiglaf was, in a sense, a hero of the poem second in nobility only to Beowulf himself: and he, through the equating of his father Wihstan with Wehha as mentioned above, was, it would seem, of the royal house of Uppsala of which the founder of the East-Anglian kingdom had first come from the family seat in Sweden. Such speculations as these may well lead to some complementary clarification of one another by the Sutton Hoo finds and *Beowulf*.[18]

Such a view would tend (a) to place the date of the composition of *Beowulf* as early as possible; and (b) to suggest a search for the exact connexion between the making of the poem and the royal house of East-Anglia. At the beginning of the eighth century, the frequently accepted date for *Beowulf,* there would still have been living old men who could remember that public burial of the Sutton Hoo treasures whose actuality the British Coroner's Inquest of Aug. 14th, 1939 had accepted as fact. So that whether we accept the statement of Nennius that the house of the Wuffingas was founded in East-Anglia by Wehha, Wuffa's father,[19] or the implication of Bede that it was Wuffa himself who was the first Anglo-Saxon East-Anglian king,

[17] *Op. cit.,* p. 139.

[18] Cf. Lindqvist, *op. cit.,* pp. 139-40.

[19] Quoted by Stenton in his Anglo-Saxon England (Oxford, 1943), p. 50.

it would be a legitimate inference that there was a real link between *Beowulf* and East-Anglia. Now Rædwald of East-Anglia who died about the year 618 had, as is well known, the title of *Bretwalda,* which implied a very considerable degree of importance for him in England as a whole: and the Sutton Hoo finds make it abundantly clear that in the third quarter of the seventh century there were men of an extraordinarily high cultural and artistic development in East-Anglia. Though we have no knowledge of East-Anglian culture in any later relevant times, there seems to be nothing that militates against a theory that there existed in East-Anglia something like that cultural environment, at the relevant time, which has made Northumbria of the age of Bede the most widely favoured place for the composition of the poem.

Nothing is known for certain of the linguistic differences that must have existed among the various types of Mercian, nor of distinctions between any of them and the dialect of East-Anglia (of which we have no written monuments before the Suffolk charters of the later tenth century). *Beowulf* might, so far as our present knowledge goes, as well have been originally Mercian as Northumbrian from a linguistic standpoint: and the reasons which have led so many scholars to prefer Northumbria have been mainly 'kulturgeschichtlich' or inferences from the absence of Mercian evidences. Yet we are in no position to deny an East-Anglian origin for the poem, since we cannot distinguish linguistically East-Anglian from Mercian, and that kingdom was absorbed into the imperium of Offa of Mercia long before the close of the 8th century.[20] Miss Dorothy Whitelock has very persuasively revived the hypothesis which would place *Beowulf's* composition at the court of King Offa of Mercia at some date in the later eighth century:[21] and even so late a date would only be a hundred years or a little more after the burial

[20] For a summary of the evidences for the date of *Beowulf,* see my ed., Introduction pp. 32-41.

[21] *The Audience of Beowulf* (Oxford, 1951), pp. 63-64.

of the Sutton Hoo treasures. Now as East-Anglia became part of Offa's realm, one might reasonably look for some East-Anglian family connexion of Offa which would explain the genesis of *Beowulf* as inspired in part as a compliment to Offa, as well as to the ancient house of the Wuffingas. In this latter case, the original language of the poem could have been that type of literary Mercian *koiné* which seems to have existed in Midland and Southern England throughout the eighth century on account of the Mercian hegemony.[22] On the other hand, as remarked above, the seemingly vivid memories of the Sutton Hoo ship-burial which lie behind the accounts of the passing of Scyld Scefing and of the hero's own funeral rites in the poem, would point rather to an earlier date for its composition.

Klaeber, in the latest Supplement to his edition (3rd, reprinted 1951), restores the MS. reading *wundini golde* in 1382: and this archaic survival would be the strongest evidence for an early date. Dobbie, though he accepts the usual emendation *wundnum golde* here in his text (as Klaeber had originally done), seems to lean rather towards the more 'orthodox' circa 700 as the most likely date for the composition of *Beowulf*.[23] Ritchie Girvan in his *Beowulf and the Seventh Century, Language and Content* (London, 1935), also produces some impressive arguments for an extremely early date. Nevertheless, while emphasizing the possible significance of the Sutton Hoo finds for the dating of *Beowulf,* one can for the present but echo Dobbie's Conclusion:—'The problem of the date and place of writing of *Beowulf* are, therefore, still unsettled, in spite of the erudition which has been brought to bear upon them during the past half-century.'[24] But the Sutton Hoo discoveries have

[22] Cf. Rudolf Vleeskruyer, ed. of *The Life of St. Chad,* Introd. (Amsterdam, 1954).

[23] *Beowulf and Judith,* ed. Elliott-Van Kirk-Dobbie (in *Anglo-Saxon Poetic Records,* vol. IV). London and New York, 1953. Cf. Introd., pp. LIII ff.

[24] Dobbie, *op. cit.,* p. LVII.

at least finally cleared away any obstacles to an early dating of the poem which its astonishing high culture and art might have suggested. The treasures, and the capacity to enjoy them displayed in *Beowulf* were, we now know, a reality. And the high aesthetic qualities shown by the *Beowulf*-poet — and by implication therefore — in his audience, had been fully demonstrated not so long before by the craftsmen of East-Anglia who worked the wondrous gold and jewelry of Sutton Hoo.

Like *Beowulf,* the Sutton Hoo finds illustrate the continuity as much as the heterogeneity of Anglo-Saxon culture. Woden and Christ seem to meet, as it were, at Sutton Hoo, just as the poem may be viewed both as a pagan poem and as a Christian didactic work symbolizing the pilgrimage of man and his conflict with the supernatural powers of darkness. One could almost set forth the Germanic ideal touched by oncoming Christianity, of the hero as prince, alike from the artefacts of Sutton Hoo and from *Beowulf*. Nor should the common rejection of Levin Schücking's dating of the poem to the end of the ninth century cause us to overlook his distinguished work on its cultural significance.[25] But the drawing of parallels and the building of new speculations on them is an endless fascination which must be restrained till clarified by further study.

It has been my purpose rather to emphasize the new lines of study suggested by Sutton Hoo than to attempt new results. For guidance throughout I have been especially indebted to the work of Mr. Bruce-Mitford, to whom students of this, the

[25] See *Wann entstand der Beowulf?* (*Beiträge zur Geschichte der deutschen Sprache und Literatur XLII,* 1917) especially also his *Das Königsideal im Beowulf* (*Englische Studien* 67, 1932), and *Heldenstolz und Würde im Angelsächsischen* (*Abhandlungen der philologisch-historischen Klasse der sächsischen Akademie der Wissenschaften,* Band XLII, 1933).

greatest archaeological discovery in Britain of our century, are more indebted than to anyone.[26]

[26] The following articles reached me too late for consideration in this paper: — *Snake-swords and Boar-helms in Beowulf* by A. T. Hatto (*English Studies* XXXVIII, 1957; *Beowulf and Archaeology* by Rosemary J. Cramp (*Medieval Archaeology* vol. I, 1957); *Beowulf and the Harp at Sutton Hoo* by J. B. Bessinger (*Toronto Univ. Quarterly* for Jan., 1958).

15

BEOWULF—AN ALLEGORY OF SALVATION?*

M. B. McNamee, S.J.

WHEN BEOWULF'S CHARACTER IS STUDIED IN THE LIGHT OF THE Christian concept of magnanimity, the idea common amongst most modern scholars that his character and that of the poem in which he figures are substantially Christian in spirit is greatly strengthened.[1] Some few scholars have gone further and suggested that the story may possibly be read as an allegory of the Christian story of salvation. Klaeber has very tentatively hinted at that notion in the introduction to his edition of the poem.

> That the victorious champion, who overcomes this group of monsters, is a decidedly unusual figure of very uncertain historical associations has been pointed out before. The poet has raised him to the rank of a singularly spotless hero, a 'defending, protecting, redeeming being,' a truly ideal character. We might even feel inclined to recognize features of the Christian Savior in the destroyer of hellish fiends, the warrior brave and gentle, blameless in thought and deed, the king that dies for his people. Though delicately kept in the background, such a Christian interpretation of the main story on the part of the Anglo-Saxon author could not but give added strength and tone to the entire poem.[2]

Gerald Walsh, in his provocative little book on *Medieval Human-*

* Reprinted, by permission of the author, and the University of Illinois Press, publishers of the *Journal of English and Germanic Philology,* from that journal, LIX (April 1960), 190-207.

[1] I have made a detailed study of this aspect of *Beowulf* in *Honor and the Epic Hero* (New York, 1960), pp. 86-117.

[2] Frederick Klaeber, *Beowulf and the Fight at Finnsburg* (New York, 1950), pp. l-li.

ism, has stated forthrightly that the poem is a Christian allegory:

> *Beowulf* is not a pagan poem; it is the creation of a Christian, possibly of a monk. The legends had come from Denmark and Sweden, but the Norsemen knew comparatively little of composition or literary creation. By the eighth century, these legends had become grist for the Christian poet's mill. They were welded together into a single allegorical song imitating the Divine Mystery of Redemption — a conception beyond the scope of the Viking's power.[3]

Professor Kennedy, although he denies in *Beowulf* any such liturgical echoes as occur in *Christ I* and any such reflection of theological dogmas as are evident in *Christ II,*[4] does concede that "the ancient tale of Beowulf's struggle with monster and dragon may well have lent itself to the uses of Christian allegory."[5] I wish to suggest in this study that as an allegory of the Christian story of salvation the *Beowulf* poem both echoes the liturgy and reflects New Testament theological dogma.

There is no doubt whatever that the *Beowulf*-poet has gone out of his way to exclude all the old pagan gods from an active place in his poem. The god referred to throughout by Hrothgar and Beowulf alike is the one, providential God of the Christians,[6] the Creator and Lord of the whole universe and the Creator and

[3] Gerald G. Walsh, S.J., *Medieval Humanism* (New York, 1942), p. 45.

[4] Charles W. Kennedy, *The Earliest English Poetry* (New York, 1943), p. 91.

[5] Kennedy, p. 98.

[6] It is true that *Wyrd* or fate is also referred to frequently in the poem, but often in such a way as to suggest that *Wyrd* is subject to the decrees of a providential God. Professor Kennedy says of the relationship of these two ideas in the poem: "Examples of this incomplete fusion of pagan and Christian will be found in a parallelism of reference to the blind and inexorable power of *Wyrd,* or Fate and to the omnipotence of a divine Ruler Who governs all things well. But even in survivals of pagan material the modifying influence of Christian thought is often evident. In both instances in which there is reference to the curse upon the dragon's treasure the poet specifically excludes from the operation of the curse one who has God's favor. Elsewhere in the poem *God* and *Wyrd* are brought into juxtaposition in such a manner as to imply control of Fate by the superior power of Christian divinity" (Kennedy, pp. 87-88).

Final Judge of man as well. Idolatry and especially devil worship are looked upon as aberrations hateful to the true God and subject to divine punishment.[7] Man's whole life is represented as under the providential care of this one, true God. In estimating the effect of the new Christian revelation upon the poem, it is important to notice that the two most fundamental certitudes which that revelation provided — certitude about man's beginnings and about his end — play an important part in the poem. Professor Gilson has reminded us that no pagan philosopher ever arrived at a clear idea either of Creation as the beginning of life nor of the final judgment and man's destiny after death.[8] Both these ideas find a definite place in *Beowulf*. The joyful hymn which is sung at Hrothgar's court and which particularly enrages the jealous Grendel is a hymn of creation telling the story of the beginnings of all things, not unlike the Creation poem of Caedmon.[9] Besides this, God is referred to throughout the poem as the Creator and Lord of all, and there is frequent reference to the

[7] See *Beowulf,* translated by Clark Hall, p. 29 [170-90], for a forthright condemnation of idolatry and more specifically of devil worship. "Sometimes they vowed sacrifices at the tabernacles of idols, — prayed aloud that the destroyer of souls would provide them help against the distress of the people. Such was their custom, — the hope of the heathen, — they remembered hellish things in the thoughts of their hearts. They knew not the Creator, Judge of deeds; they knew not the Lord God, nor, truly, had they learned to worship the Protector of the heavens, the glorious Ruler." [Note: All future references to *Beowulf* will be to the Hall translation newly edited and revised by C. L. Wrenn (London, 1950). The numbers in brackets in the references to the *Beowulf* refer to the pertinent lines of the original Old English edition of Frederick Klaeber.]

[8] Etienne Gilson, *The Spirit of Medieval Philosophy* (New York, 1936), pp. 68-69, 385-90.

[9] Hall, p. 25 [91-98]: "He who could recount the first making of men from distant ages, spoke. He said that the Almighty made the earth, a fair and bright plain, which water encompasses, and, triumphing in power, appointed the radiance of the sun and moon as light for the land-dwellers, and decked the earth-regions with branches and leaves. He fashioned life for all kinds that live and move."

judgment to come.[10] The human situation as a race fallen from grace is hinted at, too, in the fact that Grendel is represented as a monstrous offspring of the murderer Cain;[11] and the flood sent by God to destroy the sinful race is shadowed forth in the carvings of the flood on the hilt of the magic sword which Beowulf brings back from the mysterious mere.[12] All these Old Testament allusions, occurring, as it were, in asides in the poem, have led some scholars to say that all the Scriptural allusions in the poem are to the Old Testament and that they occur outside the events of the main story.[13] There is nothing from the New Testament, they claim, and nothing that expresses any specific dogma of Christianity in the main episodes of the poem. I wish to suggest here that that conclusion should not be reached too hastily.

Even more important than the idea of Creation and Final Judgment provided by divine revelation as a clue to the real meaning of life is the idea of a Redeemer sent by God to save

[10] Note the reference to the Creator and Provident God of the Christians in the quotation in n. 6. But there are repeated references to this one true God, Creator and Judge, throughout the poem. See, for example, Hall, pp. 36 [318], 39 [384], 42 [442], 44 [478], 55 [687], 56 [700], 57 [707], 67 [932], 69 [978], 74 [1057], 85 [1270], 99 [1553], 108 [1725], 109 [1750], 111 [1778], 157 [2740], 160 [2794], 163 [2874], 171 [3054].

[11] Hall, p. 25 [102-15].

[12] Hall, p. 106 [1687-95]. "Hrothgar discoursed; he scrutinized the hilt, the ancient heirloom, upon which was inscribed the rise of the primeval strife when the flood, the rushing deep, destroyed the brood of giants. They suffered terribly; that was a race alien from the eternal Lord, (and) for that the Sovereign Ruler gave them a final retribution by the surging water."

[13] Thus Klaeber (p. xlix): "Of specific motives derived from the Old Testament (and occurring in *Genesis A,* also) we note the story of Cain, the giants, and the deluge, and the song of Creation." And Kennedy (p. 88): "The Christian influence in the *Beowulf* is a matter of transforming spirit, rather than of reference to dogma or doctrine. And it is, in the main, an influence reflecting the Old Testament rather than the New. The poem contains specific references to Cain's murder of Abel, and to the stories of Creation, the giants, and the Flood. But we find no such allusions to New Testament themes as characterize, for example, the *Christ* of Cynewulf."

man from the consequences of his own sins. The Christian story of redemption in its essentials is simply this: man has fallen from a state of innocence and happiness and is in the powerful grip of Satan. Utterly helpless to save himself, he is in dire need of a Savior to redeem him from the power of sin and Satan. In the advent of Christ, man finds such a Savior. These bare facts about man's need and the historical advent of a Savior are as much a heart of the revelation of the New Testament as the story of Creation and the fact of the one true Lord and Final Judge of all were to the Old Testament.

I do not think that anyone perfectly familiar with the details of the Christian story of salvation can read *Beowulf* and not be struck by the remarkable parallel that exists between the outline of the Beowulf story and the Christian story of salvation. For the purpose of the comparison here, we may consider the poem as divided into two parts: part one concerned with the conflicts of the young Beowulf with Grendel and his dam, and part two with the mortal conflict of the aged Beowulf with the fire-dragon.

In part one we have a situation that parallels the story of salvation almost perfectly. In the first episode, dealing with the story of Hrothgar and his people, we have the spectacle of a people who are in the grip of a frightful monster who, jealous of their happiness in Heorot,[14] has left woe and sorrow in the wake of his destructive visitations. And it is emphasized in the story that neither the great and magnanimous Hrothgar himself nor anyone among his followers can do anything to save himself from the

[14] That Grendel's envy of the happiness of Hrothgar's people in Heorot is the motive of his murderous raids is stated clearly in the poem itself. Hall, p. 24 [87-91]: "Then the mighty spirit who dwelt in darkness bore grievously a time of hardship, in that he heard each day loud revelry in hall; — there was the sound of harp, the clear song of the minstrel." This motive for Grendel's incursions into Heorot parallels the traditional motive of Satan's incursions into the Garden of Eden — envy of the happiness of our first parents in contrast to his own misery in hell.

depredations of this monster.[15] Then, in the person of Beowulf, a savior, sent by God from outside, comes to them — a savior who has both the desire and the power to save them and who does actually free them from the ravages of Grendel by confronting and slaying the monster.

For an audience familiar with both the story of salvation and the ancient Nordic myths, all that would be needed to identify the story of Beowulf with that of the Christian Savior would be a clue. Miss Whitelock has rather convincingly argued[16] that the audience for which the poem was written was definitely Christian; there has never been any doubt that it was an audience familiar with the old, pagan, Nordic myths. Quite a sufficient clue for such an audience to make the identification, it seems to

[15] Hrothgar in his welcoming address to Beowulf is most emphatic in stating his own and his people's helplessness against Grendel: "It is grief to me in my heart to tell any man what Grendel with his thoughts of hate has wrought for me in Heorot of harm and sudden harassings. My troop in hall, my war-band is diminished" (Hall, p. 44 [474-477]). And when Beowulf has conquered Grendel, Hrothgar makes this public proclamation: "Many horrors and afflictions have I endured through Grendel: yet God, the King of Glory, can ever work wonder on wonder. It was but now that I despaired of ever seeing a remedy for any of my troubles, since the best of houses stood stained with the blood of battle, — an all-embracing woe for every one of the counsellors, of those who despaired of ever guarding the fortress of this people from foes, from demons and evil spirits. Now, through the might of the Lord, a warrior has done a deed which up to now we could not accomplish by our schemings" (Hall, pp. 67-68 [927-943]).

[16] Dorothy Whitelock, *The Audience of Beowulf* (Oxford, 1951). Miss Whitelock's interest in the audience of *Beowulf* is motivated by her attempt to date the composition of the poem. Incidentally, she has this to say about its Christianity: "He [the poet] was composing for Christians, whose conversion was neither partial nor superficial. He expects them to understand his allusions to biblical events without his troubling to be explicit about them. He does not think it necessary to tell them anything of the circumstances in which Cain slew Abel, or when, and why, 'the flood, the pouring ocean, slew the race of giants.' He assumes their familiarity not merely with the biblical story, but with the interpretation in the commentaries — not necessarily at first hand, but through the teaching of the Church" (p. 5). See Chapter One, *passim,* for further discussion of the same point.

me, is the fact that Grendel is repeatedly identified throughout the first episode with the powers of darkness and described as an inmate of hell.[17] If the monster that has Hrothgar's kingdom in his grip is consistently associated with the powers of hell, it would take no great stretch of imagination for an audience familiar with the Christian story of salvation and with an innate taste for the allegorical and riddles in general to see in Beowulf an allegorization of Christ the Savior — especially since, as I

[17] Professor Tolkien in a note to his article *"Beowulf:* The Monsters and the Critics," *Proceedings of the British Academy,* XXII, 278-80, calls attention to the ambiguity that hovers about the titles of Grendel. It is not clear, he claims, that Grendel is conceived by the poet as a full-fledged medieval devil; he would seem to be a kind of transitional figure — half-ogre, half-devil. But whether the terms used unequivocally spell out a medieval devil or only a man-monster symbolizing the power of evil and the forces of hell makes little difference for the allegorical meaning of the poem. In fact, for the allegory a physical monster drawn from the old myths would serve the purpose better than a theologically accurate devil as long as the monster is associated with the powers of hell. And that the poet makes inescapably clear. See for instance Hall, p. 28 [164], p. 59 [755], and most striking of all, p. 60 [787]: "A din arose, strange and mighty; a horrible fear came to the North-Danes, to everyone who heard the shrieking from the wall, — heard the adversary of God chant his grisly lay, his song of defeat, — the prisoner of hell wailing over his wound." And again his retreat and death are described in the following terms: pp. 63-64 [841-853]: "His parting from life did not seem a cause of sorrow to any of the men who saw the trail of the inglorious one, — how he, weary in spirit and vanquished in the fight, bore the tracks of his failing life away from thence, fated and fugitive, to the lake of the water-demons. Then the water was boiling with blood, the frightful surge of the waves welled up, all mingled with hot gore, — with sword-blood; the death-doomed creature had hidden himself there, and then, deprived of joys, he gave up his life, — his heathen soul in the fen-refuge; there hell received him." For an allegory this is a much more effective way of dramatizing the defeat of Satan than if he were represented as the entirely spiritual entity of theology, where any suggestion of a body and soul in Satan would be absurd. Nor does this mean that the poet did not know his theology. It merely means that he chose to borrow some of the traditional Nordic monster-lore to allegorize the overthrow of the worst monster of them all, in much the same way that Milton later retained what he knew to be an obsolete cosmography and astronomy in *Paradise Lost* because it provided a more poetic stage for the action of his poem.

have shown elsewhere, he so well exemplifies the virtues of humility and charity which Christ Himself had come to preach. The first episode, then, could very readily have appeared to such an audience as an allegorization of the essential facts of the story of salvation.

And what would such an audience make of the second episode — the descent into the mysterious mere? A great deal more, it would seem to me, than some of the modern critics make of it. The facts of the story are again quite simply told: Hrothgar's people are once more in the power of a monster. Grendel's ghoulish dam comes to revenge the death of her son, and once more Hrothgar and his followers are helpless in the face of her murderous visitations. They once more look to Beowulf for succor from this new monster. Again the Geatish hero assures them that he will save them by subduing this new threat to their peace and happiness. He goes to the mysterious mere infested with serpents, plunges into the murky waters down to the fiery cave where the monster dwells. There, in a terrible struggle with the monster, he wounds her; and, as her blood bubbles to the surface, his followers on the shore are saddened at what they think is the death of their master. Meantime, when Beowulf is almost overcome by the demon, finding the sword of Unferth useless against her, he notices a great mysterious sword on the walls of the cave and, seizing it, does the monster to death. As her blood gushes out in fiery streams, the sword melts down to the very hilt in the hot blood. But the monster is dead. Then comes the climax to Beowulf's visit to this fiery cave at the bottom of the mere. He turns to the dead body of Grendel stretched out on the floor of the cave, triumphantly hacks off his head, and, with it and the hilt of the great sword, swims up through the waters of the mere, now purified of all its serpents, and rejoins his followers amidst their great rejoicing at his triumphal return. After being greeted and feted by the grateful Hrothgar, he returns home triumphantly laden with the gifts which the grateful Hrothgar has showered upon him.

A Christian can hardly read this second episode even today without hearing all sorts of Scriptural and liturgical echoes ringing in his ears; and those echoes would have been a great deal louder for members of the *Beowulf*-poet's audience, who were much more familiar with Scripture and the impressive contemporary ritualistic ceremonies of baptism than are most modern readers of the poem.[18] From the earliest times in the Church the symbolism of the baptismal ceremony by submersion was based on a passage in Saint Paul's Epistle to the Romans (6:3-4): "Know you not that we, who are baptized in Christ Jesus, are baptized in his death? For we are buried together with him by baptism into death; that as Christ is risen from the dead by the glory of the Father, so we also may walk in newness of life." In the old baptismal ceremony, which took place on Holy Saturday immediately after the blessing of the new baptismal water as a part of the Easter vigil service, the redemptive death and burial of Christ and the sinner's death to sin were symbolized by the

[18] Allan Cabaniss in an article entitled, "*Beowulf* and the Liturgy" (*JEGP,* LIV [April, 1955], 195-201), has called attention to the possible influence of the Holy Saturday Liturgy and the Harrowing of Hell tradition on the second episode of the *Beowulf.* In a concluding paragraph of the article he says: "However heathen the original story was, it is surely reasonable to suppose that the account of Beowulf's descent into the grim fen, his encounter with the demon-brood staining the water with blood, and his triumphant emergence from it into joyous springtime is, at the least, a reflection of the liturgy of baptism; at the most, an allegory of it. That this view is not on a priori grounds impossible is evident from the quite elaborate Christian allegories of Cynewulf and of the Cædmonian *Exodus,* both approximately contemporary with the *Beowulf*-poet. Indeed the *Exodus* shows precisely the influence of the same twelve Holy Saturday prophecies. And, interestingly enough, it reflects a knowledge of just that portion of *Beowulf* with which we are here concerned. Since it has been demonstrated that the *Exodus* shows the effect of the ancient liturgy of baptism and Holy Saturday, one goes not too far afield in presuming that a similar relationship exists in reference to *Beowulf.*" I had come to the same conclusion myself before reading Mr. Cabaniss' article, and I believe that I provide further corroborative evidence for this interpretation of the second episode of *Beowulf* here and that I throw it into a broader allegorical context in the poem as a whole.

submersion of the catechumen in the baptismal waters. Christ's triumphant resurrection and the sinner's new life of grace were in turn symbolized by his emersion from the waters. The fact that the waters represented death and sin and the power of Satan in this ancient baptismal ceremony[19] is suggested by the prayers that are still said on Holy Saturday at the blessing of the new baptismal water:

Therefore may all unclean spirits, by thy command, O Lord, depart from hence; may the whole malice of diabolical deceit be entirely banished: may no power of the enemy prevail here; may he not fly about to lay his snares; may he not creep in secretly; may he not corrupt with his infection. May this holy and innocent creature be free from all the assaults of the enemy and purified by the removal of all his malice.[20]

To an audience familiar with this symbolic meaning of immersion into and emersion from waters infested by the powers of hell and

[19] A. Villien points out that the solemn symbolic ritual that surrounds the blessing of the baptismal water and the actual baptism of catechumens on Holy Saturday by immersion is amongst the most ancient in the Church, parts of it probably of Apostolic origin. See his *The History and Liturgy of the Sacraments* (London, 1932), p. 2. Besides the exorcism of Satan from the baptismal waters which occurs in the earliest *Ordos* and *Sacramentaries* very much as we find it in the present ritual for the baptism of adults, the symbolism of the anointing of the catechumen with sacred oil also is pertinent to Beowulf's struggle with Grendel. Of this anointing Villien remarks: "As for the anointing of the breast and back (*inter scapulus* [between the shoulders], as the Ritual says), we know what symbolism is represented by this. The *De Sacramentis* indicates it in a few words: the athlete of old anointed his body with oil in order that his adversary might not be able to get a grip on him; it is against the most formidable of all foes, the devil, that the catechumen is now taking up the struggle; the blessed oil of unction represents the power of Christ which will preserve him from defeat and lead him to eternal life" (pp. 34-35). This most ancient ritual, therefore, would have familiarized a Christian audience, which had witnessed it repeated dramatically each Holy Saturday, with the struggle against Satan as a hand-to-hand wrestling match. *"Unctus et quasi athleta Christi, quasi luctam hujus saeculi luctaturus"* [anointed also, like an athlete of Christ, like one about to fight the battle of the world] are the words of the *De Sacramentis,* I, ii, 4 and 5, in this regard.

[20] Dom Gaspar Lefebvre, O.S.B., *Saint Andrew Daily Missal* (Saint Paul, 1937), p. 609.

purified by the powers of God, it would have been natural to see in Beowulf's descent into the serpent-infested mere and his triumphant ascent from those waters purified of their serpents a symbolic representation of the death and burial and of the resurrection of Christ, and, in the purification of the waters, a symbol of the redemption of man from the poisonous powers of evil. Again sufficient clue for such an interpretation would have been provided for such an audience by the explicit identification of Grendel's dam and Grendel himself with the powers of hell.

The description of the cave of Grendel and his mother as a fiery cavern under the sea corresponds, too, to what was, from the time of the apocryphal Gospel of Nicodemus on up to the heart of the Middle Ages, the traditional way of representing hell. A familiar subject of literary description and artistic representation, one that goes back to at least the ninth century, is what was called Christ's *Harrowing of Hell*.[21] These descriptions were

[21] The source of the Harrowing of Hell tradition is, of course, the Apocryphal Gospel of Nicodemus, the oldest manuscripts of which date back to the fifth century, and that work was tremendously popular in England from the earliest days of Christianity there. William Henry Hulme says of its history in England: "The influence of the *Evangelium Nicodemi* was felt in English literature long before the period of the religious drama. The Gospel was doubtless introduced into England in the Latin version not very long after Christianity began to flourish there. For early English writers like Bede show perfect familiarity with its contents. And the early Christian poets utilize the story and paraphrase it in a number of their productions. An extensive account of the descent of Christ is contained in the so-called Cædmonian poems, whilst the greatest of all Old-English religious poets, Cynewulf, refers to the Harrowing of Hell in several different connections, and he reproduces much of the description in his poem on *Christ*. Cynewulf, in fact, or one of his school of poets, devoted an entire poem to the subject, though only a fragment of it has been preserved [*The Harrowing of Hell*]. In the later centuries of Old-English literature the *Evangelium Nicodemi* was turned into the Old-English prose, which is preserved in at least three different manuscripts. Besides this the story of the descent was frequently employed by writers of Old-English homilies and lives of the saints. The Gospel probably reached the climax of its popularity in English during the thirteenth and fourteenth centuries." *Introduction to the Middle English Harrowing of Hell and Gospel of Nicodemus* (London [EETS, E.S., 100] 1907),

meant to visualize the article in the Creed which states that Christ descended into hell. The minimum meaning of that tenet of the Creed is that Christ descended into Limbo to free the souls of the just from the Old Law and conduct them into their reward now that He had completed their redemption from the power of Satan. But, based on the apocryphal Gospel of Nicodemus, a tradition had grown up that Christ also descended into the very hell of Satan, where He made His victory over His old enemy felt in a very special way.[22]

In early book illuminations, especially of Anglo-Saxon and Germanic origins, Christ is frequently represented as leading souls out of fiery caverns or out of the flaming mouth of a dragon, and as making Satan, represented sometimes as a human monster and sometimes as a dragon or serpent, feel His complete triumph

---

pp. lxvii-lxviii. The seventh *Blickling Homily* on Easter Day is an excellent example of the assimilation of the Harrowing of Hell into the Old English literary tradition and provides the best background for the proper understanding of Beowulf's descent into the lake.

[22] This is the description of Christ's victory over Satan in hell as it occurs in one version of the Gospel of Nicodemus: "And, behold, suddenly Hades trembled, and the gates of death and the bolts were shattered, and the iron bars were broken and fell to the ground, and everything was laid open. And Satan remained in the midst, and stood confounded and downcast, bound with fetters on his feet. And, behold, the Lord Jesus Christ, coming in the brightness of the light from on high, compassionate, great, and lowly, carrying a chain in His hand, bound Satan by the neck, and again tying his hands behind him, dashed him on his back in Tartarus, and placed His holy foot on his throat, saying: Through all ages thou has done many evils; thou has not in any wise rested. To-day I deliver thee to everlasting fire. And Hades being suddenly summoned, He commanded him, and said: Take this most wicked and impious one, and have him in thy keeping even to that day in which I shall command thee. And he, as soon as he received him, was plunged under the feet of the Lord along with him into the depth of the abyss" ("The Gospel of Nicodemus," *The Ante-Nicene Fathers,* Translated by Rev. Alexander Roberts and James Donaldson [New York, 1908], VIII, 457). To an audience familiar with this and many other accounts of Christ's Harrowing of Hell, it would not have been difficult to see in Beowulf's climactic beheading of the dead Grendel in the fiery cave under the sea an allegorical representation of Christ's final victory over Satan.

over him by transfixing him with a sword or spear, or by binding him in chains. Again, for an audience familiar with this ancient and rich tradition, the description of Beowulf descending into the fiery cave of Grendel, of his overcoming Grendel's dam with the magic sword, and of his climaxing his visit with the triumphal beheading of the dead Grendel himself, who had been repeatedly identified with the powers of hell, would almost certainly have been taken as an allegorization of Christ's descent into hell. In Beowulf's victorious ascent from the mere, carrying the symbols of his triumph over Grendel, they could also have seen an allegorization of Christ's triumphant resurrection and victory over death, and in his victorious return to his homeland, laden with gifts from Hrothgar, a representation of Christ's triumphal ascension into heaven.

I have long suspected that the mere in this second episode of the *Beowulf* represented to the Anglo-Saxon imagination hell itself, but have had no particular evidence for such a view. I have examined a large number of Anglo-Saxon illuminated manuscripts in the British Museum, and the Bodleian and Morgan libraries, but have been unable to find any illuminations picturing hell that date back as early as the presumed ninth-century date of the *Beowulf*. There are several from the eleventh century, however, which graphically represent hell as a lake infested with dragons and man-eating, man-shaped monsters. Several illuminations in an eleventh-century Psalter (Harley Manuscript, No. 603), for instance, consistently represent hell as a lake inhabited by serpents and a great man-monster, such as that seen in Fig. 1. This illustration accompanies Psalm XXV — which treats of the great mercy of God in sparing the psalmist from his enemies. Here the illuminator has definitely interpreted the enemy as Satan and has pictured him as a man-eating man-monster emerging from the surface of a serpent-infested lake and devouring souls. In the illumination accompanying Psalm CII (not reproduced here) the souls are shown as being pitchforked into the maw of this same man-monster as it emerges from the lake. These

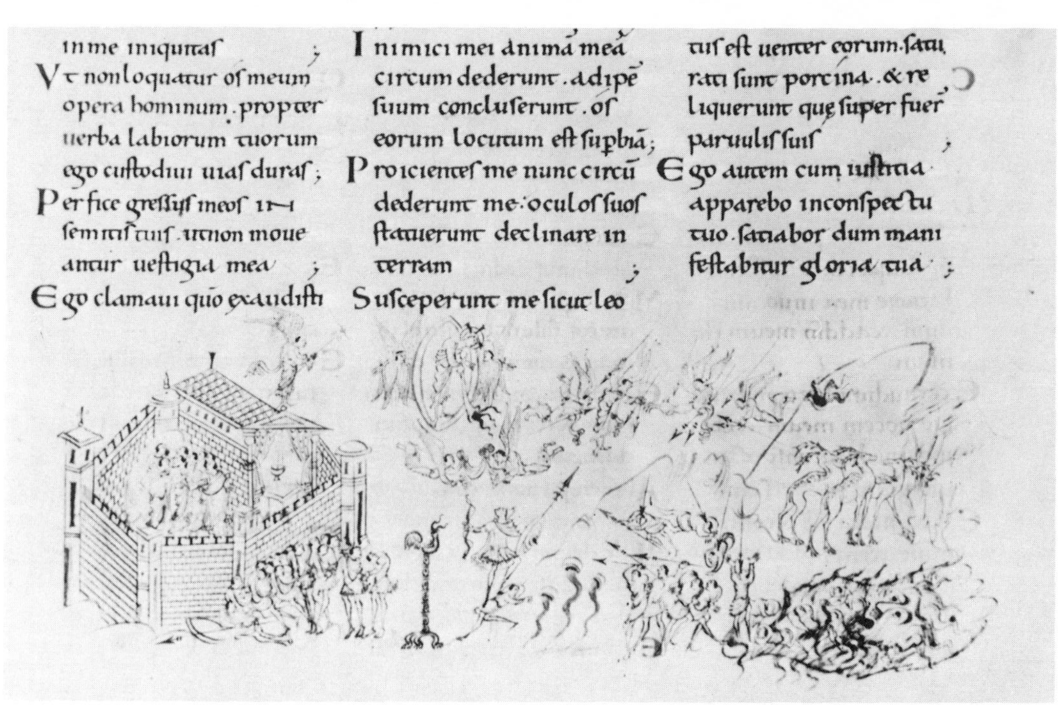

Fig. 1. Illustration of Psalm xxv. Eleventh Century, English. Harley MS. 603 f.9. Reproduced by courtesy of the British Museum.

Fig. 2. Gloucester Candlestick (*ca.* 1110).
Reproduced by courtesy of the Victoria and Albert Museum.

illuminations for the Psalter of the Harley Manuscript, No. 603, could in general be used as illustrations for the second episode of the *Beowulf*. They show that, at least by the eleventh century, the mysterious 'serpent-infested mere of Anglo-Saxon saga had provided a means of making the story of Christ and Satan and Hell graphic to the Anglo-Saxon imagination. It is my suggestion that the *Beowulf*-poet had already begun to employ this means of representing Satan and Hell in the figure of Grendel and the mysterious mere.

As a matter of fact, the use of the traditional Nordic serpent and dragon motif for symbolizing the power of Satan over mankind became something of a tradition in Anglo-Saxon and Anglo-Norman art in general. The whole symbolical treatment of the theme of redemption in the famous Gloucester paschal candlestick (*ca.* 1110) preserved in the Victoria and Albert Museum in London employs this motif (Fig. 2). The condition of unredeemed man is symbolized in the candlestick, the base and stem of which are entirely made up of little human figures enwrapped in the coils of serpentine and dragonish creatures. Man's redemption from the toils of the evil one is symbolized by the signs of the four evangelists on the knob of the candlestick, by the candle itself (the symbol of the light of truth and the saving grace of Christ the redeemer), and most unmistakably by the inscription in Latin on the rim of the cup of the candlestick: LUCIS: ON-[US]: VIRTUTIS: OPUS: DOCTRINA: REFULGENS: PREDICAT: UT: VICIO: NON: TENEBRETUR: HOMO (The duty of this light is a work of virtue, as a shining lesson it preaches that man be not darkened by sin). If my interpretation of *Beowulf* is correct, the poet had used, back in the ninth century, the Nordic material in very much the same way in which the designer of the Gloucester candlestick used it in the twelfth century — to symbolize the redemption of mankind by Christ from the grip of Satan.

If this was in any way intended by the *Beowulf*-poet, it might be asked why he was not more explicit. It might be countered that to have been more explicit would have spoiled the poem as an allegory — especially for an Anglo-Saxon audience which had such a taste for obscure allegory and the riddle of runes. All that would have been needed for such an audience is a clue sufficient to suggest the identification. The close parallel between the situation of Beowulf and the Savior would have been sufficient to fasten the allegory. And in many places the language employed by the *Beowulf*-poet is almost a direct paraphrase of the language of Scripture describing a situation in Christ's life parallel to that in which Beowulf finds himself.[23]

If this suggestion has any merit whatever, what the *Beowulf*-poet has done in the first two episodes of the poem is to tell the story of salvation twice in allegorical terms. In the first episode, he merely allegorizes the essential *facts* of the story — the need of a Savior and His advent. In the second episode, he repeats the story of man's need of a Savior from the powers of evil, but emphasizes the effects of redemption in the descent into and purification of the serpent-infested mere.

In the third and last episode of the poem, which tells of Beowulf's conflict with the fire-dragon, he allegorizes the story of salvation once again, this time dramatizing the price of salvation — the very life of the Savior Himself. The literal story is again quite simple. Beowulf's own people are being ravaged by a fiery dragon whose treasure-hoard has been disturbed by a fugitive from justice. They are powerless to save themselves from the havoc wrought by the dragon, and hence Beowulf goes out to do battle with the fire-drake. He is led out to the lair of the dragon

[23] Klaeber, in his notes to the poem, has pointed out many of the scriptural echoes which occur throughout the poem. Let me call attention here to just one typical example which subconsciously but inevitably makes one associate Beowulf with Christ. It occurs in Hrothgar's exclamation of thanks to Beowulf for having freed his people from the attacks of "demons and evil spirits." "Lo! That self-same woman who bore this child among the tribes of men may say, if she still lives, that the eternal God has been gracious to her in her child-bearing" (Hall, p. 68 [942-946]). This subtly echoes the woman's greeting of Christ in Luke 11:27: "Blessed is the womb that bore thee, and the paps that gave thee suck."

by the guilty follower who enraged the dragon in the first place. When the monster comes forth belching fire to meet his challenger, all Beowulf's followers flee in terror with one sole exception — the faithful Wiglaf, who stays with his master to the end. Beowulf succeeds in giving the dragon a mortal wound, but he himself has been mortally wounded by the beast in the struggle. He has saved his people and won for them the treasure hoarded by the dragon but at the price of his own life. He expires at the ninth hour of the day, and the poem ends with the picture of his twelve followers circling his funeral mound singing his praises to the four corners of the world.

Klaeber has observed, in his notes on this part of the poem, the close parallel between the circumstances that surround Beowulf in this last episode and those which surrounded Christ in the last hours of his life.[24] The number correspondence is exact. Beowulf is led out to his conflict by a guilty follower as Christ was betrayed into the hands of His executioners by His guilty disciple Judas. The poet notes that there are thirteen in the party going out to meet the dragon, thus paralleling Christ and His twelve apostles. When the dragon attacks, ten of Beowulf's followers flee in terror, leaving only Wiglaf, the one faithful fol-

[24] Klaeber comments, regarding the third episode: "It is especially in the last adventure that we are strongly tempted to look for a deeper, spiritual interpretation. The duality of the motives which apparently prompt Beowulf to the dragon fight may not be as unnatural as it has sometimes been considered. Still, it is somewhat strange that the same gold which Beowulf rejoices in having obtained for his people before the hour of his death is placed by his mourning thanes into the burial mound; they give it back to the earth. Nay, Wiglaf, in the depth of his sorrow which makes him oblivious of all else, expresses the wish that Beowulf had left the dragon alone to hold his den until the end of the world. The indubitably significant result of the adventure is the hero's death, and, in the structural plan of the poem, the aim and object of the dragon fight is to lead up to this event — a death, that is, which involves the destruction of the adversary, but is no less noteworthy in that it partakes of the nature of a self-sacrifice. . . . Some incidents in the encounter with the dragon also lend themselves to comparison with happenings in the garden of Gethsemane" (p. li).

lower, who remains to the end. This, too, corresponds to the situation of Christ in His last hours. Ten of His followers also deserted Him in His passion (Judas had deserted Him before the event), and only Saint John remained faithful to Him to the end. Beowulf is described, too, as expiring, like Christ, at the ninth hour. When his funeral mound has been built, his twelve disciples are described as circling it singing his praises to the four corners of the world. This again corresponds to the Apostles of Christ — twelve in number after the election of Matthias — who proclaimed the story of the Savior to the whole world after His death.

As the specific identification of the monsters in the first two episodes with the powers of hell would have been sufficient clue to enable the *Beowulf*-poet's audience to identify the story with the Christian story of salvation, so the parallel between the circumstances surrounding Beowulf's last hours and those surrounding Christ's would also have sufficed for the identification of this third episode with the Christian story as salvation. But a climactic detail is added in this third allegorization of the story which emphasizes the kind of savior — a savior who saves by losing his own life. This, of course, was the most impressive feature of the Christian story of salvation — the unselfish generosity of a Savior Who lays down His life to redeem mankind. The use of the dragon as the adversary in this final conflict would also have served as a clue to the allegory for an audience familiar with the very ancient tradition representing the fiends of hell as fire-breathing dragons.[25]

But how much of this can be represented as the intention of the *Beowulf*-poet? I make no claim here of being able to answer that question. But this much at least is true: if one were to invent a story whose every detail was designed to allegorize the story of salvation, one could not improve very much on the Beowulf

[25] The tradition of representing Satan as a dragon, of course, is based on the following passage from the *Apocalypse* (21:2): "And he laid hold on the dragon the old serpent, which is the devil and Satan, and bound him for a thousand years."

story as it stands. This fact suggests the possibility that the *Beowulf*-poet was writing in the spirit of Pope Saint Gregory, who had cautioned Saint Augustine in his zeal not to make a clean sweep of the old native Anglo-Saxon customs, myths, ceremonies, and traditions, but to adapt them to the expression of the new Christian message.[26] And if our interpretation of the poem is tenable, it would seem that the *Beowulf*-poet was proceeding in a manner exactly opposite to the procedure of the authors of poems like the *Andreas:* There an explicit Christian subject matter is told in the language and literary conventions of the old Nordic sagas; whereas in *Beowulf* the old pagan sagas are subtly reshaped and reorganized to shadow forth the essential facts of the new story of salvation. To an audience that was familiar with the substance of the Christian story of salvation, as well as with the traditional pagan myths, no more would be needed than the identification of Grendel and Grendel's dam with the powers of hell in part one, and the parallelism between the situations of Christ and Beowulf in part two to enable them to catch the allegory. It would be surprising, in fact, if this allegorical element were not present in *Beowulf,* when we see how much it permeated subsequent Anglo-Saxon and Anglo-Norman sculpture, and book illuminations.

[26] See The Venerable Bede, *The Ecclesiastical History of the English Nation* (Everyman Edition) (London, 1951), pp. 52-53: "When, therefore, Almighty God shall bring you to the most reverent Bishop Augustine, our brother, tell him what I have, upon mature deliberation on the affair of the English, determined upon, viz., that the temples of the idols in that nation ought not to be destroyed; but let the idols that are in them be destroyed; let holy water be made and sprinkled in the said temples, let altars be erected, and relics placed. For if these temples are well built, it is requisite that they be converted from the worship of devils to the service of the true God; that the nation, seeing that their temples are not destroyed, may remove error from their hearts, and knowing and adoring the true God, may the more familiarly resort to the places to which they have been accustomed." What St. Gregory is bidding St. Augustine do in the matter of pagan temples, purify them of the paganism and make them serve the purposes of Christianity, is parallel to what the *Beowulf*-poet has done with the old pagan myths, if our interpretation of the poem is defensible.

This allegorical intention would also help to explain why the poet combines the particular elements of the bear-man story and other sagas in the precise way in which he does. If our interpretation is reasonable, it was the story of salvation that was the principle of selection and arrangement for the poet. It was the outline of the story of salvation that dictated what he would take and what reject from the traditional tales to fit his allegorical intention. Thus the order of events in the cave, ending in the beheading of Grendel instead of the death of his mother, an order which differs from all comparable situations in similar traditional stories and which has consistently puzzled the critics,[27] is no puzzle at all if we see this episode as an allegorization of the Harrowing of Hell which must be climaxed by a dramatization of Christ's final victory over Hell and Satan.

This interpretation also reinforces the artistic unity and consistency of the poem as a whole. I have shown elsewhere in *Honor and the Epic Hero* how parts one and two are intimately woven together through the relationship of the characters of Hrothgar and Beowulf. They are also closely intertwined in the allegorical meaning. Part one tells the story of salvation, emphasizing the historical fact of the Savior; part two repeats the story

[27] In discussing the parallel between the second episode of the Beowulf story and the *Samsonsaga,* Klaeber calls attention to the narrative shift in the position occupied by the beheading of Grendel. "Some noteworthy innovations in the *Beowulf* account — apart from the general transformation incident to the epic setting and atmosphere — are the following. The mother of the slain Grendel leaves her cave, appears in the hall, and avenges her son in heroic fashion — an evident amplification (including a partial repetition) of the narrative. Again, Grendel, though (mortally wounded by Beowulf and) found dead in the cave, is as it were slain again and definitely disposed of by beheading. In the original form of the story, it appears, the male demon had been merely wounded; when the hero made his way to the dwelling place of the monsters, he put the wounded enemy to death (and afterwards killed the mother)" (Klaeber, p. xviii). If the poet was here allegorizing the harrowing of hell, it would be clear why he puts the beheading of Grendel in the climactic position in this episode, and why he has Beowulf mount through the waters cleansed of the serpents that had infested it, bearing triumphantly the severed head of Grendel.

but dramatizes the kind of Savior Who saved by yielding up His own life. This is also parallel to the relationship between parts one and two in the literal story in which the mature Beowulf of part two is a repetition of the mature Hrothgar of part one. Klaeber is right, then, in saying that if *Beowulf* can be interpreted as an allegory of salvation, a much fuller meaning and even greater artistic unity is discernible in the poem as a whole.

For the allegorical purposes of the poem, moreover, the conflict with the monsters is a far better vehicle than any either historical or fictional conflict on the battlefield could ever be. Historical battles are consistently kept in the background, and, as Chambers points out, we are continually given the impression that Beowulf's struggle has a far broader implication than any conflict of Odysseus with mere preternatural monsters like Polyphemus.[28] Beowulf's conflict with the monsters comes closer to that of Adam with Satan in *Paradise Lost*. It has some of the same universal implications. Although he made it in connection with specifically religious Anglo-Saxon poems, Professor Kennedy's remark is also applicable, it seems to me, to *Beowulf:*

> It cannot be forgotten that there is constantly recurring evidence in Old English religious poetry that in many instances the central unity of these religious poems develops from theological, rather than from literary, roots.[29]

[28] R. W. Chambers, "*Beowulf* and the 'Heroic Age' in England," *Man's Unconquerable Mind* (Philadelphia, 1953), p. 66. And Klaeber also suggests that the *Beowulf*-poet was content with the struggle with fabulous monsters precisely because that struggle may have suggested something far more significant. "It would indeed be hard to understand why the poet contented himself with a plot of mere fabulous adventures so much inferior to the splendid heroic setting, unless the narrative derived a superior dignity from suggesting the most exalted hero-life known to Christians" (Klaeber, p. li).

[29] Kennedy, p. 190. Still another remark of Professor Kennedy's states generically of *Beowulf* what we have tried to show more specifically: "It was natural, then, that Old English poetry should reveal this blending of pagan and Christian culture. The pagan legend of *Beowulf* was reshaped into an unmistakably Christian poem. Conversely, Christian themes were versified and adorned in the spirit, and with the detail, of the pagan heroic lay" (p. 159).

16

THE *BEOWULF* POET*

Paull F. Baum

SOME YEARS AGO (1936) PROFESSOR TOLKIEN, IN HIS BRITISH Academy lecture, created an academic stir with his complaints that the scholars had been too busy about their own concerns and had neglected the criticism of *Beowulf* as a poem.[1] Latterly, Miss Whitelock (1951) attempted to recreate the 'audience' of *Beowulf* in the interests of bringing forward its date from the early to the late eighth century.[2] Though the two subjects are not closely related, one may be used to throw light on the other.

Tolkien was attacked and defended, but the questions are still open — and little wonder, for the critical handicaps are forbidding. The language of the poem is difficult, partly owing to the state of the text and partly because the poet chose to make

* Reprinted, by permission of the author, and the editor of *Philological Quarterly*, from that journal, XXXIX (1960), 389-399.

[1] J. R. R. Tolkien, "Beowulf: the Monsters and the Critics," *Proc. of the British Academy*, XXII (1936), 245-295. This has been called a "masterful defence of the monsters against the critics." It was attacked by T. M. Gang, "Approaches to *Beowulf*," *RES*, III (1952), 1-12, and defended by A. Bonjour, "Monsters Crouching and Critics Rampant," *PMLA*, LXVIII (1953), 304-312. Cf. also Arthur G. Brodeur, "The Structure and Unity of *Beowulf*," *PMLA*, LXVIII (1953), 1183-95. Also cf. J. R. Hulbert, "The Genesis of *Beowulf*: a Caveat," *PMLA*, LXVI (1951), 1168-76, which shows how far we are from agreement on even the essential points, and warns against the dangers of "a new orthodoxy."

[2] Dorothy Whitelock, *The Audience of Beowulf* (Oxford, 1951).

it so. Very few, even of the specialists, can pretend to such a feeling for style as we bring to the appreciation of later English poets; and the others are dependent on translations of uncertain merit and fidelity. Knowing so little about whom the poet addressed, we cannot easily estimate the responses he expected: what seems remote to us may well have seemed simple to them. It would help a good deal if we knew whether he wrote to please himself, to satisfy an inner need, or for recitation to a listening audience capable of following with pleasure and understanding his often cryptic language and his often intricate plan of narrative, his ironies, and his exhilarating methods of reticence and indirection. Moreover, *Beowulf* is unique. Being the first of its kind in the vernacular, it has an honored position, but it exists, for us, in a kind of literary vacuum without historical perspective. Nothing is certainly known of its author or of his 'audience.' And its survival in a single manuscript and a different dialect some two and a half centuries after its original composition tells us little; it does not signify a continuous history of recitation or reading.

I

There are really two poems: one about Beowulf and the Danes, the other, roughly half as long, about Beowulf and the Geats. They have in common the same hero, first as a youth then as an old man, overcoming first two water-monsters and later a fire-drake. The earlier victories appear to be successful, though in delivering the Danes from Grendel and his Mother the hero has left them a prey to subsequent disaster; he has established his renown, which was paramount, but as the savior of a nation in distress his achievement was only temporary. His later victory has also a tragic irony: it brings his own death and so opens the way to disaster for his own people. Thus the two poems, or parts of the same poem, share a single theme: that beyond the hero's bravery there are forces which he cannot subdue. Valor is vanity in the end. So much any reflective reader may see.

The plan of Part I looks simple: the Danish setting, the hero's journey and reception, his fight and the celebration of his victory, his second fight and the following celebration, his return home and report of his adventures. But such is the poet's chosen method that he disguises the symmetry by making his concluding point (Hroðgar's plan to heal a feud with the Heaðobards) look like an irrelevance. This is the result of pursuing two themes at once, the plight of the Danes and their deliverance by the hero — with the necessary interchange of background and foreground. For the rest, having not much story to tell and meaning to tell none *as* story, the poet took his raw materials from the old 'lays,' and combining them with history and with folklore created something new, not exactly a heroic poem, (for there is less of that sheer delight in man-to-man fighting than we expect in heroic poems; compare the tone of the Finnsburgh Fragment with the poet's treatment of the same situation) and certainly not an epic, but a modification or adaptation to suit himself — a mixture of pagan matter treated in a somewhat non-pagan manner and of heroic matter from the legendary and historic past along with court ceremonies as he understood them. The actual fighting, including Beowulf's recapitulation, occupies less than one-tenth of the whole.

Part II, with less than a thousand lines, is another poem with the same hero. No significant differences in vocabulary, syntax, style, or meter have been found, and in the face of an improbable assumption of two men writing at about the same time in the same, or almost the same, manner, it must be taken for granted that both poems are by the same author. There are small linkages, but the subject and planning of the two Parts are different; there is a wholly new cast of characters, the emphasis is shifted, the polarity is altered. Part I had a beginning, a middle, and an end. Part II is less simple, it is more confused, the so-called digressions occupy relatively much more space (besides being more puzzling to the modern reader), and the whole is more gloomy, not only with the hero's death but also with the presage of disaster for his race.

II

One of the 'intentions' attributed to the poet is the portrayal of a virtuous pagan who might be said to manifest some of the high qualities inculcated by the new religion; and this might imply, or even signify, a semi-didactic purpose. Perhaps, as some have thought, he felt the zeal of a new convert; but if so, one would have expected him to go further. Or perhaps, as Gang conjectures, "*Beowulf,* so far from being a Christianized epic, is an attempt at a sort of secular Saints' Life," as though to prove that the heathen legends contained, latent, "a great deal of sound doctrine and Christian morality." Perhaps; or, since the divine guidance of the world, though prepotent, evidently — from the turn of events among Danes, Swedes, and Geats — leaves room for family and dynastic distress (*gyrn æfter gomene* [grief after joy]), the poet's aim might be a warning to his contemporaries, pointing a deadly parallel to the local wars he saw all about him and their inevitable outcome. Or, even more narrowly, he might mean to show that the supernatural forces which threaten mortal man can be overcome — Grendel driven off and finally beheaded, his Mother killed in her hidden haunt, the Dragon tumbled lifeless over the cliff — but the human conflicts, treachery and cowardice against loyalty and bravery, bring ineluctable doom. But if so, the poet has left these inferences to our ingenious interpretation. He was too much the artist to certify a "palpable design."

The symbolic or parabolic interpretations have a distinguished history. They go back at least to Grundtvig and they seem now to be taken for granted.[3] They are only suspect when

[3] Cf. H. V. Routh, *God, Man and Epic Poetry* (Cambridge, 1927), I, 13, 17, 21; Malone, *English Studies,* XXIX (1948), 161-72; Klaeber, 1, li; Tolkien *passim;* Arthur T. DuBois, *PMLA,* XLIX (1934), 374-405 and *ibid.,* LXXII (1957), 819-822.

they are applied to raise the epic level of the poem and to dignify the monsters — otherwise crude and merely folklorish — by assuming that they stood *in the poet's mind* for the dark forces of evil which oppress mankind and thus acquire in the reader's mind a Satanic stature. This "usury of our own minds" should not be allowed to crystallize into dogma.

Nor need we stop with the monsters. For example, if Hroðgar thought it necessary to warn Beowulf against pride, it is a short step to discovering a psychic disturbance in his own predicament. He himself has been guilty; he has erected his splendid meadhall and God is punishing him with Grendel. Grendel is specially irritated by the revelry and the sound of the harp. And Beowulf? Unbidden — or so we may suppose, though the poet is not altogether perspicuous on this point — he has crossed the seas and freed Heorot of its plague, and has thus interfered with divine justice and punishment, just as he did later when he became entangled with the accursed hoard. Moreover, Hroðgar's warning goes unheeded, for Beowulf at the end of a long and prosperous reign interferes again and stubbornly insists on fighting the Dragon in spite of his advanced age. Pride must have its fall and he is punished both by the humiliation of having to depend on Wiglaf and by his own death.

Moreover, the poem may be read not as an exaltation of manly valor and fortitude but a lament for the hopelessness of the human lot — "an heroic-elegiac poem" (Tolkien), beginning with a burial, ending with a cremation, and all that seemed so heroic in between coming to naught. But then, by superimposing a Christian orientation on those noble heathens, the poet compromised his Christian faith in God's goodness; or perhaps one should say he acknowledged the pessimism latent in Christian doctrine, a resignation to the evils of the world, without being able to hold out the hopes of relief and salvation in another life.[4]

[4] The poet shows some knowledge of the Old Testament (which aligns him with Cædmon) but none of the New (which distinguishes him from Cynewulf). The Sermon on the Mount and the Epistles of Paul have not

Thus as critical latitude broadens, puzzling difficulties deepen.

One might go further. *Beowulf* is, as Chambers said, a poem of ambiguities; and in every ambiguity may lurk a secret meaning. For example, Beowulf encounters in Part I the evils of water (especially with Grendel's Mother) and in Part II the evils of fire (the fire-drake and his cremation). With this there is a chiastic balance which ought to be significant; for in Part I Heorot's destruction by fire is prophesied and in Part II the Dragon is pushed over into the sea. And, assuming a little different position, one notes that Grendel is the agent, not the enemy of God; he was sent to punish the Danes and the poet was only adding his touch of cunning subtlety when he said *Godes yrre bær* [he bore God's anger].

One more speculation. Taking a leaf from Samuel Butler, one could argue that the poet was a woman, a learned abbess inspired, say, by Hild's success with Cædmon — or why not Hild herself? Feminine authorship would account for many things in the poem: the absence of gory fighting and lust of battle; the vagueness of detail in the wrestling match with Grendel and in the encounter with his Mother and in the final contest with the Dragon, so much interrupted by Beowulf's speeches; the touches of pathos here and there, the implied sympathy with Hildeburh, and with the Dragon; the praise of queen Hygd and queen Wealhþeow; in general, "the poet's sympathy with weak and unfortunate beings" (Klaeber); Beowulf's interest in the gold ornaments from the hoard; the feeling for harsh landscape on the way to Grendel's mere; the delicate reticence about the parentage of Fitela; the absence of gluttony and lechery (though there is abundance of mead and the duguð get drunk, drunkenness leads

touched him. The doctrines and dogmas of the Church — sin and redemption, revelation, a future life — have left little mark on his poem; at least he found no place for them. For obvious reasons there are no miracles; but the friends of Bede would have cleansed Heorot with Holy Water and vanquished the Dragon with a sign of the Cross. Beowulf seems to have followed St. Paul's exhortation to avoid women — thereby unfortunately leaving the succession open.

to nothing worse than noise and some reckless talk); the celebrations of victory in Part I by singing and racing, with none of the grosser indulgences; the pervasive manner of indirection; the extraordinary amount of talking and the tendencies to 'digress'; the pessimistic judgment on men's inability to rule successfully at home and abroad (the hero's long reign is only an apparent exception; it was far from peaceful); the crowning attribute of mildness in Beowulf; and much more. An enthusiast could write convincingly on this topic.

These, and other such hypotheses, do no harm if they are not taken too seriously. They testify to our critical industry and also — which is the point here — to our uncertainty about the fundamental criteria of the poem. They emphasize its enigmas.

III

A poem assumes readers, but since in the eighth century the *Beowulf* poet could hardly expect any considerable number of readers and since then poetry was commonly recited, read aloud with some sort of musical accompaniment —

þær wæs hearpan sweg,
swutol sang scopes —
[there was the sound of the harp, the clear song of the minstrel —]

it is usually taken for granted that the *Beowulf* poet cast himself in the role of *scop* and both recited his poem to a group of listeners and hoped that others would do the same. Miss Whitelock has computed that the poem "could easily be delivered in three sittings," and it only remains to inquire who the listeners would be. This question she has faced with courage and great learning; she presents her case with shrewd caution, avoiding over-confidence: "it would be unsafe to argue that any part of England was in the eighth century insufficiently advanced in intellectual attainments for a sophisticated poem like *Beowulf* to have been composed there and appreciated." Most admirable caution, though one might have hoped for a more positive conclusion. "The audience," she says, "would doubtless consist of both veterans and young men" in the royal retinue, as well as "an audience of sportsmen." They would probably be Christians. Remembering Alcuin's *Quid Hinieldus cum Christo* [What has Ingeld to do with Christ], she seems not to have included a monastic audience. (One wonders how much Alcuin knew about Ingeld. Saxo's spelling is Ingellus.) The men on the meadbench are slightly disguised as veterans and young men: they would have to be more temperate than the celebrants in Heorot.

For such an "advanced" audience two requisites must be met: one, a group both interested in the fearless exploits of a heathen hero, modified for Christian ears, who fought ogres and a dragon in the long ago, and sufficiently familiar with Geatish and Swedish feuds and with continental legends and sagas — Sigemund and Heremod, Hengest and the Heaðobards, and so forth — to be able to absorb easily and with pleasure the poet's somewhat abrupt allusions; and secondly, a group capable of the concentrated attention necessary to follow, while listening, a narrative as involved and circuitous ("circumambient," "static" with the illusion of forward movement), in a style as compressed and often cryptic, as that of *Beowulf.* The reasoning assumes not only a group of listeners knowledgeable on all the many topics to which the poet points and passes, as well equipped as the poet himself, and sufficiently able to fill in all that he leaves out or hints at, but *a fortiori* nimble-minded enough ("alert") *while listening* to, say, three sequences of about 1000 lines each, to pick up and drop at need the several allusions historical and traditional without losing the main pattern, to adjust and re-adjust their attention in rapid alternation to diverse matters without sacrificing their interest in the principal concern. Could such a listening audience ever have existed? Did ever a poet before or since ask so much of one?

The 'argument' was succinctly put, long ago, by Gummere: "The style of reference to the death of Hæthcyn shows how familiar the whole story must have been."[5] Miss Whitelock elaborates this. At every turn she insists that the poem would not be intelligible unless the audience was well informed—on Christian doctrine, for example, to understand a Biblical reference (the giants of *Exodus*), or on the subsequent history of Hroðgar's strife with his own son-in-law to catch the hint of *þenden* (1019), and so on. "To an audience that did not know that Hrothulf killed Hrethric, the whole section [1164 ff.] would be pointless." She dwells at length on the fourfold account of Hygelac's Frisian raid. It would ask a good deal for the audience to pick up the second hint eleven hundred and forty lines after the first unless they were well acquainted with Frankish tradition and Geatish history. It assumes "the likelihood that the poet could rely on his hearers' previous knowledge of the Geatish kings as on that of the Danish kings, and could leave it to them to supply more than he chose to tell them" — while they listened for what was coming next. And finally, "if even a few of the claims I have made are true, we must assume a subtle and sophisticated poet, and an alert and intelligent audience" later than the age of Bede.

Those elements of the minstrel style which the poet made use of, and his picture of the improvising scop at Hroðgar's court will not have deceived him, or us. He was not composing an enlarged tripartite 'lay.' "The first concern of heroic poetry," says Bowra, "is to tell of action, . . . bards . . . avoid . . . not merely moralizing comments and description of things and places for description's sake, but anything that smacks of ulterior or symbolic intentions"; "the listening audience requires single moods and effects, without complications." A bard has to hold the audience's attention, "to make everything clear and interesting."[6] This hardly describes the *Beowulf* poet and his work. The "discontinuity of action" (Tolkien) and the calculated double movement of Part II especially, with its rapid interchange of present (Beowulf and the Dragon) and the historical past is

[5] *The Oldest English Epic* (New York, 1910), p. 129.
[6] C. M. Bowra, *Heroic Poetry* (London, 1952), pp. 48, 55, 215.

the last thing a scop would submit to a group of listeners. Miss Whitelock's "we must assume" is therefore circular: if the poet wrote for an audience, the audience must have been waiting.

Who will, may hear Sordello's story told.

IV

We are still in the dark about the poet's intentions. If we knew anything precise about those lost 'lays' we might guess a little about his originality. Did he invent Grendel's Mother, for instance? and why did he give her no name? The supernatural elements were, one assumes, in the 'lays' and he accepted them; they are the folklore coefficient of heroic saga. The Scandinavian settings were, one assumes also, in his 'lays' and he had to accept them and try his best to make them interesting to his Anglian 'audience.' He would celebrate a hero whose life was dominated by a (pagan) desire for fame, who won fame by overcoming superhuman opponents, and whose last act was to order a burial mound on a conspicuous headland as a monument to his fame, and whose epitaph was *lofgeornost* [most eager for praise, glory]. But he would raise what might seem like a tale of adventure "above mere story telling"; he would make it a *poem* and load every rift with ore. So he avoided continuous narrative, intercalated fragments of story with recondite, enriching, sometimes teasing, allusions and with forward and backward glances into the historical backgrounds, and arrayed it all in a highly ornate, alembicated style, with some vestiges of the minstrel formulas to set it off. These have an odd look alongside his methods of "syntactic correlation, parallel and antithetic structure, parenthesis, and climactic progression" (Klaeber). His *style* is one of the poet's glories — and impediments. It makes his poem a tour de force, which he must have enjoyed writing and hoped others would enjoy — enjoy the peculiar strain he put upon language and relish the tension of keeping pace with his structural convolutions. But this combination is so curious, so original, in the sense of being contrived, that the whole seems more like an artifact than a poem created out of the artist's experience.

When, finally, one thinks of the modern reader, *Beowulf* suffers the drawbacks of all subjects drawn from Northern myth and legend. The Greek and Roman world is too much with us. The subject of the poem is unsympathetic to our taste and the cultivation of a taste for it is a burden. Its people are alien to us. The tribal conflicts of sixth-century Danes and Swedes have no recognizable place on our stage of history. Their names have no familiar associations; and for our confusion there are twenty-six personal names beginning with H - - -. We have some acquaintance with literary dragons, but our imagination can do little with ogres and trolls; and what is more, none of the characters in the story makes an emphatic appeal to us. Only by intervals is there a touch of human feeling or anything that speaks directly to us. There is no conception of character tested in significant human situations or any clear sense of tragic conflict, man against man or man against fate, with a catharsis which ennobles the victim through his sacrifice and the reader through contemplation of victory in death. (The hero's end is confused, for the reader, by his involvement with the heathen hoard.) The divided spirit of Hroðgar; the plight of that terrible old Ongenþeow, his queen captured and rescued and his death at the hands of a young man; the graciousness of Wealhþeow; the pathos of Hildeburh and the indecision of Hengest; the little comedy (if it be comedy) of Unferð — these seem to us undeveloped possibilities. We can see them but they are offered in passing. Like the tragic glimpses of Heremod and young Đryð, and all the so-called digressions, they are absorbed into the main 'narrative' — smaller or larger pieces of color, purple or crimson or black — with little attention to their emotional or psychological interest. Whether functional or decorative or both at once, they appear suddenly and are gone quickly, and one hardly has time to enjoy them. The poet evidently set great store by them, but his touch-and-go use of them robs them of their power. The one major character for whom we are invited to feel sympathy is the Dragon.

All this and more would make for the dullness and dimness which the late Middleton Murry saw in the poem.[7] But dullness and dimness are relative terms, and it is worth recalling that to some Racine is dull, his characters a seeming vehicle for rhetorical declamation. To your French critic Shakespeare is chaos. Even *Prometheus Bound* is a strange work unless one brings to it the right kind of sympathetic understanding; Prometheus on his rock and the Oceanides singing would be, if we were not brought up on them, as remote as Hroðgar and his trolls or Beowulf and his Dragon. The language of Aeschylus is as difficult, until one has learned it, as the language of *Beowulf*.

As literature, said Mr. Murry, *Beowulf* is "an antediluvian curiosity," and Professor Gilbert Highet, speaking as a classicist, says that "artistically *Beowulf* is a rude and comparatively unskilled poem."[8] Well, it must be conceded that *Beowulf* is a foreign masterpiece, as foreign to modern taste in subject and manner as in language. It has, however, affinities with much of Donne and some of Browning, and it looks forward, curiously, to the very modern handling of time-sequence. But it cannot be translated to our idiom because we have no language corresponding to its ideas and emotions and we have no ideas and emotions to fit its peculiar language. The poet seems to have created many of his own difficulties. He had, one surmises, his own taste of chaos and in his fashion revived it, recreated it, while at the same time he looked back to a time of ideal loyalties and heroism. Simplicity, clarity, and elegant organization were luxuries he could not afford if he was to communicate what he felt the need of expressing. Why did he try? He could expect few silent readers in his own day. He adopted a tense crowded style and a convoluted method of narration, the very antithesis of a minstrel's, most unsuited for oral recitation, and if he looked for an audience of listeners he was extraordinarily, not to say

[7] J. Middleton Murry, a review of the translation by C. K. Moncrieff, in *The Nation and the Athenæum*, 22 October 1921.

[8] Gilbert Highet, *The Classical Tradition* (Oxford, 1949), p. 24.

stubbornly, sanguine. But all the signs point (they can hardly be called evidence but they are all we have) to a very individual man, a serious and gifted poet, steeped in the older pagan tradition from the continent, moved perhaps by a pious desire to compromise his two religions, and above all delighting in his unusual skill with language (as all poets do) — all the signs point to such a poet sitting down to compose a quasi-heroic poem to please himself, in the quiet expectation of pleasing also just that "fit audience though few." Shelley said of *Prometheus Unbound* that it was "never intended for more than five or six persons." It may seem odd to picture such an ivory-towered poet in the eighth century, but *Beowulf* is unique in every sense, and in the balance of probabilities the scales incline to even this unlikely assumption: a poet as individual and apart as his style, his plan, and his subject.

17

PATRISTICS AND OLD ENGLISH LITERATURE: NOTES ON SOME POEMS*

Morton W. Bloomfield

IN RECENT YEARS, BECAUSE OF VARIOUS CONTROVERSIES ABOUT the interpretation of mediaeval literature, the term *patristics* has unfortunately come to be associated with only one aspect of Patristic activity — biblical exegesis. However, the rich theological and philosophical fare which the Fathers offer moderns comprises a great deal more than a method of hermeneutics with an accompanying biblical symbolism, however important. It is the purpose of this brief article to call attention to three passages in OE literature which can be illuminated by the writings of the Fathers whereby a sense of the meaning of the whole poems of which they are a part can be suggested if not completely attained. The interpretations here put forth will add to the steadily growing body of scholarship which is pointing to the connection between the ancient classical world, both Christian and pagan, and OE literature.

With a poem like Caedmon's *Hymn,* this connection is not to be wondered at, as it is a Christian poem in every way and a short example of a favorite ancient Christian literary genre, the poetic biblical paraphrase of an hexaemeral cast. However, even in poems not composed on Christian themes nor within Christian

* Reprinted, by permission of the author, the editor of *Comparative Literature,* and Stanley B. Greenfield, editor of *Brodeur Festschrift*. The article first appeared in *Comparative Literature,* XIV (Winter 1962), 36-37, and 39-41.

literary genres, such as *The Battle of Maldon* and *Beowulf,* we may find such connections which will not only explain particular lines but clarify the background implicit in these works and help identify the overall purpose of these poems. It has always been recognized that these a-Christian poems of the OE *corpus* are an amalgam of pagan and Christian elements, even though the proportions of both have not always been agreed upon. At present, the Germanizing interpretations, dominant for many years, seem to be on the wane and Christianizing interpretations are very common. Obviously both Christian and Germanic themes are present in these poems, but the exact determination of their relative weight is still to seek. Perhaps no general answer is possible; each poem presents a special union of the two traditions. In the last analysis, a subjective element in this task must always be present, but this factor should not blind us to whatever objective facts can be ascertained. Whatever the origin of these poems, it is clear that in their preserved and thus final form they were the products of Christians and written by Christian scribes. This does not preclude, of course, a basic heathen story. Inasmuch as the Germanic element has been extensively explored, often to the extent of claiming as Germanic dubious or even clearly erroneous themes,[1] the balance needs to be redressed. It is in the Fathers, the main literary material (along with the Bible) of the Christians who wrote or composed OE literature as it is preserved, that we can find the best sources for discover-

[1] The widespread tendency to use the word "wyrd" as evidence of Germanic paganism seems to be dangerously simplistic, for *wyrd* was soon given a Christian meaning. After all, there is a Christian meaning to fate well summed up in the term "providence." On this subject, see Bertha S. Phillpotts, "Wyrd and Providence in Anglo-Saxon Thought," *E&S,* XIII (1928), 7-27, and especially B. J. Timmer, "Wyrd in Anglo-Saxon Prose and Poetry," *Neophil,* XXVI (1940-41), 24-33, 213-228; see also his "Heathen and Christian Elements in Old English Poetry," *Neophil,* XXIX (1944), 180-185.

For a plea to use Patristics in interpreting mediaeval literature, see J. M. Campbell, "Patristic Studies and the Literature of Mediaeval England," *Speculum,* VIII (1933), 465-478.

ing the Christian materials in these poems. Even in avowedly Christian poems, like Caedmon's *Hymn,* we can still find new meanings and explanations when they are closely examined from the point of view of these basic sources. Three examples of the use of this material follow. [Sections A and C of this paper which discuss *The Battle of Maldon* and Cædmon's *Hymn* have been omitted.]

B. *Beowulf,* line 2330:

> wende se wisa þæt he Wealdende
> ofer *ealde riht* ecean Dryhtne
> bitre gebulge.

The wise one [Beowulf] supposed that he had bitterly offended the Eternal contrary to old law.

The phrase *ealde riht* is taken by most commentators on *Beowulf* to be an allusion to Old Testament law, although apparently the phrase can also be used of what we might call customary law. Klaeber, in his note on this line, writes that this phrase "is here given a Christian interpretation";[2] Wrenn similarly writes, "Here Beowulf's thoughts may be Christian, though they need not necessarily be so. But the whole tone points to Christianity and the expression *ofer ealde riht,* 'contrary to ancient law,' seems to refer to God's commandments."[3] Even Charles Donahue is extremely cautious in discussing this line, although he has pointed out how Irish tradition conceived of its pagan heroes (or at least some of them) as saints under natural law or naturally good rather than damned as outside the Judaeo-Christian tradition. He writes,

> When Beowulf heard that a dragon had destroyed his royal hall, he was troubled in his heart, the poet says, because "as a wise man, he believed that he had broken the ancient law . . ." The contents of the ancient law, in so far as they can be deduced from the poem, seem to be the traditional precepts of Germanic morality.[4]

[2] *Beowulf,* 3rd ed. (Boston, 1950), p. 211.

[3] *Beowulf* (London, etc., 1953), p. 220.

[4] "Beowulf, Ireland and the Natural Good," *Traditio,* VII (1949-51), 275.

Whether the equation of pagan with Old Testament law is due to Celtic influence or not or whether it be due to a general consciousness of the "danger of celebrating a pagan hero,"[5] it is clear that pre-Christian moral law of whatever origin was considered something of a unity before the time of the *Beowulf* poet. The tendency to assimilate the best part of paganism to the Old Testament is one way converted pagans could accept the New Law and still maintain pride of ancestry.

The problem of the "Old Law" is complicated and it cannot be solved here. The fact that the word "law" is used for a body of moral obligations would argue for Patristic influence, for law is the normal term for religious and moral obligations in the Fathers. It is also true that the law of the Old Testament which was considered binding on Christians — the moral laws — was equated for the most part with natural law, although in general this equation is later than the early Middle Ages — in St. Thomas, for instance.

But St. Thomas is discussing the Mosaic law, or the moral part of it. It is, however, often forgotten that figures like Cain to whom Grendel was assimilated lived before the promulgation of the "Old Law" on Mount Sinai and if he sinned, as he obviously did, he sinned against natural law. So did Lucifer and the rebellious angels. Subordinating pre-Mosaic Old Testament figures to pagan or natural law is not really difficult. Abel and Cain (and the devil) are the only Old Testament figures mentioned in *Beowulf*. They are Old Testament figures but not Jews, and to Christians and Jews they were the ancestors of the whole human race. Even a good man like Abraham, who lived before at least the full knowledge of the Mosaic law, was certainly saved by faith. These pre-Mosaic figures of the Old Testament provided,

[5] As Margaret E. Goldsmith argues in "The Christian Theme of *Beowulf*," *Medium Ævum*, XXIX (1960), 83. The purpose of this article may be summed up in the author's words: "I suggest that the *Beowulf* poet saw, in the legendary life of a heathen hero, an opportunity to write of this fight against the devil and the seed of Cain" (p. 101).

then, an opening of salvation for the pagan ancestors of the Germanic and Celtic peoples. If good men were saved before Sinai, then good pagans like Beowulf could be saved.[6] If bad men were damned before Sinai, then Grendel and his ilk could be damned without inconsistency.

All this is argued at length by Origen in his commentary on St. Paul's *Epistle to the Romans,* especially on Chapter VII in discussing passages like "Nay, I had not known sin, but by the law" (verse 7) and "For without the law sin was dead" (verse 8). Origen points out that there was sin in the period from Adam to Moses and that Paul was not referring merely to the Old Law but to natural law in Chapters IV and VII. To take one passage from his treatment of the subject,

> Magis ergo illud in hoc loco [one of the Pauline verses] debet intelligi esse . . . legem naturæ quæ "scripta" est "non in tabulis lapideis, sed in tabulis cordis" . . . quæ lex ab illo qui ab illo qui ab initio creavit hominem ita in principali cordis ejus ascripta est . . . [In this place, therefore, that (one of the Pauline verses) should be understood . . . as a law of nature which is "written not on tablets of stone but on the tablets of the heart" . . . which law is from him who created man from the beginning, so that it is written principally in the heart.][7]

Thus Patristic thinking helps us to see why the *Beowulf* poet could, without qualms, mingle pagan and Old Testament elements. To him there was no mixing of incompatibles in this procedure, especially as he confined his Old Testament figures to pre-Mosaic personages. The *ealde riht* refers not to Old Testament (i.e., Sinaitic) law but natural law which was implanted even in the hearts of pagans, including the pre-Mosaic "pagans"

[6] Beowulf must have been regarded by the author of the final form of *Beowulf* as a pagan, but, owing to a lack of true historical perspective, Christian sentiments of a general sort may sometimes have been attributed to him.

[7] *P.G.*, XIV, col. 1033. The whole sections of Books IV and V of this work discuss the problems involved in Paul's remarks. I owe this reference to the kindness of Mrs. Carol Kaske. Hrabanus Maurus, in *Enn. in Epp. Pauli* (*P.L.*, CXI, col. 1422), says specifically that Cain sinned against natural law.

of the Old Testament. All this helps us to solve the problem of the mingling of biblical and pagan elements in the poem.

18

THE CHRISTIAN PERSPECTIVE IN *BEOWULF**

Margaret E. Goldsmith

IF I SAY THAT *Measure for Measure* IS ABOUT CHASTITY AND charity, no one will suppose that I mean to imply that it is not a good play. When I say that *Beowulf* is about pride and covetousness, a simplification of roughly the same order, I can expect to be thought to say that it is not a poem at all, but a homily in verse. It is part of the purpose of this paper to show that *Beowulf* is a poem of the spirit, achieving its effects for the most part by poetic, not homiletic, techniques. To put this another way, *Beowulf* is not what Blake would call an Allegory, "formed by the daughters of Memory," but a poem of that greater kind which springs from Imagination, which he calls Vision.[1] Such poems stem directly from the poet's inbred beliefs about man and the universe, so that the work itself embodies his conception of reality. He may asseverate, as Blake did, that "Vision or Imagination is a representation of what

* Reprinted, by permission of the author, the editor of *Comparative Literature,* and Stanley B. Greenfield, editor of *Brodeur Festschrift.* It first appeared in *Comparative Literature,* XIV (Winter 1962), 71-80.

[1] "Vision or Imagination is a representation of what Eternally Exists, Really and unchangeably. Fable or Allegory is Form'd by the daughters of Memory. Imagination is surrounded by the daughters of Inspiration, who in the aggregate are called Jerusalem." William Blake, "Notes on A Vision of the Last Judgment," in *The Complete Writings of William Blake,* ed. G. Keynes (London, 1957), p. 604.

Eternally Exists, Really and unchangeably," or affirm, less introspectively, that poetry can speak truth:

hwilum gyd awræc
soð ond sarlic, hwilum syllic spell
rehte æfter rihte.
(*Beowulf,* lines 2108-10)
[sometimes he related a tale, true and painful;
sometimes he related a strange tale rightly.]

This kind of poetry must be both "soð ond sarlic": true, as congruent with "what Eternally Exists"; sorrowful, because "Man being in the parlous state he is, vision for him is largely a question of seeing his aberrations reflected against the stainless mirror of the real."[2] Such a poet is more intensely aware than other men of human weakness and destitution: the ultimate nakedness of the rich, the ultimate helplessness of the strong. If he is also a Christian, he has a doctrine to explain human imperfection, a promise of help in weakness, a consolation for inevitable loss. His belief in the doctrine and the hope in no way dulls his awareness of these things—it often sharpens their poignancy; but it annihilates despair. So, the *Beowulf* poet, writing of strength and riches, is synchronously aware, not only that strength and riches are transient, but that the greatest human strength is inadequate, and the greatest human wealth valueless, when the soul is in jeopardy. As an Anglo-Saxon Christian, he could lay the blame for man's parlous state upon Adam and Eve, who forfeited Paradise "þurh heora gifernesse and oferhyde" [through their avarice and pride].[3] For him, self-sufficiency and love of the world would be the denial of man's natural service to God, for which he was created. These, therefore, are the primeval sins. Alienation from God begets envy and hatred of the good, as is told in the myth of Cain. These are the sins of the second generation. It follows that, if I say that *Beowulf* is about pride and covetousness in the first

[2] G. Wingfield Digby, *Symbol and Image in William Blake* (Oxford, 1957), p. 106.

[3] *Blickling Homilies,* ed. R. Morris, EETS 58 (London, 1880), p. 24.

place, and about envy and hatred in the second place, I am asserting, in sum, that the Christian poet was writing about the human tragedy as he understood it.

Perhaps I may here rehearse some of the considerations which have led me to this view of the *Beowulf* poem. We read a story of fabulous adventures, peppered with general maxims about life, and the first question which forms in our minds is whether these maxims are necessary to the poem, or whether the author, or someone else, has scattered them broadcast, in order to lend an odor of sanctity to what might otherwise smack of heathenism. Since the publication of Professor Brodeur's book, *The Art of Beowulf* (Berkeley, 1959), this question of artistic unity need no longer be debated. Where we may still differ is over the emphasis to be given to those passages in which the poet speaks directly and not through the mouth of a character in the story. For me, these passages reinforce an impression, which grows stronger with study of the poem, that the poet was concerned with the minds and hearts of men *sub specie aeternitatis* [with respect to eternity], and only secondarily with wars and banquets and feats of swimming. One of the strongest reasons for this belief is the extraordinary way in which the poet has avoided writing an epic about a martial hero. If we compare *Beowulf* with the *Chanson de Roland,* it is plain that the earlier poet had the material, had he so wished, to write a poem of the *Roland* sort (granted some license in the matter of Beowulf's religious beliefs). It is not difficult to imagine an epic of a knightly Beowulf, the hero as the right arm of his uncle Hygelac as Roland was of Charlemagne, routing the Swedish companions with Nægling, fighting a desperate rear-guard action as the invading Geats are forced back to the Rhine, engaging in personal combat to the death with thirty of the attacking Franks, and so on. Yet, in spite of the promise of his opening lines, our poet seems to have very little interest in such battle poetry. He never allows Beowulf to move at the head of an army, or even to slay a human opponent, in any part of the main action.

These features of his life story must be deliberately suppressed; we cannot say that the poet was constrained by his well-known story, since the poem as we have it contains somewhere all these heroic elements. For some purpose of his own, the poet has minimized all the battle scenes in which Beowulf might have displayed his prowess; though the vigorous treatment of the Battle of Ravenswood, in which Beowulf has no part, shows that he lacked neither the skill nor the temper to create battle-poetry.[4] It is noteworthy, too, that Beowulf's revenge on Onela for the slaying of his king Heardred is accomplished, as it were, by proxy, and his revenge on Dæghrefn for the death of Hygelac is not told as an exciting feat in itself, but as part of the history of the *breostweorðung* [breast-ornament] which was torn from Hygelac's dead body.[5] If a martial epic of Beowulf was known to our poet, he has taken pains to recast it in quite another mold. One feature which might find a place in a poem of either kind is the hero's pride. Beowulf, like Roland (and like Byrhtnoth), possesses that arrogant self-confidence which is the special trait of the supremely noble and courageous fighter. Roland's refusal to call for help destroys the flower of France;

[4] The prominence given to the Battle of Ravenswood seems to call for some explanation, since its connection with Beowulf's life is very slight, and more significant battles are passed over in a line or so. Are we intended to see in the cruel contest *wið Hrefnawudu* [at Ravenswood] a particular example of the violence and hatred of the race of Cain, whose symbol, according to Bede, is the raven of the Ark? "significant homines in immunditia cupiditas teterrimos, ad illa quæ foris sunt in hoc mundo intentos" [but what is said about the raven . . . means that men in the dirtiness of cupidity are especially horrid, being content with those things which are all about them in this world], Beda, *In Pent. Comm., Gen.; P.L.,* XCI, col. 223. This passage is used by Huppé to elucidate lines 1446-48 of the OE *Genesis* (B. F. Huppé, *Doctrine and Poetry* [New York, 1959], p. 175). One might recall also the extraordinary raven that awakens the men of Heorot (line 1801) on the day of Beowulf's departure.

[5] See lines 2501-08.

Beowulf's insistence on challenging the dragon alone destroys the Geats. Oliver's bitter reproach to Roland:

> Mielz valt mesure que ne fait estultie
> Franceis sont morz par vostre legerie . . .
> Vostre proecce, Rollanz, mar la veïmes,[6]

[Moderation is better than reckless courage. French have died because of your recklessness. . . Your heroism, Roland, we have seen it to our sorrow.]

is matched by Wiglaf's words after Beowulf's death:

> Oft sceall eorl monig anes willan
> wraec adreogan, swa us geworden is.
> Ne meahton we gelæran leofne þeoden,
> rices hyrde ræd ænigne
> þæt he ne grette goldweard þone.
> (Lines 3077-81)

[Often must many a noble endure suffering for the will of one, as it has happened to us. We might not teach the dear prince, the guardian of the kingdom, any counsel, that he should not attack the keeper of the gold.]

If we regard his treatment of the disastrous pride of the traditional epic hero as a touchstone of the poet's Christianity, by this test *Beowulf* is revealed as a more fundamentally Christian poem than the overtly crusading poem of Roland. Beowulf's fatal pride is foreshadowed; it is treated as a sin which he must guard against when he comes to power.

This evidence of the poet's intention to put the wars into the background and the motives of men into the foreground led me to examine more closely his pointers to the meaning of the stories, both in the comments upon the action and in the emphases of the stories themselves. This approach revealed a coherence of inner design, which not only justified the sequel to the affairs at Heorot but also explained the relevance of several difficult passages.[7]

[6] *La Chanson de Roland, laisse* 131 (Gröber's numbering).

[7] Notably, lines 175-188, 1002-08, 1059-60, 1722-81, 2291-93, 2329-32, 2764-66, 3058-60, 3074-75.

It may be in place to summarize briefly here my interpretation of the poem, as previously published,[8] since what I have to say now assumes a view of the work substantially in agreement with this interpretation.

Hrothgar, King of the Danes, builds a towering hall, in which he lives prosperously, untroubled by enemies, until the terrible visitation of a hellish monster, of the race of Cain, who devours his men and parts him from his throne and treasure.[9] In retrospect, the old king recognizes this visitation as allowed by God because of his own pride in his power and his wealth. The tribulation of the Danes is brought to an end by the young champion Beowulf, whom Hrothgar hails as God-sent for their deliverance. Slowly the darker side of Heorot is revealed: it is to be destroyed, and the Scylding line cut off, through the workings of envy and murderous hatred within it. These are the sins of the generation of Cain, embodied in the destructive beast Grendel and his dam. The spiritual sons of Cain are all those who "build their cities" in this world, like Hrothgar at Heorot, pinning all their hope on a false good. God's mercy, working through Beowulf's selfless courage, reveals to Hrothgar his own folly; he then, in his new-found wisdom, warns the young hero of the dangers he will face when he comes to power. He may conquer his passions (unlike Heremod), and yet be corrupted insidiously, as Hrothgar was, by success and wealth. The second part of the poem is the realization of what Hrothgar's warning has foreshadowed, the old King Beowulf's mortal struggle with the dragon, who as a shape of the devil typifies pride, and as *goldweard* [guardian of gold] typifies covetousness. As young Beowulf's selflessness saved Hrothgar, so young Wiglaf's selfless love saves Beowulf from defeat, though it cannot save him from

[8] M. E. Goldsmith, "The Christian Theme of *Beowulf*," *Medium Ævum*, XXIX (1960), 81-101.

[9] I accept here the interpretation of lines 168-169 so convincingly argued by Brodeur, *The Art of Beowulf*, pp. 203-204, save that I should regard "ne his myne wisse" as a statement that Hrothgar did not enjoy God's favor at that time.

death. Beowulf, dying, puts off his royal adornments, and his spirit goes to face judgment among the just souls. Thus, the poet uses the heroic combats of story to typify man's unending contest with the powers of darkness, an idea implicit in the Psalms, made explicit by Paul in his Epistles,[10] and elaborated by the Fathers, in particular by Gregory the Great: "Tentatio itaque ipsa militia est, quia dum contra malignorum spiritum insidias vigilat, in bellorum procinctu procul dubio exsudat" [And so that temptation is a battle, because while one keeps vigil against the snares of the malign spirits, he toils in preparation for the wars].[11]

When I first formed this theory of the meaning of the poem some years ago, it looked a good deal more improbable than it does today. The recent spate of scholarly discoveries about the nature of Old English elegiac poetry is washing away many theories built upon the false impression that the Christian beliefs contained in them were not germane to the essential themes. The "paganism" of *Beowulf* died hard, chiefly because of widespread ignorance of what Anglo-Saxon Christianity was like. Professor Whitelock's book, *The Audience of Beowulf,* published ten years ago, showed that we have every reason to believe that the poet and his audience were grounded in the Christian faith and accustomed to listen to Christian poetry.[12] Some of the implications of this are suggested below.

Beowulf critics have been diffident in recognizing to the full that the stored mind of the hearer or reader is part of the poet's material. This fact, accepted as a truism by modern artists,[13] is

[10] *Ep. I Tim.* VI, 12; *Ep. ad. Eph.* VI, 10, 13-18.

[11] Gregorius, *Moralia; PL.,* LXXV, col. 805.

[12] D. Whitelock, *The Audience of Beowulf* (Oxford, 1951), p. 7. This pioneer book has been followed by such consolidating studies as those of M. P. Hamilton, "The Religious Principle in Beowulf," *PMLA,* LXI (1946), 309-330, and A. G. Brodeur, *The Art of Beowulf, passim.*

[13] E.g., J. M. Synge, Preface to *The Playboy of the Western World,* says "All art is a collaboration," and is quoted approvingly by modern critics.

none the less true for Anglo-Saxon poets, in spite of being ignored by the early manuals of poetic art, which concern themselves exclusively with formal structures. This critical diffidence is surprising when we consider the peculiar nature of the *Beowulf* narrative, which moves forward by "a subtle technique of allusion, reminder, and suggestion."[14] Where the allusions and reminders concern traditional heroic stories, research has always been busy, acknowledging the importance of finding the reference. Where the reminders concern Christian lore (with the exception of the explicit connection of Grendel with Cain and the giants of Genesis) scholars often silently assumed that these were out of keeping with the story of Beowulf, and hence not to be pressed. Now that scholars are accepting the importance of the Latin Fathers in the shaping of the Christian Anglo-Saxon's mental world, the critic has the task of sifting from these doctrines those which are poetically relevant.

Beowulf is not, Brodeur states, a religious poem.[15] Interpreted rather narrowly, this judgment is not to be questioned. This is not a poem of the same sort as *Crist* or *Andreas;* in essence it is neither devotional nor homiletic. Yet, as I am sure Brodeur would agree, it is by no means an *ir*religious poem or a wholly secular poem. It is a poem about the heroic life, written by a Christian poet, and such a theme could not be divorced from Christian faith and hope, save by a deliberate effort on the poet's part to recreate the past with the detachment of a scientific historian. There is no conceivable reason for the poet to adopt such a course. Nor should we expect him to chase from his mind the traditional Christian attitudes toward the Good Fight, when imagining a fight against monstrous creatures whose malice springs ultimately from the Ancient Enemy. Undeniably, *Beowulf* has a historical perspective, but even if the poet possessed the fictive power to create a wholly heathen Beowulf,

[14] Whitelock, p. 2.
[15] Brodeur, p. 31.

he and his audience would still measure the hero's beliefs about life against their own.

Can we know what the poet's beliefs were? We can assume, without debate, that his intended audience would share them, since without this assumption his allusive method would please no one but himself. Can we guess at the subjects of the Christian poetry he knew and that they were accustomed to hear? I think we can. By common consent, *Beowulf* is placed later than Cædmon's poems. We know from Bede's list of them[16] that Cædmon's verse paraphrases covered the whole of the history of man: his Creation, Fall, Redemption, and his ultimate destiny. Because of the authority conferred on them by reason of Cædmon's miraculous gift of song, these poems were no doubt recited wherever Bede's tale was known. We shall see that they cover just those subjects which Bede would have required a Christian convert to know. We are not to suppose that there was ever an evangelical stage in the conversion of the English, when an audience of baptized Christians would have been familiar with the Gospel of Christ and yet unaware of the symbolic commentaries of the Fathers. Professor Whitelock makes some general observations about the way missionaries teach the Faith,[17] but we can perhaps be more definite than this. It is relevant to note the evidence of Professor J. P. Christopher in the preface to his translation of *De catechizandis rudibus:*

> Since St. Augustine composed this treatise on such sound principles of pedagogy and psychology, it is not surprising to find that upon it are based almost all subsequent works on catechetics . . . In England, Bede and Alcuin, under whom the monastic schools reached their highest development, used *De catechizandis rudibus* and *De doctrina christiana* as textbooks.[18]

Though the reference here is to the use of these books in monastic schools, this formulation of the essentials of the Faith

[16] Beda, *Historia Ecclesiastica,* IV, lib. c. xxiv.

[17] Whitelock, pp. 6-7.

[18] St. Augustine, *The First Catechetical Instruction* (in *Ancient Christian Writers,* Vol. II), translated by J. P. Christopher (Westminster, Md., 1946), p. 8.

would spread from the priests to those whom they prepared for baptism or confirmation. The evidence of the surviving OE homilies is that in England, as elsewhere, the reverence for authority which is a dominant characteristic of the Roman Church showed itself in close repetition of patristic *sententiae* in popular sermons, so that even a lay audience might be expected to remember their chief doctrines and to recognize their favorite metaphors. For our purpose, however, we do not have to assume that every Anglo-Saxon knew his Gregory. There are signs in the secular interests of the poem that it was composed primarily for a cultured audience. Even if only a minority of the poet's hearers could have appreciated the richness of his allusions, they are there because the poet, himself an educated man, had been trained to see life like this, and expected his audience to share his attitude. It is no coincidence that Augustine's model form of instruction,[19] to be used by the priest in teaching the would-be Christian, begins, after an exhortation to think of the fleeting nature of this world's wealth and success, with the Creation, man's Fall, Cain and Abel, and the Flood, and follows the same course as the list of Cædmon's poems given by Bede. We shall recognize this approach in the *Beowulf* poem itself, with the difference that the poet, who is *not* instructing the ignorant, takes for granted the story of the Fall, and stops short of the Incarnation, since the characters in his story do not know Christ.

The other Christian teacher whose writings were particularly known to the Anglo-Saxons is of course Gregory the Great, whose mission established the Roman Church in England. It is not surprising, therefore, to find the major doctrines of both Gregory and Augustine alluded to, but never expounded, in *Beowulf*. The lines in which the most obvious Gregorian and Augustinian influence appears are suspect in the eyes of some editors,[20] chiefly on the grounds that their tone is "more Chris-

[19] *De Catechizandis Rudibus,* c. xvi, §24; *P.L.,* XL, col. 328.
[20] See the edition by C. L. Wrenn (London, 1953), pp. 67-69.

tianly homiletic than we could expect."[21] Professor Brodeur has gone a long way towards justifying the inclusion of these passages;[22] I hope to go even further in establishing their relevance.

This, then, was my starting-point: the man who wrote Hrothgar's "sermon" was conversant with the teachings of Augustine and Gregory, and was familiar with Gregory's favorite image of the soldier keeping vigil against the onslaughts of the Enemy.[23] Suppose, therefore, that this sermon in the heart of the poem was no less carefully contrived than the rest of the narrative; we may look in the latter part of the poem for the *poetic* effect of the recalling of this image. Similarly, in other places, we may find reminders of commonly-held Christian ideas which are to be recollected later in the story. The "sermon" itself no doubt seemed to the poet completely appropriate for a pre-Christian king. As Brodeur says, it is "reminiscent of the Psalms,"[24] and this not only in its majesty and wisdom, but in its humility before the King of Kings. In speaking of its Augustinian or Gregorian modes of thought, we must not forget that these have roots in the Pentateuch and the Psalms; the attitude of Hrothgar here is that of the Psalmist who says, "Bonum mihi quia humiliasti me, ut discam iustificationes tuas. Bonum mihi lex oris tui super millia auri et argenti." [It was in mercy thou didst chasten me, schooling me to thy obedience. Is not the law thou hast given dearer to me than rich store of gold and silver? (Knox)].[25]

In just the same way the poet imputes to Beowulf thoughts which he finds in the Psalms, adding a little "local color" by also putting into his mouth some proverbial phrases about *Wyrd* which men would recognize as belonging to their ancestors. This seems to me the likely explanation of the feeling some readers

[21] Wrenn, p. 67.

[22] Brodeur, pp. 182-219.

[23] Gregorius, *Moralia; P.L.*, LXXV, cols. 805 ff., sections 244, 246, 399, etc. See also Whitelock for other examples, p. 7 and p. 81.

[24] Brodeur, p. 214.

[25] Psalm CXVIII, 71-72 (Vulg.).

have that Beowulf is portrayed as a Christian, and the belief of others that he is given a heathen character. As Brodeur says, "The hero is as much a Christian as Hrothgar—and no more. The question is: did the poet really conceive either of them as a Christian?"[26] It seems to me that he thought of them as living under the Old Covenant, to be judged according to the Old Law as the Israelites were, since they had had no Revelation of God.[27] In one important passage, which Tolkien has called the manifestation of "a heathen and unchristian fear"[28] and Brodeur has equated with the Christian state of "readiness for contrition,"[29] Beowulf grieves that he has incurred God's anger unwittingly.[30] Here again, the Psalter resolves the argument: "Delicta quis intelligit? Ab occultis meis munda me." [Who knows his own frailties? If I have sinned unwittingly, do thou absolve me. (Knox)].[31]

It is not surprising that this Psalm should be in the poet's mind, for the preceding verses speak of the judgments of the Lord as more to be desired than gold, "etenim servus tuus custodit ea; in custodiendis illis retributio multa." [By these I, thy servant, live, observing them how jealously! (Knox)].

This recalls the general tenor of Hrothgar's sermon to Beo-

[26] Brodeur, p. 196.

[27] This highly controversial point cannot be debated here. I interpret the Danes' idol-worship as a falling-away from the true God, *pace* Brodeur (p. 198 et seq.). The poet may have had in mind Psalm LXXVII (Vulg.), particularly 7, 8, 22, 34, and 58. If *Drihten God* (line 181) be taken as the Lord Jesus Christ, "ne wiston" (they knew not of) would be perfectly appropriate. "Metod hie ne cuþon" (line 180) might then be interpreted to mean that the Creator was not known to them (as a Person) because they did not know Christ. Line 182, "herian ne cuþon," surely means that they had no Church to guide their prayers? I offer these suggestions tentatively, to avoid the charge of having ignored this difficulty.

[28] J. R. R. Tolkien, "*Beowulf*: The Monsters and the Critics," *Proc. Brit. Acad.,* XXII (1936), 287.

[29] Brodeur, p. 193.

[30] Lines 2327-32.

[31] Psalm XVIII, 12 (Vulg.).

wulf, as does the next verse of this Psalm, which reads, "Et ab alienis parce servo tuo. Si mei non fuerint dominati, tunc immaculatus ero; et emundabor a delicto maximo." [Keep me ever thy own servant, far from pride; so long as this does not lord it over me, I will yet be without fault, I will yet be innocent of the great sin (Knox)].

With the difficult meaning of *alienis* here we need not concern ourselves;[32] it is the last phrase which once again reminds us of the warning against the great sin of pride: as Augustine explains, "Delictum magnum arbitror esse superbiam" [I think that pride is a great sin].[33]

It would be wholly wrong to suggest that because the characters of the story live under the Old Covenant the poet has adopted an outmoded moral law for the purposes of his tale. He and his audience have a knowledge denied to Hrothgar and Beowulf, and his hearers are not expected to suspend belief. Our sense of the *depth* of the poem comes not so much from its backward look into "a darker antiquity" as from its own Christian perspective, which gives the adventures another dimension. The reminders of another world, so far from being alien to the Beowulf stories, seem to me to have a special poetic result, demonstrating "the power of reducing multitude into unity of effect" [34] which Coleridge required of a great poet.

[32] Augustine understands *"ab alienis"* to mean "from the evil persuasions of others." *Enarr. in Ps.* XVIII; *P.L.* XXXVI, col. 162). He compares *Ps.* XXXV, 2, explaining *"Non veniat,* inquit, *mihi pes superbiæ,* hoc est, *Ab occultis meis munda me, Domine; et manus peccatorum non moveant me,* hoc est, *Ab alienis parce servo tuo* [He says, *"Let not the foot of pride come upon me,"* that is, *"If I have sinned unwittingly, do thou absolve me, Lord; and let not sinners' hands move me,"* that is, *"Spare me, thy servant, from the evil persuasions of others"*]. Some commentators see in the following phrase, *"Si mei non fuerint dominati"* [If these do not lord it over me (Knox)], an echo of Gen. IV, 7, *"tu dominaberis illius"* [you shall lord it over him], where sin is imagined as waiting like a beast at the door to overcome Cain, or to be overcome by him.

[33] *P.L.,* XXXVI, col. 163, verse 15.

[34] *Biographia Literaria,* Ch. XV, § 1.

[In the concluding section of this paper, omitted here, the author cites various kinds of evidence to show that Beowulf in the second half of the poem is "still generous and beloved, but spiritually unguarded because of his pride, as Hrothgar himself had been. . . ."]